REMARRIAGE AND STEPPARENTING

REMARRIAGE
AND STEPPARENTING
Current Research and Theory

Edited by

Kay Pasley
Colorado State University

Marilyn Ihinger-Tallman
Washington State University

Guilford Press
New York   London

Dedication

To JFC and JJB—teachers, mentors, and most-valued friends—for your continued encouragement and loving support.

K.P.

To Ola, Frank, and Mona—parents and stepparent—for your strength and support when things get tough and your shared pleasure and enthusiasm when the going is easy.

M. I.-T.

© 1987 The Guilford Press
A Division of Guilford Publications, Inc.
72 Spring Street, New York, NY   10012

Printed in the United States of America

Last digit is print number: 9 8 7 6 5 4 3 2 1

Library of Congress Cataloging-in-Publication Data

Remarriage and stepparenting.

   Includes bibliographies and index.
   1. Parenting.   2. Stepparents—Family
relationships.   3. Stepchildren—Family
relationships.   4. Remarried people—Family
relationships.   5. Remarriage.   6. Parent and child.
I. Pasley, Kay.   II. Ihinger-Tallman, Marilyn.
[DNLM: 1. Child Rearing.   2. Divorce.   3. Marriage.
4. Parent–Child Relations. HQ 759.92 R384]
HQ759.92.R45   1987   306.8′4   87–17718
ISBN 0–89862–697–8
ISBN 0–89862–922–5 (pbk.)

Contributors

Constance R. Ahrons, Ph.D., Department of Family Counseling, University of Southern California, Los Angeles, California.

Eulalee Brand, Ph.D., Department of Psychology, The Pennsylvania State University at Harrisburg, Middletown, Pennsylvania.

W. Glenn Clingempeel, Ph.D., Department of Psychology, The Pennsylvania State University at Harrisburg, Middletown, Pennsylvania.

Marilyn Coleman, Ph.D., Department of Child and Family Development, University of Missouri at Columbia, Columbia, Missouri.

Frank F. Furstenberg, Jr., Ph.D., Department of Sociology, University of Pennsylvania, Philadelphia, Pennsylvania.

Lawrence H. Ganong, Ph.D., School of Nursing, University of Missouri at Columbia, Columbia, Missouri.

Jean Giles-Sims, Ph.D., Department of Sociology, Texas Christian University, Fort Worth, Texas.

E. Mavis Hetherington, Ph.D., Department of Psychology, University of Virginia, Charlottesville, Virginia.

Marilyn Ihinger-Tallman, Ph.D., Department of Sociology, Washington State University, Pullman, Washington.

Doris S. Jacobson, Ph.D., School of Social Welfare, University of California at Los Angeles, Los Angeles, California.

Kay Pasley, Ed.D., Department of Human Development and Family Studies, Colorado State University, Fort Collins, Colorado.

John W. Santrock, Ph.D., Programs in Psychology, University of Texas at Dallas, Richardson, Texas.

Sion Segal, Ph.D., Department of Psychology, The Pennsylvania State University at Harrisburg, Middletown, Pennsylvania.

Karen A. Sitterle, Ph.D., Timberlawn Psychiatric Hospital, Dallas, Texas.

Lynn Wallisch, M.A., Schizophrenia Research Project of the School of Social Work, University of Wisconsin at Madison, Madison, Wisconsin.

Preface

This volume is the product of two years of work on the part of the authors represented here. It was born out of the collective wisdom of the nine scholars who participated in the Study Group on the Effects of Remarriage and Stepparenting on Child Outcomes and the Quality of Family Life sponsored by the Society for Research in Child Development and funded by the Foundation for Child Development. This group of scholars met twice during one year to share with each other their own work and to discuss their collective knowledge about the work of others in this area. Originally there was little interest in preparing a published volume. Most of us couldn't bear the thought of making another commitment to write a formal manuscript—we all were already overburdened with such projects. However, as the second meeting evolved, we became aware that we had much to share with those who did not have the privilege of participating in our six days of discussions over the 12-month period. We had learned a good deal from each other about our own work as well as that of others, and we agreed to produce a volume which would be on the "cutting edge" of the field—one which could serve as a guideline to researchers in this area. We wanted to offer new conceptual frameworks and report the results from our most recent research.

Two additional scholars were invited to participate in this book because both were involved in projects or had produced recent work that was new and important—work we had admired. We felt honored that they agreed to join us.

In the pages that follow you will be able to judge for yourself the quality of what we offer. In the first chapter of Section I, the remarried family is placed in a historical context, tracing the incidence and changes which have occurred over time. Ihinger-Tallman and Pasley examine the differences between remarriage prior to this century and the changes which have occurred since 1900, noting the similarities and differences at two different time periods. Coleman and Ganong report the findings from studies on the "step" stereotype in Chapter 2. They report on the prevalence of stereotyping of this family form. In Chapter 3, Furstenberg provides an overview of the results of two studies on remarriage, focusing primarily on the similarities and differences in family life among first-married and remarried families. He reports on economic behavior, parenting, and child outcomes. While suggesting that there are fewer differences than originally believed, there are, nevertheless, unique issues to be faced in remarried families. Many of the findings he reports are echoed throughout other chapters in this volume.

The chapters in Section II examine the existing literature within particular theoretical frameworks and/or develop new theoretical perspectives. In Chapter 4, Clingempeel, Brand, and Segal integrate family development theory with the ecological framework in order to identify areas of needed research. Ganong and Coleman build upon an earlier comparison of the clinical and empirical literatures in Chapter 5. They identify the areas where earlier theoretical and methodological weakness have been eliminated and examine the continuing problems in both literatures. In Chapter 6, Giles-Sims applies social exchange theory to help explain power-dependency issues in remarriage. Finally, in Chapter 7, Ihinger-Tallman theorizes about a relatively unexplored area: stepsibling relationships. Drawing on Bronfenbrenner's ecological framework and Turner's theory of bonding, she derives a series of propositions about sibling and stepsibling relationships.

In Section III, Chapter 8, Hetherington reports the findings from a 6-year follow-up of her original divorce sample. The majority of those divorced mothers had remarried by 6-years postdivorce. Hetherington compares and contrasts the influence of sequential life changes (such as divorce and remarriage) on parent adjustment and parent–child relationships. In Chapter 9, Pasley explores a family process which is believed to cause stress within remarried families: the definition of family boundaries. She reports findings from a large sample of remarried couples and examines both the prevalence of boundary ambiguity and the types of remarried families which more readily experience boundary ambiguity.

In Chapter 10, Ahrons and Wallisch report the findings from a longitudinal study which followed couples 5 years postdivorce. Their chapter focuses on the relationships between stepparents and parents as they care for children within a binuclear family system. Jacobson, in Chapter 11, reports the findings from a longitudinal study of children in linked family systems— those where the child serves as the "link" between two parental households via his or her continued contact with both. She compares the visiting patterns and child outcome for several different types of linked family systems.

In Chapter 12, Santrock and Sitterle report the results of a multisource, multimethod, multimeasure study. Their chapter offers an in-depth look at the nature of interaction between stepmothers and stepchildren, comparing these families to both first-marriage families and stepfather families.

In the last section, Pasley and Ihinger-Tallman trace the history of the study of remarriage and stepparenting and summarize the changes which have occurred over time. They synthesize the content of previous chapters and identify ways they contribute to the advancement of research on this topic.

We trust that the reader will find the ideas expressed and the findings reported in this volume both challenging and enlightening. It is our hope that both students and scholars alike who elect to study this family form view the content here as enhancing their existing knowledge, guiding their future work, and encouraging their commitment to interdisciplinary dialogue.

Kay Pasley
Marilyn Ihinger-Tallman

Acknowledgments

This volume is the result of a collaborative effort on the part of many. First and foremost, we wish to express our appreciation to the Society for Research in Child Development (SRCD) whose Study Group Committee had the wisdom to take a chance and approve our proposal for a unique study group. Little did any of us know at that time we would agree to produce a volume such as this—we originally thought only in terms of a final report summarizing our activities. The Foundation for Child Development provided the funding to SRCD to support the meetings where many of the scholars represented in this volume had the opportunity to share their knowledge of the field, discuss the issues and concerns they experienced in their own work, and review and critique the work of others.

We feel most fortunate to have been able to work with the outstanding scholars represented here. They endured our many suggestions as we worked together to prepare chapters with clarity; chapters that make excellent contributions to the existing knowledge-base. The papers in this volume represent scholarly writing on the forefront in the study of remarriage and stepparenting. This book is an indication of the collective commitment of the authors who have challenged ideas and provided new ways of thinking about this family form.

Further, the content of these chapters is a tribute to the time and energy provided by the two original editors of the special series of Guilford Press which focuses on the family: Drs. Bert Adams and Reuben Hill. Both added much to improving our work. With the gentlest of hands, they offered new insights and expertise we lacked. It was our loss, and a great loss to the community of family scholars, when Reuben passed away mid-way through this project.

We are indebted to many highly skilled individuals. Excellent secretarial support was provided by Jackie Lindsay at CSU and Ruth Self at WSU. Seymour Weingarten, Editor-in-Chief at Guilford, eased our stress in bringing the project to a close. He assisted us with the management of details and showed patience and understanding as deadlines came and passed.

Lastly, this book is a tribute to the success of interdisciplinary scholarship and collaboration. Its co-editors have now worked together for 8 years (longer than most first marriages last). This project is one outcome of the joy and challenge we have shared over these years. Not all such teams work together so successfully. Perhaps the beauty of our professional relationship is based in the complementarity of our skills, interests, work styles, and personalities—and the strong friendship that has developed.

K. P.
M. I.-T.

Contents

SOCIAL AND CULTURAL CONTEXTS OF REMARRIAGE AND STEPPARENTING

1

Divorce and Remarriage in the American Family: A Historical Review

MARILYN IHINGER-TALLMAN
Washington State University
KAY PASLEY
Colorado State University

INTRODUCTION

There are strong tendencies in many of us to believe that the social norms and behaviors that are currently practiced have always existed, to compare current events and experiences with the recent past, and to assume that what one personally experiences is unique. This tendency is particularly pronounced in areas involving intimate relationships. Locked into the present as we are, we lose sight of the historical perspective concerning beliefs and practices related to love, courtship, and marriage—and remarriage. For example, the writings of social scientists, and the subsequent media dissemination of that information, have kept the public informed about changes in family life, such as the increased divorce rate, the growing number of single parent families, and the rising number of children growing up in stepfamilies. The fact that the current remarriage rate closely parallels that of an earlier time (Cherlin, 1981; Dupâquier, Hèlin, Laslett, Livi-Bacci, & Sogner, 1981; Furstenberg & Spanier, 1984; Griffith, 1980; Laslett, 1977) has not been well publicized. The relatively high rates of marital dissolution from the mid-1960s to 1980, and the correspondingly high proportion of adults and children living in families formed through remarriage is, in actuality, not too dissimilar from the rates in Europe and America in the 17th and 18th centuries. During that time, the proportion of remarriages among all marriages was on the order of 20% to 30%, a figure comparable to the current United States rate. Demographically, the two time periods are similar with regard to the incidence of remarriage, but contextually they are quite different due to the fact that divorce, not death, is the event that now precedes remarriage.

Our goal in this chapter is to describe how the experiential sequence of marriage–death–remarriage in the earlier time period shifted to the marriage-divorce–remarriage experience of today. We conclude with a discussion of the consequences for a remarried household when divorce rather than death ends a prior marriage.

HISTORICAL PERSPECTIVE

Value of Marriage

Early colonial New England life was characterized by the realities of a subsistence economy, an initial shortage of women, and a value orientation that honored matrimony and the family. In the New England colonies, the family was one of the two primary institutions, along with religion, and few people lived independent of a family. A 1689 Bristol, Rhode Island town census, for example, showed that among 70 resident families only two were headed by a single adult (Demos, 1968). In Plymouth Colony, no married person was permitted to live apart from his or her spouse except in very unusual and temporary circumstances (Demos, 1970).

Marriage was generally considered to be a civil contract rather than a religious one in New England. In a few places, however, some couples made their own contract irrespective of Church or State. Such marriages, called "disorderly" marriages, meant there was no marriage formality except by a couple joining hands and declaring themselves married. There were some attempts to stop this type of union through the use of fines or legislative acts. For example, in Rhode Island a 1647 act outlawed marriage by agreement (Calhoun, 1917). However, whichever way marriage vows were taken— religious, civil, or common law—they were generally honored for life. When a marriage ended, the most frequent cause was the death of a husband or wife.

Death and Remarriage

Remarriage following the death of a spouse was common and socially approved. Calhoun (1917) writes that men and women married the first time at an early age and remarried promptly in the event of a spouse's death. Second and even third marriages were "common among the early New Netherlanders. . . . One man, a German, appears in the chronicles as the fourth husband of his first wife and the third husband of his second wife" (p. 163). However, Demos (1970) shows that 40% of the men and 25% of the women in his Plymouth Colony study remarried only once. Demos's data showed that only 6% of men and 1% of women who lived to be at least 50 years old were married more than two times. Grigg (1977) determined from Demos's Plymouth Colony data that between 53% and 66% of all possible second marriages actually did occur:

Remarriage was the norm for survivors of first marriages in seventeenth-century Plymouth, but it was far from universal, and long succession of marriages were less common than may have been supposed. (p. 185)

Other data from the town of Woburn, Massachusetts (Keyssar, 1980) suggest that remarriage was infrequent among third generation inhabitants (data from 1701 to 1710 records). Here only 10% of the women married more than once, between 25% and 33% of the men did so, and only one man was known to have married more than twice. It is likely that Calhoun's more impressionistic data suggesting multiple marriages reflects the consequences of death among younger people, thus accounting for the greater rate of remarriage he reports. What seems quite clear, however, is that remarriage was an accepted and socially approved solution to the loss of a mate.

Records show that in some areas remarriage occurred quickly; so quickly that controls were applied to prevent rapid remarriage. Plymouth Colony records indicate that when a spouse died remarriage occurred within a relatively short time: "Often the interval was less than a year, and in a few cases less than six months" (Demos, 1970, p. 67). Puritan widows were advised to remarry immediately so as not to idolize their departed spouses (Fox & Quitt, 1980). On the other hand, in the Colony of Pennsylvania a 1690 law specified that a widow could not marry until a year after her husband's death. American Quakers were similar to Pennsylvanians, and required both widows and widowers to wait a year before remarrying (Frost, 1973).

Some of the discrepant evidence about multiple remarriers offered above may stem from regional differences. Carr and Walsh (1983) report on family life in 17th-century Maryland where health hazards were greater than in New England. These authors suggest that new immigrants frequently became ill upon arrival (usually from malaria), and many died: "Recurrent malaria made the woman who survived less able to withstand other diseases, especially dysentery and influenza. She was especially vulnerable when pregnant" (p. 324).

While life was risky for women, it was even more risky for men: "However long they lived, immigrant women in Maryland tended to outlive their husbands—in Charles County, for example, by a ratio of two to one" (Carr & Walsh, 1983, p. 328). Data suggest that in this Maryland County, women took new husbands three times more often than men took new wives (Carr & Walsh, 1983). Calhoun (1917) also commented on the same high risk for men when he reported that few men lived beyond middle age in 17th-century Virginia: "The malarial climate, exposure, and reckless habits cut them off" (p. 247). In Charles County, Maryland, marriage was likely to last only 7 years and had only a 33% chance of lasting 10 years before one partner died. Then,

remarriage was the usual and often the immediate solution for a woman who lost her husband. The shortage of women made any woman eligible to marry again, and the difficulties of raising a family while running a plantation must have made remarriage necessary. (Carr & Walsh, 1983, p. 332)

Calhoun (1917) reminds us that the fathers of Patrick Henry and Thomas Jefferson married widows, as did George Washington and James Madison.

Looking at death from the perspective of children's loss, Fox & Quitt (1980) report that about 25% of the children in 17th-century Virginia had lost one or both parents by the age of 5. Over half of these children had suffered the loss of a parent by age 13, and 70% had experienced the death of one or both parents by age 21.

Husbands generally anticipated their wives remarrying after their death and frequently planned for that eventuality. Both Demos (1970) and Carr and Walsh (1983) describe the precautions some husbands took to ensure their children were not abused or their property embezzled after their death. Sometimes premarital agreements were contracted between a widow and her future spouse to protect the widow's property rights, since the property of a 17th-century woman transferred to her husband when she married. Such premarital contracts might require the new spouse to relinquish his right to the use of the children's portion of the estate, or they might deed property to the widow that she would then control (Carr & Walsh, 1983; Demos, 1970). Some old Dutch wills in the colony of New Amsterdam specified penalties if a wife remarried. Calhoun (1917) interprets this as lack of trust in the surviving spouse to protect the rights of the children of the deceased: ". . . attempts were made to restrain wives by wills ordering forfeiture of property in case of remarriage. . . . Restraints placed by wills on remarriage were commonly in behalf of children of the first marriage" (p. 176).

Grigg (1977) studied remarriage in Newburyport, Massachusetts, at the beginning of the 19th century to determine the influence of sex and age of surviving spouse, number of minor children by age, and husband's estate valuation in the year of his or his wife's death on the likelihood of remarriage of the survivor. Grigg found that half of the widowers eventually remarried compared to only 20% of the widows. Widowers remarried more rapidly than widows with the average duration of widowhood being 1.9 years for men and 5.6 years for women. Regarding age, remarriage was most likely for people under the age of 30 and did not occur at all among the oldest 18% of either sex. Children were found to influence the likelihood of remarriage in the following manner: for widowers, children aged 5 to 15 reduced the likelihood of remarriage while older and younger children increased it. For widows, however, age of children did not affect their remarriage rate. Lastly, there was no association between a husband's valuation at the time of his wife's death and the likelihood of his remarriage. For widows, valuation was confounded with age; widows with the highest and lowest valuations were relatively old, and thus their remarriage rates were correspondingly low. A similar negative relation between wealth and remarriage was also found among women in Salem, Massachusetts in 1800 (Farber, 1972).

Fox and Quitt (1980) determined that age was an important factor in a widow's decision to remarry. They report that in the Chesapeake colonies, with their high mortality rate and imbalanced sex ratio,

> second and third marriages were the rule for women. This occurred especially in the 17th century. In New England, where wives did not become widowed usually until they were in their 50's or 60's and their children were nearly all grown up, remarriage was the exception. (p. 54)

A most critical factor affecting the remarriage rate was a change in the proportion of men to women. The sex ratio was highly imbalanced in New England by the late 18th century, in favor of men. This change served to depress the chances of remarriage for widows. For example, in 1765 the adult sex ratio was 87.9 in Woburn, Massachusetts, meaning that for every 100 women there were only about 88 men. Most widows in that community did not remarry; apparently their age and the shortage of males made marital opportunities scarce (Guttentag & Secord, 1983). On the other hand, the westward migration of men meant that the sex ratio favored females in the western settlements. Correspondingly, female marriage and remarriage rates were high. Not only do these figures indicate the influence that a shortage of one sex or the other had on remarriage rates, but they once again suggest regional differences in rates of remarriage.

Divorce and Remarriage

Early America

While death terminated most marriages during the 17th and 18th centuries, desertion did occur and divorce was not unknown. In fact, divorce was easier to obtain in the 18th century New England courts than in England during the same time period. In addition, divorce was easier to obtain in some New England colonies than in others. In Connecticut, for example, a spouse could obtain a divorce easier than in Massachusetts (Cohn, 1970). Calhoun (1917) writes that New England was more liberal in granting divorce than the south, with the middle colonies "nearer to the extreme of the conservatism of the South than the broad and liberal policy of New England" (p. 181). In colonies not permitting divorce, separations were granted. For example, Virginia law accepted the English principle disallowing divorce, but did permit legal separation. Both men and women could initiate separation, and "Virginia courts not only insured the financial security of the separated female, but also allowed her to make contracts" (Fox & Quitt, 1980, p. 407).

Not only were there regional differences with regard to the ease of obtaining a divorce, but the grounds for divorce also varied between the colonies. For example, there were four legitimate grounds for divorce in Plymouth Colony: willfull desertion, bigamy, adultery, and an inability to bear children (Demos, 1970). However, in Massachusetts between 1639 and 1692, only 40 divorces were granted by the Massachusetts magistrates for "adultery, bigamy, desertion, impotence, and affinity" (Blake, 1962, p. 36). Thus, while the possibility of divorce existed, there were not many cases of absolute divorce or even permanent separation. Blake (1962) reports that during the Dutch rule of New Netherlands only an occasional divorce was granted. After the English conquest of the colony in 1664, "divorces continued to be granted for the next eleven years" (p. 42) but they were rare. There is no clear evidence of divorce being granted in New York after that time, or during the remainder of the colonial period.

Further support for the existence of variation in grounds for divorce among the colonies comes from a Pennsylvania law of 1682 which included divorce as one of the penalties for adultery. In 1700 a number of new laws were passed and "three of these made some provision for divorce as part of the punishment designated for adultery, bestiality, and bigamy" (Blake, 1962, pp. 45–46). There is, however, no evidence to show that either absolute divorce or partial divorce (divorce from bed and board) were at all common in Pennsylvania. Of the 304 legislative decrees granted in Pennsylvania between 1769 and 1873, all but two of these decrees were granted after the War of Independence (Jacobson, 1959).

A clear sex bias is evident in the granting of divorce. Degler (1983) writes,

> Before 1773 not a single petition for divorce by a woman in Massachusetts on the grounds of adultery by a husband was accepted by the courts, though many had been from husbands alleging such behavior on the part of their wives. (p. 72)

Cott's (1983) research on divorce and the status of women in 18th-century Massachusetts also supports the sex-bias hypothesis. She found an increasing number of both petitions and decrees granted between 1692 and 1786. A sex bias in favor of men also appears in the frequent occurrence of extra-legal divorce, that is, desertion. Cott (1983) writes,

> Women's petitions against bigamous husbands revealed some of the vagaries of marriage in eighteenth century Massachusetts. . . . These cases [of bigamy] suggest the ease and perhaps the appeal of running away from one partner and finding another—the traditional "self-divorce." Husbands more frequently made such escapes and new starts than did wives. . . . Men moved more easily from place to place, it seems; certainly according to custom, they, and not women, took the initiative in deciding to marry or remarry. (p. 354)

Post-revolutionary America

After the Revolutionary War petitions from women for divorce increased dramatically. Two explanations are offered for this increase. Cott (1983) attributes the increase in divorce to an increase in wives' petitions filed for husbands' adultery. She claims that the motives for granting more divorces at this time (when they would have been refused in an earlier era) were political concerns rather than a commitment to sexual equality. Because it was felt that the new Republic's success was dependent on the virtue of its citizens, there was a new emphasis on marital fidelity. The family was viewed as the training ground for future citizens, and thus it was necessary to provide legal buttresses to support this moral ideology (p. 358). Calhoun (1918) makes a cultural claim, saying that "democratic independence in America tended to easy divorce" (p. 44). He also reports that after 1776 the majority of divorces were granted at the request of the wife, a finding confirmed by Cott's more recent (1983) data. Jacobson (1959) indicates that the practice of granting divorces to women continued. He reports that wives received 64% of the divorces in the years immediately after the Civil War, and by 1950 were receiving 72.5% of divorce decrees.

In most states the "innocent" person in a divorce action was permitted to remarry. However, states varied in their response to the "guilty" partner. Some states allowed an immediate remarriage while others withheld this privilege during the life of the former partner. The law could be evaded, however, by moving to another state, for then, as now, each state had its own divorce law. The legal confusion evident in this situation is reflected in the remarks of an American lecturer quoted in Charles Dickens's magazine *All the Year Round* (Anonymous, 1883–1884):

> A man who has been married, divorced, and remarried will, in traveling from Maine to Florida, find himself sometimes a bachelor, sometimes married to his first wife, sometimes married to his second wife, sometimes a divorced man, and sometimes a bigamist, according to the statutes of the states through which he is traveling. (pp. 90–93)

During the Victorian era there was long debate between the conservatives and liberals over divorce and the right to remarry. The conservative position stated that remarriage was "nothing less than registered concubinage" (O'Neill, 1967, p. 37) and the Catholic Church forbade it. Most of the Protestant churches allowed remarriage, although sometimes only to the innocent party in an adultery suit. Aside from varying religious doctrines, civil law permitted the divorced to remarry (O'Neill, 1967).

It was easier to get a divorce in some states than in others since each state had different divorce laws. Indiana, for example, had very liberal divorce laws. There the law allowed the court to grant a divorce for any cause it saw fit (Carlier, 1972). According to Wires (1967),

> . . . the state's courts too frequently displayed a procedural laxity that further eased the procurement of divorces. . . . Especially objectional to many observers was the fact that combined legal and judicial circumstances made it possible for residents of other states to secure divorces in Indiana with little difficulty. (p. 1)

In South Carolina, on the other hand, divorce was absolutely prohibited by its Constitution, and in New York only adultery was recognized as a ground for divorce (Blake, 1962; Calhoun, 1918). Some western states had extremely liberal divorce codes. For example, as early as 1861 the divorce code in Nevada required only 6 months residency. In 1927, this period was reduced to 3 months, and in 1931 (in reaction to an Arkansas and Idaho ruling that lowered their state residency requirements to 3 months) residency requirements were further reduced, this time to only 6 weeks (Blake, 1962; Jacobson, 1959).

By the 1860s general alarm was expressed over the "rising tide of divorce." While the early records are incomplete, Jacobson (1959) estimates that immediately prior to the Civil War the rate was about 1.2 divorces per 1,000 existing marriages. By the turn of the century the rate had increased to 4 per 1,000 marriages. In response to the rising divorce rate the New England Divorce Reform League was organized in 1881, and a national study was commissioned by Congress in 1887 (Carter & Glick, 1976). Carroll Wright (1889) wrote the *Report of the Commissioner of Labor*, the final report of that study indicating, among other things, a 157% increase in the number of divorces granted between 1867 (9,927) and 1886 (25,535). He reported also that the average duration of marriage before divorce was 9.17 years. He noted that 39.4% of divorcing couples had children.

Between 1886 and 1906 the divorce rate continued to increase. A second national survey was conducted and published as *The Marriage and Divorce Report of 1909*. Figures were calculated on a population base in this survey (as opposed to the earlier married couple standard). Twenty-seven divorces per 100,000 population were reported in 1867 compared to 86 per 100,000 in 1906. While the population in 1905 was estimated at little more than double that of 1870, divorces were six times as numerous. The report estimated that somewhere between 1 in 12 and 1 in 16 marriages would probably end in divorce (Calhoun, 1919; Carter & Glick, 1976). Divorce records kept at the turn of the century in Los Angeles also indicate a dramatic increase in the number of divorces between 1880 and 1920 (May, 1983). Validating these reports, Cherlin (1981) compiled data that show a gradual but steady rise in the divorce rate from 1860, when the first national divorce statistics were available, to the present. This gradual rise lasted until about 1960, broken only by brief increases in divorce immediately following each major war (the Civil War, World War I, and World War II). Specifically, the trends show that during the early years of the 1930s depression both marriage and divorce rates declined. By the middle of the decade, however, they began to rise once more. This gradual rise continued (except as noted above) until 1960, when the rate dramatically increased, reaching higher levels than ever previously recorded for America (Norton & Glick, 1976).

Although the divorce rate was rising, in the early 1920s brides and grooms who were remarrying were still more likely to have been widowed than divorced (Jacobson, 1959). Not until 1940 did the number of divorced men (aged 25 to 44) exceed the number of widowers; for women in this age range the corresponding point was 1950 (Glick, 1980). The rapid increase in divorce after the early 1960s created a pool of eligible remarriers so that by 1980 divorced persons constituted close to nine tenths of all persons who remarried (Glick, 1980). In Degler's (1980) comment on the 20th-century trend concerning the rise in remarriage rates among women whose marriages ended, he noted that in 1910 only 28.7% of divorced or widowed women between the ages of 50 and 54 were remarried. In 1940 the proportion was 31.3%, and in 1970 the remarriage rate among this group of women was 45.2%. Looking at the trends from another perspective, we see how over time the proportion of remarriages to all marriages changed. In 1900, only 3% of all brides were divorced; in 1930, the percentage increased to 9; and in 1978, 28% were divorced (Cherlin, 1981).

THE CURRENT PICTURE

The remarriage rate has declined in the last 15 years. Carter and Glick (1976) reported that the remarriage rate for women aged 35 to 44 peaked in 1968. Glick (1984) confirmed this decline using recent national health center statistics that showed that the remarriage rate per 1000 divorced men dropped from 229 in 1972 to only 166 in 1979 (Glick, 1984).

Sex differences in remarriage rates are reported that show that more men than women remarry after divorce. This fact continues to be as true in 1985 as it was in 1785. The median interval between marriage and divorce is now 7 years, and the median interval between divorce and remarriage is 3 years. The timing of divorce and remarriage, however, varies according to age. Glick (1980) reports that remarriages after divorce are currently most numerous between the ages of 25 and 44, while remarriages after widowhood are most numerous between the ages of 45 and 64—a not surprising finding. Census figures also show that the age of remarriage among widowed persons is increasing as the population ages. Comparing the time period 1963–1977, the median age at remarriage changed from 58.0 years to 60.1 years for widowers and from 49.7 years to 53.1 years for widows. However, the median age of remarriage for divorced men and women fell from 36.3 years for men (in 1963) to 33.6 years (in 1977) and from 31.8 years to 30.2 years for women during the same period. Census figures also show that men and women in early middle age are more likely to remarry if their marriages end by divorce rather than by death of their spouse (Glick, 1980).

A recent study of remarried-couple households reported there were 9.2 million divorced and remarried couples in the United States in 1980 (Cherlin & McCarthy, 1985). In 30% of these households only the wife had been previously married, in 35% only the husband had been married, and in 35% both spouses were previously married.

Several factors have been found to influence the remarriage rate. Education and income level, for example, differentially affect the rates for men and women. The probability of women remarrying after divorce varies negatively according to their education and income levels. That is, the higher their education and income level, the less likely women are to remarry. On the other hand, the probability of men remarrying after divorce varies positively with education and income. Higher educated and financially well-off men remarry more quickly (Glick, 1980). Remarriage rates also vary by race. Comparing blacks and whites, the first marriage rate is higher among whites than blacks. The separation and divorce rate among blacks, however, is higher than for whites. Further, although the remarriage rate for whites is higher, redivorce among them also is more common (Glick, 1980).

The incidence of redivorce after remarriage has increased over time along with the first-divorce rate. Glick (1984) has computed the most up-to-date projection of redivorce. He estimates an eventual redivorce rate of 61% for men and 54% for women in their 30s in the 1980s. These levels are slightly higher than the projected 49% who may eventually have a first divorce. Generalizing across sex, race, and education, Glick (1984) estimates for all persons under 40 years of age:

> Among those in their thirties in 1980, about 90% had married; a little over one-fourth of this 90%, or 24%, of all persons in their early thirties had ended their first marriage in divorce; about two-thirds of this 24%, or 16%, of all persons in their thirties had remarried after divorce; and . . . one-fifth of this 16%, or only 3%, of all persons currently in their thirties have already experienced redivorce. (pp. 18–19)

What is most evident in all these figures is the inherent "marriage bias" of Americans. As a people, we enter first marriage at a greater rate than people in most other countries. We also seem to have higher expectations of the marital union in that we are willing to abandon the marriage if it is perceived as unsatisfactory. This inclination has produced one of the highest divorce rates in the world. And finally, as was pointed out above, Americans subsequently recouple at a higher rate than couples in other western nations, as evidenced by a high remarriage rate (United Nations Department of International Economic and Social Affairs Statistical Office, 1985).

Thus far we have attempted to illustrate the vulnerability of first marriages during the more than 3 centuries of growth and change in America. Throughout those years, remarriage and the formation of stepfamilies have not been isolated or unusual events. Today, a high divorce rate is the indicator of the continued vulnerability of first marriages. The media, our own experience, and the experience of our friends and kin inform us that remarriage and the formation of stepfamilies are common events. However, what differentiates the past from the present is the condition under which the majority of remarriages begin, that is, the fact that remarriage follows divorce rather than death. This difference affects the nature and complexity of remarried family life, and is the subject of our final remarks.

REMARRIED HOUSEHOLDS FOLLOWING DIVORCE VERSUS DEATH

The primary condition that differentiates remarriages that follow divorce from those following the death of a spouse is the living presence of that former spouse. While the former spouse may or may not be physically present in the immediate environment, his or her presence can be made known at any time.

This fact is less relevant when the formerly married couple have no children, since there is no need for continued contact unless the couple desire it. The presence of children, however, complicates the lives of all members of a remarried household because children require continued interaction between parents—interaction which is often legally demanded as a part of custody and visitation arrangements. Thus, while divorce represents the end of the marital relationship, it does not mean the termination of the parental relationship. When children are involved, the presence of a former spouse/parent means that custody arrangements, financial support, and visitation schedules must be negotiated. During the course of childhood these arrangements may need to be renegotiated, particularly after one parent remarries. When remarriage occurs following the death of a spouse/parent, custody, visitation, and financial support do not serve to link two parental (binuclear) households, as they do after divorce.

Problematic Aspects Associated with a Binuclear Family

The quality of the relationship between parents is believed to affect parent–child visitation arrangements. Findings from several studies suggest that visitation of children on the part of a nonresidential father becomes less frequent and more irregular after divorce (Hetherington, Cox, & Cox, 1979; Furstenberg & Spanier, 1984; Wallerstein & Kelly, 1980). In part, this distancing of father and children may result from the quality of the relationship between the father and his former spouse. Negative interaction between former spouses can result in desperate behaviors, such as a biological parent "kidnapping" his or her own child. Conflict between former spouses has been reported to have a negative effect on children (Lutz, 1983). Additionally, children may come to feel a sense of rejection by their nonresidential parent if that parent does not keep his or her visitation schedule, or makes only sporadic or inconsistent contact.

If a child resides with a parent who remarries, he or she is usually expected to be involved with the newly formed family. Such an expectation is evident from the responses of 784 remarried adults who all reported that "close family ties and many shared times" was "very important" to them (Pasley & Ihinger-Tallman, 1984). For some children, such expectations can result in feelings of ambivalence and conflict, creating uncertainty about where their loyalty should reside. As adults vie for the attention and loyalty of a child, the consequence is often a feeling of dislike for the new stepparent.

On the other hand, remarriage following divorce may permit children an alternative living arrangement. Should either the residential parent or the child desire it, the child can move to his or her "other" parent's home. This possibility can generate custody battles between ex-spouses. No such alternative exists for widowed spouses, or orphaned children. Some counselors feel that an "escape" option for the children of a binuclear family may not be a good thing, since children can successfully avoid confrontation, conflict, and accountability for their actions in one parent's household if they have a second home to which they can turn. It may be a particularly bad idea to allow a change in custody when the child or adolescent is not behaving in the custodial home, as this can undermine the parental authority in *both* households (D. Mills, personal communication, February 1, 1986).

Few researchers have studied the effects of divorce versus death on stepmember adjustment. However, most of those that have done so report that the remarried couple feel they have an easier time when death ended the former marriage of one or both spouses. Duberman (1973, 1975) found stepparent–stepchild relationships were rated more positively by the adults in the family when the previous marriage was terminated by death rather than divorce. Duberman also found marital quality scores were higher for couples when a former marriage ended in death. Examining the responses of adolescents, Parish & Kappes (1980) found college students in stepfather families rated their stepfamilies more positively when the family had been broken by the death of their father versus parental divorce. Controls on sex of respondent did not alter this finding. Burgoyne and Clark's (1984) British couples felt it was easier to fulfill the role of stepparent if a previous marriage ended in death rather than divorce. Finally, Ferri's (1984) evidence from a study of British children supports this position. Her data showed a clear trend for boys and girls in both stepmother and stepfather families indicating more positive relationships when the remarriage followed bereavement rather than divorce. She writes, "Children whose parents had been divorced or separated were two and one half times as likely to be seen as 'deviant' [as indicated by a Rutter Home Behavior Score] as those whose natural father or mother had died (p. 73).

There are some scholars, however, who counter this position. Maddox (1975) suggests that stepparents who replace a deceased parent have more difficulty than those who replace a living parent. Bernard (1956) also writes that the entrance of a new parent tends to have an adverse effect after death and a benign effect after divorce.

Problematic Aspects Associated with Marital Dissolution by Death

The stepfamilies of yesteryear likely coped with more complex stepsibling relationships since the overall death rate was higher than it is today and families were larger. In 17th-century Andover, Massachusetts, the average number of children per family was 8.7, and in Hingham, Massachusetts, an average of 7.8 children survived to adulthood (Degler, 1980). Families were equally large in other colonies in the 17th and early 18th centuries. Family structure is hypothesized to have been more complex in the Southern colonies compared to New England because health was more problematic among southerners. Thus, stepsiblings and halfsiblings were more likely to be present in the southern household.

Family size began to decrease in the second half of the 18th century, especially after the Revolution. Degler (1980) reports that "the fertility of white women in the United States fell 50% between 1800 and 1900, from 7.04 in 1800 to 3.56 in 1900" (p. 181). This decrease likely reduced the complexity of stepfamily structure.

It is safe to conclude that in the past there were greater numbers of families with stepmothers rearing stepchildren, since more women/mothers died before rearing their children to adulthood. In addition to the vagaries of disease, there was a higher incidence of maternal death in childbirth than is currently experienced. Demos (1970) estimated that about 20% of maternal deaths among adult women were associated with childbirth in Plymouth Colony. When small children were in the family, a wife's death not only left the family emotionally bereft but functionally bereft as well. An early remarriage permitted a return to routinization and normalcy, but it meant stepmothers parenting their husbands' children.

If Saffady's (1973) interpretation of Sir Thomas More's experience is any indication, at least some children felt hostility, resentment, and abandonment at a parental remarriage after their other parent's death. Such biographical accounts are one of the few sources for interpreting what children felt and/or experienced in stepfamilies in the past. Folk or fairy tales are another source for culturally interpreting what children might experience as a result of living in stepfamilies, especially in stepmother families. The stories of Snow White and Hansel and Gretel tell us that stepmothers plan the death of their stepchildren, and the mistreatment of Cinderella is legendary. However, cultural stereotypes manifest in folk tales do not accurately convey the range of actual emotions and behaviors that bereaved children and surviving spouses experienced in the past. In the final analysis, we have very little evidence that describes or explains our predecessors reactions to loss, adjustments to stepfamily households, and relations between stepmembers.

CONCLUSION

The evidence indicates that in the United States marriage is a valued institution. America has a high first marriage and remarriage rate. In our century, more marriages are dissolved because of divorce than because of the death of a spouse. Yet, even when a marriage is abandoned through legal action the majority of formerly married people marry again, and do so in a relatively short time. This tendency to remarry is as true today as it was in the 17th century.

There are differences between the two time periods with respect to remarriage that were suggested in our earlier discussion. First, different motivations probably prompted the decision to remarry in the past as compared to the present. This is because successful family functioning in agrarian America depended upon a division of labor that called for two adults performing quite different tasks. This traditional division of labor is not as necessary in the urban industrialized present. Second, stepfamily interaction may have been different because of larger families, that is, more stepsiblings and halfsiblings in the family. Third, the absent parent was usually in the grave instead of alive and possibly residing in the neighborhood, and therefore his or her influence was negligible.

The historical record rarely permits a glimpse into the nature of interpersonal relationships, emotions, and experiences of stepfamily members who lived before our time. This limitation is regretful. However, the scholarship of contemporary social historians has revealed important information about the incidence of remarriage and the structure of stepfamilies. This knowledge helps put the present remarriage rate into a more balanced perspective. It also permits us to learn a lesson from the past. It is possible for contemporary students of the family to leave for future scholars a historical record that accurately describes and explains not merely incidence and structure, but information about the interpersonal complexities of stepfamily living as well.

REFERENCES

Anonymous. (1883–1884). Marriage in America. In C. Duhem (Ed.), *All the year round* (Vol. 33, pp. 90–93). London: Crystal Palace Press.

Bernard, J. (1956). *Remarriage: A study in marriage.* New York: Russell & Russell.

Blake, N. M. (1962). *The road to Reno: A history of divorce in the United States.* Westport, CT: Greenwood Press.

Burgoyne, J., & Clark, D. (1984). *Making a go of it: A study of stepfamilies in Sheffield.* London: Routledge & Kegan Paul.

Calhoun, A. W. (1917). *A social history of the American family: Vol. I, Colonial Period 1607 to 1776.* New York: Barnes and Noble.

Calhoun, A. W. (1918). *A social history of the American family: Vol. II, From Independence through the Civil War 1776 to 1865.* New York: Barnes and Noble.

Calhoun, A. W. (1919). *A social history of the American family: Vol. III, From 1865 to 1919.* New York: Barnes and Noble.

Carlier, A. (1972). *Marriage in the United States.* Boston: Arno.

Carr, L. G., & Walsh, L. S. (1983). The planter's wife: The experience of white women in seventeenth century Maryland. In M. Gordon (Ed.), *The American family in social-historical perspective.* New York: St. Martin's.

Carter, H., & Glick, P. C. (1976). *Marriage and divorce: A social and economic study.* Cambridge, MA: Harvard University Press.

Cherlin, A. J. (1981). *Marriage, divorce, remarriage.* Cambridge, MA: Harvard University Press.

Cherlin, A. J., & McCarthy, J. (1985). Remarried couple households: Data from the June 1980 current population survey. *Journal of Marriage and the Family, 47,* 23–30.

Cohn, H. S. (1970). Connecticut's divorce mechanism: 1638–1969. *American Journal of Legal History, 14*(43), 35–54.

Cott, N. F. (1983). Divorce and the changing status of women in eighteenth century Massachusetts. In M. Gordon (Ed.), *The American family in social-historical perspective* (pp. 347–371). New York: St. Martin's.

Degler, C. N. (1980). *At Odds: Women and the family in America from the revolution to the present.* Oxford: Oxford University Press.

Degler, C. N. (1983). The emergence of the modern American family. In M. Gordon (Ed.), *The American family in social-historical perspective* (pp. 61–79). New York: St. Martin's.

Demos, J. (1968). Families in colonial Bristol, Rhode Island: An exercise in historical demography. *William and Mary Quarterly, 25,* 40–57.

Demos, J. (1970). *A little commonwealth: Family life in Plymouth Colony.* London: Oxford University Press.

Duberman, L. (1973). Step-kin relationships. *Journal of Marriage and the Family, 35,* 283–292.

Duberman, L. (1975). *The reconstituted family: A study of remarried couples and their children.* Chicago, IL: Nelson-Hall.

Dupâquier, J., Hèlin, E., Laslett, P., Livi-Bacci, M., & Sogner, S. (Eds.). (1981). *Marriage and remarriage in populations of the past.* New York: Academic Press.

Farber, B. (1972). *Guardians of virtue: Salem Families in 1800.* New York: Basic Books.

Ferri, E. (1984). *Stepchildren: A national study.* Windsor, Berkshire, England: NFER-Nelson.

Fox, V. C., & Quitt, M. H. (1980). Stage VI, spouse loss. In V. C. Fox & M. H. Quitt (Eds.), *Loving, parenting, and dying: The family cycle in England and America, past and present* (pp. 49–61, 400–421). New York: Psychohistory Press.

Frost, W. J. (1973). *The Quaker family in colonial America: A portrait of the society of friends.* New York: St. Martin's.

Furstenberg, F. F., & Spanier, G. B. (1984). *Recycling the family: Remarriage after divorce.* Beverly Hills, CA: Sage.

Glick, P. C. (1980). Remarriage: Some recent changes and variations. *Journal of Family Issues, 1,* 455–478.

Glick, P. C. (1984). Marriage, divorce, and living arrangements: Prospective changes. *Journal of Family Issues, 5,* 7–26.

Griffith, J. D. (1980). Economy, family, and remarriage. *Journal of Family Issues, 1*, 479–496.

Grigg, S. (1977). Toward a theory of remarriage: A case study of Newburyport at the beginning of the nineteenth-century. *Journal of Interdisciplinary History, 8*(2), 183–220.

Guttentag, S., & Secord, P. F. (1983). *Too many women: The sex ratio question.* Beverly Hills, CA: Sage.

Hetherington, E. M., Cox, M., & Cox, R. (1979). Stress and coping in divorce: A focus on women. In J. Gullahorn (Ed.), *Psychology of women in transition* (pp. 95–128). Washington, DC: B. H. Winston & Sons.

Jacobson, P. H. (1959). *American marriage and divorce.* New York: Rinehart.

Keyssar, A. (1980). Widowhood in eighteenth-century Massachusetts. In V. C. Fox & M. H. Quitt (Eds.), *Loving, parenting, and dying: The family cycle in England and America, past and present* (pp. 425–445). New York: Psychohistory Press.

Laslett, P. (1977). *Family life and illicit love in earlier generations.* Cambridge, MA: Cambridge University Press.

Lutz, P. (1983). The stepfamily: An adolescent perspective. *Family Relations, 32*, 367–375.

Maddox, G. (1975). *The half-parent.* New York: Evans Press.

May, E. T. (1983). The pressure to provide: Class, consumerism and divorce in urban America, 1880–1920. In M. Gordon (Ed.), *The American family in social–historical perspective.* New York: St. Martin's.

Norton, A. J., & Glick, P. (1976). Marital instability past, present and future. *Journal of Social Issues, 32*, 5–20.

O'Neill, W. L. (1967). *Divorce in the progressive era.* New Haven, CT: Yale University Press.

Parish, T. S., & Kappes, B. (1980). Impact of father loss on the family. *Social Behavior and Personality, 8*, 107–112.

Pasley, K., & Ihinger-Tallman, M. (1984, October). *Consensus about values among remarried couples.* Paper presented at the Annual Meeting of the National Council on Family Relations, San Francisco, CA.

Saffady, W. (1973). The effects of childhood bereavement and parental remarriage in sixteenth-century England: The Case of Thomas More. *The Journal of Psychohistory, 1*(2), Fall.

United Nations Department of International Economic and Social Affairs Statistical Office. (1985). *Demographic Yearbook, 1983.* New York: Author.

United States Bureau of the Census (1981). Marital status and living arrangements: March, 1980 current population reports. Series p-20, *365*, 1–6.

Wallerstein, J. S., & Kelly, J. B. (1980). *Surviving the breakup.* New York: Basic Books.

Wires, R. (1967). The divorce issue and reform in the nineteenth century. *Ball State Monograph No. 8: Publications in History, No. 2.* Muncie, IN: Ball State University.

Wright, C. D. (1889). *Marriage and divorce in the United States 1867–1886.* Washington, DC: Commissioner of Labor.

2

The Cultural Stereotyping of Stepfamilies

MARILYN COLEMAN AND LAWRENCE H. GANONG
University of Missouri-Columbia

Adjunct faculty members are treated like family . . . the same system that provides us with a job also withholds from us many privileges and makes us feel like stepchildren.   —From *Faculty non-persons live in limbo* (1984).

The New Orleans show marked a coming of age for soft-ware, once the neglected stepchild of the computer business.   —Elmer-DeWitt (1984).

We got beat like stepchildren.   —Clark, cited in Shatel (1983).

Study of the family . . . has been a stepchild . . . of such realms as sociology, psychology, anthropology and home economics.   —Collins (1984).

In the great blooming, buzzing confusion of the outer world we pick out what our culture has already defined for us, and we tend to perceive that which we have picked out in the form stereotyped for us by our culture.   —Lippman (1922, p. 55).

People have a need to organize cognitively their view of the world (Fiske & Taylor, 1984). In order to make sense of the endless flow of information bombarding them, individuals actively attempt to organize stimuli into a manageable number of categories (Ashmore, 1981; Taylor, 1981).

Stereotypes are a direct function of the categorization process (Taylor, 1981). That is, categorization is a precursor of stereotyping (Jones *et al.*, 1984). Stereotypes are not formed of individuals, but of individuals as members of a social category or group. Stereotypes may be defined as a set of beliefs about the personal attributes of a group (or category) of people (Ashmore & Del Boca, 1981).

Although the process of stereotyping is functional because it simplifies cognitive organization, most stereotypes are negative (Schneider, Hastorf, & Ellsworth, 1979) and tend to increase social distance (Allport, 1954). When a stereotype is negative, such as that of the "wicked stepmother," the individuals who are stereotyped may become the object of prejudice (Ehrlich, 1973;

Schneider *et al.*, 1979). Prejudice, or "prejudgments," serve to increase social distance, and they maintain themselves by allowing a person to perceive others and their behaviors in ways that reinforce the prejudice (Snyder & Swann, 1978). In the case of the stepmother, people may interpret a stepmother's behavior as negative, though it may not be, simply because negative behavior fits the image of the "wicked stepmother," thus maintaining the prejudice and the stereotype.

Do people hold stereotypes about stepparents and stepchildren? If so, what is the nature of those stereotypes? If people hold stereotypes, do they affect behavior toward stepfamily members? In this chapter we will look at these questions regarding the issue of cultural stereotyping of stepfamilies. We will examine anecdotal and empirical evidence that indicates the existence of such a stereotype.

ANECDOTAL EVIDENCE

The examples given here illustrate the widespread use in our culture of the "stepchild" as a metaphor for neglect and abuse. Being compared to forgotten computer software, a neglected area of study, a losing basketball team, or any other low status person, place, or thing is not pleasant, and stepchildren face this comparison frequently and in diverse places. This negative image is so pervasive that one definition of the word stepchild is "one that fails to receive proper care or attention" (Webster's Seventh New Collegiate Dictionary, 1976). Interestingly, though the stereotype of the "wicked stepmother" may be more widely known, it is the term "stepchild" that is consistently used to represent a negative experience or situation. This metaphor is not limited to use by the media or the general public; anyone who has run a computer search for books and articles with the word "stepchild" in the title knows that its metaphorical use may be found in such helping professions as nursing, psychiatry, education, and child development (e.g., "Infant and group care: The stepchild of day care," "Caring, the stepchild of our medical care system") as well as in law, economics, and other fields. Wald (1981) states that the term "step-" encapsulates four basic aspects of the human experience of the steprelationship: bereavement, replacement, negative connotations, and lack of institutionalization of this family form in the constellation of families. She contends that the continued use of the prefix "step-" in a negative context and the use of the term "stepchild" as a metaphor for neglect or abuse helps perpetuate a negative bias against stepfamilies. William O. Smith spoke to this issue in his classic 1953 book, *The Stepchild*:

> From the material presented in this chapter we may conclude that there is a definite stereotype of the stepchild in popular thinking; he is a pitiable creature who suffers from cruelty and neglect. Since the term has been bandied about so

freely, the stereotype with all its sinister implications has made a deep impression, and, consciously or unconsciously, influences the reactions toward anyone who has the stepchild label attached to him. Truly, popular usage has done much to fixate the stereotype, and the stereotype has done much to make the lot of the stepchild an unhappy one. (p. 14)

Although Smith's assertions have yet to be tested empirically, this use of "stepchild" as a negative label, apparently as much in use now as 30 years ago, does seem to indicate the existence of a stereotype.

There is other anecdotal evidence for the existence of a stepfamily stereotype. Consider the euphemisms for stepfamily: blended, reconstituted, remarried, Rem, extended, second, merged, combined, reorganized. These terms are used by both professionals and the general public. Why do stepfamilies have so many alternative labels? Some writers and speakers admit they prefer to avoid using the prefix "step-" to escape what they see as its negative affective attachments (Espinoza & Newman, 1979). Jesse Bernard (1956), in her early study of remarriage, wrote, "Because of the emotional connotations of the terms stepchild, stepmother, and stepfather, they are avoided whenever possible . . . for they are, in effect, smear words" (p. 14). Alternative labels are used, therefore, to reduce biased reactions.

Many stepfamily members seek terms to describe themselves that are nonjudgmental (Wald, 1981). There are problems with using these new terms, however. First, most people have little idea of what a Rem or a reconstituted family is. Explanations of these words can be lengthy and confusing. Second, while the use of alternative family labels may help avoid "negative affective attachments," there are not suitable substitutes for stepmother, stepson, and so on. Of course, some families avoid the prefix step- by referring to each other as "mother" or "son." Some creative parents we have known refer to themselves as "Jim's sociological mother" or "Jim's father's wife" or "Jim's other mother." Brenda Maddox (1975) has suggested "mother-by-marriage" as an accurate, nonpejorative substitute for stepmother. But, she also added that "I think attempts to abolish the step term are ridiculous. . . . If the connotation is unpleasant, the reason should be faced, not glossed over with change of label" (p. 165). Such efforts to avoid the step- label provide more anecdotal evidence that a step stereotype may exist.

The most extreme method that can be employed in avoiding the step label is to deny, ignore, or otherwise refuse to recognize the reality of stepfamily status. Clinicians have identified the tendency of some stepfamilies to deny their status (Jacobson, 1980; Johnson, 1980; Visher & Visher, 1979), and researchers have reported that it is a common desire of stepfamily members to be seen by others as a "normal" family (Coleman & Ganong, 1985a; Duberman, 1975). It may be that stepfamilies remain "in the closet" in order to avoid being stereotyped by others and to prevent any consequent negative reactions.

Several clinical writers have argued that negative societal attitudes toward stepfamilies create stress for stepfamily members (Visher & Visher, 1979; Wald, 1981). It has been speculated that the tendency for stepfamily members to seek clinical or counseling services is related to social pressure and the lack of acceptance of this family form (Hutchison & Hutchison, 1979; Kompara, 1980; Visher & Visher, 1979). Jones (1978) has stated, "Interpersonal problems in a stepfamily are complicated by the mere categorization by society and itself as deviant" (p. 220). Stepparenting is considered to be difficult in part due to negative stereotypes and role ambiguity surrounding stepparenthood (Rallings, 1976).

Some clinicians have attributed negative societal attitudes toward stepfamilies to folklore (Fast & Cain, 1966; Jones, 1978; Schulman, 1972; Visher & Visher, 1979; Wald, 1981). Visher and Visher (1979) have referred to stepfamilies as "culturally disadvantaged families" because the term "step" evokes the negative imagery found in fairy tales such as *Snow White, Cinderella,* and *Hansel and Gretel.*

Folklore

Folklore about the step relationship is widespread. Smith (1953) mentioned the existence of 345 variations of the *Cinderella* folk tale alone, and folk tales about step relationships are found in the cultural–historical lore in virtually every part of the globe. The "wicked stepmother" is a prominent character in many folk tales and popular fairy tales (e.g., *Cinderella, Hansel and Gretel, Snow White*). Children are exposed very early to fairy tales, and "wicked stepmother" tales have been enduring favorites. The story of Cinderella has been traced to 9th-century China in much the same form as it is known today and has been known for hundreds of years throughout Europe, Africa, and Latin America. Variations of *Hansel and Gretel* and *Snow White* have also been tracked back centuries in countries throughout the world (Wald, 1981). These folk tales, from which our children's fairy tales are derived, have the same general structure. A mean and unloving stepmother mistreats a poor and helpless stepchild, while the father remains a passive, usually distant character. The stepchild, who is almost always good, triumphs over the stepmother, who is almost always evil. Often, there is a "reconciliation" or renewed closeness with the father (Smith, 1953).

What purposes do these tales serve? Psychoanalyst Helene Deutsch (1973) has argued that the stepmother folk themes allow the splitting of good and bad feelings for a mother onto a stepmother image. Stepmother is a symbol, therefore, representing the child's unacceptable feeling. Bettelheim (1977) defends the "wicked" stepmother in fairy tales as providing a way for children to deal with ambivalent feelings about their mothers, but other clinicians argue that young children are capable of dealing with mixed feelings toward their parents without propagating, using, or relying upon the wicked stepmother imagery of fairy tales (Radomisli, 1981). Stepfathers generally have escaped portrayal in fairy tales, but the prefix "step-" is often considered a pejorative one for stepfathers as well as stepmothers (Leslie, 1982; Wald, 1981).

Do fairy tales help create and maintain certain stereotypes about stepfamily members? The anecdotal evidence would suggest the answer is "yes." Smith (1953) cited case histories in which reading or hearing fairy tales negatively colored children's images of stepmothers and stepfathers. Fairy tales are typically the first exposure to the step relationship for young children. It would seem logical that these first images would influence the development of stereotypes about such relationships. It should be noted, however, that there is little research in general about how children learn stereotypes (Ashmore & Del Boca, 1981) and no research on children's stereotypes of stepfamily members.

EMPIRICAL EVIDENCE

Most research on the content of stereotypes has focused on the social categories of religion, race, sex, ethnic groups, and occupations. Family structure is another potentially salient cue for stereotyping, but it has been seldom investigated. Several writers have speculated that *all* non-nuclear families are viewed as dysfunctional (Cherlin, 1978; Price-Bonham & Balswick, 1980; Uzoka, 1979). It has been argued that the intact nuclear family has been used as the measure of "normalcy" against which other family forms have been judged (Bernard & Corrales, 1979; Lewis, Beavers, Gossett, & Phillips, 1976; Satir, 1982). Empirical evidence for the existence of stereotypes based upon a person's family structure is limited, however.

A series of studies by Etaugh and her colleagues have found that married persons generally are evaluated more positively than single persons (Etaugh & Foresome, 1983; Etaugh & Kasley, 1981; Etaugh & Malstrom, 1981; Etaugh & Riley, 1983). Widowed persons have been found to be evaluated more positively than divorced persons (Etaugh & Crump, 1982; Etaugh & Malstrom, 1981).

There is some evidence that children also have been stereotyped on the basis of family structure. Santrock and Tracy (1978) found that teachers' perceptions of children varied according to family structure. After viewing identical videotapes of a child playing, teachers who believed they were viewing a child from a single-parent household (parents divorced) rated the child as less happy, less emotionally well adjusted, and less able to cope with stress than did teachers rating a child whom they believed was from an intact nuclear home. A similar study of social workers, teachers, and laypersons also found that stereotypes of boys in single-parent households were more negative than stereotypes of boys believed to be in nuclear families (Fry & Addington, 1984). No differences were found between professionals and laypersons. A study done with nursing students found similar results; a child believed to reside with one parent was perceived more negatively than the same child who was believed to live with both parents (Siebert, Ganong, Hagemann, & Coleman, 1986). It should be noted that in the Etaugh series and in other studies of family structure stereotyping, remarried adults and stepchildren were not included as categories.

Negative connotations to the prefix "step-," as well as stereotypes about steprelations, are assumptions that have had little empirical test. A series of studies we have conducted provides some evidence for the existence of such stereotypes.

FOUR STUDIES OF STEPFAMILY STEREOTYPING

The first study was designed to determine whether people have more negative perceptions of the concepts of "stepmother" and "stepfather" than they do of "mother" and "father" (Ganong & Coleman, 1983). Two hundred and eight college students enrolled in introductory courses in human development or health care at a large Mid-Western university rated six family positions via a semantic differential composed of nine pairs of bi-polar adjectives. The items used were affectionate–hateful, good–bad, happy–unhappy, likeable–unlikeable, fair–unfair, loving–unloving, lenient–severe, strict–not strict, and kind–cruel. These were chosen because they were evaluative adjectives that seemed appropriate for perceptions of family role positions.

Subjects were directed to respond to the family position "in general" and not to a specific person they might know in the position. All subjects were common family positions: grandmother, brother, nephew, and cousin. The remaining two family positions for half the subjects were mother and stepfather. The other half of the subjects responded to stepmother and father. The family positions were presented at random, one to a page.

Using MANOVA, mothers were perceived more positively than stepmothers on seven of the nine scales, $F(1, 206) = 21.96, p < .0001$, and fathers were perceived more positively than stepfathers on eight of the nine scales, $F(9, 198) = 14.26, p < .0001$. An examination of responses to the other four family positions indicated no significant differences on any of the nine scales for subjects responding to mother–stepfather compared to those responding to stepmother-father. In other words, the two groups of subjects held similar views toward the family positions included as distractors (i.e., grandmother, brother, nephew, cousin). A rank order of responses to all family positions is shown in Table 2-1.

Table 2-1. Rank Orders of Mean Responses on All Family Positions for All Semantic Differential Scales

Position	Affectionate–Hateful	Fair–Unfair	Kind–Cruel	Loving–Unloving	Strict–Non strict	Lenient–Severe	Happy–Unhappy	Likeable–Unlikeable
Grandmother	1	1	1	1	1	1	1	1
Mother	2	2	2	2	6	5	4	2
Father	3	3	3	3	7	6	5	3
Nephew	4	5	5	4	2	2	2	4
Brother	5	4	4	5	4	4	3	5
Cousin	6	6	6	6	3	3	6	6
Stepmother	7	7	7	7	5	7	7	7
Stepfather	8	8	8	8	8	8	8	8

These data appear to support the contention that "step-" is a perjorative prefix, signifying a more negative image, at least for stepmothers and stepfathers. The stereotype of stepmothers and stepfathers as being less loving and less kind than mothers and fathers still seems to be in operation.

Study 2

To further investigate the possibility of family roles and/or structure as a salient social category by which people organize their perceptions of others, a second study was designed and carried out (Bryan, Coleman, Ganong, & Bryan, 1986). The study was specifically designed to compare perceptions toward stepparents and stepchildren to perceptions toward adults and children in other family structures.

Subjects were 460 female and 236 male undergraduates enrolled in human development, family living, and agricultural economics classes in two Mid-Western universities. Perceptions of stimulus persons were measured with a semantic differential. The First Impression Questionnaire (FIQ) was designed for this study and was refined through pilot testing and factor analysis. The final version of the FIQ (see Appendix 2-1) consisted of 40 items making up six factors: Social Evaluation, Potency, Satisfaction/Security, Personal Character, Activity, and Stability.

During class, students were invited to participate in a study concerning "the accuracy of first impressions." Each student was given 1 of 20 test booklets containing brief descriptions of an adult and an adolescent in a family. Respondents were asked to rate both persons on a set of bipolar scales and to fill out some demographic questions.

The 20 descriptions varied family structure (remarried, married, divorced, widowed, or never married), sex of parent, and sex of child. Writer was chosen for the occupation of the parent because it is perceived as sex neutral (Shinar, 1978). Sex of parent and sex of child were included because previous research has documented that sex is a salient characteristic on which people stereotype (Ashmore, 1981; Etaugh & Crump, 1982; Etaugh & Kasley, 1981; Etaugh & Malstrom, 1981). The parent and child stimulus paragraphs within each test booklet were randomly altered to prevent an order effect. The paragraphs were variations of the following:

> Ann (Alan) Davis is 41, married (divorce, remarried, widowed, never married), and lives in suburban Chicago with her (his) husband (wife) [if divorced, widowed or never married, this was omitted] and her (his) 17-year-old daughter (son, stepdaughter, stepson), Linda (Larry). Ann (Alan) has a master's degree from the University of Illinois and works as a writer. Linda (Larry) is a senior in high school.

The First Impressions Questionnaire booklet consisted of five pages: one page of instructions, one page with the name of the parent underlined in the stimulus paragraph followed by the 40-item FIQ, one page with the same stimulus paragraph but with the name of the child underlined followed by the 40-item FIQ, and two pages requesting demographic information.

The six factors (i.e., Social Evaluation, Potency, Satisfaction/Security, Personal Character, Activity, and Stability) were subjected to 5 (Family Structure) $\times$ 2 (Sex of Parent) $\times$ 2 (Sex of Child) $\times$ 2 (Sex of Respondent) MANOVAs. Family structure was categorized as married, widowed, divorced, remarried, and never married. Sex of respondent was included as an independent variable because there is empirical evidence that males and females consistently differ in person perception (Ashmore, 1981; Etaugh & Crump, 1982; Etaugh & Kasley, 1981; Etaugh & Malstrom, 1981). In the first MANOVA perceptions of the parent were the dependent measures, and in the second MANOVA perceptions of the child were the dependent measures.

Perceptions of the Adult Stimulus

The first MANOVA indicated significant main effects for family structure $F(6, 651) = 5.43, p < .0001$, and sex of the respondent, $F(6, 651) = 7.53, p < .001$. There were no other main effects nor were there any significant interaction effects.

An examination of the univariate analyses of variance indicated significant differences in perceptions of adults on every factor except Activity. A rank ordering of mean responses to parents in various family structures is shown in Table 2-2. Stepparents were seen more negatively than parents in nuclear families on all factors. Parents in nuclear families were perceived the most positively on all measures.

Table 2-2. Rank Order of Mean Responses for Parents and Children of all Family Structures for all Factors of the FIQ

Family Structure	Social Desirability	Potency	Activity	Satisfaction/ Security	Personal Character	Stability
Intact Nuclear	1 (2)	1 (1)	1 (1)	1 (1)	1 (1)	1 (1)
Widowed	2 (1)	2 (2)	4 (3)	3 (2)	2 (2)	2 (2)
Divorced	3 (3)	3 (3)	2 (2)	5 (5)	3 (4)	3 (4)
Stepfamily	4 (5)	5 (5)	3 (5)	2 (3)	4 (5)	4 (5)
Never Married	5 (4)	4 (4)	5 (4)	4 (4)	5 (3)	5 (3)

Note. Numbers in parentheses are rank orders for responses to the child stimulus.

Female parents (biological mothers and stepmothers) were perceived more positively (Social Evaluation, $p < .05$), as more potent (Potency, $p < .0001$) and as more active (Activity, $p = .0001$) than male parents (fathers and stepfathers). No differences were perceived for Satisfaction/Security, Personal Character, and Stability.

Female respondents perceived parents differently from male respondents on every measure except Stability. Females rated the parent stimulus more positively than males did.

Perceptions of Child Stimulus

Multivariate analyses of variance tests indicated significant main effects for family structure, $F(24,2274) = 6.63$, $p < .0001$, sex of the stimulus child, $F(6,651) = 2.68$, $p < .05$, and respondent's sex $F(6,651) = 5.86$, $p < .0001$. There was only one significant interaction effect, respondent sex by sex of the stimulus child, $F(6,651) = 2.26$, $p < .05$.

In the univariate analysis of variance, significant differences were found on all six factors for the main effect of family structure. Stepchildren were seen less positively than children from nuclear families on every measure. In fact, stepchildren were ranked lower than children from all other family structures on five of the six factors. In general, children who had never experienced family disruption were seen as more stable and as more satisfied and secure than those from less "traditional" households.

Daughters (biological and step) were perceived more positively than sons on four factors: Social Evaluation, Potency, Activity, and Personal Character. No differences were found on Satisfaction/Security and Stability factors.

Female respondents rated the stimulus child more positively than did male respondents on the Social Evaluation, Potency, Satisifaction/Security, and Personal Character factors. No differences were found on the Activity factors.

Examination of the Sex of Respondent × Sex of Stimulus Child interaction on the ANOVAs indicated that differences were found only on the Activity factor. Same-sex pairings were perceived more positively than when the sex of the stimulus child was different from that of the respondent.

Study 3

The results of Study 2 appear to support the contention often made by clinicians that a bias toward stepfamilies exists (Hutchison & Hutchison, 1979; Kompara, 1980; Palermo, 1980; Visher & Visher, 1979). If stepfamilies are at "high risk" for cultural stereotyping, it is not beyond the realm of possibility that mental health professionals are themselves susceptible to these stereotypes. Although most counselors strive to eliminate biases from the "helping relationship," studies have found that mental health professionals stereotype such client characteristics as sex (Maslin & Davis, 1975), social class (Fielding & Evered, 1978), and ethnicity (Wampold, Casas, & Atkinson, 1981). Family structure has not yet been studied as a client characteristic in relationship to counselor stereotypes, therefore, a third study was designed and executed (Bryan, Ganong, Coleman, & Bryan, 1985).

The sample consisted of 256 females and 119 males from the fields of social work and counseling psychology. Of the total sample, 123 were employed professionals, 147 were graduate students, and 105 were undergraduates. Student subjects were enrolled in counseling and social work courses at the University of Missouri. Active professionals were recruited from statewide meetings of the National Association of Social Workers, the American Association of Social Workers, and the American Association of Marriage and Family Therapy, as well as from agencies in the central-Missouri area.

The methodology was basically the same as that employed in the second study. A semantic differential was used again. The final instrument, the First Impressions Semantic Differential (FISD), consisted of 25 items loading on four factors (Evaluative, Potency, Activity, and Adjustment/Well Being). Principal component factor analysis was used to develop the final version of the FISD (see Appendix 2-2).

The procedures for this study were identical to those in Study 2. The concepts chosen for study were "parent" (father, stepfather, mother, stepmother) and "child" (daughter, stepdaughter, son, stepson). Concept combinations (e.g., father–son, stepfather–stepson, stepfather–stepdaughter) were presented within the same stimulus paragraph used in Study 2. Paragraphs varied in family structure (intact nuclear or stepfamily), sex of parent, and sex of child.

In this study four comparisons were made using a series of MANOVAs: (1) counselor's perceptions of parents in intact families versus stepparents; (2) perceptions of children in intact nuclear families versus stepchildren; (3) perceptions of stepparents and parents held by experienced and inexperienced counselors; and (4) perceptions of stepchildren and children in intact nuclear families held by experienced and inexperienced counselors. All sex combinations of parents and children were portrayed in the vignettes (e.g., mother–son, mother–daughter, stepmother–stepson, stepmother–stepdaughter).

For comparisons (1) and (2), FISD scales representing the four dependent measures were subjected to a 2 (Family Structure) $\times$ 2 (Sex of Parent) $\times$ 2 (Sex of Child) MANOVA. For comparisons (3) and (4), a four-way MANOVA, 2 (Family Structure) $\times$ 2 (Sex of Parent) $\times$ 2 (Sex of Child) $\times$ 2 (Professional Experience of Subject) was calculated using the FISD factor scores as dependent measures.

The means and standard deviations for each stimulus parent and child are shown in Table 2-3. The MANOVA for comparison (1) indicated a significant main effect for family structure, $F(4, 367) = 2.69, p < .05$, and sex of parent, $F(4, 367) = 6.45, p < .0001$. The main effect of sex of the child was not significant; there were no interaction effects. Inspection of the ANOVAs revealed that stepparents were perceived to be less potent and less well adjusted than parents in intact nuclear families. Also, stepfathers and fathers were viewed as less potent and less well adjusted than stepmothers and mothers.

For perceptions of children (comparison [2]), the MANOVA yielded a significant main effect for family structure, $F(4, 367) = 13.89, p < .0001$, but there were no other main effects and no significant interactions. Stepchildren were evaluated less positively and viewed as less potent, less active, and less well adjusted.

Table 2-3. Means and Standard Deviations for Each Stimulus Parent and Child

	Evaluative	Potency	Activity	Adjustment & Well-being
Parent Stimulus				
Nuclear Family				
M	38.21	13.01	7.40	13.98
SD	10.45	4.03	2.02	4.74
Stepfamily				
M	40.24	13.86	7.35	15.43
SD	10.64	4.60	1.98	4.65
Female				
M	38.49	12.50	7.26	14.07
SD	11.03	4.34	2.04	4.63
Male				
M	40.03	14.45	7.51	15.40
SD	10.06	4.11	1.95	4.78
Child Stimulus				
Nuclear Family				
M	42.03	16.03	7.90	15.79
SD	10.60	3.70	2.16	4.73
Stepfamily				
M	45.21	17.21	8.47	19.43
SD	10.89	4.15	2.13	5.49
Female				
M	43.38	17.07	8.52	19.09
SD	10.87	4.12	2.16	5.65
Male				
M	47.04	17.36	8.42	19.77
SD	10.73	4.23	2.13	5.25

Note. Higher mean scores denote negative direction.

For comparison (3), there was a significant main effect for family structure, $F(4,359) = 2.65$, $p = .0331$, and for sex of parent, $F(4,359) = 5.86$, $p < .0001$. A Professional Experience $\times$ Family Structure Interaction, $F(4,359) = 3.52$, $p = .0078$ was also significant. Since this comparison was concerned with professional experiences, only the Professional Experience $\times$ Family Structure interaction was analyzed further. Univariate differences were found on three factors. Examination of the pairwise mean comparison indicated that stepparents were viewed less positively by *inexperienced counselors* on the Evaluative factor and as less potent and less well adjusted than were parents in intact nuclear families. There were no differences in experienced counselors' perceptions of nuclear family parents and stepparents.

For comparison (4) there was a significant main effect for professional experience, $F(4,357) = 3.68$, $p = .0059$, and family structure, $F(4,357) = 6.72$, $p < .0001$, was the only significant interaction effect. The ANOVA comparisons for this interaction revealed a difference for the Evaluative and the Adjustment/Well Being factors. Inexperienced counselors viewed children from nuclear families more positively on these factors than experienced counselors did. Those counselors with experience did not view stepchildren differently from children in intact families.

The results of the data analyses for the first two comparisons indicate that stepparents and stepchildren are evaluated more negatively than parents and children from intact nuclear families. These results support the contention that a strong negative stereotype of stepfamily positions exists (Visher & Visher, 1979; Wald, 1981).

The results of comparisons (3) and (4) require further consideration, however. The data for these two hypotheses indicate that amount of professional experience has a significant effect on perceptions of persons from intact or stepfamilies. Only those with limited experience perceived stepparents and stepchildren differently from parents and children in nuclear families. Inexperienced helping professionals saw intact nuclear family members more positively than stepfamily members and more positively than experienced helpers evaluated target persons from either family structure.

Study 4

A fourth study was conducted with another group of inexperienced helping professionals (Blaine, Ganong, & Coleman, 1985). The sample for this study consisted of 149 nursing students enrolled in baccalaureate programs from three Mid-Western universities. Each subject was presented with a brief written vignette of a child and asked to respond with general impressions of the child and predictions about what could be expected from the child and his/her parents in the clinical setting.

The vignettes varied as to sex of the child, family structure, and diagnosis of a problem the child had. Family structure was varied in four ways, by indicating the child lived with his/her mother and father, stepmother and father, stepfather and mother, or by not conveying any information about the family as a "no information" control. The child's diagnosis was either enuresis (bedwetting) having physiological causes or enuresis having psychological causes. In the vignette, the 5-year-old child was described as coming to a clinic for a physical exam prior to beginning school in the fall.

Each subject received one of eight booklets containing a variation of the vignette. After reading the description, subjects responded to the FISD used in Study 3 and to a series of 14 questions developed to determine the predicted behavior of the child and parents in a clinical setting. These questions consisted of statements to which subjects responded on 7-point bipolar scales.

Based upon our earlier findings, it was predicted that nursing students would have lower evaluations of a child from a stepfamily than from the nuclear family or no family information groups. It was also expected that children with a diagnosed psychological problem would be perceived more negatively than children with a physical problem, and those from stepfamilies with a psychological problem would be seen least positively of all groups.

The first prediction was supported only weakly. On the FISD, stepchildren from both stepmother and stepfather households were seen more negatively on the Evaluative scale, but no differences were obtained on the Potency or Adjustment scales. On the 14 questions predicting clinical behavior, only three comparisons were significantly different. Interestingly, these three items did not relate to the child's behavior toward the nurse or other exam-related behavior but to the child's relationships to family members. In response to the item "To what extent would Jason's family be concerned for his well-being," nursing students indicated that stepchildren would have less concerned families than the no information control and nuclear family. The other items with significant differences referred to father–child interactions. The responses to the questions "To what extent would Jason respond to his father's/stepfather's/parental discipline during the exam?" and "How helpful do you think Jason's father/stepfather/parent would be to a nurse in encouraging him to be cooperative during the procedures?" resulted in fathers in stepmother households and stepfathers being seen as less helpful in managing the child's behavior than fathers in nuclear families or the gender-free "parent" from control families. No differences were found on comparable questions of mother involvement. All in all, it would seem most accurate to conclude that there were only a few differences in how the child was perceived by these nursing students.

The second prediction that psychological versus physical diagnosis would make a difference was also not supported. No differences were found in perceptions between a child with enuresis caused by psychological problems and a child with enuresis caused by physical problems. There were also no sex by diagnosis or family structure by diagnosis effects. This finding does not support other research on nurses and nursing students' reactions to differential diagnosis, but it may be because previous research focused on adults rather than on children.

DISCUSSION

Although stereotypes are not inherently bad, implications of negative stereotyping of stepfamilies by certain populations may be far-reaching. Stereotypes may cause problems for members of stereotyped groups in a number of ways. First, stereotypes distort perceptions so that what is perceived is what is believed about the group. Negative stereotypes, therefore, lead people to evaluate the stereotyped group less favorably no matter what behavior is observed. This has been called the "cognitive confirmation" effect (Darley & Gross, 1983). For example, counselors who hold negative stereotypes of stepparents and stepchildren may interpret functional behavior negatively, and, therefore, not be therapeutically effective. It also may be true that teachers who hold negative stereotypes of stepchildren may perceive their behavior more negatively than it actually is. This could have serious consequences for the stepchild's self-esteem in the school setting. To enable counselors, teachers, youth leaders, clergy, and other professionals to be more objective in their interactions with stepfamily members, professional training should be provided that disseminates information (strengths and problems) about stepfamilies. Family therapists who are or have been members of stepfamilies agree: In a study of a random selection of American Association of Marriage and Family Therapy members, Bennett (1981) found that all of those respondents who had been stepchildren or stepparents at some point in their lives indicated the need for therapists to have special training to work with stepfamilies. Only a small proportion (14%) of other therapists saw the need for special training.

The "cognitive confirmation" effect also calls into question the conclusions of studies on stepchildren based on rating by individuals who knew the children's family structure prior to the rating (Perry & Pfuhl, 1963; Touliatos & Lindholm, 1980). Previous knowledge of family structure will likely influence how behavior is evaluated. Therefore, differences in rating may be due to stereotyped perceptions rather than true behavioral difference.

Another problem of stereotyping is that beliefs about a group of people may influence behaviors directed toward members of that group. One possible consequence is that these stereotyped beliefs may influence interaction with members of the group in such a way that expected behavior is elicited (Snyder & Swann, 1978). This has been called the "behavioral confirmation" effect (Snyder & Swann, 1978) or the "self-fulfilling prophecy" (Merton, 1948). No data exist to either support or refute the "behavioral confirmation" effect as applied to family structure stereotypes.

Finally, stereotypes might also affect how members of a group perceive and value themselves. Visher and Visher (1979) report that stepfamilies often attempt to hide their status from others, indicating some awareness of the negative stereotype and the social distance it creates. There are many examples of this: Stepchildren in stepfather families often publicly use their stepfather's last name while legally maintaining their biological father's surname. There are also stepmother families where all family members share the same surname (often presenting themselves as nuclear families). Other stepfamilies often simply deny they are a stepfamily or that a remarriage has taken place (Coleman & Ganong, 1985b). In hiding their step status, stepfamily members may be perpetuating prejudicial perceptions, in that unfamiliar categories are frequently viewed more harshly than what is familiar (Livesley & Bromley, 1973). Even within the stepfamily, stereotypes of "stepparent" and "stepchild" may affect expectations of one another. It may also affect how they interpret each others' behavior and subsequent interactions with each other, especially during the early phases of stepfamily development. For example, if children whose parents remarry expect their stepparent to be "wicked" and "cruel," this expectation may, in turn, elicit negative behavior that affects stepfamily adjustment.

One outcome of prejudicial stereotyping is to create social distance (Allport, 1954). There is some indication that society has created social distance from stepfamilies by attempting to ignore them as a prominent family form. The term stepfamily is not found in most standard American dictionaries nor are any of the euphemisms mentioned. The relative absence of greeting cards for stepmothers, stepfathers, and stepchildren is another example of the symbolic avoidance of stepfamilies. Even family professionals are subject to this. For example, stepfamilies are virtually ignored in marriage and family living textbooks while less common relationships such as communes and interracial marriages are often more comprehensively covered (Nolan, Coleman, & Ganong, 1984). Robinson (1980) has postulated that the lack of research on stepfamilies is due in part to a bias against them. Sensing this negative stereotype against them, stepfamilies may deny their step status or refuse to participate in studies (Burgoyne & Clark, 1984; Coleman & Ganong, 1985b; Gibralter & London, 1984; Visher & Visher, 1979). Stepfamily researchers may contribute to this problem by their pervasive use of a deficit-comparison orientation in which stepfamilies and their individual members are deemed to be in a deficit position vis-à-vis nuclear families (Ganong & Coleman, 1984). Few attempts have been made by researchers to examine the strengths of stepfamilies, to postulate "new" models of healthy family functioning more fitting to the complexity unique to stepfamilies, or to examine their data with an attitude that different and deficient are not necessarily analogous. The deficit-comparison orientation of researchers perhaps illustrates the broader cultural views toward stepfamilies and stepfamily roles. This may indicate that researchers themselves are influenced by the negative stereotypes.

SUMMARY

Is There a Stepfamily Stereotype?

There is abundant anecdotal evidence for the existence of a stepfamily stereotype. The use of "stepchild" as a term signifying neglect and abuse and the search for alternative terms that abandon the "step-" prefix are indications that stepfamily labels serve as cognitive cues for a stepfamily stereotype. A strong argument can be made that folk tales have facilitated either the development or the maintenance of beliefs about stepmothers and stepchildren. The recognition of a step category for stereotyping appears to be widely held by clinical writers (Prosen & Farmer, 1982; Visher & Visher, 1979) and by stepfamily members themselves.

The empirical evidence for a step stereotype is also quite compelling, although many questions remain unanswered and much more research is needed before definitive conclusions can be drawn. It may be concluded from the four studies reported here that stepfamily status is a social category by which people are stereotyped. It must be noted, however, that these studies utilized a similar design: a brief written stimulus, followed by a semantic differential. The minimal cues can be seen as a stringent test for identifying social categories for stereotypes but, on the other hand, the external validity of such stimuli is low. The question remains: Would other methods of investigating step stereotypes find similar results to these studies? Other media, such as audiotapes, videotapes, and confederates should be used to elicit step stereotypes, and different instrumentation should be employed to broaden the ecological validity of these studies.

What Is the Nature of These Stereotypes?

The anecdotal evidence indicates that the stepfamily stereotype is a negative one. Stepparents shun the labels of stepmother and stepfather (Maddox, 1975), and professionals think of new terms that are less pejorative (Espinoza & Newman, 1979). Early sociological researchers (Bernard, 1956; Smith, 1953) and clinicians in recent years (Wald, 1981) have argued that the societal perception of step relations is a negative one and that this has a potentially destructive effect for stepfamilies. It can be argued that the relative absence of institutional guidelines for stepfamilies is due to an avoidance of what society deems a deviant family form (Cherlin, 1978).

From the research on this subject, it can be concluded only that step stereotypes are relatively less positive (or more negative) than stereotypes of other family structures. Generally, responses to stepmothers, stepfathers, and stepchildren were less positive than responses to mothers, fathers, and children, but the responses seldom were negative in an absolute sense. Mean scores for stepfamily positions on semantic differential items tended to be near the midpoint, with mean scores for comparison stimuli falling toward the positive side of the scales. The empirical evidence cited here supports claims that non-nuclear families are compared to nuclear families as a normal standard (Cherlin, 1978; Price-Bonham & Balswick, 1980). We cannot conclude, however, that the step stereotype is negative, just that it is more negative than for other family stereotypes.

How Widespread Are These Stereotypes?

The stereotypes appear to be widely held, although research has been limited to college students and helping professionals. Little is known about how pervasive these perceptions might be. The influence of such variables as family structure, age, exposure to stepfamily members, and education has not been investigated. Further research is needed to delineate the breadth of adherence to stepfamily stereotypes.

DIRECTIONS FOR FUTURE RESEARCH

It has been pointed out that research is needed to: (1) confirm the existence of step stereotypes using other research methods; and (2) identify the correlates of adherence to step stereotypes. Future research could also focus on the content of such stereotypes. Of more practical interest, however, are the issues of cognitive effects (Darley & Gross, 1983) and behavioral confirmation effects (Snyder & Swann, 1978). In other words, does knowledge of a target person's stepfamily status affect subsequent interpretations of the target person's behavior and motivation (cognitive confirmation), and does knowledge of a target person's stepfamily status affect behavior directed toward the target person (i.e., behavioral confirmation)? These questions are important ones because of their implications for the functioning of stepfamily members. Studies addressing these effects could shed light on many of the anecdotal arguments presented earlier in this chapter.

APPENDIX 2-1

First Impressions Questionnaire

Place an "X" in the blank which best represents how you feel about
ALAN

Honest ___:___:___:___:___:___:___	Dishonest
Insecure ___:___:___:___:___:___:___	Secure
Family Oriented ___:___:___:___:___:___:___	Not Family Oriented
Incompetent ___:___:___:___:___:___:___	Competent
Hateful ___:___:___:___:___:___:___	Affectionate
Quarrelsome ___:___:___:___:___:___:___	Congenial
Predictable ___:___:___:___:___:___:___	Unpredictable
Unloving ___:___:___:___:___:___:___	Loving
Successful ___:___:___:___:___:___:___	Unsuccessful
Fortunate ___:___:___:___:___:___:___	Unfortunate
Disrespectful ___:___:___:___:___:___:___	Respectful
Lonely ___:___:___:___:___:___:___	Not Lonely
Responsible ___:___:___:___:___:___:___	Irresponsible
Sick ___:___:___:___:___:___:___	Healthy
Satisfied ___:___:___:___:___:___:___	Dissatisfied
Cruel ___:___:___:___:___:___:___	Kind
Happy ___:___:___:___:___:___:___	Sad
Disagreeable ___:___:___:___:___:___:___	Agreeable
Fair ___:___:___:___:___:___:___	Unfair
Intelligent ___:___:___:___:___:___:___	Not Intelligent
Understandable ___:___:___:___:___:___:___	Mysterious
Impulsive ___:___:___:___:___:___:___	Deliberate
Approving ___:___:___:___:___:___:___	Disapproving
Aggressive ___:___:___:___:___:___:___	Defensive
Disobedient ___:___:___:___:___:___:___	Obedient
Sexy ___:___:___:___:___:___:___	Not Sexy
Wholesome ___:___:___:___:___:___:___	Unwholesome
Active ___:___:___:___:___:___:___	Passive
Insensitive ___:___:___:___:___:___:___	Sensitive
Changeable ___:___:___:___:___:___:___	Stable
Eager ___:___:___:___:___:___:___	Indifferent
Immoral ___:___:___:___:___:___:___	Moral
Sophisticated ___:___:___:___:___:___:___	Naive
Reputable ___:___:___:___:___:___:___	Disreputable
Ungrateful ___:___:___:___:___:___:___	Grateful
Good ___:___:___:___:___:___:___	Bad
Rude ___:___:___:___:___:___:___	Friendly
Poor ___:___:___:___:___:___:___	Rich
Independent ___:___:___:___:___:___:___	Dependent
Aimless ___:___:___:___:___:___:___	Motivated

APPENDIX 2-2

First Impressions Semantic Differential

Directions:

Rate on the following dimensions which most closely reflects your impression.

Good	___	___	___	___	___	___	Bad
Unfair	___	___	___	___	___	___	Fair
Grateful	___	___	___	___	___	___	Ungrateful
Hateful	___	___	___	___	___	___	Affectionate
Weak	___	___	___	___	___	___	Strong
Severe	___	___	___	___	___	___	Lenient
Constrained	___	___	___	___	___	___	Free
Passive	___	___	___	___	___	___	Active
Relaxed	___	___	___	___	___	___	Tense
Excitable	___	___	___	___	___	___	Calm
Obedient	___	___	___	___	___	___	Disobedient
Disrespectful	___	___	___	___	___	___	Respectful
Loyal	___	___	___	___	___	___	Disloyal
Unstable	___	___	___	___	___	___	Stable
Likeable	___	___	___	___	___	___	Unlikeable
Insecure	___	___	___	___	___	___	Secure
Competent	___	___	___	___	___	___	Incompetent
Disagreeable	___	___	___	___	___	___	Agreeable
Kind	___	___	___	___	___	___	Cruel
Unfortunate	___	___	___	___	___	___	Fortunate
Stable Family Member	___	___	___	___	___	___	Unstable Family Member
Unsuccessful	___	___	___	___	___	___	Successful
Predictable	___	___	___	___	___	___	Unpredictable
Uncooperative	___	___	___	___	___	___	Cooperative
Family Oriented	___	___	___	___	___	___	Not Family Oriented
Unhappy Home Life	___	___	___	___	___	___	Happy Home Life
Adjusted	___	___	___	___	___	___	Maladjusted
Rigid	___	___	___	___	___	___	Adaptable
Loving	___	___	___	___	___	___	Unloving
Unhappy	___	___	___	___	___	___	Happy
Congenial	___	___	___	___	___	___	Quarrelsome
Isolated Family Member	___	___	___	___	___	___	Not Isolated Family Member
Unwholesome	___	___	___	___	___	___	Wholesome
Immoral	___	___	___	___	___	___	Moral
Independent	___	___	___	___	___	___	Dependent
Not Lonely	___	___	___	___	___	___	Lonely
Satisfied	___	___	___	___	___	___	Dissatisfied
Defensive	___	___	___	___	___	___	Aggressive
Contented	___	___	___	___	___	___	Discontented
Not Jealous	___	___	___	___	___	___	Jealous

REFERENCES

Allport, G. (1954). *The nature of prejudice.* Cambridge, MA: Addison-Wesley.

Ashmore, R. D. (1981). Sex stereotypes and implicit personality theory. In D. L. Hamilton (Ed.), *Cognitive processes in stereotyping and intergroup behavior* (pp. 37–81). Hillsdale, NJ: Erlbaum.

Ashmore, R. D., & Del Boca, F. K. (1981). Conceptual approaches to stereotypes and stereotyping. In D. L. Hamilton (Ed.), *Cognitive processes in stereotyping and intergroup behavior* (pp. 1–35). Hillsdale, NJ: Erlbaum.

Bennett, P. (1981). Stepfamily survey: The final report. *Stepparent News, 2*(10), 3.

Bernard, J. (1956). *Remarriage.* New York: Dryden Press.

Bernard, C., & Corrales, R. (1979). *The theory and techniques of family therapy.* Springfield, IL: Charles C. Thomas.

Bettelheim, B. (1977). *The uses of enchantment: The meaning and importance of fairy tales.* New York: Vintage.

Blaine, D., Ganong, L., & Coleman, M. (1985). *The influence of family structure and sex on nursing students perceptions.* Unpublished manuscript, University of Missouri, School of Nursing, Columbia, MO.

Bryan, H., Ganong, L., Coleman, M., & Bryan, L. (1985). Counselor's perceptions of stepparents and stepchildren. *Journal of Counseling Psychology, 32*(2), 279–282.

Bryan, L., Coleman, M., Ganong, L., & Bryan, H. (1986). Person perception: Family structure as a cue for stereotyping. *Journal of Marriage and the Family, 48,* 169–174.

Burgoyne, J., & Clark, D. (1984). *Making a go of it: A study of stepfamilies in Sheffield.* London: Routledge & Kegan Paul.

Cherlin, A. (1978). Remarriage as an incomplete institution. *American Journal of Sociology, 84,* 634–649.

Coleman, M., & Ganong, L. (1985a). Childbearing and stepfamilies: Effects on half-siblings. Unpublished raw data.

Coleman, M., & Ganong, L. (1985b). Effects of childbearing in stepfamilies on half-siblings: Sampling procedures. Unpublished raw data.

Collins, G. (1984, December). Cited in the *Task Force for the Development of A Family Discipline, 1*(1).

Darley, J., & Gross, P. H. (1983). A hypothesis confirming bias in labeling effects. *Journal of Personality and Social Psychology, 44,* 20–33.

Deutsch, H. (1973). *The psychology of women: A psychoanalytic interpretation.* New York: Bantam.

Duberman, L. (1975). *The reconstituted family.* Chicago: Nell-Hall.

Ehrlich, H. J. (1973). *The social psychology of prejudice.* New York: Wiley.

Elmer-DeWitt, P. (1984, March 5). The stepchild comes of age. *Time,* p. 54.

Espinoza, R., & Newman, Y. (1979). *Stepparenting* (DHEW Publication No. ADM 78-579). Washington, DC: U.S. Government Printing Office.

Etaugh, C., & Crump, D. (1982). Perceptions of restricted relationships of divorced and widowed women and men. *Perceptual and Motor Skills, 55,* 223–228.

Etaugh, C., & Foresome, E. (1983). Evaluations of competence as a function of sex and marital status. *Sex Role, 9*(7), 759–765.

Etaugh, C., & Kasley, H. (1981). Evaluating competence: Effect of sex, marital status, and parental status. *Psychology of Women Quarterly, 6*(2), 196–203.

Etaugh, C., & Malstrom, J. (1981). The effect of marital status on person perception. *Journal of Marriage and the Family, 43,* 801–805.

Etaugh, C., & Riley, S. (1983). Evaluating competence of women and men: Effects of marital and parental status and occupational sex-typing. *Sex Roles, 9*(9), 943–952.

Faculty non-persons live in limbo. (1984, April). *Central Missouri State University Mule-skinner*, p. 2.

Fast, I., & Cain, A. C. (1966). The stepparent role: Potential for disturbances in family functioning. *American Journal of Orthopsychiatry, 36*, 485–491.

Fielding, G., & Evered, C. (1978). An exploratory experimental study of the influence of patients' social background upon diagnostic process and outcome. *Psychiatric Clinics, 11*, 61–86.

Fiske, S. T., & Taylor, S. (1984). *Social Cognition*. Reading, MA: Addison-Wesley.

Fry, P. S., & Addington, J. (1984). Professionals' negative expectations of boys from father-headed single-parent families: Implications for the training of child-care professionals. *British Journal of Developmental Psychology, 2*, 337–346.

Ganong, L., & Coleman, M. (1983). Stepparent: A perjorative term? *Psychological Reports, 52*, 919–922.

Ganong, L., & Coleman, M. (1984). The effects of remarriage on children: A review of the empirical literature. *Family Relations, 33*, 389–406.

Gibralter, J., & London, H. (1984, October). *A study of stepfamily interaction patterns*. Paper presented at the meeting of the National Council on Family Relations, San Francisco, CA.

Hutchison, J., & Hutchison, K. (1979). Issues and conflicts in stepfamilies. *Family Perspectives, 19*, 111–121.

Jacobson, D. (1980). Crisis intervention with stepfamilies. *New Directions for Mental Health Services, 6*, 35–42.

Johnson, H. C. (1980). Working with stepfamilies: Principles of practice. *Social Work, 25*, 304–308.

Jones, E. E., Farina, A., Hastorf, A. H., Markus, H., Miller, D. T., Scott, R. A., & French, R. (1984). *Social stigma: The psychology of marked relationships*. New York: Freeman.

Jones, S. M. (1978). Divorce and remarriage: A new beginning, a new set of problems. *Journal of Divorce, 2*(3), 217–227.

Kompara, D. (1980). Difficulties in the socialization process of stepparenting. *Family Relations, 29*, 69–73.

Leslie, G. (1982). *The family in social context* (5th ed.). New York: Oxford University Press.

Lewis, J., Beavers, W., Gossett, J., & Phillips, V. (1976). *No single thread: Psychological health in family systems*. New York: Brunner/Mazel.

Lippmann, W. (1922). *Public opinion*. New York: Harcourt, Brace, Jovanovich.

Livesley, W., & Bromley, D. (1973). *Person perception in childhood and adolescence*. London: Wiley.

Maddox, B. (1975). *The half-parent: Living with other people's children*. New York: Signet.

Maslin, A., & Davis, J. (1975). Sex role stereotyping as a factor in mental health standards among counselors in training. *Journal of Counseling Psychology, 22*, 87–91.

Merton, R. (1948). The self-fulfilling prophecy. *Antioch Review, 8*, 193–210.

Nolan, J., Coleman, M., & Ganong, L. (1984). The presentation of stepfamilies in marriage and family textbooks. *Family Relations, 33*, 559–566.

Palermo, E. (1980, April). Remarriage: Parental perceptions of steprelations with children and adolescents. *Journal of Psychiatric Nursing and Mental Health Services*, pp. 9–13.

Perry, J., & Pfuhl, E. (1963). Adjustment of children in 'solo' and 'remarriage' homes. *Marriage and Family Living, 25*, 221–223.

Price-Bonham, S., & Balswick, J. (1980). The noninstitutions: Divorce, desertion and remarriage. *Journal of Marriage and the Family, 42*, 959–972.

Prosen, S. S., & Farmer, J. H. (1982). Understanding stepfamilies: Issues and implications for counselors. *The Personnel and Guidance Journal, 60*, 393–397.

Radomisli, M. (1981). Stereotypes, stepmothers, and splitting. *The American Journal of Psychoanalysis, 41*(2), 121–127.

Rallings, E. M. (1976). The special role of the stepfather. *The Family Coordinator, 25*(4), 445–450.

Robinson, M. (1980). Stepfamilies: A reconstituted family system. *Journal of Family Therapy, 2*, 45–69.

Santrock, J., & Tracy, R. (1978). Effects of children's family structure status on the development of stereotypes by teachers. *Journal of Educational Psychology, 70*, 754–757.

Satir, V. (1982). Remaking the stepfamily's image. *Stepfamily Bulletin, 2*(3/4), 18.

Schneider, D., Hastorf, A., & Ellsworth, P. (1979). *Person perception.* Reading, MA: Addison-Wesley.

Schulman, G. (1972). Myths that intrude on the adaptation of the stepfamily. *Social Casework, 53*, 131–139.

Shatel, T. (1983, January 20). Cowboys sit tall in saddle after losing shootout at MU. *Kansas City Star*, pp. 1D, 3D.

Shinar, E. (1978). Person perception as a function of occupation and sex. *Sex Roles, 4*, 679–693.

Siebert, K., Ganong, L., Hagemann, V., & Coleman, M. (1986). Nursing students' perceptions of a child: The influence of information on family structure. *Journal of Advanced Nursing, 11*, 333–337.

Smith, W. O. (1953). *The stepchild.* Chicago, IL: University of Chicago Press.

Snyder, M., & Swann, W. (1978). Behavioral confirmation in social interaction: From social perception to social reality. *Journal of Experimental and Social Psychology, 14*, 148–162.

Taylor, S. E. (1981). A categorization approach to stereotyping. In D. L. Hamilton (Ed.), *Cognitive processes in stereotyping and intergroup behavior* (pp. 83–114). Hillsdale, NJ: Erlbaum.

Touliatos, J., & Lindholm, B. (1980). Teachers' perceptions of behavior problems in children from intact, single-parent, and step-parent families. *Psychology in the Schools, 17*, 264–269.

Uzoka, A. (1979). The myth of the nuclear family: Historical background and clinical implications. *American Psychologist, 34*, 1095–1106.

Visher, E., & Visher, J. (1979). *Stepfamilies: A guide to working with stepparents and stepchildren.* New York: Brunner/Mazel.

Wald, E. (1981). *The remarried family: Challenge and promise.* New York: Family Services Association of America.

Wampold, B., Casas, S., & Atkinson, D. (1981). Ethnic bias in counseling: An information processing approach. *Journal of Counseling Psychology, 28*, 498–503.

Webster's New Collegiate Dictionary. (1976). Springfield, MA: Merriam.

3

The New Extended Family: The Experience of Parents and Children after Remarriage*

FRANK F. FURSTENBERG, JR.
University of Pennsylvania

INTRODUCTION

During the past 2 decades, the nuclear family, the predominant family form in the United States, has appeared to be more ephemeral than was once imagined by social scientists. Historians and demographers have shown that this family form was not nearly so common in earlier times as was once thought (Cherlin, 1981; Hareven, 1978). Paradoxically the nuclear family (ironically, now referred to as the traditional family) was more common in 1950 than in 1850 because of high rates of mortality, illness, and economic uncertainty (Uhlenberg, 1974). Large numbers of people never married or never had children, and among those who did, the prospect of living a settled and secure life was much lower than is nostalgically recalled.

This family form became more prominent by the middle of the 20th century though it hardly ever lived up to its cultural ideal. As soon as it became the modal form, the nuclear family was attacked for producing conformity, stifling children, concealing marital tensions, and frustrating women's legitimate aspirations (Gordon, 1972).

These tensions helped to usher in what some have called the "post-modern" family. Change came from many directions. The extension of education, the rise of a service-based economy, the growth of the welfare state, the improvement of contraceptive technology, and legal reform (especially concerning the rights of women and children) are but a few of the conditions that have contributed to the family's transformation (Thornton & Freedman, 1983). The social, legal, and economic changes in the kinship system brought about a heightened emphasis on individual discretion. A

---

*An earlier version of this paper was presented at the "Changing Family Conference: The Blended Family," University of Iowa, Iowa City, February 9, 1984.

42

sense of obligation to kin is still strong, but these expectations have been tempered by a more voluntaristic conception of marriage and parenthood.

Although life-long monogamy is still esteemed, it is no longer expected of couples entering matrimony. In its place is a pattern of conjugal succession (Furstenberg, 1982). Couples are only expected to stay together so long as a marriage is emotionally gratifying. If it is not, the parties are permitted, even encouraged, to break the marriage contract and search for another mate. In the *National Survey of Children* (NSC), a study that will be described later in this chapter, 68% of a nationally representative sample of adolescent children and 71% of their parents agreed with the statement that "a couple should not get married unless they were prepared to stay together for life." However, three fifths of the children and close to half of the adults also agreed that "it should be easy for a couple that is unhappily married to get a divorce." The emotional quality of the relationship is the *sine qua non* of contemporary marriage. The central justification for marriage is emotional gratification, not economic cooperation or family continuity. This shift in sentiments about marriage also has implications for the strength of the parent–child bond and the nature of kinship ties more generally (Bohannon, 1970; Furstenberg & Spanier, 1984; Thornton & Freedman, 1983).

CHANGING PATTERNS OF DIVORCE AND REMARRIAGE

The changing norms of marriage and parenthood reflect a remarkable change in the actual risk of marital dissolution. The probability that an individual will divorce has tripled for those born in this century, rising from about 15% in the cohort born before World War I to 45% in the 1950s cohort (Preston & McDonald, 1979; Weed, 1980). Most current projections indicated that well over half of all those who married in the 1970s will end their unions voluntarily. Similarly, the probability of remarriage has risen accordingly so that at least a third and probably two out of five of those who wed in the past decade will remarry (Cherlin, 1981; Glick, 1984). Although the interval between divorce and remarriage has been growing, most remarriages still occur within 5 years after divorce, and many of those who do not rewed will enter a cohabitational relationship within that period (Spanier & Furstenberg, 1986).

About two fifths of divorcing couples are childless (Norton & Glick, 1976). Although marital dissolution under these circumstances may be no less painful for the individuals involved, it leaves few lasting social traces. However, most divorces involve children, and parents are frequently compelled to share childrearing responsibilities when they no longer live together. Parenting apart is a socially awkward arrangement, and most formerly married couples manage it poorly or not at all (Furstenberg & Nord, 1985).

Remarriage further complicates the life course of children of divorce.

Most young children who see their parents' marriage dissolve are likely to enter a stepfamily before they reach adulthood. Using data from the NSC conducted in 1981, it is estimated that 40% of all children will encounter divorce, and about one in four will live with a stepparent before they reach the age of 16. If we calculated as well the existence of stepparents, not living with the child, *probably a third of all children growing up today will be part of a stepfamily before they reach adulthood.* (See also Bumpass, 1984; Hofferth, 1984, for similar estimates.)

Cherlin and McCarthy (1985) have reported in a recent analysis of households with children that approximately one in six presently live with a stepparent or parents who are remarried. This figure will continue to grow if divorce and remarriage rates remain at their current levels. Clearly, not all such arrangements involve regular contact with stepparents and stepsiblings, but most children who do enter a stepfamily will have ongoing relations with a variety of steprelatives. Bumpass (1984) has estimated that a third of all children entering stepfamilies will acquire a halfsibling within 4 years, and close to two thirds will eventually have either a step- or half-sibling. Beyond the immediate household, children in stepfamilies can expect to amass a vast collection of stepkin. Clearly the boundaries of the family are being expanded by marriage at least as much as by childbearing.

What these structural changes in the form of the family imply for the quality of family life is an intriguing question in kinship research. How does the pattern of conjugal succession modify the nature of marriage, childbearing, and childrearing? Are relations with extended kin altered in response to new and complex arrangements created by divorce and remarriage? These questions will be addressed in this chapter, which reports on evidence from one completed small-scale study of divorce and remarriage and an ongoing longitudinal investigation of families interviewed from 1976 to 1981. Special attention is given to several important topics relating to family reconstitution: (1) the viability of second marriages, (2) their economic status, (3) strategies of co-parenting, and (4) the well-being of children.

Sources of Data

In the late 1970s, when I first began to examine the process of family recycling, I undertook a comprehensive review of the existing sociological literature on remarriage and stepfamilies. While this survey, no doubt, failed to uncover some references, it turned up only about a dozen studies that reported results from nonclinical samples (Furstenberg, 1979; Walker, Rogers, & Messinger, 1977). Even these studies were not methodologically sound enough to provide more than suggestive evidence on processes of remarriage and stepfamily life. The situation has improved considerably in the past few years as several major studies and countless small-scale investigations are now underway. The present volume and its predecessor published in *Family Relations* signal a scholarly commitment to empirical research on remarriage and stepfamily life (see Pasley & Ihinger-Tallman, 1984).

The evidence presented in this chapter was collected in a series of studies carried out with a number of colleagues. In the first, Graham Spanier and I followed some 200 recently divorced individuals in central Pennsylvania for a period of two and a half years, during which time about half remarried or reestablished new partnerships. Our aim was to explore how individuals redefined marriage and parenthood as they negotiated the transition from one relationship to the next. (For a full account of the results, see Furstenberg & Spanier, 1984.) The second study examines a national sample of children over a 5-year period, contrasting the development and family patterns of young adolescents whose parents experienced marital disruption with those who have continuously lived with two biological parents. This study was designed by Nicholas Zill, James Peterson, and myself to measure the consequences of marital change for the development and well-being of children (Furstenberg, Nord, Peterson, & Zill, 1983; Furstenberg & Allison, 1985). In 1976, a nationally representative sample of 2,279 children between the ages of 7 and 11 from 1,747 households were interviewed. Data on the children and family experiences were also collected from a parent, usually the child's mother. School information on the children was also obtained from teachers through a mailed questionnaire. In 1981, all the children from disrupted families and families with high marital conflict in 1976 were reinterviewed, as well as a random subsample of children in low-conflict families. Data were also collected again from parents and schools. (A full description of the study design and data collection procedures can be found in Furstenberg et al., 1983.) As an add-on to this study, a sample of the grandparents of the children was interviewed to determine how conjugal succession affects the bonds between generations (Cherlin & Furstenberg, 1986).

The Stability of Remarriages

A hotly debated issue is whether remarried persons are at special risk of redivorce. Rates of redivorce have been rising as a growing number of individuals enter second unions (Cherlin, 1978, 1981). One of the painful issues of stepfamily life is the fragility of the new marriage. In the NSC, we estimated that at least a tenth of the children in our study would see their parents divorce, remarry, and redivorce before they reached the age of 16. These figures probably understate the true incidence of this risk because they include the divorce risk only of the parent in the household, and only of parents who legally remarried, thus eliminating some of the short-lived cohabitation arrangements.

In a cogent review of the literature on remarriage, Cherlin (1978) argued that the risk of redivorce may be elevated by the absence of clear-cut guide-lines for dealing with the day-to-day dilemmas that surface in stepfamilies. He lists a number of pivotal problems such as the potential occurence of incest, the confusion over kin terms, the difficulties of exercising discipline, and division of responsibilities between residential and nonresidential parents to mention but a few. Unquestionably, as I shall show later, these problems are real ones and seem to contribute to the higher level of stress within stepfamilies and, no doubt, sometimes elevate the level of marital tensions (see White & Booth, 1985).

Oddly enough, however, when one examines the risk of marital dissolu-tion, the rates of divorce and redivorce are fairly similar in first and second marriages. Remarriers are approximately 10% more likely to become di-vorced than first marriers (56% vs. 49% [Weed, 1980]), a disparity that is not very large considering the obvious difficulties surrounding life in stepfamilies. Moreover, when this risk of divorce is examined more closely, it appears not to be exclusively attributable to the complexities of stepfamily life. Remarried couples without children seem to have as high a risk of redivorce as those with children, suggesting the possibility that personal characteristics of those who remarry account in part for their being at higher risk for divorce (Furstenberg & Spanier, 1984).

In a recent study of remarried couples, however, White and Booth (1985) specifically identified the presence of stepchildren in the home as a principal source of strain in second unions. They report that couples in complex households, especially those in which both partners are remarried and have children, are more likely to say that they should not have gotten remarried. Apparently, having stepchildren in the home diminishes the satisfactions of family life.

Some researchers have also reasoned that the divorced are different from the never-divorced if only because the former have been ideologically and psychologically prepared to end an unhappy marriage (Halliday, 1980). In contrast, the population in first marriages includes some people who are equally unhappy but unwilling or unprepared to dissolve their unions. Cou-ples in central Pennsylvania reported that virtually everyone who goes through the process of divorce and remarriage is committed to making their second marriage work. Both the qualitative case studies and survey data suggest that remarried couples think about marriage differently if they have done it before. Many, although certainly not all, approach marriage a second time with fewer illusions, less imbued with romantic expectations. They are wary of wanting too much, but determined not to settle for too little. Consequently, they are more likely to view marriage with a "third eye" and monitor the quality of their relationship than are individuals in first unions.

What they want from a marriage, however, is remarkably similar to what people in first marriages value: communication, sympathy, and trust.

Table 3-1 presents findings from the NSC in which parents were asked about their attitudes concerning marriage.

A similar profile of conjugal beliefs emerged when persons in first and subsequent marriages were compared. Roughly the same portion agreed that a good marriage should have no secrets, spouses should be one another's best friends, working women make more interesting partners, it is wrong to have sexual affairs, and individuals should not get married unless they were prepared to stay together for life. Remarried individuals were, however, significantly less committed to the principle of romantic love as a basis for marriage, more supportive of living together before marriage, a little less likely to value shared interests, but only slightly more tolerant of divorce. Generally though, conjugal expectations do not seem to vary greatly by marital status.

Consistent with previous research, the NSC data also reveal that the quality of remarriages, at least those which have survived the early years, seem to be fairly similar to the assessments offered by those in first marriages (Glenn, 1981; Glenn & Weaver, 1977; White & Booth, 1985). The great majority of both marital subgroups are positive about their relationship. In the central Pennyslvania study remarried respondents generally explained that their unsuccessful first marriage resulted from poor selection rather than

Table 3-1. General Statements from Adults about Marriage and Family Life by Family Type (Percentage of Those Who Strongly or Mostly Agree)

	Total	Nuclear	Remarried
In a good marriage, a couple should not have any secrets from each other	82	83	86
A person's spouse should be his or her most imtimate friend	92	91	94
A husband and wife are better off not sharing too many interests	13	12	18
Working women make more interesting partners in marriage	44	44	42
Marriages are better when the husband works and the wife runs the home and cares for the children	65	65	61
As long as it is secret, a sexual affair would not harm a good marriage	10	11	7
Unless a couple is prepared to stay together for life, they should not get married	74	74	74
People should not get married unless they are deeply in love	95	96	86
Living together before marriage makes a lot of sense	17	14	36
It should be easy for unhappy couples to get a divorce	43	42	46
Unweighted *ns*	(669)	(580)	(119)

from inadequate preparation or personal immaturity. But, most confess that they married for foolish reasons: a response to social pressure, romantic illusions, or to escape from home. In their second marriage, they claimed to have resisted social pressures and selected more wisely. Evidence from the central Pennsylvania studies suggests that individuals who remarry are not immune to social pressures, although they may be of a different kind than those experienced early in life (Furstenberg & Spanier, 1984).

The Economics of Remarriage

It is well known that divorce greatly alters the economic situation of adults and their dependent children. Marital instability is a source, if not *the* major source, of economic insufficiency in American families (Bane & Ellwood, 1984; Rawlings, 1980; Ross & Sawhill, 1975). While it can be safely assumed that remarriage repairs some of the damage done by divorce, it is not well known how families allocate resources when they are supporting more than one household. Most divorced fathers do not pay significant amounts of child support. In fact, the majority do not pay any money on a regular basis to their children (United States Bureau of the Census, 1979). One reason for the low level of child support may be that most divorced men have assumed support for a new household and are unwilling or unable to divide their limited resources. But we simply do not know the essential economic facts about remarriage (Weitzman, 1985).

Some economic information on stepfamilies was collected in the NSC. Less than a third of the women in second marriages were receiving child support from their first husbands. On the whole, the situation of remarried women was not very different from women in first marriages; they were just as likely to work and were no more or less likely to express anxieties about their economic situation. Remarried women, however, had somewhat lower family incomes and contributed a larger share to the household earnings than did women in first marriages. Apparently, working experience between marriages may strengthen the employment situation of females. Also, greater economic demands on the family may press remarried women into a more prominent economic role. Remarried persons probably do not make out quite as well, perhaps because of preexisting socioeconomic disadvantage or perhaps because of the loss of assets following divorce. On balance, however, remarried women are about in the same economic position in a second marriage as they would have been had they stuck it out in their first (Jacobs & Furstenberg, 1986).

An intriguing question is how families merge their economic assets and obligations. Fresh from disentangling economic interests in their first marriages, couples may be reluctant to throw everything into a "common pot." Moreover, some parents may resist new obligations such as the support of stepchildren. To my knowledge, no careful study exists of how families manage these allocations or what consequences economic exchanges have for the emotional quality of relations between the marriage partners and their children. Incidentally, the same issues arise when we turn to intergenerational relations. Grandparents, for example, must decide whether and how to assist stepgrandchildren. Qualitative evidence from the grandparent survey suggests that withholding resources from stepgrandchildren can create considerable tensions between the middle and senior generations (Cherlin & Furstenberg, 1986).

PATTERNS OF PARENTING IN STEPFAMILIES

Dividing material resources within stepfamilies raises similar issues as those facing parents in allocating their time and affection among biological and stepchildren both within and across households. In making such comparisons, it is easy to lose sight of the fact that there is as much diversity among stepfamilies as there is among families of first marriage. Not to recognize the variety of stepfamily life runs the risk of sociological stereotyping—creating distinctions between families where none exist or exaggerating only trivial differences. In fact, some differences do exist between first families and stepfamilies; however, they generally are not large enough to conclude that, typically, stepfamilies behave one way and first families another. For the most part, the overlap between the two populations is far greater than the divergence between them.

Existing research has produced conflicting accounts of the quality of relations and the general level of harmony within stepfamilies. (See, for example, the special issue of *Family Relations* edited by Pasley & Ihinger-Tallman, 1984.) Clinicians have uncovered a great deal more evidence of strain than have investigators employing survey methods on nonclinical samples (Esses & Campbell, 1984). Quite possibly, these differing results may be an artifact of the methods employed or the research design. Clinicians have searched with more probing tools but have usually examined patient populations, consisting of families who are in the process of negotiating the transition to stepfamily life. Not surprisingly, they have discovered more distress than researchers who have examined more general indications of family functioning in larger and less-select populations.

The NSC provides information about a broad and fairly representative sample of stepfamilies, some of which were longstanding units while others had been constituted only for a short time. Thus, we can contrast established and newly formed stepfamilies and compare both of these groups to never-divorced couples. Moreover, we have observations from both parents and children on a number of dimensions of family life.

A useful point of departure is to ask whether and when steprelatives are incorporated in the family system. Both parents and children were asked who specifically they included in their family. Whereas only 1% of the parents failed to mention their biological children, 15% of those with stepchildren *in the household* did not list them as family members. Similarly, just 7% of the children excluded a biological mother and 9% a father, compared to 31% of those with a residential stepmother or stepfather. Moreover, 19% of the children with siblings omitted at least one biological sibling whereas 41% of the children living with stepsiblings did not include one or more in their family. Length of time in a stepfamily, interestingly, was not related to the acknowledgment of steprelations. Apparently, time alone does not guarantee that family boundaries will be redrawn.

These figures provide a window into stepfamily life by showing that a fairly small fraction of parents and a much greater proportion of children partition biological kin and stepkin. The definition of the family provides an indirect measure of family relations among biological kin and stepkin, suggesting the possibility of serious rifts. Table 3-2 presents a more direct set of indicators measuring the quality of relationships within different family types. Parents and children were asked to rate varied dimensions of their family life over the past several months. Parents in first married families consistently rated the quality of family relations in more favorable terms than those in stepfamilies. The differences, however, are relatively small and generally not statistically significant. Moreover, in all instances, the great majority of adults, regardless of their situation, portray the quality of life in relatively rosy terms. Children are no less positive about their household ambience, although they are somewhat more influenced by their current family structure than are adults. Even so, the majority of children in stepfam-

Table 3-2. Parents' and Children's Assessment of Quality of Family Life in Last Few Months, by Family Type (Percentage Who Agreed with Listed Quality)

Quality of Family Life	Parents		Children	
	Nuclear	Stepfamily	Nuclear	Stepfamily
Relaxed	75	67	83	67
Orderly	67	66	85	74
Close	87	78	75	66
Sharing	92	91	91	81
Complex	27	39	26	34
Tense	24	30	20	30
Disorganized	27	29	20	24
Unweighted *n*s	(580)	(119)	(776)	(161)

ilies provide a positive portrait of their family life. Upon closer inspection, it turns out that most of the differences that do occur are located in stepmother families. Households with biological mothers and stepfathers receive almost identical ratings. I shall return to these differences between types of stepfamilies shortly.

When the family descriptions are examined by the longevity of the stepfamily, it can be seen that family life did not become more settled or harmonious over time. This again points to the conclusion that most families appear to be able to reconstitute in fairly short order. Perhaps, also the expectations of members in newly formed families are more modest and consequently produce fewer discontents. Finally, we must consider the possibility that children who experience divorce and remarriage early in life may encounter more adjustment problems than those who encounter family disruption in later childhood (see Furstenberg & Allison, 1985; Wallerstein & Kelly, 1980).

In addition to these subjective appraisals of family life, a good deal of information on family routines and practices was obtained from the adolescents and their parents. Table 3-3 compares reports of family contact in first marriages and stepfamilies. The picture that emerges in Table 3-3 is not unfamiliar by now. On most items, children in the two family types offer rather similar depictions of the level of interaction. Stepfamily members are almost as likely to go to the movies, go shopping with the child, work on some project together, or play a game or sport during a specific time interval. They are somewhat less likely to have gone out to dinner together or taken a trip, and children in stepfamilies are noticeably less likely to have received help on homework.

In the bottom section of Table 3-3, the household expectations and family rules as reported by parents and children are displayed. Again the data reveal rather little variation by family form. Children in stepfamilies are somewhat more likely to be called upon to help out with certain household chores, perhaps because they played a larger role in household maintenance during the divorce. In other respects, there is little to distinguish the family types. The application of rules, the children's participation in rule making, and their response to family regulations are nearly identical. Parents and teens in stepfamilies report arguing about rules slightly more frequently.

Overall, though, the daily character of stepfamily life does not appear to differ greatly from the perception of life of members in first-married households. Moreover, once again, we did not discern differences in family interaction and routines among more recently formed stepfamilies as compared to long-lasting ones. Indeed, contrary to expectation, there was a slight tendency for families reconstituted in the past 3 years to report higher levels of positive interaction and lower levels of conflict, but the differences are neither large nor entirely consistent.

Table 3-3. Percent Who Replied "Yes" on Questions of Family Interaction, Rules, and Expectations by Family Type

	Parents		Children	
	Nuclear	Stepfamily	Nuclear	Stepfamily
Within the last month have you and your parents:[a]				
attended movies			23	23
gone out to dinner			66	52
gone shopping			70	63
taken a trip			41	28
Within the last week have you and your parents:[a]				
done things together			49	53
school work			34	19
played game			42	43
In your home, are you regularly expected to help out with:				
straightening your room	98	96	96	97
keeping rest of house clean	81	75	82	80
doing the dishes	64	69	60	69
cooking	35	38	32	43
Are there any rules about:				
watching TV	61	70	33	35
keeping your parents informed about your whereabouts	99	91	94	92
doing homework	84	91	76	75
dating and going to parties	76	74	70	64
Do you argue about the rules?				
(often or sometimes)	56	52	41	48
How often do your parents talk over important decision with you?				
(often)	62	60	64	60
Unweighted *n*s	(580)	(119)	(776)	(161)

[a]Not asked of parents.

Despite this pattern of similarity, it is clear that stepfamilies do face a set of problems not experienced in nuclear units. In the NSC, adults with both biological and stepchildren were asked their views about certain features of stepfamily life. The results (presented in Table 3-4) show that most parents acknowledge difficulties in assuming the stepparent role. A majority said that it was more difficult to be a stepparent and most reported some reservations about their ability to give love and affection and to discipline their stepchildren. A substantial proportion perceived that their stepchildren did not entirely accept them as parents.

This table also shows some significant shifts in these sentiments according to how long the stepparent and child have lived together. Stepchildren are harder to love and discipline in the early years of remarriage, and stepparents are more likely to be regarded as friends rather than parents. On the other hand, children become more difficult to manage in long-term stepfamilies, presumably as they enter adolescence. Apparently, only some of the distinctions between biological and step-children subside over time. Moreover, it is important to recognize that families with severe strains may not have survived, and thus, the NSC data may overstate the positive trajectory of adjustment. The limitations of these cross-sectional impressions point to the desirability of carrying out longitudinal research on the adaptation to stepfamily life over a fairly long period of time, simultaneously examining the situations of children and parents who may not adjust at the same pace or end up at the same place. Furthermore, in this preliminary overview, we have ignored age and gender distinctions, a theme which will be explored in a later report on the NSC.

Further information on the quality of relations between children, their biological parents and stepparents are presented in Table 3-5. These data show trivial or no differences in the quality of relations between children and their biological parents, living in nuclear and stepfamilies. The levels of closeness, affection, and identification are about the same in the two family types.

Table 3-4. Parents Opinions about Stepfamily Life by Length of Time in a Stepfamily (Percentage of Those Who Agree Somewhat or Very Much)

	< 3 years	3–7 years	> 7 years	Total
It is more difficult to discipline your stepchild(ren) than your own child(ren)	70	53	43	53
It is generally harder to love your stepchild(ren) than to love your own child(ren)	52	46	40	47
You find it easier to think of yourself as a friend than a parent to your stepchild(ren)	61	54	47	53
It is harder to be a stepparent than a natural parent	47	47	66	53
Your child(ren) would have had fewer problems with two natural parents than with one natural parent and one stepparent	64	41	33	43
Your stepchild(ren) can't think of you as a real parent	70	33	61	49
You've had problems getting your parents to accept your stepchild(ren) as grandchild(ren)	10	34	20	20
Unweighted *n*s	(8)	(18)	(14)	(40)

Table 3-5. Quality of Relations between Children and Their Biological Parents or
Stepparents as Reported by Children, by Family Type

Family Type	Mother			Father		
	b-m[a] b-f	b-m s-f	s-m b-f	b-f b-m	b-f s-m	s-f b-m
Say often or sometimes argue with parent	46	45	67	33	36	32
Report parent spends enough time	80	71	74	75	61	76
Report parent given enough affection	96	90	81	93	88	79
Say often do things together with parent	34	33	22	43	39	23
Feel extremely or quite close to parent	87	84	44	81	86	56
Want to be like parent when they grow up	72	65	33	73	78	44
Unweighted *ns*	(776)	(134)	(27)	(776)	(27)	(134)

[a]b = biological, s = stepparent, m = mother, f = father.

When it comes to relations with stepparents, the story is quite different. There are huge disparities in children's feelings toward step and biological parents. Parents and their non-biological children alike report less intimacy. Children are less likely to report doing things with stepparents, much less likely to feel close to them, and most do not want to be like them when they grow up. Other data not shown in this table seem to corroborate the children's perceptions that their stepparents are less involved in their care and supervision. A higher proportion of biological parents in stepfamilies complain that their spouse assumes too little responsibility for childrearing and does not have a great deal of influence over the child.

Large as the variations in Table 3-5 are, it is important to note that the majority of parents and children in stepfamilies have fairly or very positive relations. Although they are distinctly more distant from stepparents than from biological parents, most children express benign, if not lavishly positive sentiments. This fact may help to explain why the impressions of family life reported earlier were not so very different for step- and first-marriage families.

Are there specific conditions that account for the variation among stepfamilies? A series of possible explanations was explored to explain the differences just described. First of all, children's experiences were contrasted in stepmother and stepfather households. Although there were only a small number of stepmother families in the cohort ($n = 27$), it is clear that relations between children and stepmothers are more stressful than relations between children and stepfathers. For example, 44% of children say that they feel "extremely" or "very close" to their stepmothers as compared to 56% of children reporting about their stepfathers. Similarly, 34% of the children say they want to be "quite a bit" or "very much" like their stepmothers when they grow up, whereas 44% of the children with stepfathers give a similar response.

Families with residential stepmothers are, of course, unusual. Typically, mothers do not relinquish or lose custody. Therefore, we can assume that patterns of parenting that preceded the divorce and the divorce process itself often differed from what transpired in stepfamilies in which the mother retained custody. (Alternatively, fathers may have been given responsibility for a child who was not, for one reason or another, able to adjust to the mother's household.) Previous analysis revealed that nonresidential mothers maintain closer contact with their children than do nonresidential fathers (Furstenberg *et al.*, 1983). Consequently, the possibility of competition between biological mothers and stepmothers looms larger. A substantial minority of fathers in stepmother households frequently reported that dealings with their former spouse put a strain on their current marital relationship. Many also said their former spouse interfered with the stepmother's relationship to the child. Respondents in families with stepfathers were much less likely to lodge similar complaints of interference.

Next, the effect of contact with the nonresidential parent on the child's relationship with the stepparent was examined. Children were just as attached to their stepfathers when they continued to see their biological father on a regular basis as when contact was intermittent or nonexistent. Although the number of stepmother families is too small to produce reliable findings, children appear to have more difficulty handling simultaneous relations with two mothers (Furstenberg, 1987). This finding seems to be corroborated by the views of the adult respondents who reported greater competition between mothers and stepmothers than between fathers and stepfathers.

One might expect that these difficulties become resolved over time. Contrasting stepfamilies of differing duration, no consistent pattern in the quality of relations between children and their stepparents could be discerned. Not enough families are captured in the earliest stages of transition to ascertain how long it takes for children to establish an intimate bond with a stepparent, if such a bond is formed at all, but ties between children and their stepparents do not become progressively stronger over time. Again, this result might be explained by the fact that younger children seem to be most vulnerable to the adverse effects of marital disruption. And, it is not possible to examine separately the age of the child at the time of separation and the duration of remarriage. Were it possible to consider each of these influences on the quality of relations between stepparents and their children, one might find that the duration of remarriage has a positive effect on the strength of the parent–child bond.

To sum up, the findings on the nature of stepfamily life reveal a rather mixed picture that neither supports the dire descriptions of many clinical researchers nor substantiates the completely rosy view of some survey researchers. Stepfamilies do have more different types of problems than do first-marriage families. While relations between biological parents and their children are quite similar among family types, children in stepfamilies frequently do experience problems in establishing close ties with their stepparents. Given sufficient time, most children establish relatively close ties to their stepparents, especially their stepfathers, but a sizable minority report troubled relations with stepparents in adolescence.

Nonetheless, the vast majority of stepfamilies appear to function rather well. Indeed, there was little to distinguish the overall description of family life, offered by both parents and children, in step- and first-marriage families. This seems to suggest that an absence of positive relations between stepparents and children typically does not disturb the overall family functioning, or that there are compensations that offset the relatively weak dyadic ties between stepparents and children. However, again it must be noted that the sample screens out the stepfamilies that did not survive. These may include a disproportionate number of complex families which White and Booth (1985) describe as families at risk of disruption.

THE CONSEQUENCES OF REMARRIAGE FOR CHILD DEVELOPMENT

A critical question is how relations within stepfamilies affect the child's performance outside the family. In an ongoing analysis, the development of children in families of first marriages, single-parent households, and stepfamilies is being compared. Provisional results reveal that on a variety of outcomes including mental health, school achievement, social adjustment, and anti-social behavior, children are better off when they come from families of stably and happily married parents than when they do not. Children in stepfamilies perform about the same as children in single-parent households, when background differences are taken into account. Both are somewhat less well adjusted at home and in school than adolescents who are living with both biological parents (Furstenberg & Allison, 1985).

It is important to put the magnitude of the risk associated with family structural differences into perspective. The great majority of children in stepfamilies are not experiencing problems if we rely on reports of their parents, their own self-reports, or evaluations from their teachers. In other words, if we were trying to predict whether a child was prone to emotional or academic problems, it would help only a little to know the marital history of his or her parents. Clearly, however, marital disruption does impose some kind of developmental risk that is neither erased generally nor aggravated by remarriage.

If these preliminary findings hold up, these results will have important practical implications for those who work with families. Most of all, they suggest that we should take great care not to stigmatize stepfamilies. As we have seen from the data presented, stepfamilies operate differently from nuclear families in certain respects, but these differences are not typically hazardous to children. In our zeal to prevent or ameliorate problems, we sometimes define dangers that do not exist. To paraphrase an old addage, let us not manufacture a solution to a problem that is worse than the problem itself.

Our challenge, then, is how to identify families truly in need of services. Researchers can help to make finer discriminations by identifying specific processes that lead to family malfunctioning or promote successful adaptation to stressful situations.

SOURCES OF SUPPORT TO THE CHILD IN A STEPFAMILY

One important determinant of the child's capacity to cope with family disruption is how parents manage the situation. Most existing research focuses on the period during the divorce itself. It seems highly plausible that the amount of conflict between the parents and the way that they separate has an effect on the child's subsequent adjustment, but the data from the NSC do not show that the divorce process itself has a long-term effect on the child's sense of well-being unless parents sustain a high level of conflict after the marriage dissolves.

The popular impression that many divorced couples are unable to disengage is not substantiated. Indeed, we found just the opposite to be true. The overwhelming majority completely severed their ties and in so doing abandoned the prospect of collaborative childcare. Fully half of the noncustodial parents in the NSC had not had any personal contact with their children in the previous year. Most of those who had seen their child at all did so only on an occasional basis. Noncustodial mothers had more interaction with their children than did fathers, but males comprised nearly 90% of the noncustodial parents. Only one in six managed to see their children as often as once a week on the average during the year preceding the survey (Furstenberg *et al.*, 1983).

Even if we confine our attention to the small minority of cases in which noncustodial parents maintain regular contact with their children, parents still operated without regard for one another. More than half of these coparenting couples said they "rarely" or "never" discussed matters about the childcare. Elsewhere we have described this postmarital arrangement as "parallel parenting," rather than coparenting, a term that seems to imply more sharing than customarily occurs.

While at first glance this pattern of parallel parenting might seem highly undesirable, it has some beneficial consequences. The potential for conflict is reduced between the formerly married couples by segregating their activities. It probably also reduces strain between parents and stepparents by minimizing the capacity of each to observe the other. Relatively few parents report interference by their former spouse in their current marital relations or in their present spouse's relations with their children. While competition between parents and stepparents undoubtedly occurs, most couples manage to contain it by restricting contact except on ritual occasions. Naturally, we are all familiar with exceptions where former and current spouses and their respective children build close family ties, but this is rare according to the data from the NSC.

In coping with transitions, children are frequently sustained by relations outside the nuclear family. Grandparents, in particular, are often figures of stability. To observers of black family life, this finding is nothing new (Hill, 1977; Stack, 1974). Extended kin have a preeminent position in systems where conjugal ties are weak or insecure. Divorce strengthens the lineage ties of the custodial parent (usually on the mother's side) while the bonds to the noncustodial parent's family (usually on the father's side) are often attenuated (Cherlin & Furstenberg, 1986). This pattern is far from inevitable. When noncustodial parents remain involved as caretakers, associations between the child and extended kin remain strong. Typically this does not occur.

The contraction of the kinship network after divorce is usually temporary because of the acquisition of new relatives through remarriage. Remarried respondents in the NSC were asked if their parents had problems accepting their new grandchildren; four fifths reported no such difficulties. In the central Pennsylvania study, children were almost as likely to see their stepgrandparents as frequently as their biological grandparents, even though some remarriages had only recently occurred. Evidence from qualitative case studies reveals that grandparents often showered attention on their grandchildren acquired by marriage, partly as a means of strengthening their bonds to the middle generation (Furstenberg & Spanier, 1984).

Divorce then may expand a child's kinship network if it is followed by remarriage. Little is known about how families manage the competing claims of various sets of grandparents, but in central Pennsylvania we learned that the more children see one side of the family, the more they are likely to see of the other sides. Thus, it appears that the kinship network is more like an accordion than a pie. The children we studied seemed to have little difficulty accepting the existence of five, six, or more sets of grandparents and what to the outside observer, appeared like a bewildering array of aunts, uncles, and cousins. The pattern of conjugal succession may have the consequence of enlarging the pool of kin available to children. How enduring these ties will be in later life is another issue that deserves future research. The recent survey of grandparents indicates that relations among stepgrandparents and their stepgrandchildren are likely to be emotionally thin, unless they are established when the child is young and nurtured by frequent contact (Cherlin & Furstenberg, 1986).

CONCLUSION

It is tempting to try to attach a bottom line to the changes that have taken place in our family system. Most accounts reckon the costs of divorce and remarriage to families without mentioning some of the offsetting conditions. The objective of this chapter has been to assess some of the potential consequences of moving from a system of life-long monogamy to one in which marriage is treated as a conditional contract. I have mentioned how this transformation is changing conceptions of marriage, parenthood, and kinship. In the United States, we seem to be moving from a kinship system where family membership was an obligation, whether or not it offered much gratification, to one where the search for gratification has become paramount. The question that looms large is what this will mean for the viability of the family and its capacity to fulfill its principal mission, the nurturance and training of future generations. Most observers are at least troubled by the changes that have taken place, feeling that children's interests often come last.

The results presented here probably will not console those who believe that the pattern of conjugal succession is creating chaos and disintegration in what was otherwise a strong and effective family system. While such a view cannot be dismissed, much of the evidence reviewed here is not as alarming as some might fear. Family life has become less predictable and secure, but it has also become more flexible and, at least sometimes, more rewarding. Whether accommodation to the interests of adults means that the family is not serving the needs of the children remains to be confirmed. For now, it is in our interest to monitor closely the changes that are taking place and their potential effects on the next generation.

REFERENCES

Bane, M. J., & Ellswood, D. T. (1984). Single mothers and their living arrangements. Unpublished manuscript, Harvard University.

Bohannon, P. (1970). *Divorce and after*. Garden City, NY: Doubleday.

Bumpuss, L. (1984). Children and marital disruption: A replication and update. *Demography*, *21*, 71–82.

Cherlin, A. J. (1978). Remarriage as an incomplete institution. *American Journal of Sociology*, *81*, 634–650.

Cherlin, A. J. (1981). *Marriage, divorce, remarriage*. Cambridge, MA: Harvard University Press.

Cherlin, A. J., & Furstenberg, F. F., Jr. (1986). *The New American Grandparent.* New York: Basic Books.

Cherlin, A. J., & McCarthy, J. (1985). Remarried couple households: Data from the June 1980 Current Population Survey. *Journal of Marriage and the Family, 47,* 23–30.

Esses, L., & Campbell, R. (1984). Challenges in researching the remarried. *Family Relations, 33,* 415–424.

Furstenberg, F. F., Jr. (1979). Recycling the family: Perspectives for researching a neglected family form. *Marriage and Family Review, 2*(1), 12–22.

Furstenberg, F. F., Jr. (1982). Conjugal succession: Reentering marriage after divorce. In P. B. Baltes & O. G. Brim, Jr. (Eds.), *Life-Span Development and Behavior* (Volume IV; pp. 107–146). New York: Academic Press.

Furstenberg, F. F., Jr. (1987). Marital disruption and child care. In S. B. Kamerman & A. J. Kahn (Eds.), *Child Support in International Perspectives.* Beverly Hills, CA: Sage.

Furstenberg, F. F., Jr. & Allison, P. A. (1985). *How divorce affects children: Variations by age and sex.* Paper presented at the Society for Research in Child Development, Toronto.

Furstenberg, F. F., Jr., & Nord, C. W. (1985). Parenting apart: Patterns of childrearing after divorce. *Journal of Marriage and the Family, 47,* 893–904.

Furstenberg, F. F., Jr., Nord, C. W., Peterson, J. L, & Zill, N. (1983). The life course of children of divorce: Marital disruption and parental conflict. *American Sociological Review, 48,* 656–668.

Furstenberg, F. F., Jr., & Spanier, G. B. (1984). *Recycling the family: Remarriage after divorce.* Beverly Hills, CA: Sage.

Glenn, N. O. (1981). The well being of persons remarried after divorce. *Journal of Family Issues, 2,* 61–75.

Glenn, N. O., & Weaver, C. (1977). The marital happiness of remarried divorced persons. *Journal of Marriage and the Family, 39,* 331–337.

Glick, P. C. (1984). Marriage, divorce, and living arrangements: Prospective changes. *Journal of Family Issues, 5*(1), 7–26.

Gordon, M. (1972). *The nuclear family in crisis: The search for an alternative.* New York: Harper & Row.

Halliday, T. C. (1980). Remarriage: The more complete institution? *American Journal of Sociology, 86,* 630–635.

Hareven, T. K. (Ed.). (1978). *Transitions: The family and the life course in historical perspective.* New York: Academic Press.

Hill, R. B. (1977). *Informal adaptations among Black families.* Washington, DC: National Urban League.

Hofferth, S. L. (1984). Updating children's life course. *Journal of Marriage and the Family, 47,* 93–116.

Jacobs, J. A., & Furstenberg, F. F., Jr. (1986). Changing places: Conjugal careers and women's marital mobility. *Social Forces, 64,* 714–732.

Norton, A. J., & Glick, P. C. (1976). Marital instability: Past, present, and future. *Journal of Social Issues, 32,* 5–20.

Pasley, K., & Ihinger-Tallman, M. (Eds.). (1984). Special issue of *Family Relations: Remarriage and stepparenting. 33*(3).

Preston, S. H., & McDonald, J. (1979). The incidence of divorce within cohorts of American marriages contracted since the Civil War. *Demography, 16,* 1–25.

Rawlings, S. W. (1980). Families maintained by female householders 1970–1979. *Current Population Reports: Special Studies Series P-23,* No. 107. Washington, DC: U. S. Government Printing Office.

Ross, H. L., & Sawhill, I. V. (1975). *Time of transition: The growth of families headed by women.* Washington DC: The Urban Institute.

Spanier, B. G., & Furstenberg, F. F., Jr. (1987). Remarriage and reconstituted families. In M. B. Sussman & S. K. Steinmetz (Eds.), *Handbook of marriage and the family* (pp. 419–434). New York: Plenum Press.

Stack, C. (1974). *All our kin*. Chicago: Aldine Press.

Thornton, A., & Freedman, D. (1983). The changing American family. *Population Bulletin, 38.*

Uhlenberg, D. (1974). Cohort variations in family life cycle experiences of U.S. females. *Journal of Marriage and the Family, 36,* 284–292.

United States Bureau of the Census (1979). Current Population Reports, Series P-23, No. 84. *Divorce, child custody, and child support.* Washington, DC: U.S. Government Printing Office.

Walker, K., Rogers, J., & Messinger, L. (1977). Remarriage after divorce: A review. *Social Casework, 58,* 276–285.

Wallerstein, J. S., & Kelly, J. B. (1980). *Surviving the breakup: How children and parents cope with divorce.* New York: Basic Books.

Weed, J. A. (1980). National estimates of marriage dissolution and survivorship: United States. *Vital and Health Statistics*: Series 3, Analytic Statistics: No. 19. DHHS Publication No. (PHS) 81-1403. Hyattsville, MD: National Center for Health Statistics.

Weitzman, L. J. (1985). *The divorce revolution: The unexpected social and economic consequences for women and children in America.* New York: Free Press.

White, L. K., & Booth, A. (1985). Stepchildren in remarriages. *American Sociological Review, 50,* 689–698.

CONCEPTUAL AND THEORETICAL ISSUES IN CONTEMPORARY RESEARCH

4

A Multilevel–Multivariable–Developmental Perspective for Future Research on Stepfamilies

W. GLENN CLINGEMPEEL
The Pennsylvania State University
EULALEE BRAND
The Pennsylvania State University
SION SEGAL
The Pennsylvania State University

A major theme of recent reviews and critiques of the stepfamily literature (e.g., Esses & Campbell, 1984; Ganong & Coleman, 1984) is that little research attention has been given to the variety and complexity of factors that may influence the quality of stepfamily relationships and child outcomes. Most studies have focused on a narrow range of research issues (e.g., comparisons of stepfamilies and nuclear families on child outcomes; comparisons of first and second marriages on marital quality or stability). Thus, a plethora of potentially important questions remain unexamined.

We propose a multilevel–multivariable–developmental perspective as an overarching conceptual framework that may serve, heuristically, to broaden the foci of future research on stepfamilies. Borrowing from Bronfenbrenner's (1979) multilevel conceptualization of the ecology of human development, factors that influence the quality of stepfamily relationships and child outcomes may operate at three levels of analysis: stepfamily household, extrahousehold network, and social institution. The stepfamily household level consists of the individual characteristics of family members and the nature of their interrelationships. The extrahousehold network level consists of the informal social networks of members of the stepfamily and may include kin and friends who live in other households. The social institution level includes the formal and quasi-formal institutions (e.g., policies of worksettings, schools, the legal system, mass media, church, and government agencies) which may influence variables at both the "stepfamily household" and "extrahousehold network" levels of analysis.

At each of the three levels of analysis there are multiple variables that may influence the quality of family relationships and child outcomes in stepfamilies. Moreover, the levels are conceived of as nested ecological systems that can be represented spatially as concentric circles (Bronfenbrenner, 1979). The stepfamily household level occupies the innermost circle and is embedded within a second circle signifying the extrahousehold network level that, in turn, is contained within a third and outermost circle representing the social institution level of analysis. The levels are interdependent and thus variables at one level may affect, both directly and indirectly, variables at the other levels.

We also propose that future research should examine stepfamilies over time and should consider the various stages of family development. After remarriage, stepfamilies may encounter, with varying degrees of certainty, specific life cycle changes (e.g., shifts in custody arrangements, birth of a child to the current marriage) that may alter the nature of relationships both within and outside the stepfamily household. Consequently, long-term as well as short-term sequelae of living in a reconstituted family should be examined.

This chapter has two major goals: (1) to demonstrate the heuristic utility of a multilevel–multivariable–developmental perspective; and (2) to elucidate lacunae in the stepfamily literature and propose guidelines for expanding the range of questions addressed. Consistent with these heuristic goals, we discuss multiple classes of dependent variables and examine a variety of research directions in less detail rather than focus on a single class (e.g., child outcomes) in great detail. However, even with our attention to breadth, the complexity of this topic has meant that we were necessarily selective and that potentially important issues (e.g., factors which influence the quality of sibling relationships) were, in some cases, given little attention.

We do not attempt to review comprehensively and critique the extant empirical literature. Recent reviews are available elsewhere on the effects of remarriage on children (e.g., Ganong & Coleman, 1984) and on differences between the quality and stability of first and second marriages (e.g., Furstenberg & Spanier, 1984). Our emphasis is on future inquiry rather than past findings.

THE STEPFAMILY HOUSEHOLD LEVEL

Most research on stepfamilies has focused on the stepfamily household level of analysis. Nevertheless, many empirical issues have received little or no attention from stepfamily researchers. We shall attempt to elucidate some of these issues within three major classes of predictor variables: family structure, demographic and personality characteristics of family members, and intrahousehold relationship variables.

Family Structure

Stepfamilies may assume myriad structural forms. We propose a taxonomy of structural variations derived from two defining criteria: (1) presence/absence and custody status of wife's children from a prior marriage; and (2) presence/absence and custody status of husband's children from a prior marriage. For each spouse, three possibilities are considered including absence of children from the prior marriage, presence of children from the prior marriage and custody of all children, and presence of children from the prior marriage and custody of no children.[1] By considering the three options independently for husband and wife, nine combinations, or structural types of families, can be delineated. We are not designating as a "stepfamily" the combination where one or both spouses are remarried but neither spouse has children from the prior marriage. Thus, our taxonomy includes eight structural variations of stepfamilies. The descriptive labels and defining criteria or the eight types are presented in Figure 4-1.

The descriptive labels for the eight types of stepfamilies are formed by adding one of three "custody status" terms including *residential* (spouse or spouses with children from a prior marriage have custody of all children), *nonresidential* (spouse or spouses with children from a prior marriage have custody of none of these children), and *mixed* (one spouse is a residential biological parent and one spouse is a nonresidential biological parent) to one of three "sex of stepparent" terms including *stepfather family* (only the husband is a stepparent), *stepmother family* (only the wife is a stepparent), and *stepparent family* (both husband and wife are stepparents). Six of the eight descriptive labels are based on a 2×3 crossing of two custody status terms (residential, nonresidential) with the three sex-of-stepparent terms. Logically, the term "mixed" can be linked only with the term "stepparent family." However, we add on a parenthetical expression to mixed stepparent family, either "(stepfather type)" or "(stepmother type)," to distinguish between families where the wife is the custodial parent and the husband is the noncustodial parent, designated as "mixed stepparent family (stepfather type)," and families where the husband is the custodial parent and the wife is the noncustodial parent, designated as "mixed stepparent family (stepmother type)."

This taxonomy broadens the typical definition of stepfamilies to include nonresidential stepfamilies where neither spouse has custody of children from a prior marriage but either the wife is a nonresidential biological parent (nonresidential stepfather family), the husband is a nonresidential biological parent (nonresidential stepmother family), or both spouses are nonresidential biological parents (nonresidential stepparent family). This scheme also distinguishes residential stepparent families, where both spouses have custody of

Wife's Presence/Absence and Custody Status of Children from Prior Marriage

Husband's Presence/Absence and Custody Status of Children from Prior Marriage	Absence of children from prior marriage	Presence of children and custody of none	Presence of children and custody of all
Absence of children from prior marriage	Remarried Family[a] (if one or both spouses were previously married)	Nonresidential Stepfather Family	Residential Stepfather Family
Presence of children and custody of none	Nonresidential Stepmother Family	Nonresidential Stepparent Family	Mixed Stepparent Family (Stepfather Type)
Presence of children and custody of all	Residential Stepmother Family	Mixed Stepparent Family (Stepmother Type)	Residential Stepparent Family

[a]This type is not subsumed under our definition of stepfamilies.

Figure 4-1. Descriptive labels and defining criteria for nine structural types of stepfamilies.

all children from prior marriages, from mixed stepparent families, where one spouse is a custodial parent and one spouse is a noncustodial parent.

We have limited our initial taxonomy to eight types because we believe a parsimonious scheme is more likely to be adopted by stepfamily researchers. The choice of presence/absence and custody status of children from prior marriages of each spouse as defining criteria was guided by our assumption that these criteria would delineate structural variations of stepfamilies with probable differences on qualitative dimensions of family relationships (e.g., variations may differ on permeability of boundaries, loyalty conflicts, and the nature of problems faced by family members). The validity of this assumption awaits empirical verification.

The extant stepfamily literature includes very few empirical studies which have examined the quality of family relationships and child outcomes in the structural types delineated by our taxonomy. Most research has compared children living (or adults who have lived) in residential stepfather families, nuclear families, and/or single parent families on measures of psychosocial adjustment or cognitive functioning (e.g., Bowerman & Irish, 1962; Burchinal, 1964; Chapman, 1977; Kellam, Ensminger, & Turner, 1977; Langer & Michael, 1963; Oshman & Manosevitz, 1976; Perry & Pfuhl, 1963; Santrock, 1972).[2] Thus, primarily only one of the eight types of stepfamilies in our taxonomy (residential stepfather families) has been included in research on child outcomes. Studies of family structure effects on the quality of intrahousehold relationships (e.g., marital satisfaction) also have ignored, for the most part, the other seven structural types of stepfamilies and compared nuclear families with residential stepfather families.

From an epistemological perspective, it would be advantageous for stepfamily researchers to include other structural variations of stepfamilies in their research designs and to compare different types of stepfamilies with each other. The appropriateness of a comparison group depends upon the theoretical question addressed, and, in many cases, comparisons among types of stepfamilies may yield more theoretically meaningful results than comparisons of stepfamilies with nuclear families. The lack of attention to structural variations may have resulted, in part, from the ubiquitous "deficit family" bias (Marotz-Baden, Adams, Bueche, Munro, & Munro, 1979) which assumes that nuclear families are "normal" and deviations from it may engender negative outcomes for family members. Given limited resources, researchers may have felt compelled to recruit a nuclear family group and thus forego another structural type of stepfamily. Hopefully, family researchers will move beyond this bias in designing future studies of reconstituted families.

The majority of studies that compare structural types of stepfamilies have focused on potential differences between residential stepmother and residential stepfather families. Both researchers (e.g., Brand, Clingempeel, &

Bowen-Woodward, in press; Clingempeel, Brand, & Ievoli, 1984) and clinicians (e.g., Visher & Visher, 1979) have speculated that residential stepmothers may have more difficult and ambiguous roles than stepfathers due to negative stereotypes (e.g., the "wicked stepmother" portrayals) and cultural norms establishing the sacrosanctness of biological motherhood. However, recent studies have found few differences between these family forms regarding the quality of family relationships and child outcomes. Two studies found no significant differences in the quality of stepparent–stepchild relationships (Clingempeel, Brand, & Ievoli, 1984; Ferri, 1984), and one study (Clingempeel & Brand, 1985) found no differences in marital quality. In addition, few differences on measures of children's social adjustment have been associated with these structural types (Clingempeel & Segal, 1986; Ferri, 1984).

While there actually may be few differences between residential stepmother and residential stepfather families, it is also possible that limitations in current conceptualizations and operational definitions of relationship dimensions have impeded our capacity to detect differences. Stepmothers and stepfathers may differ in their proclivity to develop roles as parent figures or adult friends, but no studies of stepparent–stepchild relationships have assessed friendship or companionship dimensions as well as the typical parenting dimensions (e.g., warmth, control) derived from studies of nuclear families. The stepparent may not become a parent figure and measures of relationship quality should reflect this possibility. The development and validation of measures of role strain and role ambiguity associated with stepparenting also may be prerequisites to detecting differences between types of stepfamilies. As is true for all areas of family research, a major task for stepfamily researchers in the future lies in the domain of construct development, refinement, and measurement.

The presence or absence of noncustodial children from the prior marriage of each spouse is a structural dimension that distinguishes among several types of stepfamilies in our taxonomy. Despite clinical evidence and theory suggesting that visiting stepchildren may alter family relationships and child outcomes in stepfamilies (Visher & Visher, 1979; Wald, 1981), very few empirical studies have compared stepfamilies differing on this dimension.

Nonexistent are studies of stepfamilies where neither spouse has custody of children from a prior marriage but one or both spouses are nonresidential biological parents. The three types of "nonresidential stepfamilies" (see Figure 4-1) may have been ignored because they are not subsumed under typical definitions of stepfamilies that require that at least one spouse have custody of at least one child from a prior marriage. Studies that compare these types of remarried couples who have no children from former conjugal unions may yield information on the impact of visiting stepchildren on the quality of remarriages. The effects of custody arrangements on the quality of stepparent–stepchild relationships may be determined from research that compares residential stepfamilies with their nonresidential counterparts.

A few empirical studies examining the effects of structural complexity on the quality of relationships within the stepfamily household have compared residential stepfather families, which have a relatively simple structure (the residential stepfather has no children from a prior marriage), with mixed stepparent families (stepfather type), which have a more complex structure (the residential stepfather is also a nonresidential biological parent). Three studies found that persons in mixed stepparent families exhibited lower marital quality (Clingempeel, 1981; Clingempeel & Brand, 1985; Pasley & Ihinger-Tallman, 1982), and one study (Clingempeel, Ievoli, & Brand, 1984) found that these structural variations did not differ on the quality of step-father–stepchild relationships. No studies have examined the effects of structural complexity on the social and cognitive development of children, and no studies have compared mixed stepparent families (stepmother types) with residential stepmother families on family dynamics or child outcomes.

In addition to focusing attention on structural variations, a taxonomy of stepfamily types may facilitate comparability of studies and communication among researchers. There is some evidence in the extant stepfamily literature of a "confusion of labels" problem in which the same descriptive terms have been used to describe different types of stepfamilies. For example, Furstenberg and Spanier (1984) used the term "complex stepfamily" to describe stepfamilies where both spouses have children from prior marriages regardless of custody arrangements (this term does not differentiate among four distinct types in our taxonomy); Clingempeel (1981) used the term more narrowly to describe stepfamilies where the residential stepfather was also a nonresidential biological parent (mixed stepparent family [stepfather type] in our taxonomy). Similar definitional problems may be avoided if future stepfamily research is guided by a consensually agreed-upon and sufficiently differentiated taxonomy of structural variations.

A final note should be added to our discussion of "family structure" variables. The life events that distinguish among the eight stepfamily types in our taxonomy are not randomly assigned to American adults, but instead are differentially associated with a variety of demographic factors as well as personal characteristics of family members. Residential stepmother and residential stepfather families may differ naturally on several dimensions because the process and conditions under which fathers remarry and obtain custody of children, or obtain custody of children and remarry, may differ from mothers. Several factors (e.g., mental disturbance of mothers, close father–child relationships) have been related to father custody (Sanders & Spanier, 1979), but the possibility of unknown concomitants cannot be discounted (e.g., fathers who obtain custody may differ from mothers on assertiveness, nurturance, and other specific personality characteristics). Similarly, persons who marry, have children, divorce, and remarry may differ in both known and unknown ways from persons who have not experienced one or more of these life events. One implication for stepfamily researchers is that differences in family dynamics and child outcomes associated with various family structures may not be determined by family structure per se but may stem from factors usually, but not always, associated with the formation of these structural variations. Consequently, studies of the impact of family structure may need to distinguish between the effects of the definitional criteria of family type (e.g., remarried fathers in residential stepmother families will always have custody of at least one child from a prior marriage) and the effects of factors usually associated with the definitional criteria (e.g., remarried fathers with custody of their children will usually be more assertive and nurturant than remarried fathers without custody of their offspring).

Demographic and Personality Characteristics of Family Members

The characteristics of parents, stepparents, and children may mediate the quality of intrahousehold family relationships and child outcomes in stepfamilies. The sex of a stepchild is a potentially important variable. Despite evidence for sex differences in childhood psychopathology (e.g., Links, 1983; Werner & Smith, 1979) and in response to marital discord and divorce (e.g., Hetherington, Cox, & Cox, 1979; Wallerstein & Kelly, 1980), the sex of a stepchild has rarely been an independent variable in research on stepfamilies. Three recent studies have found that girls have more difficulty in relationships with stepfathers than boys (Clingempeel, Brand, & Ievoli, 1984; Clingempeel, Ievoli, & Brand, 1984; Santrock, Warshak, Lindbergh, & Meadows, 1982). One study, (Clingempeel, Brand, & Ievoli, 1984) found that girls also had more problematic relationships with stepmothers. However, these studies used small and select samples of stepfamilies and thus generalizability of findings is limited.

A few studies have examined sex of stepchild as a mediator of child outcomes in stepfamilies. Chapman (1977) and Santrock (1972) found that boys, but not girls, obtained higher scores on measures of cognitive development in stepfather families than in mother custody, single-parent families. At least one study (Oshman & Manosevitz, 1976) found the same pattern of results on social adjustment measures. Recently, Ferri (1984) found that girls were rated as more deviant by their parents in both stepmother and stepfather families. Ferri also reported that girls in stepmother families had more contacts with the police than girls in nuclear families and were the only family group in which teachers rated girls as more deviant than boys. Thus, girls in stepmother families may be especially vulnerable to family dissolution and reconstruction. The existing research on sex differences has given little attention to family relationship variables. Little is known about how boys and girls in stepfamilies differentially affect and are affected by the quality of relationships with family members.

The age of the stepchild may also mediate the quality of family relationships and child outcomes in stepfamilies. Children of different ages will vary in developmental tasks, salient settings (e.g., home, school, and neighborhood), and social/cognitive competencies. Thus, they may respond differently to parental remarriage and the entry of a stepparent into the home. Two studies that compared children of different ages on the quality of stepparent–stepchild relationships (Bowerman & Irish, 1962; Duberman, 1975) have found that relationships were more difficult with adolescent than with younger, school-age children. Ferri (1984) found no relationship between the child's age at the time the stepfamily was formed and the quality of stepparent–stepchild relationships. However, Ferri did report a differential pattern for boys and girls. Relationships were most positive for 5- to 11-year-old boys and least positive for girls in this age range. These results suggest that future studies of stepparent–stepchild relationships should examine sex-of-child–age-of-child interactions. No studies to date have examined how children of different ages adjust over time to parental remarriage. However, several longitudinal studies of stepfamilies are currently in progress.[3]

Problem-solving strategies, coping styles, and personality characteristics of adults and children may affect the quality of family relationships and child outcomes in stepfamilies. The level of interpersonal reasoning and locus of control orientation in children have been related to children's divorce adjustment (e.g., Kurdek, Blisk, & Siesky, 1981) and may be related to remarriage adjustment as well. The temperament of the child may also be an important variable. Temperamentally difficult children have been found to be more vulnerable to a variety of life changes and stressors than temperamentally easy children (Rutter, 1979). Parents and stepparents may differ on personality characteristics that may alter the quality of relationships within the stepfamily. The purported ambiguity of steprelationships would suggest that tolerance of ambiguity, social adaptability, and resourcefulness are personality traits that may be important predictors.

Childrearing values, problem-solving strategies, and coping mechanisms may vary across races and social classes. Yet, the majority of research on stepfamilies has focused on Caucasian, middle-class samples. Three studies conducted more than 2 decades ago found that stepparent–stepchild relationships become more positive with increases in socioeconomic status (SES) (Bernard, 1956; Bowerman & Irish, 1962; Langer & Michael, 1963). One recent study (Ferri, 1984) found that higher SES was associated with more positive stepparent–stepchild relationships in residential stepfather families and less positive stepparent–stepchild relationships in residential stepmother families. Thus, the relations between SES and the quality of stepparent–stepchild relationships depended upon the sex of residential stepparent.

No studies have examined racial differences in the quality of family relationships and child outcomes in stepfamilies. Despite both theoretical speculation and empirical data suggesting that black families use different coping mechanisms (e.g., greater use of kin as support systems) in response to marital disruption and other life changes than white families (Hill, 1977; Nobles, 1978; Stack, 1974), the black stepfamily has received no research attention. Studies of the effects of divorce and remarriage on parents and children of other non-Caucasian races and other cultures are also lacking.

Future research on factors that may affect the quality of family relationships and child outcomes in stepfamilies should examine the mediating role of various demographic and psychological characteristics of family members, including: (1) sex of stepchild; (2) age of stepchild; (3) personality characteristics of children including level of interpersonal reasoning and locus of control; (4) personality characteristics of adults including tolerance of ambiguity, social adaptability, and resourcefulness; (5) SES-determined factors (e.g., income and educational level of parents and stepparents); (6) SES-related factors (e.g., household density; and (7) race of parents and stepparents. Greater epistemic progress may come from studies that include multiple predictors and that assess possible interactions among predictors.

Intrahousehold Relationship Variables

Relatively few studies of stepfamilies have focused on the interdependencies of intrahousehold relationships (husband–wife, parent–child, sibling) and the extent to which qualitative dimensions of these relationships mediate children's cognitive and social development. Moreover, studies that have addressed these issues typically have focused on a narrow range of relationships and relationship dimensions and have relied exclusively on questionnaire measures.

Rare in the stepfamily literature are studies of the "effects" of qualitative dimensions of the remarried couples' relationship on stepparent–stepchild relationships and children's psychological adjustment. Brand and Clingempeel (1987) recently completed a multimethod–multisource study of qualitative dimensions of marital relationships as mediators of the quality of stepparent–stepchild relationships and children's psychological adjustment in 40 stepfather families and 22 stepmother families (with half of each type having a male, and half having a female, 9- to 12-year-old "target" child). All stepparent couples had been married less than 3 years. Positive dimensions of both dyads were assessed by questionnaire (perceptions of relationship events) and behavioral measures (proportions of positive communication behaviors emitted during structured interaction tasks). Children's psychological adjustment was assessed via a self-concept questionnaire and parent ratings of deviant behaviors.

Their results indicated that the mediating role of marital quality differed depending upon type of stepfamily and sex of stepchild. In stepfather families, the correlations revealed patterns similar to those obtained in studies of nuclear families. Stepfathers both perceived and behaved toward stepchildren of both sexes more positively to the extent positiveness characterized their marital relationship. Higher marital quality also was associated with better psychological adjustment of stepchildren. In stepmother families, striking differences in the "effects" of marital quality were obtained for male and female stepchildren. For stepmother families with boys, more positive marital relationships were associated with more positive stepmother–stepson relationships and better psychological adjustment of stepsons. For stepdaughters, more positive marital relationships were associated with less positive step-mother–stepdaughter relationships and lower psychological adjustment scores.

The negative association between marital quality and positive dimensions of the stepmother–stepdaughter relationship and girl's psychological adjustment may stem from the special nature of girls' relationships with biological parents prior to the father's remarriage and the changes in these relationships following remarriage. Girls may be awarded to fathers after divorce primarily in cases of exceptionally close father–daughter relationships and/or distant mother–daughter relationships (Sanders & Spanier, 1979). Consequently, girls in the custody of fathers may acquire a more privileged status with more adult-like roles (e.g., confidant to father) than other sex-of-child–sex-of-custodial-parent groups. After the father remarries, stepmothers who exhibit more positive behaviors to fathers or who are ostensibly happier in their marriages may be perceived by stepdaughters as greater competitors for the father's personal resources (time and affection) and as greater intruders on the daughter's roles acquired during the single parent stage (e.g., confidant, household manager). In fact, more positiveness in the remarriage may result from greater reallocations of the fathers' time and affection from daughters to new spouses. Furthermore, due to differential socialization of females, stepmothers may try harder and earlier on to become parent figures to girls, and these parenting efforts may exacerbate loyalty conflicts for stepdaughters (who perceive responding positively to stepmothers as disloyal to biological mothers).

Contrary to the experience of girls, boys in stepmother families may perceive increasing positiveness in the father–stepmother marriage as augmenting rather than supplanting previously positive dimensions of biological parent–child relationships. During the single-parent stage, boys may develop a male friend type of relationship with fathers (centering on companionship and joint activities) rather than the nurturant, wife-like relationship developed with girls. Consequently, positiveness in the marital relationship may be perceived as an additional support system and not an encroachment upon the father–son relationship.

These explanations are necessarily speculative due to several methodological limitations: (1) no data were obtained on the custodial parent–child relationship and how it changed from pre- to post-remarriage; (2) children's perceptions of the extent to which positive dimensions of relationships with biological parents were supplanted or augmented by marital positiveness were not assessed directly; and (3) the findings were based on correlations across groups and not on within-stepfamily interdependencies.

Residential parent–child relationships may mediate child outcomes in stepfamilies. The entry of a stepparent into the household may alter the disciplinary practices of the residential biological parent who may, for example, become stricter and exert tighter controls as a direct result of support from another adult. It is also possible that residential parents initially may redirect their time and affection from biological children to the new marital relationship. As a result, children may resent the residential parent (whose remarriage also has vitiated their hopes for reconciliation of biological parents) and parent–child relationships may become strained. In a national survey of adolescents and their families in Great Britain, Ferri (1984) found that boys, but not girls, in stepfather families had less-positive relationships with biological mothers than their counterparts in nuclear families.

The quality of the stepparent–stepchild relationship also may have an impact on child outcomes and the quality of relationships within the stepfamily household. Crosbie-Burnett (1984) examined the self-reported behaviors, emotions, and cognitions of parents, stepparents, and children in 87 Caucasian, stepfather families. She found that a mutually supportive stepparent–stepchild relationship was a better predictor of overall happiness within the family than the quality of the marital relationship. In preliminary analyses of a National Survey of Children (Furstenberg, Nord, Peterson, & Zill, 1983; Furstenberg & Seltzer, 1983), findings showed that the quality of the stepparent–stepchild relationship was a better predictor of child adjustment than the quality of the child's relationship with the nonresidential biological parent.

Using the same data as the Brand and Clingempeel (1987) study, Clingempeel and Segal (1986) found that the quality of stepparent–stepchild relationships was more strongly related to child outcomes (especially for female stepchildren) in stepmother families than stepfather families. In residential stepmother families, more positive stepmother–stepchild relationships were associated with lower parent ratings of aggression and inhibition for children of both sexes and higher self-esteem scores for female stepchildren. Few significant findings were obtained in residential stepfather families. This study underscored the importance of examining family structure–process interactions as mediators of child outcomes. Collapsing across type of stepfamily would have obscured the significant correlations between the family process and child outcome measures.

Sibling and stepsibling relationships may mediate child outcomes in stepfamilies. Biological siblings may constitue an important support system during stressful life events and when parenting practices become disturbed

(Bank & Kahn, 1975). Family scholars have theorized that siblings develop closer and more cohesive relationships in response to family dissolution and reconstitution (e.g., Ihinger-Tallman, personal communication, May, 1984), but there is little empirical data substantiating this claim. One study (Ferri, 1984) found that adolescents in stepfamilies reported more conflict with siblings than adolescents in nuclear families.

Virtually nonexistent are studies of relationships among stepsiblings and the effects of these relationships on child outcomes. In one exception, Duberman (1973) examined adult perceptions of stepsibling relationships. She found that stepsiblings living in the same household had closer relationships than stepsiblings living apart and that opposite sex stepsibling relationships were closer than those of the same sex. Children with stepsiblings may confront a number of difficult tasks. Previously unshared territory (e.g., room, toys) and time with parents may need to be reapportioned among stepsiblings. The child's ordinal position in the family may be altered (e.g., the previously oldest child may be displaced by older stepsiblings) with concomitant changes in familial roles and responsibilities. In some cases, children may be displaced from a familiar environment and forced to share a household with stepsiblings who have lived there for some time. Since stepsiblings are nonconsanguinal kin, opposite sex teenage stepsiblings may experience conflict stemming from the ambiguity of incest taboos governing stepsibling relationships.

Future research that focuses on intrahousehold relationship variables as predictors should examine two major questions: (1) What are the relations between qualitative dimensions of various family relationships and children's outcomes; and (2) What are the relations between qualitative dimensions of sets of dyadic relationships within the stepfamily household (e.g., husband–wife and parent–child, stepparent–stepchild and sibling)? In addressing these questions we recommend that researchers examine a greater variety of dyadic and triadic relationships (including relationships among siblings and stepsiblings). We also recommend that researchers design studies so that these questions can be assessed separately for different sex of stepchild and type of stepfamily groups.

THE EXTRA-HOUSEHOLD NETWORK LEVEL

Relationships with persons living outside the stepfamily household may affect the quality of intrahousehold relationships. There is a substantial body of research documenting social network influences on nuclear and single-parent families (see Lee, 1979, for a review). In stepfamilies, outside relationships may be even more important. Remarriage after divorce engenders two new classes of kin which may interact with members of the stepfamily household and affect family functioning: (1) stepkin, who may include stepparents, stepgrandparents, stepsiblings, and other relatives of residential and nonresidential stepparents; and (2) "quasi-kin," a term coined by Bohannon (1970) to refer to former spouses, husbands and wives of former spouses, and bloodkin of former spouses. Thus, in comparison to nuclear families, persons in stepfamilies may encounter a larger and more complex kinship network.

Relationships with Former Spouses and Other Quasi-Kin

Relationships with these new classes of kin may also lack institutional guidelines or role prescriptions. No societal norms demarcate appropriate and inappropriate types of interaction between former spouses (e.g., whether they should have dinner together to discuss the children). This lack of institutional guidelines may challenge the coping styles and "role-creation" skills of stepfamily members. Cherlin (1978) proposed an "incomplete institution" hypothesis to account for the higher divorce rate in stepfamilies than in nuclear families. Using both complexity and ambiguity of relationships as explanatory mechanisms, Cherlin argued that interactions with former spouses and other quasi-kin (stemming from the visitation of children) lack institutional role prescriptions and thus engender role strain for the remarried couple. He predicted that, if all else were equal, the greater the frequency of contact with quasi-kin, the greater the probability of divorce in remarriages.

Cherlin's theory stands out in an area lacking in theory, and it has sparked alternative explanations and interpretations (e.g., Furstenberg & Spanier, 1984; Halliday, 1980). To date, only three published empirical studies have provided data relevant to Cherlin's prediction (Clingempeel, 1981; Clingempeel & Brand, 1985; Furstenberg & Spanier, 1984). Clingempeel (1981) conducted a multimethod study of frequency of the face-to-face contact with quasi-kin and marital quality in 40 stepfather families in Virginia. Rather than the linear and negatively correlated relationship predicted by Cherlin, Clingempeel found a curvilinear pattern. Persons in stepfather families who maintained moderate frequencies of contact with quasi-kin exhibited better marital quality than did persons who maintained either high or low frequencies of contact. However, Clingempeel and Brand (1985) replicated the study with a Pennsylvania sample of stepfather families and found that the frequency of contact with quasi-kin and marital quality were unassociated. Furthermore, data from the National Survey of Children (Furstenberg *et al.*, 1983) and from a study of 359 remarried couples from Spokane County, Washington (Pasley, Ihinger-Tallman, & Coleman, 1984) revealed that relationships with ex-spouses rarely were sources of disagreements in remarriages.

It may be important for stepfamily researchers to give more attention to qualitative dimensions of the former spouse relationship (e.g., intensity of conflict, degree of cooperative parenting) as mediators of the quality of remarriages. The extant studies have focused on relationships with former spouses but other quasi-kin (e.g., former in-laws, husbands and wives of ex-spouses) may also affect the quality of remarriages and should become targets of future studies. No studies have examined the "effects" of the quantity and quality of adult contacts with quasi-kin on other intrahousehold dyadic relationships (e.g., parent–child, stepparent–stepchild) or child outcomes. Also needed are studies that challenge and offer alternatives to the assumption that greater role ambiguity results in lower marital quality. One alternative explanation is that role ambiguity is also "role flexibility" and that the greater behavioral options may be a positive factor in the marriages of some stepparent couples. A focus on strengths rather than weaknesses is long overdue as a conceptual guide to research on reconstituted families (Clingempeel & Brand, 1985).

Nonresidential Parent–Child Relationships

The frequency of visits and the quality of the nonresidential parent–child relationship may mediate the quality of relationships within the stepfamily household and child outcomes. While frequency of visits from noncustodial fathers is a common predictor variable in divorce research (e.g., Hetherington, Cox, & Cox, 1978; Wallerstein & Kelly, 1980), it has been virtually ignored when the residential parent remarries and a stepfamily is formed.

The stepparent–stepchild relationship is one intrahousehold dyad that may be affected by the quantity and quality of the child's contacts with the nonresidential parent. Frequent visits from the nonresidential parent could reduce children's fears that the stepparent is a parent replacement, resulting in more positive stepparent–stepchild relationships and better outcomes for children. Another possibility is that frequent contacts with the nonresidential parent would increase role ambiguities for the residential parent and stepparent (due to a greater probability of increased interaction between ex-spouses and between residential stepparent and nonresidential biological parent), prevent the development of a cohesive stepparent–stepchild relationship, and ultimately translate into negative consequences for children. A third possibility is that an active child-care role by the nonresidential parent would result in the stepparent developing more of an "adult friend" rather than "acquired parent" relationship with the stepchild.

Only two studies have examined the relations between frequency of child contact with the nonresidential parent and the quality of the stepparent–stepchild relationship (Clingempeel & Segal, 1986; Furstenberg & Seltzer, 1983). In a multimethod study of stepparent–stepchild relationships in stepmother and stepfather families, Clingempeel and Segal (1986) found that, for girls in residential stepmother families, more frequent visits with the nonresidential mother were associated with less positive stepmother–stepdaughter relationships. The relationship between frequency of visits and quality of the stepparent–stepchild relationship was nonsignificant for boys in stepmother families and for children of both sexes in residential stepfather families.

Furstenberg and Seltzer's (1983) findings from the National Survey of Children were consistent with the Clingempeel and Segal data. In stepfather families, they found that regular contact with nonresidential fathers did not adversely affect stepfather–stepchild relationships. However, in stepmother families, regular contact with nonresidential mothers was related to lower-quality relationships with stepmothers. They did not report results separately for male and female stepchildren.

Studies are needed that go beyond "frequency of visitation" and assess the "effects" of qualitative dimensions of the nonresidential parent–child relationship on the quality of intrahousehold dyadic relationships (e.g., stepparent–stepchild, husband–wife) and child outcomes. This would increase the relevance of research to child-custody policy. To date, empirical research aimed at determining the advantages and disadvantages of joint versus sole custody have ignored, with a few exceptions (e.g., Clingempeel & Reppucci, 1982; Furstenberg & Spanier, 1984), what happens when one or both biological parents remarry, the next stage in the life cycle for 75% of divorced persons.

Residential Stepparents' Relationships with Nonresidential Children

Residential stepparents may also be nonresidential biological parents and have contact with biological children who live in the home of a former spouse. Stepparents in these *mixed stepparent families* (see our taxonomy) face the problem of balancing their personal resources, including time, affection, and money, between stepchildren who they live with and biological children who live elsewhere. Moreover, they may be tempted to treat biological children preferentially when they do see them, and this may engender resentment in stepchildren and current spouses. In the absence of norms, negotiating the optimal balance may be especially difficult.

Several studies have compared stepfamilies where the residential stepparent does and does not have nonresidential biological children on the quality of husband–wife and stepparent–stepchild relationships (e.g., Clingempeel, 1981; Clingempeel, Ievoli, & Brand, 1984). However, these studies have largely ignored qualitative dimensions of the stepparents' relationships with nonresidential children.

Studies are needed that examine the quantity and quality of stepparents' contacts with nonresidential biological children as predictors of the quality of husband–wife and stepparent–stepchild relationships. It may be important to assess perceptions of stepfamily members and quasi-kin (current and former spouses, stepchildren and biological children) regarding both the actual and ideal proportions of the stepfathers' personal resources given to stepchildren and biological children. The magnitude and direction of interindividual differences may affect the quality of relationships among stepfamily members. Stepparents who give substantially more to biological children than the "ideal" desired by their spouses and stepchildren may experience accusations of favoritism and greater conflict within the stepfamily household. On the other hand, stepparents who give considerably less to biological children than the "ideal" desired by biological children and former spouses may experience more conflict from the "nonresidential children" household. Intraindividual actual–ideal disparities in perceptions of personal-resource distributions also may have an impact on the quality of intrahousehold relationships. Stepparents who perceive themselves as giving much less to their biological children than their intraindividual ideal may experience guilt and intrapsychic turmoil that may interfere with the development of positive relationships with stepchildren. These speculations need to be examined in future research on stepfamilies.

Children's Relationships with Kin of Biological Parents and Stepparents

The quality and quantity of child contacts with kin of both biological parents and stepparents are predictor variables that should receive more attention. When divorced parents remarry, children may inherit an expanded kinship network consisting of possibly four biological grandparents, four stepgrandparents, two stepparents, stepsiblings, and other consanguinal kin of stepparents. As a result, children may be exposed to a greater diversity of interaction, activities, and settings, and competence in making friends and in adapting to new social situations may be developed (Riley, 1982).

However, a greater number of potential kin does not necessarily mean that more kin are functional in the lives of children. Two questions are critical: (1) Do kin of the nonresidential parent maintain contact and play a role in the child's life after divorce and remarriage? and (2) Do kin of the residential stepparent, including stepgrandparents, play an active role in the child's life? Furstenberg and Spanier (1984) addressed these questions in their longitudinal study of 204 central-Pennsylvania parents. They found that, at 2½ years after marital separation (when 35% had remarried and 13% were cohabiting), approximately 75% of the children saw their paternal grandparents at least two or three times a year. However, the frequency of contact was related to frequency of visits by nonresidential fathers who ostensibly served as a link to the third generation. Furstenberg and Spanier also reported that children in stepfamilies had almost as much contact with stepgrandparents as they did with biological grandparents on the side of the residential parent.

Studies are needed that attempt to replicate these findings with larger and more representative samples. In addition, it may be important for researchers to investigate the relations between the quantity and quality of child contacts with various grandparent figures and specific outcomes in cognitive and social development. Greater attention should be given to the conditions under which children develop close relationships with stepgrandparents (and other blood kin of the stepparent) and view them as relatives or nonrelatives. Finally, the role that grandparents and stepgrandparents play in the lives of children should be assessed from the perspective of all three generations (grandparents, parents, children).

THE SOCIAL INSTITUTION LEVEL

The social institution level of analysis has received the least attention by stepfamily researchers. Very few studies have examined how the policies and practices of formal social institutions (e.g., family courts, work settings, schools) affect the quality of relationships within the stepfamily household and children's developmental outcomes. Rather than a discussion of multiple social institutions, we focus on the mass media as one institution that may have an impact on stepfamilies.

The portrayal of stepfamilies in the mass media (e.g., television, radio, popular books) may alter the attitudes and behaviors of persons living in reconstituted families. The effects of the mass media on stepfamilies could stem from direct exposure of stepfamily members to media coverage of their lifestyle or manifest themselves indirectly through influencing how others relate to and perceive stepfamily members. Clinicians have suggested that the media has reinforced negative stereotypes and created problems for stepfamilies (e.g., Perkins & Kahan, 1979; Visher & Visher, 1979), but no empirical research has directly tested this assertion. We suggest four areas for future research: (1) content analyses of how stepfamilies are portrayed and the types of information presented about stepfamilies in various media sources; (2) studies of the effects on stepfamilies of direct exposure to mass media portrayals and discussions of their lifestyle; (3) studies of perceptions of stepfamilies held by various subpopulations and the role of the media in reinforcing, altering, or creating these perceptions; and (4) studies of the effects of media dissemination of research findings on the validity of these findings over time.

Traditional folklore and popular fairy tales (e.g., *Hansel and Gretel, Cinderella*) have depicted stepparents as mean and cruel. Systematic data are lacking on how stepparents (and stepfamilies) are portrayed in more recent popular books. Coleman, Ganong, and Gingrich (1985) performed a content analysis of adolescent fiction to determine "common themes" related to living in stepfamilies. Content analysis of other media sources (e.g., television portrayals, newspaper articles) may also be illuminating. For example, "how-to-parent" books are widely read by nuclear family members (Clarke-Stewart, 1978), and, in recent years, "how-to-stepparent" and self-help books written specifically for stepparents have proliferated. Yet, systematic surveys of the popularity and the kinds of advice given in various primers are unavailable. Recently, Pasley and Ihinger-Tallman (1985) conducted a content analysis of all articles on remarriage and stepfamilies published between 1940 and 1980 in popular American magazines (e.g., *Good Housekeeping, Redbook*). Several findings were noteworthy: (1) the number of stepfamily articles has increased substantially over 4 decades; (2) stepfamily articles in recent years have relied more on empirical sources and mental health professionals and have focused on a greater diversity of stepfamily issues; and (3) the majority of articles are directed toward women or general audiences.

The relations between the media portrayal of stepfamilies and stereotypes held by various subpopulations need to be studied. As a first step, the prevalence of various perceptions (or stereotypes) of stepparents and stepfamilies across subpopulations might be assessed (see Chapter 2 in this volume). A few studies have found that negative stereotypes of stepparents were held by college students (Ganong & Coleman, 1983) and human service professionals and trainees (Bryan, Ganong, Coleman, & Bryan, 1985). Replications of these studies with similar as well as other subpopulations are needed to establish the generalizability of these findings. Survey or interview studies of persons not living in stepfamilies could assess the portrayals of stepfamilies they see, hear, or read about and how these portrayals have affected their perceptions and beliefs. Finally, studies could examine the extent to which persons who hold and do not hold negative stereotypes of stepfamilies behave differently toward stepfamily members.

Members of stepfamilies may alter their behaviors and attitudes as a direct result of reading "how-to-stepparent" books and hearing "expert" discussions of stepfamily issues on television and radio talk shows. Moreover, these and other media sources may play an important role in establishing normative guidelines on topics of concern to stepfamily members (e.g., what is the appropriate role of the stepparent in childbearing?). We suggest that surveys with a representative sample of stepfamilies should address the following kinds of questions: Where do stepfamilies obtain information relevant to specific stepfamily issues? What kinds of information are stepfamilies obtaining from various media sources? To what extent are members of stepfamilies altering their attitudes and behaviors as a result of exposure to the media? What media sources are having the most impact?

The dissemination of research findings via the mass media and the resulting public awareness of these findings may invalidate empirical results. Stepfathers who learn of research suggesting that stepparents have more difficult relationships with opposite sex stepchildren may invest greater effort in developing positive relationships with their stepdaughters and thus invalidate this finding. Explanatory constructs may also be subject to "enlightenment effects." For example, the dissemination of research findings may foster the development of norms and institutional guidelines for steprelationships, and thus "role ambiguity" (the hypothetical causative mechanism in Cherlin's incomplete institution hypothesis) may become obsolete over time. Of course, it is possible that the dissemination of research findings would have a validating rather than invalidating effect, and thus stepfamilies would "conform to" rather than "deviate from" the findings of social science research. Gergen (1973) called for a science of enlightenment effects in which the consequences of disseminating research findings are examined empirically. We echo Gergen, and believe this strategy may be useful in increasing our understanding of mass media effects on stepfamilies.

TOWARD AN INTEGRATION OF LEVELS

Our discussion of a multilevel–multivariable perspective for stepfamily research has focused on multiple variables at each of three levels of analysis and their potentially independent effects on the quality of family relationships and child outcomes in stepfamilies. However, a demonstration of the heuristic utility of this approach requires some attempt to elucidate interdependencies of variables within and between levels of analysis. Variables within each level of analysis as well as between levels may be correlated with each other (or even causally related) or may be interactive (the effects of one variable may depend upon the level of other variables).

Within the stepfamily household, we have given examples of research that examines the interdependencies of variables across the three subclasses (family structure, demographic and personality characteristics of family members, intrahousehold relationships), and we have attempted to elucidate the heuristic utility of this strategy. However, variable interdependencies within the extrahousehold network and social institution levels of analysis also need to be examined in future stepfamily research. The quality and quantity of interactions between members of the stepfamily household and extrahousehold network including former spouses, nonresidential parents and children, grandparents and grandchildren, and former in-laws may be interrelated. For example, more conflictual relationships between ex-spouses may be related to less-frequent visits of children by nonresidential fathers which, in turn, may be related to less-frequent visits by paternal grandparents. Social institution factors may also be interdependent. The extent to which stepfamilies are portrayed by the mass media as either deviant or as alternative lifestyles may influence both the family life curricula of the schools and the policies of family courts regarding the rights of stepparents.

Research that examines the mechanisms by which various social institutions influence each other ultimately may increase our understanding of the ways stepfamilies are influenced by the multiple social contexts in which they are embedded.

Variables at the social institution and extra-household network levels of analysis also may be interrelated, and these between-level interdependencies may have implications for the quality of relationships within the stepfamily household. Mass media portrayals of ex-spouse relationships as necessarily conflictual may engender more difficult relationships between these quasi-kin which, in turn, may lead to problems between remarried couples. Family courts favorable to joint custody may produce a more even distribution of contact between children and both biological parents (and sets of grandparents) which may increase the likelihood that stepparents become adult friends rather than parent figures to stepchildren. Thus, social institution factors may affect members of the stepfamily household indirectly via direct influences on members of the extra-household network. Stepfamily researchers may need to take into account indirect paths of influence in formulating hypotheses, choosing data-analysis strategies, and interpreting results.

It may also be important for stepfamily researchers to examine the interdependencies of social institution factors and the types of stepfamilies outlined in our taxonomy. The child custody policies of family courts (e.g., proclivity to award custody of children to mothers or fathers after divorce and remarriage) may alter the prevalence of various stepfamily structures (e.g., residential stepmother families). In turn, this may have implications for interdependencies between variables at the extra-household network and stepfamily household levels. An increase in residential stepmother families may result in more children having regular contact with nonresidential parents (since nonresidential mothers generally visit more frequently than nonresidential fathers) which may alter the childrearing roles played by same sex parents and stepparents.

Stepfamily researchers who attempt to examine interdependencies of variables within and between levels of analysis may want to follow Bronfenbrenner's (1979) recommendations to include as many predictor variables as possible in research designs and to pay particular attention to potential higher-order interactions among predictors. In stepfamily research, interaction effects may be the rule and main effects the rare exception. Similarly, intercorrelated predictor variables may not be uncommon. It is likely, for example, that qualitative dimensions of various family subsystems (e.g., husband–wife, stepparent–stepchild) are interdependent. Understanding the nature of these interdependencies may be important for interpreting their role in mediating child outcomes. When multicollinearity is expected, structural equations and confirmatory factor analysis may be the preferred data-analysis strategies (Miller, Rollins, & Thomas, 1982).

Finally, stepfamily researchers will need to consider reciprocal causation and bidirectional influence mechanisms. In this chapter, we have construed the quality of family relationships and child outcomes largely as dependent variables and social institution and extra-household network factors exclusively as independent variables. However, the quality of family relationships and children's social and cognitive development can be considered as "causes" as well as "effects." In longitudinal studies, researchers may want to use cross-lagged panel techniques (see Campbell & Stanley, 1966) to analyze relative strengths of bidirectional paths between variables.

A FAMILY DEVELOPMENT PERSPECTIVE

The characteristics of individual family members, the nature of relationships within and outside the stepfamily household, and the policies and practices of social institutions may change over time. Time-related changes in the functioning of families may be viewed from a family development perspective (Duvall, 1977; Hill & Rogers, 1964; Nock, 1979). According to this perspective, families progress through a series of stages, coinciding with ubiquitous life-cycle changes (e.g., birth of first child, departure of last child from the home) which may alter role relationships among family members. After remarriage, life cycle changes may include shifts in custody arrangements of children from prior marriages, birth of a child to the current marriage, redivorce, and age-related transitions of children (e.g., preschoolers become school-age children with concomitant changes in competencies, salience of settings, stressors, and social supports).

The birth of a child to the remarriage—an expectable life cycle event for a high proportion of stepparent couples (Hill, 1986)—may illustrate the heuristic merits of the family development perspective. In first marriages, the birth of a first child engenders stressful tasks for the married couple associated with the assignment of child-care roles and the demands of a new infant. In stepfamilies, where at least one spouse already has a biological child from a prior marriage, family members may confront a variety of additional stressors.

The timing of the new infant may be important in determining the ease or difficulty of the stepfamilies' adjustment. A concatenation of stressors may occur if the birth of a child occurs before the developmental tasks associated with the transition to remarriage have been mastered.

One developmental task of newly formed stepfamilies is the reallocation of the personal resources (e.g., time, energy, affection) of the residential biological parent from the child to the new spouse. If a child is born to the remarriage prior to the resolution of this task, the stepfamily may compound the stressor events with which they must cope and thus prolong the time needed to adjust. In this situation, children from the prior marriage will have experienced two temporally contiguous events (remarriage of custodial parent, birth of half sibling), both of which may translate into less time and affection from the residential, biological parent. Children who have not yet adjusted to the losses associated with the entry of a stepparent into a single-parent household may experience even greater difficulties when a new half-sibling reduces even more the parents' personal resources available for them.

The determination of the role of the stepparent in childrearing is a second developmental task that, if still problematic when a child is born to the remarriage, may exacerbate adjustment difficulties for the stepfamily. Stepparents who had been working with their spouses and stepchildren to develop a consensus regarding the stepparents' limit setting and nurturance roles now may need to divert attention from this task and focus instead on the care of the new infant. Moreover, a stepparent who has a biological child with the current spouse may have diminished interest in developing a relationship with stepchildren with whom there are no biological ties. Consequently, the stepparent–stepchild relationship, which otherwise would have improved steadily, might now deteriorate, and the time needed for the stepparent to be integrated into the household may be extended.

The adjustment of stepfamily members may be especially difficult if age-related transitions of children overlap with both the unresolved developmental task of adjustment to remarriage and the new tasks associated with the birth of a child to the stepparent couple. There is empirical evidence that divorced persons who remarry and return to childbearing most often do so when their children from a prior marriage are experiencing the transition from preadolescence to adolescence (Hill, 1986). In these situations, parents and stepparents must simultaneously confront the developmental tasks of emerging adolescence (e.g., independence seeking, development of sexual identity, and dating competencies), the demands of a new infant, and the yet-to-be-mastered tasks associated with family reconstitution (e.g., the determination of the role of the stepparent in childrearing). Moreover, individuals, dyadic relationships within stepfamilies (e.g., the marital relationship), and the family as a whole may be on different life-cycle tracks with conflicting developmental tasks (McGoldrick & Carter, 1980; Sager *et al.*, 1983). The infant's need for nurturance and continuous care may conflict with the need of the stepparent couple for romantic bonding; and the independence strivings of the adolescent may oppose an overarching goal of the new stepfamily—to achieve unity and cohesion.

A family development perspective accentuates the importance of separating the short-term, crisis-related effects of critical transitions from long-term sequelae. In the short run, the birth of a child to the remarriage would increase stressors upon the stepfamily. However, the new child provides a parenthood bond between spouses and a biological bond between halfsiblings. In the long run, these new ties may foster a more cohesive stepfamily. Similarly, the entry of a stepparent into a single parent household initially may engender resentment in children and disrupt the parent–child relationship. However, over time, children may benefit from stepparents who serve as additional support systems and sources of cognitive and social stimulation.

A family development perspective also suggests that the spacing and timing of life-cycle events that occurred prior to the remarriage may have an impact upon stepfamilies. The length of the intermarriage interval (or the total time from biological parents' separation from ex-spouse to remarriage or cohabitation with the current spouse) may be an important predictor of the family's adjustment. An especially lengthy intermarriage interval may mean that developmental tasks associated with divorce and single parenthood have been mastered. However, a lengthy interval may also result in parent–child roles that are overly rigid and resistant to change required by the entry of a stepparent. An unusually short interval may not allow enough time for mastery of developmental tasks associated with the transition from a nuclear to a single-parent family. As a result, stressors may concatenate after remarriage, and the adjustment of family members to the new stepfamily may be adversely affected. Clinicians and family therapists have frequently asserted that "emotional baggage" from the previous marriage and divorce may interfere with the development of a well-functioning stepfamily (e.g., Hansen & Messinger, 1982; Sager *et al.*, 1983; Visher & Visher, 1979), but no empirical studies have tested this assertion. The relation between length of intermarriage interval and adjustment to a stepfamily may be curvilinear with best adjustment associated with intervals of intermediate length. This is speculation, however, and empirical research is needed here.

In demarcating "stages," stepfamily researchers may want to consider the point at which the couples begin "living together" rather than the point at which they remarry as the more meaningful criterion. Stepparent couples who have been remarried only 6 months but who have lived together several years before the remarriage probably should not be considered new stepfamilies experiencing a state of equilibrium. By the wedding day, the stepparent–stepchild relationship in these families already may have progressed through several stages. Premarital cohabitation has been the target of several studies of first marriages (e.g., Bentler & Newcomb, 1978; DeMaris & Leslie, 1983), and a few studies have examined its role in remarriage (DeMaris, 1984; Hanna & Knaub, 1981; Pink & Wampler, 1985).

A family development perspective underscores the importance of temporal factors in predicting the ease or difficulty of family reorganization following remarriage and the psychological adjustment of stepfamily members. This perspective also accentuates several needs for methodological advances that should become priorities for future research: (1) the need to determine empirically the developmental tasks (with concomitant levels of stress upon family members) that coincide with the critical transitions of remarriage, birth of a child to the remarriage, and redivorce; (2) the need to develop reliable and valid methods of assessing the extent to which developmental tasks have been mastered; (3) the need to develop strategies for assessing the spacing of developmental tasks associated with critical transitions and the degree of concatenation of tasks and stressors (the extent to which new tasks emerge before earlier tasks have been mastered); and (4) the need to develop methods for examining the extent to which developmental tasks of individuals, dyadic and triadic relationships, and entire families are conflicting.

CONCLUSION

We have proposed a multilevel–multivariable–developmental perspective for future research on stepfamilies. The adoption of this perspective by stepfamily researchers has at least three interrelated epistemological advantages (see Clingempeel, Flescher, & Brand, in press, for a discussion of epistemological advantages associated with additional proposals for future research on stepfamilies). First, it focuses attention on a greater variety of factors that may have an impact on stepfamilies. To date, a relatively narrow range of research questions have been examined, and many potentially important variables have been given little attention. Consequently, we believe that errors of omission may have limited our knowledge of stepfamilies even more than errors of measurement.

Second, this perspective fosters multidisciplinary research. The conceptual and methodological biases of social science disciplines are well established (e.g., Campbell, 1969; Endsley & Brody, 1981). Family scholars from psychology and sociology departments may raise different research questions, assess different variables, and focus on conceptual issues at different levels of analysis. Consequently, important research questions that lie at the crosspoints of several disciplines may remain unexamined, and the development of an integrated knowledge base may be impeded. By focusing attention on variables, levels of analysis, and research questions that extend across several disciplines, a multilevel–multivariable–developmental approach stimulates research that transcends disciplinary boundaries.

Third, this approach accentuates the importance of developmental and temporal factors to our understanding of remarriage and stepfamilies. The quality of family relationships and children's social and cognitive development are not frozen at a point in time as implied by much of the existing stepfamily research. The assumption that families, the nature of relationships among family members, and individuals change over time and in accordance with life events and changing social contexts is a major focus of a multilevel–multivariable–developmental perspective.

Finally, a qualifying comment is in order. We are not suggesting that single studies could incorporate all of the components of this perspective. Clearly, the feasibility of such ventures is questionable. Rather, we hope the conceptual framework presented in this chapter will encourage stepfamily researchers as a collectivity to examine a broader array of research questions.

NOTES

1. Given the rarity of split custody arrangements (where one or both spouses have custody of some but not all children from prior marriages), structural variations derived from split custody are not included in our taxonomy.

2. These global comparisons have yielded, in most cases, negligible differences on child outcomes. However, a few studies have found that stepchildren are less well adjusted than children in nuclear families (e.g., Bowerman & Irish, 1962; Ferri, 1984; Langer & Michael, 1963); and there is some evidence that boys in stepfather families perform better on cognitive tasks that their counterparts in single parent families (e.g., Chapman, 1977; Santrock, 1972).

3. These studies include C. Ahrons (University of Wisconsin), W. G. Clingempeel (The Pennsylvania State University), and E. M. Hetherington (University of Virginia), and F. F. Furstenberg (University of Pennsylvania).

REFERENCES

Banks, S., & Kahn, M. D. (1975). Sisterhood–brotherhood is powerful: Sibling sub-systems and family therapy. *Family Process, 14,* 311–317.

Bentler, P. M., & Newcomb, M. D. (1978). Longitudinal study of marital success and failure. *Journal of Consulting and Clinical Psychology, 46,* 1053–1070.

Bernard, J. (1956). *Remarriage: A study of marriage.* New York: Russell and Russell.

Bohannan, P. (1970). Divorce chains, households of remarriage, and multiple divorces. In P. Bohannon (Ed.), *Divorce and after,* (pp. 127–139). New York: Doubleday.

Bowerman, C. E., & Irish, D. P. (1962). Some relationships of stepchildren to their parents. *Marriage and Family Living, 24,* 113–131.

Brand, E., & Clingempeel, W. G. (1987). Interdependencies of marital and stepparent–stepchild relationships and children's psychological adjustment: Research findings and clinical implications. *Family Relations, 36,* 140–145.

Brand, E., Clingempeel, W. G., & Bowen-Woodward, K. (in press). Family relationships and children's psychological adjustment in stepmother and stepfather families: Findings and conclusions from the Philadelphia Stepfamily Research Project. In E. M. Hetherington & J. Arasteh (Eds.), *Divorce, Remarriage and Child Outcomes.* Hillsdale, NJ: Erlbaum.

Bronfenbrenner, U. (1979). *The ecology of human development.* Cambridge, MA: Harvard University Press.

Bryan, H., Ganong, L., Coleman, M., & Bryan, L. (1985). Counselor's perceptions of stepparents and stepchildren. *Journal of Counseling Psychology, 32,* 279–282.

Burchinal, L. G. (1964). Characteristics of adolescents from unbroken, broken, and reconstituted families. *Journal of Marriage and the Family, 26,* 44–51.

Campbell, D. T. (1969). Ethnocentrism of disciplines and the fishscale model of omniscience. In M. Sheriff & C. W. Sherif (Eds.), *Interdisciplinary relationships in the social sciences.* Chicago, IL: Aldine.

Campbell, D. T., & Stanley, J. C. (1966). *Experimental and quasi-experimental designs for research.* Chicago, IL: Rand McNally.

Chapman, M. (1977). Father absence, stepfathers, and the cognitive performance of college students. *Child Development, 48,* 1155–1158.

Cherlin, A. J. (1978). Remarriage as an incomplete institution. *American Journal of Sociology, 84,* 634–650.

Clarke-Stewart, K. A. (1978). Popular primers for parents. *American Psychologist, 33,* 359–369.

Clingempeel, W. G. (1981). Quasi-kin relationships and marital quality in stepfather families. *Journal of Personality and Social Psychology, 41,* 890–901.

Clingempeel, W. G., & Brand, E. (1985). Structural complexity, quasi-kin relationships, and marital quality in stepfamilies: A replication, extension, and clinical implications. *Family Relations, 34,* 401–409.

Clingempeel, W. G., Brand, E., & Ievoli, R. (1984). Stepparent–stepchild relationships in stepmother and stepfather families: A multimethod study. *Family Relations, 33,* 465–474.

Clingempeel, W. G., Flescher, M., & Brand, E. (in press). Research on stepfamilies: Paradigmatic constraints and alternative proposals. In J. P. Vincent (Eds.), *Advances in family intervention, assessment, and theory* (Vol. 4). Greenwich, CT: JAI Press.

Clingempeel, W. G., Ievoli, R., & Brand, E. (1984). Structural complexity and the quality of stepfather–stepchild relationships. *Family Process, 23,* 547–560.

Clingempeel, W. G., & Reppucci, N. D. (1982). Joint custody after divorce: Major issues and goals for research. *Psychological Bulletin, 91,* 102–127.

Clingempeel, W. G., & Segal, S. (1986). Stepparent–stepchild relationships and the psychological adjustment of children in stepmother and stepfather families. *Child Development, 57,* 474–484.

Coleman, M., Ganong, L., & Gingrich, R. (1985). Stepfamily strengths: A review of the popular literature. *Family Relations, 34,* 583–589.

Crosbie-Burnett, M. (1984). The centrality of the step relationship: A challenge to family theory and practice. *Family Relations, 33,* 459–463.

DeMaris, A. (1984). A comparison of remarriage with first marriage on satisfaction in marriage and its relationship to prior cohabitation. *Family Relations, 33,* 443–449.

DeMaris, A., & Leslie, G. R. (1983, April). *Cohabitation with the future spouse: Its influence upon marital satisfaction and communication.* Paper presented at the annual meeting of the Southern Sociological Society in Atlanta, GA.

Duberman, L. (1973). Step-kin relationships. *Journal of Marriage and the Family, 35,* 283–292.

Duberman, L. (1975). *The reconstituted family: A study of remarried couples and their children.* Chicago, IL: Nelson-Hall Publishers.

Duvall, E. M. (1977). *Family Development* (5th ed.). Philadelphia, PA: Lippincott.

Endsley, R. C., & Brody, G. H. (1981). Professional isolation of child and family specialists as revealed in a time series analysis of parent–child relations research methods. *Family Relations, 30,* 5–15.

Esses, L. M., & Campbell, R. (1984). Challenges in researching the remarried. *Family Relations, 33,* 415–424.

Ferri, E. (1984). *Stepchildren: A national study.* Berkshire, England: Nfer-Nelson Publishing Company.

Furstenberg, F. F., Jr., Nord, C. W., Peterson, J. L., & Zill, N. (1983). The life course of children of divorce: Marital disruption and parental contact. *American Sociological Review, 48,* 656–668.

Furstenberg, F. F., Jr., & Seltzer, J. A. (1983, April). *Divorce and child development.* Paper presented at a Meeting of the Orthopsychiatric Association, Boston, MA.

Furstenberg, F. F., Jr., & Spanier, G. B. (1984). *Recycling the family: Remarriage after divorce.* Beverly Hills, CA: Sage.

Ganong, L., & Coleman, M. (1983). Stepparent: A pejorative term? *Psychological Reports, 52,* 919–922.

Ganong, L. H., & Coleman, M. (1984). The effects of remarriage on children: A review of the empirical literature. *Family Relations, 33,* 389–406.

Gergen, K. J. (1973). Social psychology as history. *Journal of Personality and Social Psychology, 26,* 309–320.

Halliday, T. C. (1980). Remarriage: The more complete institution? *American Journal of Sociology, 86,* 630–635.

Hanna, S. L., & Knaub, P. K. (1981). Cohabitation before remarriage: Its relationship to family strengths. *Alternative Lifestyles, 4,* 507–522.

Hansen, J. C., & Messinger, L. (Eds.). (1982). *Therapy with remarriage families.* Rockville, MD: Aspen Systems Corporation.

Hetherington, E. M., Cox, M., & Cox, R. (1978). The aftermath of divorce. In J. H. Stevens, Jr., & M. Mathews (Eds.), *Mother–child, father–child relations* (pp. 149–176). Washington, DC: National Association for the Education of Young Children.

Hetherington, E. M., Cox, M., & Cox, R. (1979). Family interactions and the social, emotional, and cognitive development of children following divorce. In V. C. Vaughn & T. B. Brazelton. *The family: Setting priorities.* (pp. 89–128). New York: Science and Medicine Publishers.

Hill, R. (1977). *Informal adoption among black families.* Washington, DC: National Urban League Research Department.

Hill, R. (1986). Life cycle stages for types of single parent families: Of family development theory. *Family Relations, 35,* 19–29.

Hill, R., & Rogers, R. H. (1964). The developmental approach. In H. T. Christensen (Ed.), *Handbook of marriage and the family.* Chicago, IL: Rand.

Kellam, S. G., Ensminger, M. E., & Turner, J. (1977). Family structure and the mental health of children: Concurrent and longitudinal community-wide studies. *Archives of General Psychiatry, 34,* 1012–1022.

Kurdek, L. A., Blisk, D., & Siesky, A. E. (1981). Correlates of children's long-term adjustment to their parents' divorce. *Developmental Psychology, 17,* 565–579.

Langer, J. S., & Michael, S. T. (1963). *Life stress and mental health.* New York: Free Press.

Lee, G. R. (1979). Effects of social networks on the family. In W. R. Burr, R. Hill, I. Nye, & I. Reiss (Eds.), *Contemporary theories about the family* (Vol. I, pp. 27–56). New York: Free Press.

Links, P. S. (1983). Community surveys of the prevalence of childhood psychiatric disorders: A review. *Child Development, 54,* 531–548.

Marotz-Baden, R., Adams, G. R., Bueche, N., Munro, R., & Munro, G. (1979). Family form or family process? Reconsidering the deficit family model approach. *The Family Coordinator, 28,* 5–14.

McGoldrick, M., & Carter, E. A. (1980). Forming a remarried family. In E. A. Carter & M. McGoldrick (Eds.), *The family life cycle: A framework for family therapy* (pp. 265–294). New York: Gardner.

Miller, B. C., Rollins, B. C., & Thomas, D. L. (1982). On methods of studying marriages and families. *Journal of Marriage and the Family, 44,* 851–871.

Nobles, W. W. (1978). Toward an empirical and theoretical framework for defining black families. *Journal of Marriage and the Family, 40,* 679–688.

Nock, S. L. (1979). The family life cycle: Empirical or conceptual tool. *Journal of Marriage and the Family, 41*, 15–26.

Oshman, H. P., & Manosevitz, M. (1976). Father absence: Effects of stepfathers upon psychosocial development in males. *Developmental Psychology, 12*, 479–480.

Pasley, K., & Ihinger-Tallman, M. (1982). Stress in remarried families. *Family Perspectives, 16*, 181–190.

Pasley, K., & Ihinger-Tallman, M. (1985). Portraits of stepfamily life in popular literature: 1940–1980. *Family Relations, 34*, 527–534.

Pasley, K., Ihinger-Tallman, M., & Coleman, C. (1984). Consensus styles among happy and unhappy married couples. *Family Relations, 33*, 451–458.

Perkins, T. F., & Kahan, J. P. (1979). An empirical comparison of natural-father and stepfamily systems. *Family Process, 18*, 175–183.

Perry, J. B., & Pfuhl, E. H. (1963). Adjustment of children in "solo" and "remarriage" homes. *Marriage and Family Living, 25*(2), 221–223.

Pink, J. E., & Wampler, K. S. (1985). Problem areas in stepfamilies: Cohesion, adaptability, and the stepfather–adolescent relationship. *Family Relations, 34*, 327–335.

Riley, M. W. (1982, October). *Families in an aging society*. Key address at a meeting of the National Council on Family Relations, Washington, DC.

Rutter, M. (1979). Protective factors in children's responses to stress and disadvantage. In M. W. Kent & J. E. Rolf (Eds.), *Primary prevention of psychopathology: Promoting social competence and coping in children*, (Vol. 3; pp. 121–140). Hanover, NH: University Press of New England.

Sager, C. J., Walker, E., Brown, H. S., Crohn, H., & Rodstein, E. (1983). *Treating the remarried family*. New York: Brunner/Mazel.

Sanders, R., & Spanier, G. B. (1979). Divorce, child custody, and child support. *Current Population Reports*, U. S. Bureau of the Census, Series P-23, No. 84.

Santrock, J. W. (1972). Relation of type and onset of father absence to cognitive development. *Child Development, 43*, 455–469.

Santrock, J. W., Warshak, R., Lindbergh, C., & Meadows, L. (1982). Children's and parents' observed social behavior in stepfather families. *Child Development, 53*, 472–480.

Stack, C. (1974). *All our kin: Strategies for survival in a black community*. New York: Harper & Row.

Visher, E. B., & Visher, J. B. (1979). *Stepfamilies: A guide to working with stepparents and stepchildren*. New York: Brunner/Mazel.

Wald, E. (1981). *The remarried family: Challenge and promise*. New York: Family Service Association of America.

Wallerstein, J. S., & Kelly, J. B. (1980). *Surviving the breakup: How children actually cope with divorce*. New York: Basic Books.

Werner, E. E., & Smith, R. S. (1979). An epidemiologic perspective on some antecedents and consequences of childhood mental health problems and learning disabilities: A report from the Kauai longitudinal study. *Journal of the American Academy of Child Psychiatry, 18*, 296–306.

5

Effects of Parental Remarriage on Children: An Updated Comparison of Theories, Methods, and Findings from Clinical and Empirical Research

LAWRENCE H. GANONG AND MARILYN COLEMAN
University of Missouri—Columbia

An assumption held by a number of researchers and clinicians [is] that research on family relations can inform clinical practice.
—R. J. Gelles, 1982

The dialogue between researchers and clinicians is a myth.
—D. Ransom, 1983

THE REVIEW OF THE LITERATURE ON CHILDREN OF STEPFAMILIES

As researchers who are also practitioners. we have long been puzzled by what seemed to be a lack of interaction between family researchers and clinicians. For example, as we prepared a reference list for a graduate course on remarriage and stepfamilies, it was our impression that there seemed to be two distinct bodies of professional literature focusing on stepchildren: one in which researchers examined one set of variables, and another in which clinicians viewed quite a different set of variables. It appeared that this was a case of the "blind men and the elephant," with researchers and clinicians describing what they found to be true about the "elephant," but neither description sounding like they were examining the same animal.

As family scholars, this apparent absence of dialogue between researchers and clinicians concerns us. Such professional segregation may restrict the development of knowledge about stepchildren and their families by retarding progress in theory, research, and application.

As a result of this concern, a review of the literature on stepchildren was conducted to compare findings from clinical work to empirical research

94

results (Ganong & Coleman, 1986). The purposes of this review were: (1) to assess the congruence of foci of researchers and clinicians interested in stepchildren, and (2) to compare what is known about stepchildren based on empirical research to information derived from case studies, clinical research, and clinical opinion. For this review, the terms "clinical" and "clinician" were defined broadly to include all applied family professionals (such as family life educators, teachers, clergy, psychologists, etc.).

To generalize the findings in this first review, few similarities between the empirical and clinical work were identified (Ganong & Coleman, 1986). The main similarities were the use of a "deficit-comparison" framework and an appreciation of the influence of family functioning on stepchildren's adjustment. Dissimilarities between the two bodies of literature included difference in (1) consideration of stepfamily complexity, (2) data-gathering methods, (3) focus of interest, and (4) conclusions drawn. We found that there was abundant evidence indicating that researchers and clinicians interested in stepchildren were professionally segregated and that there was little indication of any communication between the two professional groups (Ganong & Coleman, 1986).

There were, however, encouraging signs for future dialogue. Several studies underway when the comparative review was completed (late 1984) were headed by persons with strong applied (clinical) interests (e.g., Ahrons's Bi-nuclear Family Project, Jacobson's Project Step, and Clingempeel and Hetherington's longitudinal study in Philadelphia). It was also apparent that some recent research had been stimulated by the clinical literature (Crosbie-Burnett, 1984; Halperin & Smith, 1983; Lutz, 1983). It may be that a dialogue has begun (i.e., clinicians are influencing researchers and researchers are informing clinicians). If so, then recent publications should show signs of greater convergence than was found when comparing earlier work. The purpose of this review is to update the earlier comparative examination of clinical and empirical writing on stepchildren. This review will serve two functions: (1) the information derived from each body of literature will be compared and summarized, and (2) any changes in the conceptual frameworks, foci, methodologies, and general conclusions will be identified for both clinical and empirical work.

Methods

Both this and the earlier comparative review were limited to literature published in books and journals. References were obtained from computer searches of major research banks (i.e., National Institute of Mental Health, Educational Research Information Center [ERIC], Psychological Abstracts), from bibliographies compiled by the Stepfamily Association of America (Bohannan, 1981) and by the National Council on Family Relations, from suggestions of colleagues, and from standard library search procedures. Over 400 references were reviewed. Empirical research was selected for review if the main focus of the study was the effects on children of parental remarriage, having a stepparent, or living in a stepfamily. For the clinical literature the criteria were: (1) that a main focus be on counseling, educating, or providing assistance to stepchildren and stepfamilies, and (2) that the report be in a clinically oriented book or journal written either by a practitioner or for counselors, teachers, or other applied helping professionals. First-person accounts written by stepparents or stepchildren were excluded, as were publications in popular periodicals. A total of 52 empirical studies and 89 clinical references are included. Of these, 19 empirical and 18 clinical references comprise the new or previously unreviewed sample of literature that will be specifically examined in this updated comparative review. Appendices 5-1 and 5-2 show data from all reviewed work, including references from our previous reviews (Ganong & Coleman, 1984, 1986). References not included in prior reviews are shown with an asterisk.

The two bodies of literature were compared on: theoretical approaches, methodology, type of stepfamily, problems and issues (for clinical), dependent variables (for empirical), miscellaneous variables examined or considered, and conclusions drawn. Further, changes in each body of literature over time were examined by looking at their characteristics in three time periods: pre-1970, 1970–1979, and 1980–1986.

Results and Discussion

Theory

In our earlier review, we found that clinicians wrote more often from a theoretical perspective than did researchers (Ganong & Coleman, 1986). Nearly three fourths of the clinical references discussed stepchildren from clear theoretical positions (see Appendix 5-1), while the underlying framework for most research was an atheoretical position that has been labeled "the deficit-family model" (Marotz-Baden, Adams, Bueche, Munro, & Munro, 1979) or the "deficit-comparison" (Ganong & Coleman, 1984, 1986). In the deficit-comparison approach stepchildren are compared to children living in a nuclear family, with the expectation that stepchildren will be living in a deficit environment. The primary assumption underlying this approach is that variations from the "intact" nuclear family (e.g., stepfamilies) produce undesirable effects on children.

Clinicians have been more aware than researchers of problems inherent in the deficit-comparison perspective and have argued against comparing stepfamilies to nuclear families because of basic structural and developmental differences (Fishman & Hamel, 1981; Visher & Visher, 1979). Although the deficit-comparison assumption is still popular, researchers now appear to be abandoning this model and are becoming more sophisticated theoretically in their approach to stepchildren and their families (e.g., Clingempeel, Ievoli, & Brand, 1984; Clingempeel & Segal, 1986; Ganong & Coleman, in press). However, progress in abandoning the nuclear family as a comparison group is slow; nearly half of the studies reported since 1983 include a nuclear family comparison.

The theoretical approach favored by most clinicians has been systems theory; nearly half of the publications were based on systems theory or a combination of systems theory and another conceptual framework (Ganong & Coleman, 1986). It appears that researchers are also increasingly using systems theory (see Appendix 5-2); nearly one third of the latest studies utilized a family systems framework (Clingempeel, Brand, & Ievoli, 1984; Clingempeel & Segal, 1986; Garbarino, Sebes, & Schellenbach, 1984; Kennedy, 1985; Pink & Wampler, 1985). Prior to 1984, only two studies had utilized a systems framework (Fox & Inazu, 1982; Perkins & Kahan, 1979).

Seventy-eight percent of the clinical references published since 1980 are based at least partly on the systems framework. In contrast, researchers study stepchildren from a greater variety of theories than clinicians do and are still more likely to eschew theory altogether. In general, researchers in recent years have utilized theory more often than their predecessors (47% of the updated 19 studies compared to 23% of the studies done before 1984). Three studies examined data to test Cherlin's incomplete institution hypothesis (Clingempeel, Ievoli, & Brand, 1984; Furstenberg & Spanier, 1984; White & Booth, 1985). Another group of recent studies has been atheoretically descriptive in nature but without a deficit-comparison underpinning (Ferri, 1984; Furstenberg & Nord, 1985; Ganong & Coleman, in press; Knaub, Hanna, & Stinnett, 1984; White, Brinkerhoff, & Booth, 1985). Given the limited state of knowledge regarding stepchildren and their families, these studies have yielded valuable information and can be springboards for future theoretically based study.

In summary, it appears that the two literatures continue to share a tendency to perceive stepfamilies and stepchildren within a problem-oriented framework. For clinicians, this is understandable since their clientele includes children and families who have problems and are seeking help more often than those making a relatively trouble-free adjustment to stepfamily living. Researchers study stepchildren and other stepfamily members who are functioning well; however, the "deficit-comparison" attitude tends to restrict vision by limiting research to comparisons of stepchildren to children living in other family structures. This orientation is not conducive to assisting either clinicians or researchers in asking questions that will broaden understanding of stepfamily dynamics, identify stepfamily strengths, and improve clinical practice, but rather leads again and again over well-trod ground. There is encouraging evidence, however, that researchers are beginning to abandon this limiting view.

Methodology

Clinicians and researchers utilize different methods to study stepchildren and their families (see Table 5-1). This is not unexpected since the purposes for data collection are not the same.

According to our initial review of 37 empirical studies (Ganong & Coleman, 1984), research on stepchildren has been characterized by: (1) the tendency to collect self-report data from a single respondent, usually an older child (30 studies); (2) a reliance on surveys, with data gathered once from a respondent (35 studies); (3) use of only one method of gathering data (34 studies), usually questionnaires developed by the researchers (18 of those 34 studies); and (4) nonprobability sampling techniques (30 studies). Empirical data were usually collected in group settings such as school classrooms. The dearth of multitrait–multimethod studies, of longitudinal studies, and of

Table 5-1. Comparisons of Characteristics of Research and Clinical Work On Stepchildren

Characteristics	Research	Clinical
Theory	Mostly atheoretical, deficit-comparison framework	Mostly systems, with role, family development, psychoanalytic
Purpose	Studying relationships, behavior, attitudes	Changing relationships and individual behavior
Method	Mainly self-report methods	Clinical observations of people seeking assistance
Sample	Usually nonprobability samples, volunteers, or school groups	Usually people who are having problems or want help
Setting	Usually field settings (especially classrooms) or laboratories	Usually offices; sometimes homes
Types of Stepfamilies	Most often stepchildren from step father households	All kinds of stepfamilies discussed, including noncustodial households
Design	Usually data gathered once, such as surveys	Repeated observations over time
Subjects	Usually one person, most often the stepchild	Usually several family members
General Conclusions	Generally, few differences are found between stepchildren and children from other family structures	Stepfamilies inherently have problems and difficulties, therefore, stepchildren have adjustment problems

studies obtaining responses from multiple family members has been criticized as a major weakness of this research (Esses & Campbell, 1984; Ganong & Coleman, 1984).

Some of the recent empirical studies have addressed these weaknesses. In nine studies, data were collected from multiple respondents in a family, usually the parent, stepparent, and stepchild (Clingempeel, Brand, & Ievoli, 1984; Clingempeel, Ievoli, & Brand, 1984; Crosbie-Burnett, 1984; Garbarino *et al.*, 1984; Pink & Wampler, 1985). Ferri (1984) utilized one adult and child along with school personnel as informants, and Knaub, Hanna, and Stinnett (1984) sampled spouses. Surveys continue to be the most frequently used methodology (see Appendix 5-2), although some of these are longitudinal rather than one-time-only designs (Ferri, 1984; Furstenberg & Nord, 1985; Furstenberg & Spanier, 1984; White & Booth, 1985). The appearance of longitudinal studies is encouraging since they address a critical weakness in research on stepchildren. One of these studies has a large national sample from England (Ferri, 1984) and two are nationally drawn samples from the United States (Furstenberg & Nord, 1985; White & Booth, 1985). Data from Ahrons's Bi-nuclear Family Project, Clingempeel and Hetherington's Philadelphia study, and Koren's Portland study will also supplant the lack of longitudinal research when published.

The use of only one method of gathering data, usually a questionnaire, has continued to be characteristic of empirical research, with the series of studies by Clingempeel and colleagues as notable exceptions. Neither has there been a move toward the use of paper and pencil instruments of known reliability and validity. The series of studies by Clingempeel and colleagues again are exceptions to this, as are three other recent studies designed to measure stepfamily functioning (Garbarino *et al.*, 1984; Kennedy, 1985; Pink & Wampler, 1985).

For clinicians, articulating the process by which conclusions are drawn seems to be a minor concern; seldom did clinical writers explain the sources upon which their information was based (Ganong & Coleman, 1986). The methodologies of clinicians include: descriptions of programs, case studies, literature reviews, interviews, and clinical impressions. The most frequently used method was impressionistic (i.e., drawing conclusions without either providing rationale or citing sources). In our earlier comparative review, 26 references (37%) were based entirely on clinical impressions and 27 (38%) utilized a combination of clinical impression and other methods. The second most frequent type of clinical publication was the description of an educational or counseling program. Case studies and literature reviews were published by a small percentage of clinicians.

No new methodologies were employed in the recent clinical articles we reviewed (see Appendix 5-1). The only difference between the recent reports and the earlier ones is that literature reviews are now the most often published pieces (61%) and clinical impressions are less frequently reported (only one was based solely on clinical impressions). It may be that literature reviews, case studies, and other clinical research techniques are becoming more heavily relied upon. Between 1970 and 1979, 44% of the clinical writers relied solely on clinical impressions for their data. This dropped to 34% from the period 1980–1983, and 25% for 1984–1986. In contrast, few clinical writings before 1980 were based on clinical research methods, whereas several post-1980 publications were based on clinical or empirical research (e.g., Ahrons & Perlmutter, 1982; Fishman & Hamel, 1981; Messinger, 1984; Wald, 1981; Wallerstein & Kelly, 1980).

In contrast to researchers, clinicians usually collected data from several family members (Ganong & Coleman, 1986). Although Johnson (1980) advocated that clinicians should consider the ecological environment of a stepfamily, not many have done this, preferring to focus on internal family dynamics instead. Societal attitudes (e.g., negative images of stepfamily members) were sometimes mentioned by clinicians but the impact of specific societal systems (e.g., schools, legal systems) on stepchildren was not often identified. We note that researchers have not been much better about considering nonfamilial influences.

Overall, in the first comparative review, we concluded that: (1) clinicians focused more on processes of interaction among stepfamily members, (2) clinicians referred more to long-term developmental changes in individuals and relationships than researchers did, (3) repeated observations were more characteristic of clinical studies, (4) clinicians tended to emphasize children's adjustments during the transition period following parental remarriage, and (5) both clinicians and researchers tended to use nonprobability samples (Ganong & Coleman, 1986). There has been some convergence between researchers and clinicians since 1984, although our earlier conclusions are still valid for the entire 141 references reviewed. The updated research review reflects a greater interest in stepfamily processes, more studies of changes in individuals and relationships over time, and more use of repeated measurement. Researchers' use of representative samples, although still characteristic of only a minority of studies, increases researchers' ability to generalize their results and provides a normative framework for clinicians.

Clinicians have generally done a better job than researchers of considering the complexity of stepfamily structures (Ganong & Coleman, 1986). Clinicians contend that this complexity distinguishes stepfamilies from other family forms and is a major cause of difficulty for stepchildren's adjustment and adaptation. For example, clinicians frequently discussed differences between: stepmother and stepfather households; stepchildren whose parents were divorced and those with a decreased parent; stepchildren who do and do not have stepsiblings; and stepchildren who live full-time with a stepparent and those who live in more than one household (Ganong & Coleman, 1986).

Researchers, on the other hand, have tended to ignore the complexity of stepfamilies to the point where crucial distinctions between different types of stepfamilies have not been made and critical variables have not been assessed (Ganong & Coleman, 1986). In our earlier comparative review, it was found that basic variables such as type of stepfamily household (i.e., stepmother, stepfather, or a combination where both adults are stepparents) and the cause of dissolution of the child's original family (i.e., death of a parent or divorce) were seldom measured. Less than half of the studies included stepchildren from both stepmother and stepfather households, only one included nonresidential stepchildren (Duberman, 1973), and just three assessed children from complex stepfamily households (Burchinal, 1964; Clingempeel, Ievoli, & Brand, 1984; Duberman, 1973). About one third of the studies included both children whose parent had died and those whose parents divorced, another third studied only stepchildren whose parents divorced, and the other third did not measure cause of family dissolution (Ganong & Coleman, 1986).

Several other family structure characteristics considered significant by clinicians were relatively ignored by researchers. For example, age at dissolution of parents' marriage, years resided in a single-parent household, age at parental remarriage, years resided in the stepfamily household, custody arrangements, residence, birth order, number of siblings, stepparents' age, presence of halfsiblings, stepsiblings, and extended family were stepfamily characteristics under-examined by researchers (Ganong & Coleman, 1986).

When researchers ignore the complexity of the stepchildren's family situations, their ability to generalize findings is reduced. Conclusions drawn from data in which important variables have not been measured or controlled may be questioned. Research that examines the relationship between independent and dependent variables too simplistically is generally less valuable to clinicians because it fails to reflect "real-world" situations (Blood, 1976).

It appears that clinical writers continue to point out that stepfamilies are complex environments structurally, interpersonally, and emotionally (e.g., Roberts & Price, 1985; Stanton, 1986). Understanding the complex nature of stepfamily life is held to be necessary to understanding stepchildren (Mills, 1984). Researchers increasingly indicate their sensitivity to this complexity and, as a result, in more of the recent research efforts have been made either to control for stepfamily variation (e.g., Clingempeel & Segal, 1986; Pink & Wampler, 1985) or to measure variables that were previously under-investigated. For example, all but 4 of the 19 most recent empirical studies controlled for cause of previous family dissolution (8 studies) or measured whether parental death or divorce was the cause (7 studies). A majority (11 studies) assessed the length of time a child had lived with the stepparent and some researchers included such previously under-examined variables as number of siblings (5 studies), years spent in a single-parent household (5 studies), birth order (2 studies), and presence of a halfsibling (1 study). Sex of stepparent (7 studies) and sex of stepchild (6 studies) are variables that more researchers are considering important to investigate. Although it appears that researchers are gradually attending more to the complexity of stepfamily structures than they once did, it would be wrong to conclude that researchers have reached a par with clinicians in this regard. Indeed, many structural variables continue to be ignored by researchers, with the result that quite diverse family backgrounds are grouped together in studies of stepchildren. It is too early to argue that Blood's (1976) complaint that researchers examine the relationship between independent and dependent variables too simplistically has been resolved.

Dependent Variables or Issues/Problems

A comparison of the "dependent variables" examined by researchers and the "issues" and problems identified by clinicians indicated that the two groups have not agreed upon which dimensions to focus their attention (Ganong & Coleman, 1986). The issues clinicians identified most frequently included: adjustment to stepfamily formation (62 studies); role confusion within the stepfamily (56 studies); loyalty conflicts (57 studies); dealing with loss and mourning (42 studies); and conflicts between co-parents (41 studies). Of these five issues only role confusion, loyalty conflicts, and dealing with loss and mourning have been empirically investigated (Furstenberg & Nord, 1985; Lutz, 1983; Strother & Jacobs, 1984). Researchers most frequently examined: self-concept (14 studies); perceptions of biological and/or stepparents (9 studies); perceived relationships with parents and stepparents (11 studies); and mental health and psychosomatic complaints (9 studies).

Appendix 5-3 presents the dependent variables and issues/problems. In order to facilitate summarizing the literature, conceptual categories identified in Appendix 3 were developed by the authors (Ganong & Coleman, 1986). It should be noted that even though the development of these categories was methodically done, there remains the possibility that some of these issues/ problems could have been placed in different categories. The clusters for dependent variables were based on an earlier review of research (Ganong & Coleman, 1984). For research, the five conceptual categories were: *Psychological Adjustment, Family Relations, Social Behaviors, Social Attitudes,* and *Cognitive Performance.* For clinical work, the categories were: *Family Dynamics, Transitional Adjustments, Incomplete Institution, Emotional Responses,* and *Stepfamily Expectations.*

In the past, three areas (i.e., Social Behaviors, Social Attitudes, and Cognitive Performance) investigated by researchers were virtually ignored by clinicians (Ganong & Coleman, 1986). Conversely, the effects of Stepfamily Expectations on stepchildren and Transitional Adjustments to stepfamily living were issues discussed by clinicians but ignored by researchers. The clinical category "Incomplete Institution," named after Cherlin's (1978) incomplete institution hypothesis, had generated some empirical interest (e.g., Clingempeel, Ievoli, & Brand, 1984; Lutz, 1983).

Although both groups of family professionals focused on the psychological effects of parental remarriage on the child (listed as Psychological Adjustment, Emotional Responses in Appendix 5-3), there was virtually no overlap in the variables/issues examined (Ganong & Coleman, 1986). Researchers investigated self-image, personality characteristics, and mental health as outcome variables related to parental remarriage, while clinicians examined emotional responses more directly related to stepfamily adaptation such as mourning and feeling unwanted.

Both clinicians and researchers focused on family functioning but processes and process outcomes in the family were the emphases of clinicians while the emphasis of researchers was on stepparent–stepchild and parent–child relationships and stepchildren's perceptions of their family (Ganong & Coleman, 1986). Clinicians considered processes in the entire stepfamily system (sometimes including two households), and various subsystems (dyads, triads, etc.) were discussed in analyzing stepchildren in their families. Stepfamily relationships that might indirectly affect stepchildren (i.e., marital relationships of parents, other parent–child or stepparent–stepchild dyads) were included by clinicians but rarely studied by reseachers. Although researchers and clinicians recognized the importance of family influences on stepchildren, clinicians especially viewed family dynamics as significant. Researchers did not examine family variables to the same extent as clinicians and overall there was little congruence between researchers' dependent variables and clinicians' issues/problems (Ganong & Coleman, 1986).

Have the foci of interests of researchers and clinicians converged in recent years? The answer to this question is somewhat mixed. It remains true that the researchers' categories of Social Behavior, Social Attitudes, and Cognitive Performance continue to be ignored by clinicians. This may be due to the tendency of clinicians with a strong family orientation to identify various behavior and attitudinal problems of stepchildren as being merely indicators or symptoms of family adjustment problems.

The absence of societal guidelines and supports for remarried families (i.e., Incomplete Institution) continues to be a concern for clinicians. In the updated clinical references, the absence of legal ties between stepfamily members (6 studies), the lack of kinship terms (2 studies), and no societal rituals to help support stepfamilies (3 studies) were mentioned, as were two problems related to the lack of clear guidelines for stepfamily members: role confusion (10 studies) and issues concerning money (5 studies). Several researchers also have examined, at least in part, Cherlin's incomplete institution hypothesis (Clingempeel, Brand, & Ievoli, 1984; Furstenberg & Spanier, 1984; White & Booth, 1985). This indicates some degree of overlap in interest between clinicians and researchers.

Similarly, there appears to be an increasing amount of overlap in researchers' and clinicians' focus on family functioning. Researchers still seem to be most interested in the stepparent–stepchild dyads and stepchildren's perceptions of their parents and stepparents (e.g., Ganong & Coleman, in press; White, Brinkerhoff, & Booth, 1985), but there is a growing number of studies of whole-family functioning (Clingempeel, Brand, Ievoli, 1984; Clingempeel & Segal, 1986; Garbarino *et al.*, 1984; Kennedy, 1985; Pink & Wampler, 1985) and of indirect effects (Knaub *et al.*, 1984; Tropf, 1984; White & Booth, 1985). This convergence of interests probably has been facilitated by the use of various systems models by researchers.

In recent years, clinically identified problems that have received some empirical attention include:

- poor communication (Clingempeel, Ievoli, Brand, 1984; Clingempeel & Segal, 1986);
- child membership in two households (Furstenberg & Nord, 1985; Furstenberg & Spanier, 1984; Strother & Jacobs, 1984);
- relations with extended kin (Furstenberg & Spanier, 1984);
- nonresidential parent–child bonds following remarriage (Furstenberg & Nord, 1985; Strother & Jacobs, 1984; Tropf, 1984);
- low cohesion (Garbarino *et al.*, 1984; Kennedy, 1985; Pink & Wampler, 1985);
- sexually charged atmosphere (Russell, 1984);
- co-parental conflicts (Tropf, 1984).

Overall, there remains a general separation of interests by researchers and clinicians. Researchers do seem to be more aware of clinically inspired issues, however, and there has been an attempt by some researchers to investigate those issues.

Demographic Variables Examined

In the past, few demographic variables have been examined by either researchers or clinicians (Ganong & Coleman, 1986). Race and social class were seldom assessed by researchers. Clinicians seemed to focus on white, middle-class stepfamilies and mentioned neither race nor social class as having an influence on stepfamilies or stepchildren (Ganong & Coleman, 1986). In the latest "sample" of research studies, however, over half mentioned race and 50% mentioned social class. Samples still are basically white and middle class, although larger and more representative samples have broadened this a bit. Clinicians continue to generally ignore demographic variables.

Conclusions

Differing conclusions have been drawn by researchers and clinicians in the past (Ganong & Coleman, 1986). The research literature, for the most part, has not reported significant differences between stepchildren and children from other family structures on such variables as cognitive performance, psychosomatic complaints, personality characteristics, social behavior, family relationships, and social attitudes, despite using a deficit-comparison model as the conceptual base (Ganong & Coleman, 1984). The clinical literature, on the other hand, has generally reported that stepchildren and their families inherently are beset by problems and difficulties. Since clinical writers have been more prolific than researchers, their influence on the perception of stepchildren and stepfamilies by family professionals has likely been greater. This negative orientation may have helped reinforce an image of stepchildren and stepfamilies as deviant and dysfunctional.

The problem-oriented view continues, although many clinicians have identified potential benefits available to stepchildren. A recent series of literature reviews written for applied family professionals was designed to balance the negative orientation of most clinical writers by identifying strengths of stepfamilies (Coleman, Ganong, & Gingrich, 1985; Coleman, Ganong, & Gingrich, 1986; Coleman, Marshall, & Ganong, 1986) and by examining the content of text books to see if strengths were included (Nolan, Coleman, & Ganong, 1984). Despite this series and other efforts (e.g., Mills, 1984; Papernow, 1984; Skeen, Covin, & Robinson, 1985), most clinical writers continue to draw rather pessimistic conclusions about stepchildren.

Both clinicians and researchers have shown increasing interest in stepchildren and their families. Of the 89 clinical works reviewed, 4 were published prior to 1970, 18 were published in the 1970's, and 67 have been published since 1980. Of the 58 empirical studies, 7 were published before 1970, 16 were published in the 1970s, and 35 were published since 1980. It would be logical to assume that this growing interest has been stimulated by the increase in divorce and remarriage during the past few decades.

The clinical literature has undergone subtle, but perhaps important, changes since 1970. As was stated earlier, clinical writers seem to be relying less on clinical impressions and more on other ways of gathering information. Of particular interest is the greater use of research-related methods such as surveys (e.g., Messinger, 1984) and literature reviews. Reliance on such methods appears to imply that perhaps clinicians are not so segregated from their research-oriented colleagues. We will discuss this point later.

A second trend in the clinical literature has been in the area of model building. Systems theory has been dominant in the clinical literature since 1970. Beginning in the late '70s, several clinicians combined systems and developmental constructs in efforts to conceptualize models of stepfamily development (Kleinman, Rosenberg, & Whiteside, 1979; Ransom, Schlesinger, & Derdeyn, 1979; Walker & Messinger, 1979). These initial efforts were closely followed by others (McGoldrick & Carter, 1980; Mills, 1984; Osborne, 1983; Papernow, 1984; Whiteside, 1983). Concurrent to the building of these developmental models was the proposal of alternative "ideologies" or paradigms for well-functioning stepfamilies (Draughon, 1975; Fishman & Hamel, 1981; Visher & Visher, 1979). Other clinical writers did not propose new models or ideologies, but instead discussed ways to work with stepchildren and their families from well-grounded theoretical positions (Goldner, 1982; Johnson, 1980; Roberts & Price, 1985; Stanton, 1986). There has been a considerable number of attempts to build models or apply existing models to stepfamilies. One result has been the generation of literally dozens of testable hypotheses and propositions.

A final change in the clinical literature over time has been a slight increase in the number of clinicians who have extended their attempts to understand the impact of parental remarriage on children beyond the family system by including other social systems and cultural influences. Several clinicians have looked at isolated influences such as the legal system, and a few have offered broader analyses (Stanton, 1986; Visher & Visher, 1979; Wald, 1981).

Two characteristics of the clinical literature on stepchildren have changed little. First, many intervention programs have been conducted, but few have been subjected to rigorous and careful assessment. Second, with the exception of the extra-family emphasis mentioned earlier, few new clinical issues/problems have been identified in the past decade (the time period in which 90% of the clinical references have been written). Consequently, many clinical writers have done little but restate what has already been written.

The empirical literature has also changed in important ways. There has been a gradual shift away from the deficit-comparison approach toward a greater use of theoretical frameworks. Prior to 1970, 86% of the studies on stepchildren were based at least partly on the deficit-comparison model. In the decade of the 1970s, this dropped to 75%, and since 1980 only 43% of the research has used this framework. At the same time, the use of systems, role, social learning, and other theories has increased.

There has also been an increase in studies using multiple respondents. Actually, the percentage of researchers using respondents outside the family (e.g., teachers) has decreased, but this has been more than offset by studies using multiple family members as respondents. The number of studies with multiple respondents is still relatively low, however: just under one third of the studies reported since 1980.

Finally, unlike the clinical writers, researchers have broadened their range of interests, as indicated by the study of new dependent variables and the increased attention to independent variables related to stepfamily complexity (e.g., length of time in stepfamily). Researchers continue to lavish attention on certain variables (e.g., self-concept, perceptions of parents), but since 1983 there has been evidence that empirical interests are expanding.

On the other hand, there is little evidence that researchers in general have changed their sampling methods, the size of their samples, or the target age of stepchildren under study. Data collection methods have also not changed much except for two series of observational studies (headed by Santrock and Clingempeel) and the handful of longitudinal designs mentioned earlier in this chapter. Whether these become trends in research on stepchildren remains to be seen.

SUMMARY

In spite of recent trends, it must be noted that few similarities between the empirical and clinical studies could be identified. The primary similarities remain the deficit-comparison approach underlying investigations in both areas and a shared appreciation for the influence of family functioning on stepchildren's adjustment. Dissimilarities between empirical and clinical work continued to be readily identifiable. The major distinctions are differences in consideration of stepfamily complexity, data-gathering methods, focus of interests, and conclusions drawn.

Continuing evidence indicates that researchers and clinicians interested in stepchildren are, in general, professionally segregated. There is minimal evidence demonstrating communication between the groups. There is some congruence of foci, of course, but the classic research–practice split seems to prevail.

A crude measure of this segregation is how frequently researchers cite clinical references and clinicians cite researchers. To check for "cross references," we examined the references of the books and articles published since late 1984 and coded each reference as clinical, empirical, or other (e.g., self-help book, newspaper articles). Our own publications were excluded since we had purposely tried to bridge clinical and empirical work; therefore, they were not representative of other work reviewed. Of the clinical reports, four engaged relatively heavily in cross-referencing but only Roberts and Price (1985) and Skeen *et al.* (1985) had as many as a third of their citations from empirical sources. Most clinical writers were as likely to cite self-help books as they were research. Thirty-eight percent of these recent clinical works failed to cite any research. It should be noted that Census Bureau references and other demographic studies were counted as research; for some clinicians, this was the only research cited. Researchers were no more likely than clinicians to cross-reference. Only Kennedy (1985) and Strother and Jacobs (1984) took one third or more of their citations from clinical sources. Knaub *et al.* (1984) and Pink and Wampler (1985) also contained several clinical references. Researchers most often cited other empirical reports. It should be noted that some recent research clearly has been stimulated by clinical writing (Crosbie-Burnett, 1984; Halperin & Smith, 1983; Strother & Jacobs, 1984) and three on-going research projects are being directed by clinicians (Ahrons's Bi-nuclear Family Project, Jacobson's Project Step, and Clingempeel and Hetherington's Philadelphia study). However, greater exchange between the two groups of professionals potentially could enhance and stimulate research effects as well as improve clinical practice.

Greater intercourse also could aid in building a body of knowledge about stepchildren and their families. In the absence of a substantial knowledge base, the literature that exists contributes to a "Whoozle" effect (Gelles, 1980). A Whoozle effect occurs when a particular finding reported in one study is subsequently cited by others without consideration of possible limitations to the study and without efforts to replicate the findings. Frequent citations of a study over the years result in the findings being treated as "facts." The original caveats regarding methodological or sampling characteristics are forgotten, but the findings and conclusions are not (Gelles, 1980).

The literature on stepchildren illustrates the Whoozle effect. Often the initial investigation is not an empirical study with well-defined sampling and measurement techniques, but is a report of clinical impressions based on data gleaned via clinical observations from a unique sample of unknown size and characteristics. This means that much of what is "known" about stepchildren comes from clinical data bases. For example, frequent references are made in both the self-help and clinical literature to loyalty conflicts for stepchildren. This assertion was based on clinical impressions. Not until recently was this assertion empirically tested and not supported (Lutz, 1983; Strother & Jacobs, 1984), yet this is one of the most well-known "facts" about stepchildren. The Whoozle effect is enhanced when reviewers neglect to distinguish between results drawn from empirical research and those emanating from clinical work. The failure of most previous reviews on stepchildren and stepfamilies to make such distinctions may contribute to the pervasiveness of the deficit-comparison, problem-oriented framework.

What Can Clinicians Learn from Researchers?

Clinicians seem to rely primarily on observations of stepchildren and their families. Self-report scores from well-constructed instruments could be more useful and more accurate than clinical interviews or observations (Olson, 1983). By using a multimethod approach to family assessment, self-reports could be combined with careful observations to provide a more thorough assessment (Cromwell & Peterson, 1981).

Clinicians could benefit by more carefully assessing and evaluating the efficacy of their intervention efforts. Clinicians should look to researchers for methods and measures applicable to assessing their interventions.

Clinical works would be more valuable to researchers if clinicians took greater care in generalizing from their data. Clinicians could also learn from researchers to be more explicit in reporting the source of their impressions. In some clinical studies virtually no mention was made regarding the sample (i.e., total sample size, sample composition) or methods by which conclusions were drawn.

Clinicians often seem to develop a skewed view of the world, perhaps because their data are based on individuals or families in trouble. More assertively employing normative data on nonclinical samples of stepchildren would help to balance this image and enable clinicians to provide more hope to stepfamily clients (Chilman, 1983).

What Can Researchers Learn from Clinicians?

From the clinical literature researchers appear to be gaining a greater appreciation of the value of observing and conceptualizing stepfamily interaction and of considering the complexity of stepfamilies. Although only a few empirical studies of stepchildren have measured multiple levels of the family system, there appears to be a beginning of a trend away from simplistic designs that ignore important variables. Researchers can continue to learn from clinicians the value of looking at the whole family, including various subsystems that may indirectly affect stepchildren. Although considering the structural complexity of stepfamilies may seem prohibitive in terms of the time and money required, researchers could help control for complexity by focusing on specific subgroups by using purposive sampling. A greater reliance on theory to guide stepfamily research would also lessen the need for large (and expensive) sampling procedures (Reiss, 1983). The consideration of changes within the stepfamily over time (e.g., Ferri, 1984; Furstenberg & Nord, 1985) can enhance our understanding of the development of stepfamily systems and the effects of transitions on children in stepfamilies; more longitudinal research or panel studies would help in this regard.

Finally, researchers can continue to learn meaningful questions to ask by attending to the questions raised by clinicians. Clinician-inspired questions probably number in the hundreds. In recent years, researchers have begun to ask some of these questions. However, many remain to be answered by careful investigations. The following, derived from our initial comparative review, represents a sample list of questions stimulated by clinical work that have not been systematically studied, or have been examined in only one or two investigations (Ganong & Coleman, 1986). The questions have been organized by clinical categories from Appendix 5-3.

Family Dynamics

1. What problems are encountered in establishing and developing boundaries within the stepfamily and within the suprastepfamily systems?

2. What effect does the co-parental relationship have on child development and child adjustment to remarriage?

3. Do children experience loyalty conflicts? If so, how are these conflicts resolved? What loyalty conflicts create the most stress for stepchildren? Which of the following loyalty conflicts have been experienced, those: between stepparent and biological parent of the same sex; between extended family kin and stepfamily kin; between biological siblings and stepsiblings; between the custodial parent and the noncustodial parent; between the custodial parent and the custodial stepparent?

4. What effects do different stepparent role-taking behaviors have on children's development and adjustment?

5. What effects do stepsiblings have on each other? Are there sex differences in adaptation to stepsiblings?

6. Do sibling relationships change after parental remarriage? How do stepsiblings affect sibling relations?

7. What effects do changes in sibling constellation have on a child's adjustment?

8. What effect does previous parenting experience by the stepparent have on stepchildren's adjustment and behavior?

9. How do space and residence issues affect child adjustment?

10. What effect does parental reproduction in remarriage (i.e., birth of a half-sibling) have on older children in stepfamilies?

11. What effect does stepparent adoption have on stepchildren? How is the decision to adopt made?

12. How are discipline decisions made? Who does most of the disciplining? Do children have a role in defining the stepparent's disciplinarian role? How are stepchild–stepparent relationships developed? How are these relationships defined?

13. How are stepchild–stepgrandparent relationships developed? How are these relationships defined by stepfamily members?

14. What effects do changes in custody patterns have on the adjustment of stepchildren? What effect does joint custody have on children's adjustment to parental remarriage?

15. What custody patterns are related to the most cooperative stepparent–stepchild relationships? What effect does joint custody have on the development of stepparent–stepchild relationships?

16. How do family patterns developed in the single-parent household affect stepfamily relationships and the adjustment of stepchildren?

17. How do stepchildren define their role? How do they define their stepparents to others?

18. What, if any, problems are caused by stepparents and stepchildren having different surnames? How prevalent is it that stepchildren change their surname to avoid embarrassment, and so forth?

19. What effect does the remarriage of a noncustodial parent have on children?

20. How are rules developed and maintained in stepfamilies, especially those involved with such issues as: discipline, eating habits, division of labor, attitudes toward sexual behavior, use of alcohol and drugs, responsibilities, manners, expression of positive feelings, and expression of negative feelings?

21. What effects do the previous marital experiences of the stepparent have on stepchildren's adjustment and the development of stepparent–stepchild relationships?

22. What effects do the previous parenting experiences of remarried adults have on child adjustment and development?

23. How long does it take for stepfamilies to become integrated?

24. What are the differences in adjustment between stepchildren from complex stepfamilies and those from simple stepfamilies?

25. Are children bothered by the remarried parent's displays of affection for each other?

26. Do stepmothers or stepfathers receive more social support (if there is a difference)?

27. Do stepmother family members or stepfather family members receive more social support (if there is a difference)?

28. What effect does the stepparent–noncustodial biological parent relationship have on child behavior and adjustment?

29. What, if any, is the relationship between the number of children in the household and the number of problems experienced by the children?

30. Are children better adjusted if they continue ties with a noncustodial parent?

31. How are value differences resolved in the stepfamily?

32. How does lack of control over household decisions affect stepchildren?

33. Are children involved in parental decisions to remarry and in planning for remarriage? How are children informed and prepared for the remarriage of parents?

34. How are new relatives introduced to children? When are new relatives introduced to children?

Transition

1. What effect does age at parental remarriage have on children's adjustment and the relationship between the stepparent and the stepchild?

2. Is there a relationship between personal and interpersonal flexibility and ease of adjustment in transition to stepfamily life?

3. How are rituals and celebrations in stepfamilies developed?

4. What is the effect of family processes or rules on stepchildren: disci-

pline, eating habits, division of labor, attitudes toward sexual behavior, use of alcohol and drugs, responsibilities, manners, expression of positive and negative feelings?

Incomplete Institution

1. What effect does the lack of legal relationships between stepparents and stepchildren have on the adjustment of stepchildren and the development of a positive stepparent–stepchild relationship?

2. How do stepchildren decide what to call stepparents? What are the effects of different names for stepparents on child adjustment and stepfamily integration?

3. How do stepchildren define themselves to themselves and other people?

4. How does the distribution and expenditure of money and other resources affect stepparent–stepchild relations? What effect does child support from a noncustodial parent have on the development of stepparent–stepchild bonding?

5. What effect do the attitudes of professional helpers such as counselors and school teachers have on the stepchild's adjustment?

Emotional Response

1. What feelings do stepchildren experience (i.e., about parental remarriage, the stepparent, stepsiblings, noncustodial parent, changes facing them)? How are these feelings resolved? What long-term emotional responses are there?

2. What is the relationship between the number of people added to the family, the amount of complexity, and the stress experienced by stepchildren?

Expectations

1. How do myths about stepchildren, stepparents, and stepfamily life affect the expectations and behavior of stepchildren?

2. What effect does a negative "step" image have on stepchild adjustment?

3. How do the expectations of the stepchildren themselves affect the perceived relationship with stepparents and stepsiblings?

4. Does a negative image of steprelationships have a self-fulfilling prophecy?

If clinicians were influencing researchers and empirical research was influencing clinical methodology, the body of literature would be quite different than what we have found it to be. If there was more interaction between the two professional groups, the kinds of questions being asked would look more like those listed above. A merged perspective needs to receive attention soon before the study of stepchildren and their families becomes mired in tradition, leaving stepfamilies to struggle with the "mixed messages" beamed at them from two quite divergent groups of stepfamily "experts."

APPENDIX 5-1

Summary of Clinical Work

Authors	Theory	Methodology	Type of Stepfamily	Issues Examined
Ahrons & Perlmutter (1982)	systems	description of therapy, research	SF, SM[a]	A,B,C,E[b]
Anderson, Larson, & Morgan (1981)	not given	program description	SF, SM	A,B
Baideme & Serritella (1981)	systems	program description	SF, SM	A,B,C,D,E
Barrows (1981)	systems	clinical impressions	SF, SM	A,C,D,E
Bitterman (1968)	psychoanalytic	clinical impressions	SF, SM	A,B,C,D,E
Coleman & Ganong (1980)	not given	program description	SF, SM	A,B,C,D,E
Coleman & Ganong (1985)*[c]	not given	lit. review, clinical impressions	SF, SM	A,B,C,D,E
Coleman, Ganong & Gingrich (1985)*	stereotyping, social learning	lit. review	SF, SM	A,B,C,D,E
Coleman, Ganong & Gingrich (1986)*	stereotyping, social learning	lit. review	SF, SM	A,B
Coleman, Ganong, & Henry (1984)	not given	lit. review, advice to teachers	SF, SM	C,E
Coleman, Marshall, & Ganong (1986)*	social learning	lit. review	SF, SM	A,B,C,D,E
Crohn, Sager, Brown, Rodstein, & Walker (1982)	systems, learning theory, "insight" theories	case study, clinical impressions	SF, SM	A,B,C,D,E
Crohn, Sager, Rodstein, Brown, Walker, & Beir (1981)	systems	program description, clinical impressions	SF, SM	A,B,C,D,E
Dolan & Lown (1985)*	not given	lit. review	SF, SM	A,B,C,E
Draughon (1975)	role, psychodynamic	clinical impressions	SM	A,C
Egan, Landau, & Rhode (1979)	not given	case studies, clinical impressions	SF, SM	A,C,D

APPENDIX 5-1 (Continued)

Summary of Clinical Work

Authors	Theory	Methodology	Type of Stepfamily	Issues Examined
Engebretson (1982)	not given	lit. review, clinical impressions	SM	A,B,C,D,E
Fast & Cain (1966)	role	clinical impressions of 50 case records	SF, SM	A,B,C,D,E
Fishman & Hamel (1981)	systems	interviews	SF, SM (all complex)	A,B,C,E
Framo (1981)	systems	program description, clinical impressions	SF, SM	A,C,E
Friedman (1981)	systems	case study, clinical impressions	SF, SM	A,B,C,D,E
Gardner (1984)*	not given	clinical impressions	SF, SM	A,B,C,D
Goldenberg (1982)	not given	clinical impressions	SF, SM	A,B
Goldner (1982)	developmental, systems	case study, clinical impressions	SF, SM	A,B,C,E
Goldstein (1974)	systems	clinical impressions	SF, SM	A,C
Gray & Pippin (1984)*	not given	lit. review	SF, SM	A,B,C,E
Greif (1982)	not given	clinical impressions	SF	A,D
Heilpern (1943)	psychoanalytic	case study, clinical impressions	SF, SM	A,B
Herndon & Combs (1982)	systems	clinical impressions	SF, SM	A,B,C,D
Hutchison & Hutchison (1979)	not given	program description, lit. review	SF, SM	A,B,C,D,E
Isaacs (1982)	systems	case study, clinical impressions	SF, SM	A,B,C,E
Jacobson (1979)	not given	program description, clinical impressions	SF, SM	A,B,C,D,E
Jacobson (1980a)	crisis theory	program description, lit. review, clinical impressions	SF, SM	A,C,D,E
Jacobson (1980b)	not given	lit. review, clinical impressions	SF, SM	A,B,C,D,E

APPENDIX 5-1 (Continued)

Summary of Clinical Work

Authors	Theory	Methodology	Type of Stepfamily	Issues Examined
Johnson (1980)	ecological	clinical impressions	SF, SM	A,B,C,E
Jones (1978)	systems	lit. review, clinical impressions	SF, SM	A,B,C,D,E
Kent (1980)*	systems	lit. review	SF, SM	A,B,C,E
Kleinman, Rosenberg, & Whiteside (1979)	systems	case study, clinical impressions	SF, SM	A,B,D
Kompara (1980)	role	lit. review, clinical impressions	SF, SM	A,B,C,D,E
McGoldrick & Carter (1980)	systems	case studies, lit. review, clinical impressions	SF, SM	A,B,C,D,E
Messinger (1984)*	systems	survey, lit. review, clinical impressions	SF, SM	A,B,C,D,E
Messinger & Walker (1981)	systems	program description, lit. review, clinical impressions	SF, SM	A,B,C,D,E
Mills (1984)*	systems, developmental	clinical impressions, lit. review	SF, SM	A,B,C,D,E
Mowatt (1972)	psychodynamic	program description, clinical impressions	SF	A,C,E
Nolan, Coleman, & Ganong (1984)*	not given	lit. review	SF, SM	A,B,C,D,E
Osborne (1983)	not given	clinical impressions	SF, SM	A,B,E
Papernow (1984)*	Gestalt, systems, developmental	case history research, clinical impressions	SF, SM	A,B,C,D,E
Perlmutter, Engel, & Sager (1982)	systems	case study, clinical impressions	SF, SM	A,C,D
Pill (1981)	systems	program description	SF, SM	A,B,C,D,E
Pino (1981)	none	lit. review, clinical research	SF, SM	A,B
Podolsky (1955)	psychodynamic	clinical impressions	SF, SM	A,B,C,E
Poppen & White (1984)*	not given	lit. review	SF, SM	A,B,C,D,E
Prosen & Farmer (1982)	developmental, systems	lit. review, review of programs	SF, SM	A,B,C,D,E

APPENDIX 5-1 (Continued)

Summary of Clinical Work

Authors	Theory	Methodology	Type of Stepfamily	Issues Examined
Ransom, Schlesinger, & Derdeyn (1979)	systems	case study, clinical impressions	SF, SM	A,C,D
Roberts & Price (1985)*	systems	lit. review, clinical impressions	SF, SM	A,B,C,D,E
Robinson (1980)	systems, psychodynamic	clinical impressions	SF, SM	A,B,C,D,E
Robson (1982)	Piaget–Erikson	clinical impressions	SF, SM	A,B
Rogers (1981)	psychodynamic	clinical impressions	SF, SM	A,B,D
Sager, Brown, Crohn, Engel, Rodstein, & Walker (1983)	systems, eclectic	case study, program description, clinical impressions	SF, SM	A,B,C,D,E
Sager, Brown, Crohn, Rodstein, & Walker (1980)	not given	lit. review	SF, SM	A,B,C,D,E
Sager, Walker, Brown, Crohn, & Rodstein (1981)	systems, eclectic	description of therapy, clinical impressions	SF, SM	A,B,C,D,E
Satir (1972)	systems	clinical impressions	SF, SM	A,C
Schlesinger & Stasiuk (1981)	not given	interviews with stepparents	SF, SM	A,B,C,D,E
Schulman (1972)	psychodynamic	clinical impressions	SF, SM	A,E
Schulman (1981)	developmental, systems	case study, clinical impressions	SF, SM	A,B,C,D,E
Serritella (1982)	psychoanalytic	clinical impressions	SF	A
Skeen, Covi, & Robinson (1985)*	not given	lit. review	SF, SM	A,B,C,D,E
Skeen, Robinson, & Flake-Hobson (1984)	not given	lit. review, advice to teachers	SF, SM	A,B,C,D,E
Stanton (1986)*	systems, developmental, crisis intervention	lit. review, clinical impressions	SF, SM	A,B,C,D,E
Theis (1977)	not given	clinical impressions	SF, SM	A,B,C,D
Today's Child (1981)	not given	clinical impressions	SF, SM	B,D,E
Turnbull & Turnbull (1983)	not given	program description, clinical impressions	SF, SM	A,B,C,D

APPENDIX 5-1 (Continued)

Summary of Clinical Work

Authors	Theory	Methodology	Type of Stepfamily	Issues Examined
Visher, E., & Visher, J. (1978a)	systems	clinical impressions, case studies	SF, SM	A,B,C,D,E
Visher, E., & Visher, J. (1978b)	systems	clinical impressions	SF, SM	A,B,C,D,E
Visher, E., & Visher, J. (1979)	systems	clinical impressions	SF, SM	A,B,C,D,E
Visher, E., & Visher, J. (1982a)	systems	clinical impressions	SF, SM	A,B,C,D
Visher, E., & Visher, J. (1982b)	systems	clinical impressions	SF, SM	A,B,C,D,E
Visher, J., & Visher, E. (1981)	systems	clinical impressions	SF, SM	A,B,C,D,E
Visher, J., & Visher, E. (1982)	systems	clinical impressions	SF, SM	A,B,C,D,E
Wald (1981)	developmental, systems, role, others	case study, clinical impressions, lit. review	SF, SM	A,B,C,D,E
Waldron & Whittington (1979)	systems	clinical impressions	SF, SM	A,B,C,E
Walker & Messinger (1979)	systems	program description, clinical impressions	SF, SM	A,B,C,D
Wallerstein & Kelly (1980)	developmental, psychodynamic	interviews	SF, SM	A,B,C
Whiteside (1981)	systems	case study, program description, clinical impressions	SF, SM	A,B,C,D,E
Whiteside (1982a)	systems	clinical impressions	SF, SM	A,B,C,D
Whiteside (1982b)	family development	clinical impressions	SF, SM	A,B,C,D,E
Whiteside (1983)*	developmental	lit. review	SF, SM	A,B,C,D,E
Whiteside & Auerbach (1978)	systems, psychodynamic	interviews, case records	SF, SM	A,B,C,D
Wood & Poole (1983)*	none	lit. review	SF, SM	A,B,C,D,E

[a]"SF" refers to stepfather; "SM" to stepmother; both are post-divorce.

[b]Letters in the Issues Examined column refer to the following code: A = Family Dynamics; B = Transition and Adjustment; C = Incomplete Institution; D = Emotional Responses; E = Expectations.

[c]Asterisks indicate references added since previous Ganong and Coleman (1986) review.

APPENDIX 5-2

Attributes of Research on Stepchildren

Studies	Theory	Independent Variables	Dependent Variables	Sampling Procedure	Age	Total N	Stepfamily N	Types of Stepfamilies	Method	Results
Bernard (1956)	none	death or divorce of parents; living with mother or father	stability, self-sufficiency, dominance, attitudes toward remarriage	nonprobability: college students, informants who were friends of stepfamily members	college students	112[h] 2,009	112[h] 2,009	SF, SM	questionnaires (including Bernreuter Personality [Inventory], interviews of stepchildren and informants	no differences in stability, self-sufficiency, dominance between stepchildren and BPI norms; stepchildren had positive attitudes toward parents
Nye (1957)	deficit comparison	family structure[a]	psychosomatic illness, delinquent behavior, adjustment to parents	25% regular interval samples of 3 high schools	students, grades 9–12	780	NR[j]	NR	questionnaire developed by researcher	no differences in adjustment to school, church attendance, delinquent companions; stepchildren better adjusted to parents, had fewer psychosomatic complaints, less delinquent behavior than children from unbroken, unhappy families
Bowerman & Irish (1962)	deficit comparison	family structure,[b] death or divorce of parents, sex	relationship to parents	nonprobability	students, grades 7–12	29,000	2,145	SF, SM	questionnaire	stepchildren were not as close to parents as nuclear family children; stepchildren felt more rejection & discrimination, stepmothers fared worse than stepfathers
Langner & Michael (1963)	psychoanalytic, deficit comparison	remarriage/continued singlehood of parent	mental health	random sample of adults in midtown Manhattan	adults, 20–59 years	1,660	186	SF, SM	interviews, researcher ratings	children whose parent remarried had poorer mental health than single-parent or nuclear family children; majority of stepchildren "got along" well with their step-parents
Perry & Pfuhl (1963)	deficit comparison	family structure[c]	delinquent behavior, psychosomatic complaints, grades	systematic sample of high school students from 3 communities	students, grades 9–12	2,350	267	SF, SM	questionnaire	no difference in psychosomatic complaints, grades, delinquent behavior between stepchildren and those in single-parent families

Study	Theoretical approach	Independent variables	Dependent variables	Sampling	Sample	N	Stepfamily N	Stepfamily type	Measurement	Findings
Burchinal (1964)	deficit comparison	family structure,[a] SES, sex	illness proneness, nervousness, anxiety, fright reactions, school social relations, days absent, number of friends, number of school activities, attitude toward school, attitude toward teachers	nonprobability; junior & senior high school students from one community	students, grades 7 & 11	1,566	210	SF, SM, complex	questionnaire (included Minnesota Test of Personality)	no differences in personality characteristics, grades, school and community activities, number of friends, school attitudes, days absent
Rosenberg (1965)	deficit comparison	family structure,[a] death or divorce of parents	self-esteem; psychosomatic complaints	random selection of 10 public high schools in New York State: subjects were grade 11 and 12 students in attendance the day of administration	students, grades 11 & 12	5,024	262	SF, SM	questionnaire (Rosenberg Self-Esteem Scale)	stepchildren had lower self-esteem and more psychosomatic complaints
Kaplan & Pokorny (1971)	deficit comparison	family structure,[a] death or divorce of parents; age at parental remarriage; sex, race, SES	self-derogation	3-stage probability sample design; random selection of blocks, dwelling units, & household respondents	adults	500	54	SF, SM	interviews and questionnaires (Rosenberg Self-Esteem Scale)	generally, stepchildren not different in self-esteem from those in intact homes
Santrock (1972)	social learning, deficit comparison	family structure[d]	IQ, academic achievement	nonprobability; volunteers from 4 high schools and 5 junior high schools who had an absent father plus a random sample of father present (8 of these were dropped)	junior & senior high school students	343	NR	SF	school records	remarriage had a positive influence on boys' cognitive development but not on girls'
Duberman (1973)	none	parental age, education, religion, SES, residence, sex, age of children, influence of halfsibling, parent's prior marital status	family integration, stepparent-child relationships; stepsibling relationships	random sample of parents who had remarried 1965–1968 drawn from county marriage license records	adults	88[f]	88[f]	SF, SM complex	interviews, researcher ratings	relationships between stepparents and children and between stepsiblings were generally positive

APPENDIX 5-2 (Continued)

Studies	Theory	Independent Variables	Dependent Variables	Sampling Procedure	Age	Total N	Stepfamily N	Types of Stepfamilies	Method	Results
Spreitzer & Riley (1974)	none	family structure;[a] death or divorce of parents; birth order; family authority structure; age at family disruption; age left home; relationship with mother, father, brother, sister	singlehood	secondary analysis of probability sample of applicants of social security benefits from 3 regions	adults	2,454	128	SF, SM	interviews	no relationship between growing up with a stepparent and adult singlehood
Wilson, Zurcher, MacAdams, & Curtis (1975)	deficit comparison	family structure[c]	characteristics of demographic, religious stratification, political views, crime; general interpersonal relationships; family relationships; personal evaluation	secondary analysis of 2 data sets: modified multistage area probability sample; and a multistage probability design to select schools, followed by selection of 25 boys	adults, 10th grade students	2,869	122	SF	questionnaire	no differences between those who had lived in a stepfather family and nuclear family persons on several social and psychological characteristics
Oshman & Manosevitz (1976)	social learning, deficit comparison	family structure[d]	psychosocial functioning	nonprobability; volunteer college students	college students	125	39	SF	questionnaire (Ego-Identity Scale)	no differences on psychosocial functioning
Chapman (1977)	deficit comparison	family structure[d]	field independence; scholastic aptitudes	nonprobability; college students	college students	96	32	SF	questionnaire (Embedded Figures Test), SAT scores	for males, stepfathers attenuated the effects of father absence; for females, father presence or absence was not related to cognitive performance
Kalter (1977)	deficit comparison	family structure, sex	15 symptom categories	records from a psychiatric clinic	children, 7–17+ years	387	55 (14.5%)	NR	case records	more children of divorce in clinic than expected; stepchildren's problems differed from other family structures

Study	Theoretical orientation	Independent variables	Dependent variables	Sampling	Age/grade	N	N	Family type	Method	Findings
Dahl, McCubbin & Lester (1976)	social learning; deficit comparison	family structure[d]	personal adjustment; social adjustment	nonprobability; stepfamilies drawn from 215 MIA[k] families and 2 matched groups	mean age of 10.8 years	42	14	SF	interviews, questionnaire (California Personality Inventory)	children in reunited families were better adjusted than stepchildren
Kellam, Ensminger, & Turner (1977)	deficit comparison	family structure,[a] income, number of adults, number of children	psychological well-being, social adaptation	50% random sample of 1964 first graders in a community; 100% of the 1966 class	students, grade 1	2,242	105	SF, SM	interviews; ratings by researchers, mothers, teachers, and children	no differences, but stepfather family children were nearly as often "at risk" as single-mother children
Blechman, Berberian, & Thompson	none	sex, age, social class, peer drug use, parental employment, number of parents' absence, cause of parents' absence, parental remarriage	reported drug use	random sample of students in 37 junior and senior high schools near New Haven, CT	junior & senior high school students	3,690	NR[i]	NR	questionnaire	remarriage of parents did not contribute significantly to variance in drug-use levels
Bohannon & Yahraes (1979)	none	family structure[e]	friends, quality of family relations, school behavior, grades	random sample of households in San Diego stratified by income, ethnicity, neighborhood; plus snowball technique	approximately 14 years	190[f]	106[f]	SF	interview	no differences in school behavior, friends, many behavioral characteristics
Parish & Copeland (1979)	deficit comparison	family structure,[d] evaluation of parents	self-concept	nonprobability; college students	college students	206	8	SF	questionnaire (Personality Attribute Inventory [PAI])	self-concept and evaluation of stepfathers correlated more highly than self-concept and evaluation of father
Parish & Taylor (1979)	deficit comparison	family structure,[f] grade, sex	self-concept	nonprobability; classes from a grade school	students, grades 3 & 8	406	15	SF	questionnaire (PAI)	no difference in concept (intact family children vs. stepfather family children)
Perkins & Kahan (1979)	systems deficit comparison	family structure[e]	family concept	nonprobability; volunteers who answered newspaper ads	12–15 years	40[f]	20[f]	SF	questionnaire (Family Concept Q Sort)	psychological adjustment, satisfaction with family, reciprocal understanding, perceived goodness, and potency higher in nuclear families
Raschke & Raschke (1979)	deficit comparison	family structure,[a] perceived conflict	self-concept	nonprobability; volunteers	students, grades 3, 6, 8	289	32	SF, SM	questionnaire (Piers–Harris Self-Concept Scale)	family structure was not related to self-concept
Palermo (1980)	none	age at parental remarriage, age at death or divorce, sex	stepparent–stepchild relationship	nonprobability; volunteers from Remarried, Inc.	younger than 18 years	50[f] / 204	50[f] / 204	SF, SM	questionnaire	age of stepchild was not related to parental perceptions of closeness of children

APPENDIX 5-2 (Continued)

Studies	Theory	Independent Variables	Dependent Variables	Sampling Procedure	Age	Total N	Stepfamily N	Types of Stepfamilies	Method	Results
Parish & Kappes (1980)	deficit comparison	family structure,[a] cause of father loss, sex	evaluation of (step) parents	nonprobability; college students	college students	421	15	SF	questionnaire (PAI)	stepfathers replacing deceased fathers viewed significantly more favorably than those replacing divorced fathers
Parish (1981b)	deficit comparison	family structure,[a] sex	self-concept, evaluation of parents	nonprobability; grade school volunteers	students in grade school	606	NR	SF	questionnaire (Personal Attribute Inventory for Children [PAIC])	no difference on family structure for concordance on mother/self descriptions. Intact father/self description did not differ from divorced but were significantly higher than divorced remarried. Presence of stepfather reduced concordance with biological father
Parish & Nunn (1981)	deficit comparison	family structure,[a] happiness of family	self-concept, evaluation of parents	nonprobability	students, grades 5–8	132	NR	SF	questionnaire (PAIC)	self-concepts of children from "happy" families not related to evaluation of mother, father, or stepfather; self-concepts of children from "unhappy" families were related. Death of father was not related to children's evaluations of parents but divorce was
Fox & Inazu (1982)	role, systems	parent's marital history, age at parent's marriage disruption, number of parental marriages, family structure[a]	companionship with mother; home management; participation in parenting others; companionship with mother; home management; participation in parenting others; and self-supervision	clustered, stratified sample (race, sex, birth date)	14–16 years	449	52	SF	interviews	no relationship found between marital history of mothers and various characteristics of the mother–daughter relationship

Study	Approach	Independent variables	Dependent variable	Sampling	Population				Instrument	Findings
Parish & Dostal (1980)	deficit comparison	family structure[a]	self-concept evaluation of parents	nonprobability	11–14 years	738	NR	NR	questionnaire (PAIC)	children from stepfamilies did not vary in self-concept from intact or divorced nonremarried. Mothers in intact families were rated more favorably than in step- or singleparent families. Family structure related to evaluation of fathers
Touliatos & Lindholm (1980)	deficit comparison	family structure[d], sex, social class, grade	school behavior problems	nonprobability; all children in school system	students, grades K–8	3,644	298	SF, SM	questionnaire (Behavior Problem Checklist)	stepchildren with a stepmother had more conduct problems, those with stepfathers had more conduct problems and socialized delinquency
Ganong, Coleman, & Brown (1981)	social learning; deficit comparison	family structure[a], sex	attitudes toward marriage, divorce, marital roles, family size	nonprobability; selected high schools	15–17 years	321	48	SF, SM	questionnaire (Hill Attitude to Marriage Scale; Hardy Divorce Scale)	no differences in adolescent's attitudes toward marital roles, family size. Stepchildren were more positive about divorce
Parish (1981a)	deficit comparison	family structure[d], happiness of family	self-concept	nonprobability; college students	college students	349	NR	SF	questionnaire (PAI)	self-concept did not differ by family type; single parent and stepchildren evaluated biological father more negative than in intact families
Parish (1982)	deficit comparison	family structure[d], sex	locus of control	nonprobability	college students	711	NR	SF	questionnaire (Rotter's I-E)	males from divorced remarried families were more external than males from intact families and non-remarried families where the father had died
Parish & Philip (1982)	deficit comparison	family structure[a]	self-concept	nonprobability	students, grades 3–8	376	12	NR	questionnaire (PAIC)	pre- & post self-concept changed significantly for intact family children but not divorced, non-remarried, or divorced-remarried

APPENDIX 5-2 (Continued)

Studies	Theory	Independent Variables	Dependent Variables	Sampling Procedure	Age	Total N	Stepfamily N	Types of Stepfamilies	Method	Results
Santrock, Warshak, Lindbergh, & Meadows (1982)	deficit comparison	family structure,[d] sex	parent behaviors (control, encourage independence, & intellectually meaningful verbal interaction, attentive, authoritarian, authoritative, permissive, maturity); child behaviors (warmth, self-esteem, anxiety, demandingness, maturity, sociability, independence)	nonprobability; recruited via friends and organized group	6–11 years	36[f]	12[f]	SF	observations	basically no differences in interpersonal behavior between children from stepfather, single parent, and intact families
Santrock, Warshak, Elliott (1982)	deficit comparison	family structure,[f] sex	same as Santrock et al. (1982) above	nonprobability	6–11 years	64[h]	12[h]	SM	observations	boys showed less competent social behavior in stepmother families than girls in stepmother families or boys in nuclear families; no differences for stepdaughters
J. Parish & T. Parish (1983)	deficit comparison	family structure[d]	self-concept	nonprobability	students, grades 5–8	471	55	SF	questionnaire (PAIC)	children's self-concepts were related to evaluations of families in nuclear and stepfamilies
Boyd, Nunn, & Parish (1983)*	deficit comparison	marital status, parents' marital status[a]	evaluation of self, parents	nonprobability	college students	980	not given	SM, SF	questionnaire	few differences; no differences in evaluation of mom; married respondents whose widowed parents remarried had lowest self-concept; single respondents from divorced single-parent families had lowest evaluation of dads

Study	Theoretical framework	Independent variables	Dependent variables	Sampling	Population	N	Subsample	Type	Method	Findings
Nunn, Parish, & Worthing (1983)*	deficit comparison	family structure[a]	self-concept, school, home adjustment, peer relations, evaluations of mother, father, and family	nonprobability	students, grades 5–10	566	99	SM, SF	questionnaire	intact family children had highest self-concept, evaluations of mother, father, family; home and school adjustment; stepchildren were more anxious
T. Parish & J. Parish (1983)*	deficit comparison	family structure,[a] family concept	self-concept	nonprobability	students, grades 5 & 8	472	63	SM, SF	questionnaire	family structure had both a positive and negative effect on self-concept
Halperin & Smith (1983)	deficit comparison, role	family structure,[c] race, sex	ratings of (step)father	nonprobability	10–12 years	140	70	SF	adjective checklist	stepchildren perceived both stepfathers and biological fathers more negatively than intact family children saw their fathers
Lutz (1983)	none	time in stepfamily, cause of family dissolution, stepsiblings, sex of stepparent & stepchild, halfsiblings	sources of stress found in clinical literature on stepchildren	nonprobability	12–18 years	103	103	SF, SM	questionnaire	issues of divided loyalty and discipline were most stressful, stepfamily life may not be as stressful as literature suggests
Booth, Brinkerhoff, & White (1984)	social learning	parental divorce conflict, remarriage, control variables such as age, religion, parental education, semester data gathered	courtship activity	nonprobability	college students	2,151	NR	NR	questionnaire	parental remarriage has little effect; cohabitation similar to intact family, lower than single-parent offspring, premarital sex more frequent (no difference if age at parental divorce is controlled)
Coleman & Ganong (1984)	social learning	family structure,[a] family integration, sex	divorce and marriage attitudes, marriage role expectations	nonprobability convenience	15–22 years	1,191	126	SM, SF	questionnaire	no differences in attitudes toward marriage, divorce, marriage roles
Clingempeel, Brand, & Ievoli (1984)	Cherlin's incomplete institution hypothesis	family structure	child love, child detachment, verbal/nonverbal behavior life stress, stepparent love, stepparent detachment	marriage license records, Philadelphia	9–12 years, adults	32[i]	32[i]	SF, SM	observation, self-report	no difference in quality between stepfather–stepchild and stepmother–stepchild relations; stepdaughters lower than stepsons in positive verbal behaviors toward stepparents

APPENDIX 5-2 (Continued)

Studies	Theory	Independent Variables	Dependent Variables	Sampling Procedure	Age	Total N	Stepfamily N	Types of Stepfamilies	Method	Results
Clingempeel, Ievoli & Brand (1984)*	systems, Cherlin's incomplete institution	sex of stepparent, sex of stepchild	stepparent–stepchild relations, love and detachment of adults and children	marriage license records, newspaper ads	9–12 years, adults	32[i]	32[i]	SF, SM	observation, questionnaire	stepparent—stepdaughter relationships in both stepmother and stepfather families were more problematic than stepparent–stepson relationships no other significant differences
Ferri (1984)*	not given	family structure[a]	economics and social background, family relations, educational aspirations & attainment, behavioral & social adjustment	all children from UK born in 1 week in 1958	7, 11, 16 years (longitudinal) & adults	11,688 (at 16)	121 (at 16)	SF, SM	self-report, reports by parents and teachers	for those with stepfathers less well-off economically, steprelationships were somewhat less satisfactory; no differences in attitudes toward marriage; educational aspirations were low for stepfather and single mother families; stepfather children had more behavioral problems; no differences in educational achievement; boys with stepfathers had more health problems
Garbarino, Sebes, & Schellenbach (1984)*	systems	level of risk for adolescent abuse	family structure,[b] family dynamics, parent behavior, child behavior, life events	referrals of families at risk for destructive adolescent parent relations	10–16 years, adults	62[i]	9[i]	not given	questionnaires (Family Adaptability and Cohesion Scales [FACES], Adolescent-Family Inventory of Life Events [A-FILE], Childhood Behavior Checklist [CBC], others) and interviewer ratings	more stepparents than expected had high risk for abuse group

Study	Theory	Independent variables	Dependent variables	Sampling	Age	N		Family type	Method	Findings
Crosbie-Burnett (1984)	systems	marital happiness stepfather–stepchild relations, discipline, perceived nurturance	overall family happiness	nonprobability: volunteers from stepfamily organizations, newspaper ads, referrals	adolescents, median age = 15 years; adults	87	87	SF	self-report	stepfather–stepchild relations accounted for 59% of overall family happiness variance; marital happiness accounted for 10%
Russell (1984)*	none	family structure[e]	incestuous abuse	probability sampling of households	adults (18+ years)	930	29	SF	interviews	stepfathers more likely to be sexually abusive than biological father
Tropf (1984)*	role	family structure[c]	voluntary contributions for support, telephone contacts, personal visits	nonprobability	adult males	101	76	SF	interviews	support increases after father remarries, decreases after mother remarries; visits decrease after either remarry but visiting length increases, visit frequencies are affected by distance, religion, SES, ex-wife's attitude
Strother & Jacobs (1984)*	not given	length of time in stepfamily	stress related to stepfamily living	nonprobability	13–18 years	63	63	SF, SM	questionnaire	level of stress was not high; time in stepfamily was not related to stress
Furstenberg & Spanier 1984)*	Cherlin's incomplete institution hypothesis	family structure	contact & closeness to children, parental competence, relations with extended kin	marriage license records from one county	adults	181	104	SF, SM	interviews, questionnaires	
Knaub & Hanna (1984)*	none	sex of child, age at parental remarriage, parental cohabitation, attitudes toward stepparent and remarriage, frequency of visits with noncustodial parent	family strengths	randomly from marriage license records	10–24 years, mean age = 12.9 years	44	44	SF, SM	questionnaire	parental cohabitation and perception of family adjustment related to perceived strengths; children saw families as having considerable strengths
Knaub, Hanna, & Stinnett (1984)*	none	sex of parent, being custodial parent, attitudes, family income, sought help after remarriage	family strengths	randomly from marriage license records	adults	80	80	SF, SM	questionnaire	attitudinal enviornment, higher income, & no help sought after marriage most related to family strengths perceived

APPENDIX 5-2 (Continued)

Studies	Theory	Independent Variables	Dependent Variables	Sampling Procedure	Age	Total N	Stepfamily N	Types of Stepfamilies	Method	Results
Furstenberg & Nord (1985)*	none	family structure[c]	relations between former spouses, childcare responsibility of nonresidential parent, child's adjustment to family	nationally representative	not given, adults also respondents	1,208	191	SF, SM	telephone interview	children have little contact with non-residential parent, contact is social rather than instrumental, children use a different scale to evaluate outside parent
White & Booth (1985)*	Cherlin's incomplete institution hypothesis	number of marriages, presence of stepchildren	divorce, marital quality	nationwide panel chosen through random digit dialing	children (age not given), adults	2,034 (1980) 1,578	134	SF, SM	telephone interview	presence of stepchildren is related to lower family satisfaction and divorce, stepfamilies empty the nest sooner than biological families
Kennedy (1985)*	systems, deficit comparison	family structure,[a] age at family separation, sex of stepparent, halfsiblings, family size	adaptability, cohesion, stress	nonprobability	17–22 years	631	50	SF, SM	questionnaire	no differences on adaptability, nuclear more cohesive, stepfamilies most stressful; halfsibling, age at transition, family size not related to perceptions of family
Pink & Wampler (1985)*	systems, deficit comparison	family structure[c]	quality of family functioning, quality of stepfather–adolescent dyad, ideal functioning	nonprobability	12–18 years, adults	56[f] families	28[f]	SF	questionnaire (FACES, B-LRI, others)	stepfamilies had lower cohesion, adaptability, regard, unconditionality; stepfathers reported less positive and more negative communication than biological fathers; no differences in adolescents or ratings

Study	Theory	Independent variables	Dependent variable	Sampling	Sample	N	N	SF/SM	Method	Findings
White, Brinkerhoff, & Booth (1985)*	socialization theory	family structure,[a] sex of custodial parent, cause of disruption	attachment to parents	nonprobability	college students	2,135	111	SF, SM	questionnaire	no differences between attachment to custodial parent and child-adult bonds in intact families; remarriage affect closeness to fathers; stepmothers less close than stepfathers, post-death ties to stepparent lower than post-divorce
Clingempeel & Segal (1986)*	systems	sex of stepparent and child, free of nonresidential parent's visits, time in stepfamily, quality of step dyad	social adjustment of children	marriage license and ads	9-12 years	60[f]	60[f]	SF, SM	questionnaires, observations	few significant findings for those with stepfathers for girls with stepmothers; less frequent visits with mother and longer time in stepfamily were related to positive relation with stepmothers
Ganong & Coleman (in press)*	none	sex of stepparent, sex of stepchild	perceptions of parents and steparents	nonprobability	15-22 years	126	126	SF, SM	questionnaire	few sex differences in how children perceive relations with stepparent; stepdaughter/father is less close than others; in general, stepchildren feel at least moderately close to stepparents

Family structure is defined in several ways:
[a] stepfather-stepmother-nuclear-single parent
[b] stepfather-stepmother-nuclear
[c] remarried-solo parent
[d] stepfather-nuclear-single parent
[e] stepfather-nuclear
[f] stepmother-nuclear-single parent
[g] stepmother-stepfather
[h] data were from two samples (stepchildren and informants)
[i] number denotes family rather than individuals
[j] NR = Not reported.
[k] Missing in Action: Families where husband was absent due to disappearance in Vietnam War.

APPENDIX 5-3

Comparison of Dependent Variables (Research) and Issues/Problems (Clinical)

Research	Clinical
Psychological Adjustment	*Family Dynamics*
Psychological Well-Being[a]	Loyalty[e]
Mental Health[a]	Co-Parental Conflicts
Locus of Control	Biological Parent–Child Bonds[f]
Psychosocial Functioning[b]	Jealousy
Psychosomatic Illness	Custody[g]
Psychosomatic Complaints	Sibling Relations
Self-Concept[a]	Couple Relations[h]
Evaluation of Self[a]	Idealization of Absent Parent[f]
Personal Adjustment[a]	Pseudomutuality
Self-Esteem[a]	Scapegoating
Stability[b]	Child Born of Remarried Parents
Self-Sufficiency[b]	Sexually Charged Atmosphere[i]
Dominance[b]	Push for Cohesion
Illness Proneness	Surnames
Nervousness	Turf or Space Issues
Anxiety and Fright Reactions	Two Households
Self-Derogation[a]	Boundary Issues
Stress[a]	Triangulation
Aggressiveness[c]	Rejection by Stepparents
Inhibition	Extreme Intimacy[j]
Loss and Mourning[d]	Discipline[f]
Family Relations	Competition and Rivalry
Concept of Parents[f]	Grandparents[n]
Relationship to Parents[f]	Stepchild Expelled from Remarried
Parent–Child Relationships[f]	Parent's Relationship
Companionship with Mother[f]	Subgroups Within Family
Adjustment to Parents[f]	Rejection of Stepparent[f]
Evaluation of Parents[f]	Low Cohesion[j]
Family Concepts[j]	Poor Communication[j]
Quality of Family Relations[j]	Exclusion of Parental Child
Family Integration[j]	Scapegoating Noncustodial Parent
Family Relations[j]	Stepmothers Who Lack Experience[m]
Parent Behaviors	Stepsibling Relations[k]
Child Behaviors	*Transitional Adjustments*
Stepsibling Relations[k]	Adjustment to Change
Home Management Participation	Conflict in Merging
Parenting Self and Others	Myths of Instant Love
Attitudes to Parental Remarriage	No Shared Rules
Role Confusion[l]	Lack of Shared Rituals
Loyalty Conflicts[e]	Child Not Told Prior to Marriage
Parental Competence[m]	No Shared History
Relations with Extended Kin[n]	Child's Age at Parental Remarriage
Family Adaptability	Lifestyle Difference
Family Cohesion[j]	Holidays
Family Strengths	Birth Order Changes
Home Adjustment	Lack of Privacy
Ideal Family Functioning	Increased Activity
Incestuous Abuse[i]	Time between Marriages
Parents' Marital Quality[h]	*Incomplete Institution*
Parental Divorce	Role Confusion[l]

APPENDIX 5-3 (Continued)

Comparison of Dependent Variables (Research) and Issues/Problems (Clinical)

Research	Clinical
Child Support[g]	No Legal Ties
Telephone Contacts with Noncustodial Parents[g]	No Societal Rituals
Visitation[g]	Family Identity Confusion[j]
Noncustodial Parent's Involvement[g]	Kinship Terms
	How Much to Parent?
Social Behaviors	No Model for Stepparent–Child Relations
Social Adaptation	How Much Affection to Show
Delinquent Behavior[c]	How to Show Affection
Singlehood	Money Issues
Reported Drug Use[c]	*Emotional Responses*
Number of Friends	Guilt
School Behavior Problems[c]	Loss, Mourning[d]
Peer Relations	Feel Unwanted
Days Absent from School	Reuniting Fantasies
Number of School Activities	Ambivalence
Teacher Attention	Child's Feeling Responsible for Parent's
Social Adjustment	Loneliness, Stress, Emotions, or
School Adjustment	Greater Vulnerability
Social Attitudes	Identity Confusion[a]
Family Size Preferences	Fear of Being Misunderstood
Attitude toward Marriage Roles	Anger[c]
Divorce Attitudes	Fear of Family Breaking Up
Marriage Attitudes	Rebellion[c]
Attitude toward School	Self-Worth[a]
Attitude toward Teachers	Lack of Control[o]
Religious Views	*Stepfamily Expectations*
Political Views	Stepfamily Same as Nuclear Family
Cognitive Performance	Stepparentt as Rescuer
IQ	Higher Expectations
Achievement	"Love Conquers All"
Grades	Negative Image
Field Independence	Wicked Stepparent
Scholastic Aptitude	

Note. Terms with the same superscript letter indicate some degree of overlap in concepts as defined by researchers and clinicians. Terms with no superscripts in the empirical categories were not examined by clinicians and those with no superscripts in the clinical categories were not investigated by researchers.

REFERENCES

Chapter References

Ahrons, C., & Perlmutter, M. (1982). The relationship between former spouses. In J. C. Hansen & L. Messenger (Eds.), *Therapy with remarried families* (pp. 31–46). Rockville, MD: Aspen.

Blood, R. (1976). Research needs of a family life educator and marriage counselor. *Journal of Marriage and the Family, 38,* 7–12.

Bohannon, P. (1981). *Stepfamilies: A partially annotated bibliography.* Palo Alto, CA: Stepfamily Association of America, Inc.

Burchinal, L. G. (1964). Characteristics of adolescents from unbroken, broken, and reconstituted families. *Journal of Marriage and the Family, 26,* 44–51.

Cherlin, A. (1978). Remarriage as an incomplete institution. *American Journal of Sociology,* November, 634–650.

Chilman, C. S. (1983). Remarriage and stepfamilies: Research results and implications. In Eleanor D. Macklin & R. H. Rubin (Eds.), *Contemporary families and alternative lifestyles* (pp. 147–163). Beverly Hills, CA: Sage.

Clingempeel, G., Brand, E., & Ievoli, R. (1984). Stepparent–stepchild relationships in stepmother and stepfather families: A multimethod study. *Family Relations, 33,* 465–473.

Clingempeel, G., Ievoli, R., & Brand, E. (1984). Structural complexity and the quality of stepfather–stepchild relationships. *Family Relations, 33,* 465–473.

Clingempeel, G., & Segal, S. (1986). Stepparent–stepchild relationships and the psychological adjustment of children in stepmother and stepfather families. *Child Development, 57,* 474–484.

Coleman, M., Ganong, L., & Gingrich, R. (1985). Stepfamily strengths: A review of the popular literature. *Family Relations, 34,* 583–589.

Coleman, M., Ganong, L., & Gingrich, R. (1986). Strengths of stepfamilies identified in professional literature. In S. Van Zandt (Ed.), *Building family strengths* (Vol. 7, pp. 439–451). Lincoln, NE: University of Nebraska.

Coleman, M., Marshall, S., & Ganong, L. (1986). Beyond Cinderella: Relevant reading for young adolescents about stepfamilies. *Adolescence, 21,* 553–560.

Cromwell, R., & Peterson, G. (1981). Multisystem–multimethod assessment: A framework. In E. Filsinger & R. Lewis (Eds.), *Assessing marriage: New behavioral approaches* (pp. 38–54). Beverly Hills, CA: Sage.

Crosbie-Burnett, M. (1984). The centrality of the step relationship: A challenge to family theory and practice. *Family Relations, 33,* 459–463.

Draughon, M. (1975). Stepmother's model of identification in relation to mourning in the child. *Psychological Reports, 36*(1), 183–189.

Duberman, L. (1973). Step-kin relationships. *Journal of Marriage and the Family, 35,* 283–292.

Essex, L. M., & Campbell, C. (1984). Challenges in researching the remarried. *Family Relations, 33,* 415–424.

Ferri, E. (1984). *Stepchildren: A national study.* Windsor, UK: NFER-Nelson.

Fishman, B., & Hamel, B. (1981). From nuclear to stepfamily ideology: A stressful change. *Alternative Lifestyles, 4*(2), 181–204.

Fox, G. L., & Inazu, J. K. (1982). The influence of mother's marital history on the mother–daughter relationship in black and white households. *Journal of Marriage and the Family, 44,* 143–153.

Furstenberg, F., Jr., & Nord, C. (1985). Parenting apart: Patterns of childrearing after marital disruption. *Journal of Marriage and the Family, 47,* 893–904.

Furstenberg, F., Jr., & Spanier, G. (1984). *Recycling the family: Remarriage after divorce.* Beverly Hills, CA: Sage.

Ganong, L., & Coleman, M. (1984). Effects of remarriage on children: A review of the empirical literature. *Family Relations, 33,* 389–406.

Ganong, L., & Coleman, M. (1986). A comparison of clinical and empirical literature on children in stepfamilies. *Journal of Marriage and the Family, 48,* 309–318.

Ganong, L., & Coleman, M. (in press). Stepchildren's perceptions of their parents. *Journal of Genetic Psychology.*

Garbarino, J., Sebes, J., & Schellenbach, C. (1984). Families at risk for destructive parent–child relations in adolescence. *Child Development, 55*, 174–183.

Gelles, R. J. (1980). Violence in the family: A review of research in the seventies. *Journal of Marriage and the Family, 42*(4), 873–885.

Gelles, R. J. (1982). Applying research on family violence to clinical practice. *Journal of Marriage and the Family, 44*(1), 9–20.

Goldner, V. (1982). Remarriage family: Structure, system, future. In J. C. Hansen & L. Messenger (Eds.), *Therapy with remarried families* (pp. 187–206). Rockville, MD: Aspen.

Halperin, S., & Smith, T. (1983). Differences in stepchildren's perceptions of their stepfathers and natural fathers: Implications for family therapy. *Journal of Divorce, 7*, 19–30.

Johnson, H. C. (1980). Working with stepfamilies: Principles of practice. *Social Work, 25*, 304–308.

Kennedy, G. (1985). Family relationships as perceived by college students from single-parent, blended, and intact families. *Family Perspective, 19*, 117–126.

Kleinman, J., Rosenberg, E., & Whiteside, M. (1979). Common developmental tasks in forming reconstituted families. *Journal of Marital and Family Therapy, 5*(2), 79–86.

Knaub, P., Hanna, S., & Stinnett, N. (1984). Strengths of remarried families. *Journal of Divorce, 7*, 41–55.

Lutz, P. (1983). The stepfamily: An adolescent perspective. *Family Relations, 32*, 367–375.

Marotz-Baden, R., Adams, G., Bueche, N., Munro, B., & Munro, G. (1979). Family form or family process? Reconsidering the deficit family model approach. *The Family Coordinator, 28*, 5–14.

Messinger, L. (1984). *Remarriage: A family affair.* New York: Plenum Press.

McGoldrick, M., & Carter, E. A. (1980). Forming a remarried family. In E. A. Carter & M. McGoldrick (Eds.), *The family life cycle: A framework for family therapy* (pp. 265–294). New York: Gardner Press.

Mills, D. M. (1984). A model for stepfamily development. *Family Relations, 33*, 365–372.

Nolan, J., Coleman, M., & Ganong, L. (1984). The presentation of stepfamilies in marriage and family textbooks. *Family Relations, 33*, 559–566.

Olson, D. (1983, October). *Family systems–behavioral medicine: Emerging research and methodology.* Paper presented at the Family Systems–Behavioral Medicine Workshop, Wayzatta, MN.

Osborne, J. (1983). Stepfamilies: The restructuring process. *Marriage and Divorce Today, 8*(40), 1–3.

Papernow, P. (1984). The stepfamily cycle: An experiential model of stepfamily development. *Family Relations, 33*, 355–363.

Perkins, T. F., & Kahan, J. P. (1979). An empirical comparison of natural father and stepfather family systems. *Family Process, 18*, 175–183.

Pink, J., & Wampler, K. (1985). Problem areas in stepfamilies: Cohesion, adaptability, and the stepfather-adolescent relationship. *Family Relations, 34*, 327–335.

Ransom, J. W., Schlesinger, S., & Derdyn, A. P. (1979). A stepfamily in formation. *American Journal of Orthopsychiatry, 49*(1), 36–43.

Ransom, D. (1983, October). *Family systems–behavioral medicine: Defining an emerging field.* Paper presented at the Family Systems–Behavioral Medicine Workshop, Wayzata, MN.

Reiss, D. (1983, October). *Theory construction.* Paper presented at the National Council on Family Relations, St. Paul, MN.

Roberts, T. W., & Price, S. (1985). A systems analysis of the remarriage process: Implications for the clinician. *Journal of Divorce, 9*, 1–25.

Russell, D. (1984). The prevalence and seriousness of incestuous abuse: Stepfathers vs. biological fathers. *Child Abuse and Neglect, 8*, 15–22.

Skeen, P., Covi, R. B., & Robinson, B. (1985). Stepfamilies: A review of the literature with suggestions for practitioners. *Journal of Counseling and Development, 64,* 121–125.

Stanton, G. W. (1986). Preventive intervention with stepfamilies: Social role of stepchildren. *American Sociological Review, 50,* 689–698.

Strother, J., & Jacobs, E. (1984). Adolescent stress as it relates to stepfamily living: Implications for school counselors. *The School Counselor, 31,* 97–103.

Tropf, W. D. (1984). An exploratory examination of the effect of remarriage on child support and personal contacts. *Journal of Divorce, 7,* 57–73.

Visher, E. B., & Visher, J. S. (1979). *Stepfamilies: A guide to working with stepparents and stepchildren.* New York: Brunner/Mazel.

Wald, E. (1981). *The remarried family: Challenge and promise.* New York: Family Service Association of America.

Walker, K., & Messinger, L. (1979). Remarriage after divorce: Dissolution and reconstruction of family boundaries. *Family Process, 18,* 185–192.

Wallerstein, J., & Kelly, J. (1980). *Surviving the breakup.* New York: Basic Books.

White, L., & Booth, A. (1985). The quality and stability of remarriages: The role of stepchildren. *American Sociological Review, 50,* 689–698.

White, L., Brinkerhoff, D., & Booth, A. (1985). The effect of marital disruption on child's attachment to parents. *Journal of Family Issues, 6,* 5–22.

Whiteside, M. (1983). Families of remarriage: The weaving of many life cycle threads. In J. Hansen & H. Liddle (Eds.), *Clinical implications of the family life cycle* (pp. 100–119). Rockville, MD: Aspen.

Clinical References Reviewed

Ahrons, C., & Perlmutter, M. (1982). The relationship between former spouses. In J. C. Hansen & L. Messenger (Eds.), *Therapy with remarried families* (pp. 31–46). Rockville, MD: Aspen.

Anderson, J., Larson, J., & Morgan, A. (1981). PPSF/Parenting program for stepparent families: A new approach for strengthening families. In N. Stinnett (Ed.), *Family strengths 3: Roots of well-being* (pp. 351–360). Lincoln, NE: University of Nebraska Press.

Baideme, S. M., & Serritella, D. A. (1981). Planning conjoint family therapy with the remarried family. In A. S. Gurman (Ed.), *Questions and answers in the practice of family therapy* (Vol. 1, pp. 338–341). New York: Brunner/Mazel.

Barrows, S. E. (1981). An interview with Emily and John Visher. *American Journal of Family Therapy, 9*(3), 75–83.

Bitterman, C. M. (1968). The multimarriage family. *Social Casework, 49,* 218–221.

Coleman, M., & Ganong, L. H. (1980, Fall). (Step)parent education: A proposal. *Journal of Children and Youth,* 28–37.

Coleman, M., & Ganong, L. (1985). Remarriage myths. *Journal of Counseling and Development, 64,* 116–120.

Coleman, M., Ganong, L., & Gingrich, R. (1985). Stepfamily strengths: A review of the popular literature. *Family Relations, 34,* 583–589.

Coleman, M., Ganong, L., & Gingrich, R. (1986). Stepfamily strengths: A review of professional literature. In S. Van Zandt (Ed.), *Building family strengths* (Vol. 7, pp. 439–451). Lincoln, NE: University of Nebraska Press.

Coleman, M., Ganong, L. H., & Henry, J. (1984). What teachers should know about stepfamilies. *Childhood Education, 60*(5), 306–309.

Coleman, M., Marshall, S., & Ganong, L. (1986). Beyond Cinderella: Relevant reading for young adolescents about stepfamilies. *Adolescence, 21,* 553–560.

Crohn, H., Sager, C., Brown, H., Rodstein, E., & Walker, L. (1982). A basis for understanding and treating the remarried family. In J. C. Hansen & L. Messenger (Eds.), *Therapy with remarried families* (pp. 159–186). Rockville, MD: Aspen.

Crohn, H., Sager, C., Rodstein, E., Brown, H., Walker, L., & Beir, J. (1981). Understanding and treating the child in the remarried family. In I. Stuart & L. Abt (Eds.), *Children of separation and divorce.* New York: Van Nostrand Reinhold.

Dolan, E., & Lown, J. M. (1985). The remarried family: Challenges and opportunities. *Journal of Home Economics, 78,* 36–41.

Draughon, M. (1975). Stepmother's model of identification in relation to mourning in the child. *Psychological Reports, 36,* 183–189.

Egan, M. W., Landau, E. D., & Rhode, G. (1979). The ex-spouses and the reconstituted family. *Family Perspectives, 13,* 69–81.

Engebretson, J. (1982). Stepmothers as first-time parents: Their needs and problems. *Pediatric Nursing, 8,* 387–390.

Fast, I., & Cain, A. C. (1966). The stepparent role: Potential for disturbances in family functioning. *American Journal of Ortho-psychiatary, 36,* 485–491.

Fishman, B., & Hamel, B. (1981). From nuclear to stepfamily ideology: A stressful change. *Alternative Lifestyles, 4*(2), 181–204.

Framo, M. D. (1981). Common issues in recoupled families and therapy interventions. In A. S. Gurman (Ed.), *Questions and answers in the practice of family therapy* (Vol. 1, pp. 333–337). New York: Brunner/Mazel.

Friedman, L. J. (1981). Common problems in stepfamilies. In A. S. Gurman (Ed.), *Questions and answers in the practice of family therapy* (Vol. 1, pp. 329–332). New York: Brunner/Mazel.

Gardner, R. (1984). Counseling children in stepfamilies. *Elementary School Guidance and Counseling, 19,* 40–49.

Goldenberg, I. (1982). Therapy with stepfamilies involved in joint custody. In A. S. Gurman (Ed.), *Questions and answers in the practice of family therapy* (Vol. 2, pp. 219–221). New York: Brunner/Mazel.

Goldner, V. (1982). Remarriage family: Structure, system, future. In J. C. Hansen & L. Messinger (Eds.), *Therapy with remarried families* (pp. 187–206). Rockville, MD: Aspen.

Goldstein, H. S. (1974). Reconstituted families: The second marriage and its children. *Psychiatric Quarterly, 48*(3), 433–440.

Gray, B. J., & Pippin, G. D. (1984). Stepfamilies: A concern health education should address. *Journal of School Health, 54,* 292–294.

Greif, J. B. (1982). The father–child relationship subsequent to divorce. In J. C. Hansen & L. Messinger (Eds.), *Therapy with remarried families* (pp. 47–57). Rockville, MD: Aspen.

Heilpern, E. P. (1943). Psychological problems of stepchildren. *Psychoanalytic Review, 30,* 163–196.

Herndon, A., & Combs, L. (1982). Stepfamilies as patients. *Journal of Family Practice, 15*(5), 917–922.

Hutchison, I. W., & Hutchison, K. R. (1979). Issues and conflicts in stepfamilies. *Family Perspectives, 13,* 111–121.

Isaacs, M. B. (1982). Facilitating family restructuring and relinkage. In J. C. Hansen & L. Messinger (Eds.), *Therapy with remarried families* (pp. 120–143). Rockville, MD: Aspen.

Jacobson, D. (1979). Stepfamilies: Myths and realities. *Social Work, 24*(3), 202–207.

Jacobson, D. (1980a). Stepfamilies. *Children Today, 9*(1), 2–6.

Jacobson, D. (1980b). Crisis intervention with stepfamilies. *New Directions for Mental Health Services, 6,* 35–42.

Johnson, H. C. (1980). Working with stepfamilies: Principles of practice. *Social Work, 25,* 304–308.

Jones, S. M. (1978). Divorce and remarriage: A new beginning, a new set of problems. *Journal of Divorce, 2*(3), 217–227.

Kent, M. O. (1980). Remarriage: A family systems perspective. *Social Casework, 61,* 146–153.

Kleinman, J., Rosenberg, E., & Whiteside, M. (1979). Common developmental tasks in forming reconstituted families. *Journal of Marital and Family Therapy, 5*(2), 79–86.

Kompara, D. R. (1980). Difficulties in the socialization process of stepparenting. *Family Relations, 29,* 69–73.

McGoldrick, M., & Carter, E. A. (1980). Forming a remarried family. In E. A. Carter & M. McGoldrick (Eds.), *The family life cycle: A frame work for family therapy* (pp. 265–294). New York: Gardner Press.

Messinger, L. (1984). *Remarriage: A family affair.* New York: Plenum Press.

Messinger, L., & Walker, K. N. (1981). From marriage breakdown to remarriage: Parental tasks and therapeutic guidelines. *American Journal of Orthopsychiatry, 51*(3), 429–438.

Mills, D. M. (1984). A model for stepfamily development. *Family Relations, 33,* 365–372.

Mowatt, M. (1972). Group psychotherapy for stepfathers and their wives. *Psychotherapy: Theory, Research, and Practice, 9*(4), 328–331.

Nolan, J., Coleman, M., & Ganong, L. (1984). The presentation of stepfamilies in marriage and family textbooks. *Family Relations, 33,* 559–566.

Osborne, J. (1983). Stepfamilies: The restructuring process. *Marriage and Divorce Today, 8*(40), 1–3.

Papernow, P. (1984). The stepfamily cycle: An experiential model of stepfamily development. *Family Relations, 33,* 355–363.

Perlmutter, L. H., Engel, T., & Sager, C. J. (1982). The incest taboo: Loosened sexual boundaries in remarried families. *Journal of Sex and Marital Therapy, 8*(2), 83–96.

Pill, C. J. (1981). A family life education group for working with stepparents. *Social Casework, 62*(3), 159–166.

Pino, C. J. (1981). Remarriage and blended families. *Family Perspectives, 15,* 79–87.

Podolsky, E. (1955). The emotional problems of the stepchild. *Mental Hygiene, 39,* 49–53.

Poppen, W. A., & White, P. N. (1984). Transition to the blended family. *Elementary School Guidance and Counseling, 19,* 50–61.

Prosen, S. S., & Farmer, J. H. (1982). Understanding stepfamilies: Issues and implications for counselors. *The Personnel and Guidance Journal, 60,* 393–397.

Ransom, J. W., Schlesinger, S., & Derdeyn, A. P. (1979). A stepfamily in formation. *American Journal of Orthopsychiatry, 49*(1), 36–43.

Roberts, T. W., & Price, S. (1985). A systems analysis of the remarriage process: Implications for the clinician. *Journal of Divorce, 9,* 1–25.

Robinson, M. (1980). Stepfamilies: A reconstituted family system. *Journal of Family Therapy, 2,* 45–69.

Robson, B. (1982). A developmental approach to the treatment of children of divorcing parents. In J. C. Hansen & L. Messinger (Eds.), *Therapy with remarried families* (pp. 59–78). Rockville, MD: Aspen.

Rogers, R. (1981). Stepparents and stepchildren. *Medical Aspects of Human Sexuality, 15*(9), 68F–68P.

Sager, C., Brown, H., Crohn, H., Engel, T., Rodstein, E., & Walker, L. (1983). *Treating the remarried family.* New York: Brunner/Mazel.

Sager, C. J., Brown, H., Crohn, H., Rodstein, E., & Walker, E. (1980). Remarriage revisited. *Family and Child Mental Health Journal, 6,* 19–33.

Sager, C. J., Walker, E., Brown, H., Crohn, H., & Rodstein, E. (1981). Improving functioning in the remarried family system. *Journal of Marital and Family Therapy, 7*, 3–13.

Satir, V. (1972). *Peoplemaking.* Palo Alto, CA: Science and Behavior Books.

Schlesinger, B., & Stasiuk, E. (1981). Children of divorced parents in second marriages. In I. R. Stuart & L. E. Abt (Eds.), *Children of separation and divorce* (pp. 19–35). New York: Van Nostrand Reinhold.

Schulman, G. (1972). Myths that intrude on the adaptation of the stepfamily. *Social Casework, 53*, 131–139.

Schulman, G. (1981). Divorce, single-parenthood, and stepfamilies: Structural implications of these transitions. *International Journal of Family Therapy, 9*, 87–112.

Serritella, D. A. (1982). Stepfathers-stepdaughters: Sexual issues in the remarried family. In A. S. Gurman (Ed.), *Questions and answers in the practice of family therapy* (Vol. 2, pp. 222–224). New York: Brunner/Mazel.

Skeen, P., Covi, R. B., & Robinson, B. (1985). Stepfamilies: A review of the literature with suggestions for practitioners. *Journal of Counseling and Development, 64*, 121–125.

Skeen, P., Robinson, B., & Flake-Hobson, C. (1984). Blended families: Overcoming the Cinderella myth. *Young Children, 39*(3), 64–74.

Stanton, G. W. (1986). Preventive intervention with stepfamilies. *Social Work, 67*, 201–206.

Theis, J. M. (1977). Beyond divorce: The impact of remarriage on children. *Journal of Clinical Child Psychology, 6*(2), 59–61.

Today's Child. (1981). Generous adults needed to free youngsters to find happiness in 'remarried' household. *30*(3), 4.

Turnbull, S. K., & Turnbull, J. M. (1983). To dream the impossible dream: An agenda for discussion with stepparents. *Family Relations, 32*, 227–230.

Visher, E. B., & Visher, J. S. (1978a). Common problems of stepparents and their spouses. *American Journal of Orthopsychiatry, 48*(2), 252–262.

Visher, E. B., & Visher, J. S. (1978b). Major areas of difficulty for stepparent couples. *International Journal of Family Counseling, 6*(2), 70–80.

Visher, E. B., & Visher, J. S. (1979). *Stepfamilies: A guide to working with stepparents and stepchildren.* New York: Brunner/Mazel.

Visher, E. B., & Visher, J. S. (1982a). Children in stepfamilies. *Psychiatric Annals, 12*(9), 832–841.

Visher, E. B., & Visher, J. S. (1982b). Stepfamilies in the 1980s. In J. C. Hansen & L. Messinger (Eds.), *Therapy with remarried families* (pp. 105–119). Rockville, MD: Aspen.

Visher, J. S., & Visher, E. B. (1981). How therapists can help with stepfamily integration. In A. S. Gurman (Ed.), *Questions and answers in the practice of family therapy* (Vol. 1, pp. 332–337). New York: Brunner/Mazel.

Visher, J. S., & Visher, E. B. (1982). Stepfamilies and stepparenting. In N. Walsh (Ed.), *Normal family processes* (pp. 331–353). New York: Guilford.

Wald, E. (1981). *The remarried family: Challenge and promise.* New York: Family Service Association of America.

Waldron, J. A., & Whittington, R. (1979). The stepparent/stepfamily. *Journal of Operational Psychiatry, 10*(1), 47–50.

Walker, K. N., & Messinger, L. (1979). Remarriage after divorce: Dissolution and reconstruction of family boundaries. *Family Process, 18*(2), 185–192.

Wallerstein, J., & Kelly, J. (1980). *Surviving the breakup.* New York: Basic Books.

Whiteside, M. (1981). A family systems approach with families of remarriage. In I. Stuart & L. Abt (Eds.), *Children of separation and divorce.* New York: Van Nostrand Reinhold.

Whiteside, M. (1982a). The role of explicit rule-making in the early stages of remarriage. In A. S. Gurman (Ed.), *Questions and answers in the practice of family therapy* (Vol. 2, pp. 214–218). New York: Brunner/Mazel.

Whiteside, M. (1982b). Remarriage: A family developmental process. *Journal of Marital and Family Therapy, 4*, 59–68.

Whiteside, M. (1983). Families of remarriage: The weaving of many life cycle threads. In J. Hansen & H. Liddle (Eds.), *Clinical implications of the family life cycle* (pp. 100–119). Rockville, MD: Aspen.

Whiteside, M., & Auerbach, L. S. (1978). Can a daughter of my father's new wife by my sister? Families of remarriage in family therapy. *Journal of Divorce, 1*, 271–283.

Wood, L., & Poole, S. (1983). Stepfamilies in family practice. *The Journal of Family Practice, 16*, 739–744.

Empirical Studies Reviewed

Bernard, J. (1956). *Remarriage: A study of marriage.* New York: Holt, Rinehart, & Winston.

Blechman, F. A., Berberian, R. M., & Thompson, W. D. (1977). How well does number of parents explain unique variance of self-reported drug use? *Journal of Consulting and Clinical Psychology, 45*, 1182–1183.

Bohannon, P., & Yahraes, H. (1979). Stepfathers as parents. In E. Corfman (Ed.), *Families today: A research sampler on families and children.* National Institutes of Mental Health Science Monograph. Washington, DC: U.S. Government Printing Office.

Booth, A., Brinkerhoff, D., & White, L. (1984). The impact of parental divorce on courtship. *Journal of Marriage and the Family, 46*, 85–94.

Bowerman, C., & Irish, D. (1962). Some relationships of stepchildren to their parents. *Marriage and Family Living, 24*, 113–121.

Boyd, D., Nunn, G., & Parish, T. (1983). Effects of marital status and parents' marital status on evaluation of self and parents. *Journal of Social Psychology, 119*, 229–234.

Burchinal, L. G. (1964). Characteristics of adolescents from unbroken, broken, and reconstituted families. *Journal of Marriage and the Family, 26*, 44–50.

Chapman, M. (1977). Father absence, stepfathers, and the cognitive performance of college students. *Child Development, 48*, 1155–1158.

Clingempeel, G., Brand, E., & Ievoli, R. (1984). Stepparent–stepchild relationships in stepmother and stepfather families: A multimethod study. *Family Relations, 33*, 465–473.

Clingempeel, G., Ievoli, R., & Brand, E. (1984). Structural complexity and the quality of stepfather–stepchild relationships. *Family Process, 23*, 547–560.

Clingempeel, G., & Segal, S. (1986). Stepparent–stepchild relationships and the psychological adjustment of children in stepmother and stepfather families. *Child Development, 57*, 474–484.

Coleman, M., & Ganong, L. (1984). Effect of family structure on family attitudes and expectations. *Family Relations, 33*, 425–432.

Crosbie-Burnett, M. (1984). The centrality of the step relationship: A challenge to family theory and practice. *Family Relations, 33*, 459–463.

Dahl, B. B., McCubbin, H. L., & Lester, G. R. (1976). War-induced father absence: Comparing the adjustment of children in reunited, non-reunited, and reconstituted families. *International Journal of Sociology of the Family, 6*, 99–108.

Duberman, L. (1973). Step-kin relationships. *Journal of Marriage and the Family, 35*, 283–292.

Ferri, E. (1984). *Stepchildren: A national study.* Windsor, UK: National Federation for Educational Research-Nelson.

Fox, G. L., & Inazu, J. K. (1982). The influence of mother's marital history on the mother-daughter relationship in black and white households. *Journal of Marriage and the Family, 44*, 143–153.

Furstenberg, F., Jr., & Nord, C. (1985). Parenting apart: Patterns of childrearing after marital disruption. *Journal of Marriage and the Family, 47*, 893-904.

Furstenberg, F., Jr., & Spanier, G. (1984). *Recycling the family: Remarriage after divorce.* Beverly Hills, CA: Sage.

Ganong, L., & Coleman, M. (in press). Stepchildren's perceptions of their parents. *Journal of Genetic Psychology.*

Ganong, L., Coleman, M., & Brown, G. (1981). Effect of family structure on marital attitudes. *Adolescence, 16*, 281-288.

Garbarino, J., Sebes, J., & Schellenbach, C. (1984). Families at risk for destructive parent-child relations in adolescence. *Child Development, 55*, 174-183.

Halperin, S., & Smith, T. (1983). Differences in stepchildren's perceptions of their stepfathers and natural fathers: Implications for family therapy. *Journal of Divorce, 7*, 19-30.

Kalter, N. (1977). Children of divorce in an outpatient psychiatric population. *American Journal of Orthopsychiatry, 47*, 40-51.

Kaplan, H. B., & Pokorny, A. D. (1971). Self-derogation and childhood broken home. *Journal of Marriage and the Family, 33*, 328-337.

Kellam, S. G., Ensminger, M. E., & Turner, J. (1977). Family structure and the mental health of children: Concurrent and longitudinal community-wide studies. *Archives of General Psychiatry, 34*, 1012-1022.

Kennedy, G. (1985). Family relationships as perceived by college students from single-parent, blended, and intact families. *Family Perspective, 19*, 117-126.

Knaub, P., & Hanna, S. (1984). Children of remarriage: Perceptions of family strengths. *Journal of Divorce, 7*, 73-90.

Knaub, P., Hanna, S., & Stinnett, N. (1984). Strengths of remarried families. *Journal of Divorce, 7*, 41-55.

Langner, L., & Michael, S. (1963). *Life stress and mental health.* New York: Macmillan.

Lutz, P. (1983). The stepfamily: An adolescent perspective. *Family Relations, 32*, 367-375.

Nunn, G., Parish, T., & Worthing, R. (1983). Perceptions of personal and familial adjustment by children from intact, single-parent, and reconstituted families. *Psychology in the Schools, 20*, 166-174.

Nye, F. (1957). Child adjustment in broken and unhappy homes. *Marriage and Family Living, 19*, 356-361.

Oshman, H. P., & Manosevitz, M. (1976). Father absence: Effects of stepfathers upon psychosocial development in males. *Developmental Psychology, 12*, 479-480.

Palermo, E. (1980). Remarriage: Parental perceptions of steprelations with children and adolescents. *Journal of Psychiatric Nursing and Mental Health Services, 18*, 9-13.

Parish, J., & Parish, T. (1983). Children's self-concepts as related to family structure and family concept. *Adolescence, 18*, 649-658.

Parish, T. (1981a). Young adults' evaluations of themselves and their parents as a function of family structure and disposition. *Journal of Youth and Adolescence, 10*, 173-178.

Parish, T. (1981b). Concordance of children's descriptions of themselves and their parents as a function of intact versus divorced families. *Journal of Psychology, 107*, 199-201.

Parish, T. S. (1982). Locus of control as a function of father loss and the presence of stepfathers. *Journal of Genetic Psychology, 140*, 321-322.

Parish, T., & Copeland, T. (1979). The relationship between self-concepts and evaluations of parents and stepfathers. *Journal of Psychology, 101*, 135-138.

Parish, T., & Dostal, J. (1980). Evaluations of self and parent figures by children from intact, divorced, and reconstituted families. *Journal of Youth and Adolescence, 9*, 347-351.

Parish, T., & Kappes, B. (1980). Impact of father loss on the family. *Social Behavior and Personality, 8*, 107-112.

Parish, T. S., & Nunn, G. D. (1981). Children's self-concepts and evaluations of parents as a function of family structure and process. *Journal of Psychology, 107*, 105-108.

Parish, T., & Parish, J. (1983). Relationship between evaluations of one's self and one's family by children from intact, reconstituted, and single-parent families. *Journal of Genetic Psychology, 143*, 293–294.

Parish, T., & Philp, M. (1982). The self-concepts of children from intact and divorced families: Can they be affected in school settings? *Education, 103*, 60–63.

Parish, T., & Taylor, J. (1979). The impact of divorce and subsequent father absence on children's and adolescent's self-concepts. *Journal of Youth and Adolescence, 8*, 427–432.

Perkins, T. F., & Kahan, J. P. (1979). An empirical comparison of natural father and stepfather family systems. *Family Process, 18*, 175–183.

Perry, J. B., & Pfuhl, E. (1963). Adjustment of children in "solo" and remarriage homes. *Marriage and Family Living, 25*, 221–223.

Pink, J., & Wampler, K. (1985). Problem areas in stepfamilies: Cohesion, adaptability, and the stepfather–adolescent relationship. *Family Relations, 34*, 327–335.

Raschke, H. J., & Raschke, V. J. (1979). Family conflict and children's self-concepts: A comparison of intact and single-parent families. *Journal of Marriage and the Family, 41*, 367–374.

Rosenberg, M. (1965). *Society and the adolescent self-image*. Princeton, NJ: Princeton University Press.

Russell, D. (1984). The prevalence and seriousness of incestuous abuse: Stepfathers vs. biological fathers. *Child Abuse and Neglect, 8*, 15–22.

Santrock, J. W. (1972). Relation of type and onset of father absence to cognitive development. *Child Development, 43*, 455–469.

Santrock, J., Warshak, R., & Elliott, G. (1982). Social development and parent–child interaction in father-custody and stepmother families. In M. E. Lamb (Ed.), *Non-traditional families: Parenting and child development* (pp. 289–314). Hillsdale, NJ: Erlbaum.

Santrock, J. W., Warshak, R., Lindbergh, M., & Meadows, L. (1982). Children's and parents' observed social behavior in stepfather families. *Child Development, 53*, 472–480.

Spreitzer, E., & Riley, L. E. (1974). Factors associated with singlehood. *Journal of Marriage and the Family, 36*, 533–542.

Strother, J., & Jacobs, E. (1984). Adolescent stress as it relates to stepfamily living: Implications for school counselors. *The School Counselor, 31*, 97–103.

Touliatos, J., & Lindholm, B. W. (1980). Teachers' perceptions of behavior problems in children from intact, single-parent, and stepparent families. *Psychology in the Schools, 17*, 264–269.

Tropf, W. D. (1984). An exploratory examination of the effect of remarriage on child support and personal contacts. *Journal of Divorce, 7*, 57–73.

White, L., & Booth, A. (1985). The quality and stability of remarriages: The role of stepchildren. *American Sociological Review, 50*, 689–698.

White, L., & Brinkerhoff, D., & Booth, A. (1985). The effect of marital disruption on child's attachment to parents. *Journal of Family Issues, 6*, 5–22.

Wilson, K. L., Zurcher, L. A., MacAdams, D. C., & Curtis, R. L. (1975). Stepfathers and stepchildren: An exploratory analysis from two national surveys. *Journal of Marriage and the Family, 37*, 526–536.

6

Social Exchange in Remarried Families

JEAN GILES-SIMS
Texas Christian University

Social exchange theory has emerged in sociology and social psychology as a distinct approach to understanding human relationships (Blau, 1964; Emerson, 1962, 1972, 1976; Homans, 1974; Nye, 1979; Thibaut & Kelley, 1959). The approach directs attention to the nature of the exchange relationship and how exchange processes lead to different outcomes. The unit of analysis is the social relationship rather than individual actors or their actions, and theoretical and empirical development focuses on the value of costs and rewards exchanged, the effect of alternative sources of rewards, the effects of balance/ imbalance in power and dependency on a relationship, and how exchange rules develop over time to govern the social exchange.

In this chapter, social exchange theory concepts and principles are applied to analyze the unique character of exchange in remarried families. Propositions are developed to predict specific aspects of: mate selection, power-dependency, the process of developing stepfamily norms, the impact of different exchange rules, and how changes in value and alternatives influence the degree of balance in remarried families. Whenever existing empirical evidence to support these propositions is available, it is applied, and finally, case studies from an exploratory study of 40 stepfamilies are used to illustrate exchange processes in balanced and imbalanced remarried families.

PRINCIPLES AND CONCEPTS OF SOCIAL EXCHANGE THEORY

In Nye's (1979) elaboration of exchange theory and the family, he states:

> The general principle or most general propositions of the theory under consideration is that humans avoid costly behavior and seek rewarding statuses, relationships, interaction, and feeling states to the end that their profits are maximized. Of course, in seeking rewards they voluntarily accept some costs;

likewise in avoiding costs, some rewards are foregone, but the person, group, or organization will choose that best outcome available, based on his/her/its perceptions of rewards and costs. (p. 12)

The statement emphasizes that humans can and do make rational choices to maximize profitable alternatives. However, exchange theorists disagree about the degree to which humans rationally assess the costs and rewards associated with each set of actions compared to those associated with alternative actions. Recent developments within exchange theory have modified the effects of rational choice (Cook & Emerson, 1978) and how exchange rules emerge as norms to govern long-term relationships (Emerson, 1976). These modifications indicate a tendency for social exchange theory to converge with role theory (Emerson, 1976; Goode, 1973).

Social exchange theory uses a vocabulary that often overlaps with a lay vocabulary. However, in some cases the meanings are very specific. It is necessary here to provide definitions and illustrations of several basic concepts that are used to aid analysis of exchange processes within remarried families.

Rewards refers to physical, social, or psychological experiences or statuses that a person enjoys or finds gratifying. A reward can be thought of as a socially administered positive reinforcement (Emerson, 1976). These differ somewhat by individual preference, but individuals learn what people in their culture generally define as gratifying and tend to develop a shared conception of rewards.

Costs include punishments and adverse stimuli encountered in a social transaction. *Rewards foregone* refers to rewards lost once a decision or choice is made or never experienced because of the choice made (Emerson, 1976) and to any experience that one must have when another experience would be more pleasurable. *Punishments* are any experiences defined as unpleasant by an individual. Again, costs may be individually defined, but people tend to develop a shared definition of what is costly within specific cultures.

Value refers to the magnitude of the reinforcement associated with different experiences. Rewards vary in value as do costs, depending in part on individual preference for that experience and also on the availability of similarly reinforcing experiences from alternative sources.

Value thresholds or standards of evaluating alternative sources of cost or rewards are called *comparison levels* (Thibaut & Kelley, 1959). This concept plays a crucial role in the evaluation of power or dependency in a social relationship.

Balance/imbalance in social relationships reflects the *power-dependency* aspect of social exchange. If the power of A over B is equal to the power of B over A, the relationship is balanced. In an unbalanced relationship either A or B may have greater power. The person with lesser power in an unbalanced relationship has greater dependency. Power is an aspect of the social relationship rather than an attribute of the actor (Emerson, 1962) and depends on both the value of what each receives from the other and the alternatives each person has to receive the same or similar valued rewards elsewhere.

Balanced relationships are *reciprocal* and imbalanced relationships are *nonreciprocal*. The tendency for long-term relationships to become reciprocal has been labeled the "norm of reciprocity" (Gouldner, 1960), but Emerson (1972) points out that the norm of reciprocity may simply reflect "widespread human recognition of contingencies intrinsic to all social exchange" (p. 61).

Over time, norms emerge for actions based on a history of repeated exchanges. These *exchange rules* emerge between participants in ongoing exchange relationships. Examples of exchange rules include rationality, group gain, altruism, equity, or competition (Emerson, 1976). When reciprocity and balance mark the exchange relationship, actors are likely operating under an *equity exchange rule*, but relationships may also be balanced under other rules such as *traditional marital* exchanges because of the value placed on the rewards of those traditional exchanges.

The focus of power-dependency and emerging norms within social exchange relationships opens up the possibility of looking at cohesion within social relationships and studying balancing operations—changes in the power-dependency relations that tend to reduce power advantage (Emerson, 1962). Also, these concepts provide the tools to analyze how exchanges become balanced or imbalanced, how they can be changed over time, and how norms may develop that modify the need for constant negotiation and assessment of costs and rewards for each interaction.

MATE SELECTION IN REMARRIAGE

Social exchange theory states that partners in an exchange will try to attain a balance so that rewards received compensate for the value of costs expended (Homans, 1974). This economic analysis is easy to understand in formal, business-like relationships, but increasingly this model has been applied to the investigation of intimate personal relationships. This kind of prediction does not necessarily suppose a deliberate and constant calculation of benefits and costs by parties in a relationship (Guttentag & Secord, 1983). This striving for balance may occur below the level of awareness, and people may act with only vaguely defined notions of expecting a return, but the norm of reciprocity (Gouldner, 1960) indicates both that those who give to others expect a return and that those who receive experience an obligation to return in similar kind.

In selecting mates, social exchange theory assumes that people weigh and evaluate the value of costs and rewards to be exchanged (Scanzoni, 1972;

Walster, Berscheid, & Walster, 1973). This approach also predicts that people will choose partners from relationships in which they are receiving benefits that they feel they deserve on the basis of their own contributions. Evidence of this process comes from the pattern of homogamy in marriage and from studies of the quality of relationships that vary in degree of equity. Partners in inequitable relationships experience distress. Those receiving less than fair or equitable rewards tend to feel angry and resentful, and those receiving more than equitable rewards feel guilty (Walster *et al.*, 1973).

Remarried partners tend to be less homogamous than first marrieds (Peters, 1976; Dean & Gurak, 1978), and male and female remarriage prospects differ considerably. The tendency for men to marry women younger than themselves increases as men get older, thus the age difference between partners is greater in remarriages than first marriages (Glick & Norton, 1977; Spanier & Glick, 1980). Given this pattern, men are more likely than women to remarry partners who have not been married before (U.S. Bureau of the Census, 1977), reducing the chances that divorced or widowed women will remarry at all. Furstenberg and Spanier's (1984) analysis of vital and health statistics indicates that ". . . about 1 in 8 American men eligible to remarry does so each year, compared to 1 in 25 women" (p. 38). The greatest differential exists for widowed men and women due to lower life expectancy rates of men and the norm of men marrying younger women, but still, divorced men remarry at a 60% higher rate than divorced women (Furstenberg & Spanier, 1984).

When women are in greater supply for remarriage than men, the exchange differs from what one would expect when men and women are relatively equally available. Guttentag and Secord's (1983) analysis of the economic exchanges at marriage during the late middle ages in Europe among Orthodox Jews and among early American settlers found that an oversupply of marriageable girls shifted the economic balance of marriage arrangements to become steadily more unfavorable for women compared to the relatively favorable conditions when there had been an oversupply of eligible men. Together this information suggests our first proposition:

> P_1 *The greater the oversupply of women eligible for remarriage, the more unfavorable the remarriage balance of costs and rewards will be to the female relative to that experienced by the male.*

To achieve and maintain an exchange relationship, people must offer desirable partners enough to entice them to enter into and maintain a relationship with them—to accept the costs of associating with them. A person will be less desirable if they present a higher cost-to-reward balance than other available partners. A person will accept a higher cost-to-reward balance in a partner when other possible partners are in short supply.

All people choosing marriage partners are affected by the overall sex ratio in the larger society at any given time, but remarrieds differ from first marrieds in at least two ways that figure into the usual evaluation of costs and rewards. Remarrieds have a prior marriage history that may leave them with ties to former partners and, in the majority of divorce cases, with obligations to support and/or parent children from that prior marriage. In the remarriage market, these obligations are likely to be interpreted as costs.

Former partners present the potential for financial costs and loyalty conflicts, both of which may affect the availability of resources to devote to the new marriage. The effect of ties to former partners on remarriage chances has not been adequately investigated separate from the issue of shared children, but the following proposition can be deduced from social exchange principles:

   P_2 *Within each gender group, the greater the costs associated with ties to former partners, the lower the remarriage rate and the greater the chances that new marriage partners will present a similar cost/reward balance.*

Males and females cannot be directly compared to each other solely on the basis of this variable because the sex ratio also directly influences rates of remarriage and chances of remarriage to particular partners.

Children present potential costs, including financial obligations and ongoing parenting responsibilities, and potential rewards, including the benefits associated with having children. The effect of these costs and rewards on any particular exchange relationship in remarriage depends on the value associated with each. For example, a person who brings children to a remarriage will be more attractive to a potential partner who highly values children than to one who does not value the rewards associated with children. Children are generally considered a reward in a marital relationship, but stepchildren present a complex mixture of costs and rewards. Thus, it is difficult to hypothesize about the effect of children on remarriage possibilities.

A number of studies have examined the effect of both presence of children and number of children on a mother's chances of remarriage. Some have found that those women with children when their last marriage ended were less likely to remarry and that the greater the number of children, the less the chance of remarriage (Becker, Landes, & Michael, 1977; Sweet, 1973; Thornton, 1977). Others have found that the number of children a woman has leads to no significant effect on remarriage probabilities (Hannan, Tuma, & Groeneveld, 1977; Wolf & MacDonald, 1979). Looking just at the presence of children and age of the woman, Koo and Suchindran (1980) have found that women who divorce before age 25 have a decreased likelihood of remarriage if they have children, for women divorcing between 25 and 34, there is no effect, and among women over 35 the presence of children increases the likelihood of remarriage. These discrepant findings suggest that other factors than mere presence of children and number of children determine the chances of remarriage for women. Those factors would include the value the new partner places on children, the availability of other potential partners, the value of costs and rewards presented by alternative partners, and the value of costs and rewards presented in exchange by new male partners.

Men's chances of remarriage also may depend on whether they have children in their custody. However, men tend to have more opportunities to remarry because of the sex ratio. Glick (1984) indicates that men who have custody of children tend to remarry quickly and that these men tend to be relatively affluent, thus able to attract potential partners. We need to know more about both chances of remarriage for parents and the characteristics of new partners. We suggest the following as a possible hypothesis for future research.

> P_3 *The effect of children on a person's chances of remarriage will depend on the level of costs associated with children from a prior marriage, the value the new partner places on children, the availability of other potential partners, and the value of costs and rewards presented in the exchange by the new partner.*

It is more likely that a balanced relationship will occur when each partner presents similar costs and rewards associated with children than when significantly higher costs are presented by one partner. However, heavy costs of one partner may be balanced in the exchange by the other partner's costs of a different nature. For example, women with children may be likely to marry men who also have children, or who really want children, or who are significantly older, or who have other characteristics that are perceived as costs on the remarriage market. Men with children from prior marriages are likely to experience similar conditions as women in mate selection, but the favorable sex ratio will modify the effect of costs and rewards associated with former marriage partners and children from prior marriages.

After people have chosen remarriage partners, the effects of the sex ratios and the level and types of costs and rewards partners exchange continues. Most importantly, these factors effect the power-dependency relationship between the remarried partners.

POWER AND DEPENDENCY IN REMARRIAGE

The person presenting the greater costs to a relationship or having the fewest alternative sources to attain desired rewards is most dependent on the relationship. Conversely, the person who provides the greatest rewards and who has the better chances of attaining desired rewards elsewhere has greater power (Emerson, 1962, Guttentag & Secord, 1983). Generally, these principles apply to remarriage relationships as they do to first marriages:

> P_4 *The greater the relative costs a person brings to remarriage, the greater the dependence on the relationship, and the higher the relative value of resources that one brings to a remarriage, the greater the power in the relationship.*

> P_5 *The greater the relative chances of attaining desired rewards outside the relationship, the lower the dependence and the greater the power in the relationship.*

Since men have a greater number of alternative partners for remarriage and are least likely to bring the costs of day-to-day responsibility for children from a prior marriage to a remarriage, these principles suggest that men will have greater power than women in remarriage. However, limited empirical evidence suggests this is not the case. In a study of conjugal power structure, Centers, Raven, and Rodrigues (1971) found that husbands in remarriages have lower power than husbands in first marriages. This does not imply that women in remarriages are dominant, but rather that they are more likely to be closer to their husbands in power than women in first marriages.

If men and women in remarriages share power more equally than couples in first marriages, we need to understand what factors associated with remarriage lead to this difference. Centers *et al.* (1971) suggested that prior divorce and remarriage might undermine people's confidence and make them more fearful of further marital failure, thus reducing their power. However, there is no reason to suggest that this is more likely to be true for men than for women. Still other factors need to be taken into consideration.

Guttentag and Secord (1983) have suggested that groups with unfavorable sex-ratio opportunities react to this situation in two basically different ways. On the one hand, women in a disadvantaged situation may emphasize the subordinate feminine role, do things specifically to please a man, and place greater importance on motherhood and homemaking. On the other hand, this same situation may lead other women to reduce their dependence on men and attempt to equalize the power relationship by seeking and maintaining outside resources that can be used as a basis for power in the relationship.

When women experience divorce, they face defining who they are as persons separate from a relationship, perhaps for the first time in their lives (Bohannan, 1970). The psychic costs to this process are higher and some women opt to remarry as soon as possible to end this process, while others who relish their new found independence are reluctant to give it up when they remarry (Goetting, 1982).

Together this information suggests that power and dependence in remarriage relationships depend in part on the balance in independent alternatives each partner has, and that these alternatives are not limited to chances for remarriage, but extend to the option to remain single and independent. Looking at the importance of which type of accommodation women choose to cope with the sex ratio problem, we can predict that:

> P_6 *The greater the independent resources and the greater the acceptance of the alternative of remaining single, the greater the power women will have in remarriage.*

The acceptance of remaining single for women depends on independent financial resources, feelings of competence to raise children alone, and general approval of the role of singlehood for adult women. Women who do not have independent financial resources, who do not feel competent to raise their children alone, or who do not accept the role of being single as a viable lifestyle for adult women are likely to try to remarry as soon as possible. If they find a potential partner who values the subordinate feminine role, they likely will remarry fairly quickly and establish a traditional marriage arrangement. Because of their dependence on being married, they may accept a marriage partner who presents higher costs than would a woman who is not dependent, or they may accept a relationship with a significant imbalance in power. Similarly, men who are very dependent on marriage as a lifestyle may accept a partner who presents higher costs than would a man who was not as dependent.

The dependence on marriage may be related to the ongoing parental responsibilities, although the direction of the effect that children have is not clear. Having children does provide an ongoing family, and single parents and children tend to form very tightly bound relationships (Keshet, 1980). But the role of being a single parent presents extraordinary financial and psychic demands. Therefore, the dependence of a divorced or widowed parent on remarriage depends on the level of costs relative to rewards in the single-parent status and the relative availability of other resources to meet the demands of that role. Friends, relatives, stable incomes, and the availability of sexual partners, as well as the value associated with family roles, contribute to the degree to which a single parent actively seeks remarriage and to the likelihood of attaining a remarriage relationship that is balanced in power and dependence.

Thus far, a market analysis of costs and rewards has been used as a basis for predicting outcomes in remarriage relationships. However, in ongoing relationships norms emerge that govern behavior, and increasing commitment modifies the effect of a strictly economic analysis.

DEVELOPING STEPFAMILY NORMS

To make predictions about behavior in long-term relationships, we need a theory that takes into account the effect of repetitive exchanges with specific partners. Recent modifications of social exchange theory that emphasize the effect of norms provide a basis for further refinement of explanations of social exchange in remarriage. Cook and Emerson (1978) have noted that:

> To the extent that specific social actors are drawn into repetitive exchange with one another (whether through reciprocal reinforcement in casual interpersonal attraction, through institutional arrangements such as marriage or long-term employment contracts, or through collectively or normatively enforced systems of obligation such as kinship systems), the market structure brought to the situation by economic analysis is imperfect and traditional microeconomic theory loses its precision. (p. 737)

Normative concerns operate to constrain the use of power in exchange networks where there is commitment to the partner and to the maintenance of the relationship. Norms governing behavior tend to emerge over time following periods of bargaining and negotiation. This suggests that:

> P_7 *The first year or two of remarriage will be marked by higher levels of bargaining and negotiation than subsequent years.*

Little research exists that examines how remarried families actually negotiate the definition of parental and stepparental roles (Cherlin, 1978; Furstenberg, 1980). However, research has consistently documented the lack of institutionalized norms for these roles (Cherlin, 1978; Duberman, 1975; Fast & Cain, 1966; Giles-Sims, 1984; Kompara, 1980; Messinger, 1976; Rallings, 1976; Visher & Visher, 1979), the stress associated with conflicting, ambiguous norms (Cherlin, 1978; Visher & Visher, 1979), and low value consensus (Pasley, Ihinger-Tallman, & Coleman, 1984).

Institutionalized roles offer the benefits of clear expectations, opportunities to learn how to play those roles through the experience of persons in them and a clear indication of what consequences result from failure to meet the expectations. In addition, when people perceive their role expectations clearly, they are likely to perform them better and feel better about themselves, which in turn influences the satisfaction of other people in the family (Burr, Leigh, Day, & Constantine, 1979). Thus, the convergence of role theory and social exchange theory leads to the following predictions:

> P_8 *The greater the shared definition of norms for stepfamily roles, the greater will be the individual feelings of well-being.*

Cohesion is also problematic when one or both remarriage partners experience value conflict or the potential for value conflict in a relationship (Emerson, 1972). Thus,

> P_9 *The greater the shared definition of norms and values within the stepfamily, the greater will be the stepfamily cohesion.*

The emergence of consistently shared norms and value consensus also interacts with other factors of the exchange relationship to influence individual and relationship satisfaction. If one person's comparison level of alternatives differs from the other person's because they have greater availability or alternative sources of rewards, then the point at which they will consider leaving the relationship also differs (Emerson, 1976). Thus,

> P_{10} *Persons with greater alternatives and greater power will be more likely to seek alternatives to the relationship at a higher overall level of value consensus than persons with fewer alternatives. Less-powerful persons with fewer alternatives will tolerate a relationship with lower overall value consensus longer than more powerful persons because the available alternatives are less attractive.*

However, over time the value of rewards provided within the stepfamily changes compared to the perceived value of rewards of alternative relationships. Commitment to the relationship also tends to increase the perceived value of costs associated with leaving and seeking a new relationship. Together, these theoretical propositions cannot be adequately addressed with existing empirical research, but they do suggest important areas for further research.

Independent of norms for particular stepfamily roles, remarried couples as well as first-married couples tend to develop normative definitions that cover the exchange relationship based on their ideas about desired family roles and distribution of resources among those roles. Variations in these exchange rules also affect outcomes in remarried families.

EXCHANGE RULES IN REMARRIAGE

An *exchange rule* is a normative definition of a situation that forms among or is adopted by participants in exchange relationships (Emerson, 1976). Exchange rules tend to emerge in repeated exchange relationships much as do norms for particular roles. But exchange rules focus specifically on the rules that govern the exchange relationship. Meeker (1971) contributed the original idea of exchange rules to explain how some exchange relationships varied from the strictly economic model. Some examples of exchange rules include rationality, group gain, altruism, competition, reciprocity, and status consistency (Emerson, 1976).

These last two examples have features in common with variation in contemporary marital structures. General role expectations for the traditional relationship establish a basis for exchange by allocating the provider role to the husband who receives in exchange for financial support the expressive support of his wife and the instrumental tasks of child and home care. Thus, the traditional marriage relationship exchange rules emphasize maintaining consistency with traditional status roles of males and females in society and in marriage.

On the other hand, in less-traditional relationships, sometimes called "equal partner" (Scanzoni & Scanzoni, 1981) or "parallel" (Ross, Mirowsky, & Huber, 1983), partners exchange both instrumental and expressive rewards and emphasize the need for equity and reciprocity in male–female relationships and marriage. If an equity exchange rule is operating between two people, then one cannot try to maximize his/her own gain at the expense of loss to the other (Emerson, 1976).

Economic anthropologists report that reciprocity or equity is the most common rule operating in long-term close kinship relationships (Emerson, 1976). But equity, and possibly altruism, is most likely to emerge as an exchange rule when parties enjoy a balance of power.

As Guttentag and Secord (1983) have noted, the overall imbalance of power that results from the sex ratio leads women as a lower power group to choose between two basically different ways of coping, pursuing very traditional feminine roles or seeking and maintaining outside resources to balance the greater alternatives available to males.

This distinction between traditional exchange rules and equity exchange rules at this point is merely categorical definition. No existing research on remarriage either classifies remarrieds on the basis of these exchange rules or compares outcomes in these different types of remarried families. But we can glean some hints of what to expect from research on married couples in general. Ross *et al.* (1983) found the greatest overall well-being in "parallel" marriages, but "traditional" marriages closely approached the "parallels," and the lowest well-being was found in two "transitional" types in which there was inconsistency between desired marital structure and that which they actually had. Thus, we could predict that:

> P_{11} *The greater the degree of consistency between desired exchange relationships and actual exchange rules, the greater the well-being of individuals and the greater the cohesion of the remarried family.*

Remarried people vary in their ideas about the structure of marriage as do first marrieds, but some of the unique characteristics of remarried families influence the degree to which the remarried family is able to attain consistency with their desired family structure. The ongoing parental obligations to parent and/or support children from prior marriages directly affects this possibility. Women may continue to work following remarriage, even though they do not wish to, either because they need to help support their own children or because their husbands are financially contributing to the support of children in other households. On the other hand, remarried women may continue to work following remarriage because they are reluctant to give up the contributions that outside resources make to balancing the power relationship within the marriage or simply because they choose this more independent role for intrinsic reasons. In some cases their own expectations will not be consistent with those of their husbands. If the inconsistency problem is directly identified with the remarriage situation, then resentment is likely to be directly focused on the costs associated with the obligations brought into the relationship from the prior marriage. For example, second wives may resent working to help offset money going to support a former wife or children, and remarried men may resent financial obligations to support children brought into the relationship from a wife's prior marriage.

Remarried people operating under a traditional exchange rule who are financially able to have the husband be the primary provider are less likely to experience problems with men taking over financial responsibilities of a stepchild than those in a remarriage with traditional exchange rules who are forced into dual-earner roles because of prior obligations. Remarriages operating under equity exchange rules are likely to experience problems primarily if the partner with the greater power begins to perceive that the level of rewards being received is approaching his/her comparison level of alternatives. Remarriages operating under either traditional exchange rules or equity exchange rules may be balanced because the value placed on the costs and rewards received shifts depending on the preferred marital structure. When A is approximately as dependent on B as the reverse, balance occurs, but the degree of balance changes if changes occur in the value of costs and rewards offered both in this relationship and in alternative ones. Looking at these principles of social exchange theory opens up the possibility of predicting how and why balanced or imbalanced relationships change over time.

Balanced/Imbalanced Remarriage Exchanges

Marriage relationships virtually require some degree of mutual dependence, making it more or less imperative that each partner be able to influence the other's actions to some degree. Marital power is the degree to which a partner can both influence the partner's actions and act without constraint from that partner. The power of A over B in a marital exchange equals the dependence of B on A in a balanced exchange. Balanced relationships tend to be reciprocal; imbalanced relationships are nonreciprocal, and social relationships may be balanced in power and dependency at different levels (Emerson, 1962). Balance does not neutralize power, and as was pointed out above, both traditional- and equity-type marriages may be balanced because of the degree of interdependence and the value placed on rewards received under each exchange rule compared to the value of costs expended.

Imbalanced relationships tend to be unstable because partners each experience distress. Those receiving less than fair rewards tend to feel angry and resentful, and those receiving more than fair rewards feel guilty (Walster *et al.*, 1973). They either break down because the cost/reward balance has reached the subsistence level for one person and the comparison level indicates available alternatives or because the relationship becomes more balanced.

Different patterns of exchange are expected to occur in stepfather, stepmother, and stepfather–stepmother families (three different types of remarriages). These patterns vary primarily with the amount of obligation and contact with children from prior marriages, and the degree of balance in the marriage will depend in part on the level and value of costs and rewards presented in these three types of remarriages.

P_{12} *The greater the similarity in level and value of costs and rewards associated with children from prior marriages, the greater will be the balance in a remarriage.*

Based on this prediction, we expect that balance will be easiest to attain in a stepfather–stepmother remarriage. But, balance can also be attained in remarriages where obligations to residential stepchildren are similar in level and value to other costs presented by the stepparent (e.g., obligations to nonresidential stepchildren).

Theoretically, a parent who brings the costs of children from a prior marriage to a remarriage will accept similar levels of costs in a potential partner or will present higher overall rewards or alternative sources of rewards to balance a relationship. But the stepfamily exchange relationship may also become balanced in other ways.

P_{13} *The greater the value the stepparent has for the parenting role, the lower the perceived value of costs associated with having children and the greater the possibility of balance in the exchange.*

P_{14} *The greater the alternative sources for attaining similar levels of rewards outside the remarriage relationship, the lower will be the dependence of the parent on the stepparent and the lower will be the need for costs associated with children to be balanced by other similar levels of costs in order for a relationship to become balanced.*

Also,

> P_{15} *The greater the rewards presented to the stepparent for efforts to meet stepparenting obligations, the greater will be the likelihood of attaining balance in a relationship.*

A relationship in which a parent (A) has greater power than a stepparent (B) can become more balanced through any of four basic types of changes in values or alternatives: (1) if B reduces motivational investment in goals mediated by A; (2) if B cultivates alternative sources for gratification of those goals; (3) if A increases motivational investment in goals mediated by B; or (4) if A is denied alternative sources for achieving those goals (Emerson, 1962). These principles can be applied to develop suggestions for balancing operations in remarriage relationships that suffer because of a power imbalance.

For example, Keshet (1980) reports that single parents and their children often form a tightly bound system and exclude the stepparent from that system. If the stepparent wants both access to the family system and to the role of parent to the children, and their partner blocks that access, an imbalance occurs in the dyadic power. This imbalance could be reduced (1) by the stepparent reducing his/her desire for the parent role; (2) by the stepparent seeking alternative sources for this type of gratification; (3) by the parent providing the stepparent more access, credit, or status in the parental role; or (4) by the parent becoming more dependent on the stepparent because of changes in the chances of attaining alternative sources of rewards. The first and third options represent changes in values and the second and fourth changes in alternatives.

We expect that remarriage exchange relationships will become more balanced over time, but the chances of this happening depend on a number of factors. We expect that stepparental investment in the children will increase over time neutralizing the emphasis on costs, and that parents will increase the level of rewards the stepparent receives for their efforts. It follows that these rewards will increasingly outweigh the value of the costs. We also expect that the costs of seeking alternative relationships will increase over time, thus neutralizing the effect of potential alternative sources of rewards. Another important possibility includes change in the parent's and/or stepparent's relationship with children which in turn may affect the remarriage relationship. Children are prominent actors in remarried families, and their role in relation to remarriage balance has never been adequately addressed. In those cases in which changes do not lead to more balanced relationships over time, we expect dissatisfaction with the relationship and an increase in chances of dissolution.

To illustrate the importance of balance in remarriage exchanges, we need to explore the exchange rules couples have incorporated into their marital relationship, the relative balance in the value of costs and rewards present in the remarriage relative to those available elsewhere, and how these have changed over time. To begin this effort, we present and briefly analyze case studies from an exploratory study of remarriage exchange relationships.

CASE STUDIES OF REMARRIED FAMILIES

The case studies presented below are from an in-depth interview study of one or both adult partners in 40 remarriages, including at least one child under 18 from a prior marriage. Subjects were recruited from a pool of 76 stepfamilies identified by a random sample telephone survey of 1009 households in 1983-1984 in a Southwestern urban area. Interviews included both structured questionnaires and semi-structured interviews which were taped and transcribed. In the interviews subjects were asked questions from an outline of nine different topics: (1) definition of their family and preferred family structure; (2) the history of their relationship from 6 months prior to the remarriage to the present time (of the study); (3) the role of parents and stepparents; (4) emotional trust between parents and children; (5) money and children; (6) conflict between family members; (7) relationships with ex-spouses; (8) goals for their relationship and progress toward goals; and (9) rewards of the stepfamily structure.

Preliminary analysis of these in-depth interviews has indicated support for several social exchange propositions, particularly those linking balance in the relationship to overall satisfaction and those that focus on consistency between preferred family structure and actual family structure. Short descriptions of five different cases help illustrate these processes.

DAVE AND MARY

Dave and Mary married after Dave's divorce. His two children who had been living with Dave and his parents came to live with them. Mary, who was 5 years younger than Dave and never married before, described their life during the 6 months prior to their marriage:

> It was very loving, very warm feeling, very family-close-knit type thing. I already did feel like part of the family. I already did have some responsibility for the children, and I cared and did a lot for him to help him out. I felt like I was more rewarded at that time than I do now.

Dave and Mary had a baby after 2 years, but now after 4 years of marriage she is seriously considering a divorce because:

I feel like I've had all the responsibility and I'm tired, basically. It's not that I don't love the two other kids or him, it's just that you get tired from just taking everything—discipline, school, everything—making sure that they have everything that they need, totally—and him not taking part.

Dave brought the costs of two children into the marriage, and Mary was willing to accept those costs. At first their relationship seemed balanced because she valued children and the marital role, but over time Dave did not take a part in the child rearing and did not provide Mary with the rewards of appreciation. He also increasingly spent evenings and weekends on other activities outside the family. When we interviewed Mary, she planned to file for divorce and custody of the baby, returning his two children to him. She has a fulltime professional job and views being a single parent as preferable to the costs of being a stepmother and wife without any significant help or rewards. Her comparison level provided an alternative to an unsatisfactory marriage.

TIM AND BEVERLY

In another stepmother family, we found a similar basic structure, but a very different social-exchange process. Tim had his two children alone with him for 6 months before he married Beverly, who was 2 years younger and divorced but without children. She recalls how she felt when Tim told her he was getting the kids.

I can remember that he called and said that Sheila wanted him to take the kids. He was scared to tell me. We were dating and he was scared to tell me, but I said it was great. I was surprised, but I realized that they were his kids and how he felt about them. I was glad for him. I really didn't give it that much thought. I loved him enough that if that was what it took, then I would gladly take them. There have been times when I wished that things were different—when I had to come home because there were children, which I hadn't been used to doing. There were times when I wished that things could be a little easier.

Despite her realization of difficulty, Beverly feels positive about her marriage and about the children. Tim values her role in relation to the children and also participates in their upbringing. They had an 8-month-old baby at the time of the interview. When asked whether any one parent had more say over decisions about the children, she responded:

On the day-to-day activities—I don't think so. On anything important, it's usually discussed anyway, unless it's something that comes up without the opportunity to do something.

He indicated his respect for her and his affirmation when asked if there were instances when he was upset about how she made decisions regarding his children:

Perhaps at first . . . she had never really been around children. I knew she was expecting more out of them than they were really capable of. They weren't mature enough to do that. I let her go ahead and learn on her own. I might mention it to her later, but I would let her deal with the children.

She valued his support and in turn showed her appreciation:

He was excellent. Sometime I'd say "Hey, I don't think I handled that well." And he would say, "Yes, I know." He was excellent. He has not said, these are my kids and you do this and such.

Beverly continued to work at her executive secretary position and was planning a small business venture that provided her with an alternative to the relationship, but she had no interest in pursuing alternatives. She had come to strongly value her stepchildren for themselves and the support and strong appreciation she received from her husband. Together they described feelings of security, love, and sharing within their family. Tim's dependence on Beverly as a stepmother, her choice to fill that role in favor of other alternatives, and the consistency between an equity exchange rule and actual practice contributed to their overall balanced relationship.

WAYNE AND CAROL

Eighteen months prior to our interview, Wayne had married Carol who was 5 years older than himself and became a stepfather to her 10-year-old son. Wayne had been a full-time college student the preceding year and was about to graduate. During that year, he took responsibility for his stepson after school while his wife worked. Intense conflict marked their relationship, and they had become violent with each other on a few occasions. Wayne found establishing a parental role with his stepson stressful, partially because he felt blocked by Carol. He expressed both his frustrations and his doubts about the relationship continuing.

From what I've seen, I know this about myself, it takes people a while to get used to situations. You know, a person has grown up with their father, they loved their father pretty much. But the way it is now, he had a strong bond with his father. He doesn't need me. He has his mother and his father. I, at this point, am only a hassle to him, so to speak. He could do very well without me being here. But I figure as time goes on, he's ten and in a couple more years, he'll begin to see a little over a time period that I'm not just somebody to give him a hard time, I'm going to be fair and as long as I'm fair with him, I feel that sooner or later, he's going to have to give in a little bit, start cutting me some slack, too. But I figure, if we are not to the point within two years where we can get along with one another without making others miserable, I would consider other alternatives. If you and your wife are working on it together, then things should be changing in a couple of years. If they are not, then either your wife's not helping you or you are being a jerk or something. That's what I say, if in two years, things haven't changed to a certain extent, and your wife is still not on your side then you may as well quit because you're never going to go anywhere with it.

Carol had a full-time job in sales to provide alternative financial support, but their age difference meant that Wayne could more easily find alternative relationship partners. Carol depended on the parental responsibility Wayne provided but failed to reward him for it. Wayne depended on Carol to support him so that he could finish college, but he was soon to graduate and had been offered a well-paying position in sales. Their mutual dependence had provided some balance to their relationship despite the conflicts, but for balance to continue after Wayne's alternatives are realized would require a significant increase in the rewards he receives in the relationship from both Carol and the child.

SHARON AND CHUCK

In contrast, Sharon and Chuck strongly believe that their relationship will continue, partly because of the adjustment process they experienced, including many discussions about expectations for stepparents and children and their attempts to attain an equitable exchange relationship. Sharon and Chuck married in their mid-thirties, 7 years prior to the interview. Sharon, who is 3 years younger, had two children from a prior marriage and Chuck's two children from his prior marriage visit frequently, spending about 2 months total time with them each year. Sharon and Chuck both work full-time and share parenting and household responsibilities. When asked how she and Chuck work out their relationships with the two different sets of kids, Sharon indicated:

> This is something that we have discussed. As long as they live in our home, they will be as much a part of this family as the other two. I'll never be able to love them to the degree that I love my two kids, but when they are all four together there are no differences. I'm sure there is a difference for Chuck, too, but as long as he is fair and respects and loves my children, I can accept that. One thing I feel very strongly about is equality—whatever we do for one, we do for all four. If we could not make a joint decision about his kids, I would go along with his decision. If I could not live with what he decided about my kids, he would probably go my way, but we have never reached that point. I think it has to be the natural parent's making the ultimate decision. I respect his decisions. Usually if I don't agree, I'll tell him and we try to work around it. We always manage to get to a decision we can both be happy with.

Sharon and Chuck share parenting and financial responsibility for the household, and both are committed to continuing their relationship. The overall well-being of both partners and cohesion within the stepfamily were among the best of all the remarried families interviewed. However, Sharon reported that during the first 2 years they had to constantly negotiate day-to-day challenges. At the time of the interview, the need for that kind of bargaining had decreased considerably.

VIRGINIA AND JIM

Whereas, Sharon and Chuck share parenting and provide for each other's children, Virginia and Jim had divided up the responsibilities as a way to achieve an acceptable balance in their marriage. Jim, a well-paid professional, married Virginia, who is 11 years younger, 4 years before the interview. Each of them had three children from prior marriages. Virginia's three lived with them full-time and Jim's part-time. Trial and error in their adjustment process lead them to defining each natural parent as responsible for his/her own children.

> The first six months were terrible, the second six months were bad but not as terrible. With each year that follows, things begin to be more adjusted. There was some give and take, and boundaries were set and [there was] more clear understanding of what was acceptable. We did go for counseling. I don't know if we could have made it without it. Because of counseling, we try to discipline and take care of our own children.

One of the problems that Jim and Virginia have faced is that sometimes Virginia, who is in a much lower paying job and receives child support infrequently, sometimes has to ask Jim for help. She feels guilty about this because it is inconsistent with their basic exchange rule. At these times, she is more dependent on Jim than is comfortable for her, and this disrupts the balance in their relationship.

SUMMARY

In this paper I have applied abstract exchange principles to try to explain processes of mate selection in second (and subsequent) marriages as well as patterns of power and dependence, norm formation, and the effects of variation in exchange rules on stepfamily interaction. Several testable hypotheses have been discussed and will be briefly summarized here.

Remarriages are less homogamous than first marriages, particularly in age. Social exchange theory predicts that the sex ratio which favors males in the search for new partners will lead to a higher rate of remarriage for males and a greater chance of remarrying younger and never-married partners.

Their more advantaged positions (because of greater demand and more alternative opportunities) also means that men may be able to establish a more favorable balance of costs and rewards in remarriage than women.

The cost and rewards of children from prior marriages contributes to the overall assessment of new relationships. The specific effect will depend on the level of costs associated with those children, the value the new partner holds of children, and the value and availability of alternatives compared to the value of costs and rewards in the new relationship.

The greater the relative costs a person brings to a relationship, the lower the degree of power and the greater the dependence on that relationship. In the remarriage market men have greater choice of potential alternative partners and are also more likely to have independent means of financial support which may mean lower dependence on remarriage among men than women, although other factors need to be taken into consideration. Men may be dependent on a new relationship in the expressive area or in some cases for a substitute in the mother role. Women may also have independent alternatives to remarriage either through alternative partners or acceptance of remaining single. In each case, greater outside alternatives will lead to lower dependence at least in the initial stages of the formation of a remarriage relationship.

Remarriages are marked by adjustment periods with high levels of bargaining and negotiation, but, over time, shared values and shared definitions of norms tend to emerge and contribute to individual well-being and overall cohesion. However, when problems in adjustment are significant, we expect that those persons with greater power and less dependence will seek alternatives to the remarriage sooner than those remarried persons who are more dependent. The more available and rewarding the alternatives, the more likely people experiencing problems in the remarriage will leave the remarriage.

Strict economic assessments lead to better prediction for ad hoc groups or new exchange relationships than for more established relationships. This is because, over time, commitment diminishes the impact of social-exchange processes, and also because exchange rules tend to develop, thus guiding the interaction. People will think less about whether they are getting a fair deal in macro-economic terms after they have made a firm commitment. However, assessment continues of the degree to which their actual relationship meets their expectations for a satisfying relationship. The greater the similarity in level and value of costs and rewards brought into the relationship, the greater will be the chance the marriage exchange will be balanced, and those with higher value consensus are more likely to experience relationship satisfaction. We expect that more balanced relationships are more likely to continue and be satisfying than imbalanced ones. This was illustrated with the case studies presented.

Of course, other factors influence the chances of high satisfaction in remarriage than those presented here, particularly characteristics of the exchange relationship with children. These and other issues require much more extensive exploration. Hopefully, the preliminary attempt to utilize this framework to develop propositions presented here will motivate other researchers to address all of these issues. However, there are many theoretical and methodological issues that need to be developed further before direct application can be successful.

It is difficult to objectively assess the value of costs and rewards presented in a remarriage exchange and to compare them to those available from alternative sources. Since the value of different conditions brought to the remarriage (e.g., children, relationships with former spouses) are quite subjective, the problem of measuring and comparing these values is considerable. Emerson (1972) suggests a direct behavioral solution to this measurement problem. If partners A and B are in a balanced relationship, direct observation indicates that initiations by A and B in experimental situations are equally probable. Readiness to and ease of leaving a relationship and ability to attain goals in the relationship are other behavioral indicators that can be used to assess degree of balance in power. If power is unbalanced in B's favor, A will initiate more and vice versa. Also, if A has more power than B, A will be able to leave a relationship easier, and if A wishes to stay, he/she will be able to achieve his/her own goals within the relationship more often than B. These experimental findings suggest that power could be determined by observing whether A, over time, offers respect, appreciation, and ego boosts to B more often than the reverse, and whether A seeks alternative sources of gratification more frequently than B. Direct observation of behavior with standardized coding criteria represents a strong research model.

However, the kind of self-report offered in the case studies presented here indicates that marriage partners are quite aware, and can indicate a subjective assessment, of both power and dependence and the degree of balance/imbalance in a relationship. Further research could usefully address the degree to which partners share these subjective assessments and also how assessments of parent–child exchanges affect the remarriage relationship.

Findings on what types of exchange processes lead to greater balance, greater consistency in norms and values, and the development of exchange rules that match expectations would be useful in predicting problems in remarriage. In addition, we need to focus research on the development of remarried families to determine what social factors influence changes in commitment over time, in values of costs and rewards associated with new partners and children, and in the costs of seeking alternative relationships. The more we can specify the processes that lead remarriages to become balanced and imbalanced, the greater will be our chances of both predicting trouble in remarriage and developing ways to alleviate those problems.

ACKNOWLEDGMENTS

Preparation of this chapter was supported by a grant from the Texas Christian University Research Fund. The author wishes to thank Cynthia Bruss for her assistance in this research.

REFERENCES

Becker, G. S., Landes, E. M., & Michael, R. T. (1977). An economic analysis of marital instability. *Journal of Political Economy, 85*, 1141–1187.

Blau, P. (1964). *Exchange and power in social life.* New York: Wiley.

Bohannan, P. (1970). *Divorce and after.* Garden City, NY: Doubleday.

Burr, W., Leigh, G. K., Day, R., & Constantine, J. (1979). Symbolic interaction and the family. In W. R. Burr, R. Hill, F. I. Nye, & I. L. Reiss (Eds.), *Contemporary theories about the family* (pp. 42–111). New York: Free Press.

Centers, R., Raven, B., & Rodrigues, A. (1971). Conjugal power structure: A re-examination. *American Sociological Review, 36*, 264–278.

Cherlin, A. (1978). Remarriage as an incomplete institution. *American Journal of Sociology, 84*(3), 634–650.

Cook, D., & Emerson, R. (1978). Power, equity and commitment in exchange networks. *American Sociological Review, 43*, 721–739.

Dean, G., & Gurak, D. T. (1978). Marital homogamy the second time around. *Journal of Marriage and the Family, 40*, 559–570.

Duberman, L. (1975). *The reconstituted family: A study of remarried couples and their children.* Chicago: Nelson-Hall.

Emerson, R. (1962). Power-dependence relations. *American Sociological Review, 27*, 31–41.

Emerson, R. (1972). Exchange theory: Part I. A psychological basis for social exchange. In J. Berger, M. Zelditch, & B. Anderson (Eds.), *Sociological theories in progress* (pp. 38–57). New York: Houghton Mifflin Co.

Emerson, R. (1976). Social exchange theory. In A. Inkeles, J. Coleman, & N. Smelser (Eds.), *Annual Review of Sociology* (pp. 335–362). Palo Alto: Annual Reviews, Inc.

Fast, I., & Cain, A. C. (1966). The stepparent role: Potential for disturbances in family functioning. *American Journal of Orthopsychiatry, 36*, 485–491.

Furstenberg, F. F., Jr. (1980). Reflections on remarriage. *Journal of Family Issues, 1*, 443–453.

Furstenberg, F. F., Jr., & Spanier, G. (1984). *Recycling the family.* Beverly Hills, CA: Sage.

Geotting, A. (1982). The six stations of remarriage: Developmental tasks of remarriage after divorce. *Family Relations, 31*, 213–222.

Giles-Sims, J. (1984). The stepparent role: Expectations, behavior, and sanctions. *Journal of Family Issues, 5*, 116–130.

Glick, P. C. (1984). Marriage, divorce and living arrangements: Prospective changes. *Journal of Family Issues, 5*, 7–26.

Glick, P. C., & Norton, A. I. (1977). Marrying, divorcing, and living together in the U. S. today. *Population Bulletin, 32*(5), 3–39.

Goode, W. J. (1973). *Explorations in social theory.* New York: Oxford University Press.

Gouldner, A. W. (1960). The norm of reciprocity. *American Sociological Review, 25*, 161–178.

Guttentag, M., & Secord, P. F. (1983). *Too many women?* Beverly Hills, CA: Sage.

Hannan, M. T., Tuma, N. B., & Groeneveld, L. P. (1977). Income and marital events: Evidence from an income-maintenance experiment. *American Journal of Sociology, 82*, 1186–1211.

Homans, G. (1974). *Social behavior: Its elementary forms.* New York: Harcourt Brace Jovanovich.

Keshet, J. K. (1980). From separation to stepfamily. *Journal of Family Issues, 1*(4), 517–532.

Kompara, D. R. (1980). Difficulties in the socialization process of stepparenting. *Family Relations, 29*, 69–73.

Koo, H. P., & Suchindran, C. M. (1980). Effects of children on women's remarriage prospects. *Journal of Family Issues, 1*, 497–515.

Meeker, B. F. (1971). Decisions and exchange. *American Sociological Review, 36*, 485–495.

Messenger, L. (1976). Remarriage between divorced people with children from previous marriages: A proposal for preparation for remarriage. *Journal of Marriage and Family Counseling, 2*, 193–200.

Nye, F. I. (1979). Choice, exchange, and the family. In W. R. Burr, R. Hill, F. I. Nye, & I. L. Reiss (Eds.), *Contemporary theories about the family* (pp. 1–41). New York: Free Press.

Pasley, K., Ihinger-Tallman, M., & Coleman, C. (1984). Consensus styles among happy and unhappy remarried couples. *Family Relations, 33*, 451–457.

Peters, J. F. (1976). A comparison of mate selection and marriage in the first and second marriages in a selected sample of the remarried divorced. *Journal of Comparative Family Studies, 7*, 483–491.

Rallings, E. M. (1976). The special role of stepfather. *The Family Coordinator, 25*, 445–449.

Ross, C. E., Mirowsky, J., & Huber, J. (1983). Marriage patterns and depression. *American Sociological Review, 48*, 809–823.

Scanzoni, J. (1972). *Sexual bargaining.* Englewood Cliffs, NJ: Prentice-Hall.

Scanzoni, L. D., & Scanzoni, J. (1981). *Men, women, and change.* New York: McGraw-Hill.

Spanier, G. B., & Glick, P. C. (1980). Paths to remarriage. *Journal of Divorce, 3*, 283–298.

Sweet, J. A. (1973). Differentials in remarriage probabilities. Working Paper 73-29. Madison, WI: Center for Demography and Ecology.

Thibaut, J., & Kelley, H. (1959). *The social psychology of groups.* New York: Wiley.

Thornton, A. (1977). Decomposing the re-marriage process. *Population Studies, 31*, 383–392.

United States Bureau of the Census (1977). Current population reports, Series P-20, No. 312. Marriage, divorce, widowhood, and remarriage by family characteristics: June, 1975. Washington, DC: U. S. Government Printing Office.

Visher, E. B., & Visher, J. S. (1979). *Stepfamilies: A guide to working with stepparents and stepchildren.* New York: Brunner/Mazel.

Walster, E., Berscheid, E., & Walster, G. W. (1973). New directions in equity research. *Journal of Personality and Social Psychology, 25*, 151–176.

Wolf, W. C., & MacDonald, M. M. (1979). The earning of men and remarriage. *Demography, 16*, 389–399.

7

Sibling and Stepsibling Bonding in Stepfamilies

MARILYN IHINGER-TALLMAN
Washington State University

INTRODUCTION

One of the frequent laments of students of child development and socialization is that there are few systematic studies of sibling behavior. This lacuna is even more evident when we consider the growing phenomena of stepsibling interaction, where data are virtually nonexistent. This essay is an attempt to establish a framework within which to begin considering research in this area. It sets forth the beginnings of a theory that tries to explain the processes whereby: (1) sibling bonding is affected by the divorce and subsequent remarriage of a parent or parents, and (2) sibling bonding develops or fails to develop between previously unrelated children in a stepfamily.

My intent here is to establish the criteria for explaining how sibling bonds are formed, how they are affected by a parental decision to divorce, and how children bond with new stepsiblings upon parental remarriage. Such a conceptualization is important, for if Dunn (1983) is correct in saying that sibling connections are relevant to the development of a sense of self, an essential first step is to identify and describe the dynamics of sibling attachment—before studying the relationship between such attachment and the development of a sense of self.

Bank and Kahn (1975; 1982) are among the few contributors to the socialization literature who have focused on the sibling as a socializing agent. They note, in accord with Dunn (1983), that siblings contribute to one another's identity formation. Siblings also serve as defenders/protectors of one another; they interpret the outside world to each other, and they teach each other about equity, coalition formation, and the processes of bargaining and negotiation. Siblings mutually regulate each other's behavior and offer direct services, such as teaching skills, serving as a buffer against parents, and lending money and other material goods (Bank & Kahn, 1975; Schvaneveldt & Ihinger, 1979).

As a sub-group within the family, siblings also help establish and maintain family norms. They are key contributors to the development of a family culture, and they help write family "history." Siblings are important to intergenerational continuity and thus have an impact on the larger kin system. In matrilineal societies for example, siblings play a key role with uncles holding a position of ultimate authority in the lives of their sisters' children (Hunter College Women's Studies Collective, 1983). Sororate and Levirate custom in "primitive" societies means the replacement of a "defunct wife by her sister or other female kin" or the "inheritance of a dead man's wife by his brother or other male kin" (Stephens, 1963, p. 194). In 19th-century English and American novels aunts are depicted as playing key socialization roles (see, for example, the novels of Jane Austen, Louisa May Alcott, and Edith Wharton). Social historians also have written of the close friendships that existed between mothers and daughters, female cousins, and sisters in 19th century America. Smith-Rosenberg (1983) writes,

> . . . the extended female network—a daughter's close ties with her own sisters, cousins, and aunts—may well have permitted a diffusion and a relaxation of mother–daughter identification and so have aided a daughter in her struggle for identity and autonomy. (p. 420)

The Scheme of Things: Borrowing for Theory-Building

One cannot understand the intimate relationships between a child and his or her siblings without first understanding how the conditions surrounding the family affect interaction between siblings and define each family's particular experience (Garbarino, 1982). Bronfenbrenner's (1979) ecological model permits an examination of both family and community factors and it was used as a guide for the present theoretical effort. The ecological model conceptualizes a set of interlocking social structures. The individual organism is embedded in these structures which overlap and interact, and which help explain "how the individual develops interactively with the immediate social environment and how aspects of the larger social context affect what goes on in the individual's immediate settings" (Garbarino, 1982, p. 21). Bronfenbrenner (1979) labels these structures the *microsystem* (the actual setting in which the child experiences reality), the *mesosystem* (relationships, or links between settings, i.e., between microsystems) and the *exosystem* (situations having impact on a child's development but in which the child does not actually play a direct role). Finally, the *macrosystem* is the larger social structure in which the other three are embedded—the "broad ideological and institutional patterns of a particular culture or subculture" (Garbarino, 1982, p. 24).

The theory to be developed below places siblings within this four-tiered framework. Specific dimensions of the family microsystem within which siblings, stepsiblings, and halfsiblings are embedded and in which their reality is created are discussed. While the microsystem level is where most of our attention is focused, the theory also takes into account conditions in the mesosystem, exosystem, and macrosystem which affect sibling bonding. Dimensions of the mesosystem that are considered important include "quasi-kin"[1] relationships, home–school relationships, and home–"other" parent's home relationships. Exosystem influences include the legal system, especially adjudication processes and norms of custody and visitation assignment, while macrosystem norms and values create an accepting environment in which stepfamilies function, or an unaccepting one that brings shame and/or embarrassment to children because their (step)family is atypical.

Structural variables, however, are not sufficient to establish the elements necessary for sibling interaction. Differences in personality also play a critical role in influencing these processes (Elder, in press). The discussion that follows is organized to integrate Bronfenbrenner's four structures within a framework that also takes into account personality influences. My goal is to specify the variables, relationships, and conditions that predict a specific set of behavioral outcomes, manifest as positive or negative sibling/stepsibling relationships.

In summary, the theory proposed here attempts to explain how and why sibling and/or stepsibling bonds develop—or fail to develop. The focus is on the formation of new bonds as well as on delineating how established sibling bonds change under conditions of family dissolution and remarriage. Because there is reason to think that the process may be different when stepfamily formation follows the death of a parent, the theoretical scope of the theory is limited to bonding that occurs in families that have experienced marital dissolution through divorce. Lastly, while the focus of this discussion is not on the parent–child relationship, nor the stepparent–stepchild relationship, it is obvious that parents can and do influence sibling/stepsibling bonding processes and a complete theory would include these relationships.

SIBLING BONDING: CONCEPT AND PROCESS

Bank and Kahn (1982) define the sibling bond as "a connection between the selves, at both the intimate and the public levels, of two siblings; it is a 'fitting' together of two people's identities" (p. 15). Rubin (1985) writes that bonding can be a strong emotional connection, without implying intimacy. According to Turner (1970) bonds bring group members together, keep them together, and cause them to interact. A bond exists when some value of the individual is felt to be fostered by association and interaction. The benefit gained from group membership is one of the most effective bonds holding members together. Turner points out that there may also be instrumental gains from group membership, and consequently some bonds may be based partially on instrumental considerations as well as affection. There are also bonds that develop between those who have shared an experience that left some deep impression in memory. Such experiences and impressions help shape common attitudes. The bonding process clearly fosters interdependency and shifts the focus to an emphasis on "we" and "us" rather than "you" and "I."

Bonding is a process, not a static condition, and bonds are subject to continuous change, even in established relationships (Turner, 1970). Turner suggests that the study of behavior, when relationships are disturbed or broken, may expose ties or bonds that are hidden. For example, siblings who otherwise might have been observed to be competitive and distant may display cooperative, intimate behaviors after a parental divorce.

Mutual bonding does not necessarily mean that each person is tied to the other by the same kind of bond. Superior and subordinant statuses dictate different patterns of interaction, expectations, and response. Identification processes also differ, depending on status. In the case of siblings, status differences are manifest in age and sex differences, as well as socioeconomic differences when siblings/stepsiblings reside in different households. In interracial stepfamilies, racial differences among siblings may be the source of differential status (Baptiste, 1984).

According to Turner (1970) new bonds emerge and old bonds become intensified when family members are closely involved with one another over a period of time. However, the emergence of new bonds is neither automatic nor inevitable. The degree to which they appear or fail to appear is affected by the state of the initial bonds and the situation within which the relationship exists.

The privacy associated with family behavior is one situation that fosters bonding. Family behavior is characterized by its private nature and lack of formality. Turner writes, "the shared freedom to yield to impulses forbidden outside the family is a bond that develops if conditions are favorable to the family" (1970, p. 87). He sees the family as a group that is especially conducive to eliminating reserve. At the same time, within this private unit that is sheltered from the eyes of the community, there exists a degree of privacy that separates family subsystems, that is, spouses from children and children from parents. Bank and Kahn (1982) suggest that a willingness to respect and maintain each other's privacy serves as "a powerful bond of loyalty among siblings" (p. 323).

Associated with a relaxation of reserve is a stabilization of self/other conceptualizations, of the internal "picture" (perception) we have of the traits, personalities, characteristics, and so forth of ourselves and other family members. Since family interaction is not limited to only one sphere of behavior, self/other conceptualizations are developed from and apply to a whole range of activities. Thus, the range of "unhampered, unreserved emotional and behavioral expression is equally wide" (Turner, 1970, p. 86). This point becomes important when an established family unit expands to include "new" members, such as a stepparent or stepsiblings. The addition of new siblings can be the source of a redefinition of the "self." Compared to a new stepsister or stepbrother a child can suddenly feel smarter, more attractive, more awkward, for example, than before the comparison was made.

To summarize, six key concepts specified by Turner (1970) are used to conceptualize the processes involved in sibling/stepsibling bonding: group membership and, implicitly, access to one another; shared experiences; availability of conditions that foster intimacy and privacy; interdependency; status differences; and self/other conceptualizations. In the following discussion these concepts will be more fully developed to show how sibling attachment develops or fails to develop in families.

Conditions in the Microsystem that Facilitate Bonding

It is in the microsystem that "reality" is first defined for children. That is, within the family environment children learn what constitutes effective communication, permissible limits of expressing emotions and feelings, norms of justice and fairness, and how to bargain and negotiate for what one needs or wants. That is not to say that effective communication as defined by the family is necessarily "good" communication, or that the learned negotiation skills are useful in other environments. It only means that what the child first learns in the family becomes "normal" or expected. The child must experience exchanges with other people in other environments before the first lessons learned in the family context begin to be modified.

Many of the behaviors, attitudes, and expectations children learn in the family are learned with brothers and/or sisters. These shared experiences help to promote intimacy, and develop the self/other conceptualizations discussed earlier. Bank and Kahn (1982) propose two conditions that allow strong sibling bonds to develop: high access (or the possibility for siblings to be available to one another) and insufficient parental influence. (I will discuss the consequences of the latter condition later in the chapter.) These authors suggest that when other relationships are emotionally fulfilling, the sibling bond will be weak and unimportant. They note that accessibility (which depends upon age, sex, and spacing) "during the developmentally formative years is the almost routine accompaniment of an influential sibling relationship" (p. 10). Thus, in order for intimacy to develop between siblings, they must first be viewed as meeting each other's emotional needs, and they must have access to one another. Given high (or at least moderately high) access, a setting is created for shared experiences. Given shared experiences, intimacy will develop. Connecting these ideas with Turner's (1970) suggestion that people develop bonds because of perceived benefit of association, or some other felt value, it is proposed that:

> P_1 *In family environments where (1) sibling access is high, (2) children share common experiences, and (3) siblings meet each other's needs, sibling bonds will be strong.*

It should be clear that strong sibling bonds develop under conditions of interdependency. Tallman and Gray (1984) have included the interdependency concept in a theory of group formation and commitment. The focus of their theory is resource exchange and has been formalized to a greater extent than the previous works I have drawn from. The principles of this commitment theory can be used to explain how siblings within a family might develop strong attachments to one another. Generalizing from Tallman and Gray's (1984) ideas about group commitment to the sibling group, it is suggested that a child's reliance on siblings entails mutual dependence (dependence on another sibling in the group for specific rewards), or interdependence (reliance on the group as a whole for rewards that can only be obtained by the group's collective efforts). Therefore, sibling bonding can be conceived first as a function of an individual sibling's dependencies on other siblings, and second on their dependency on the sibling group's collective rewards resulting from exchanges with others in the environment. Third, reiterating Turner's (1970) description of the family environment as one that fosters opportunities to exhibit a wide range of behaviors, emotions, and exchanges, Tallman and Gray's (1984) proposition is applied to sibling bonding. That is, the more domains of rewards that are exchanged within the sibling group, the greater the probability that siblings will be dependent on one another. Finally, the closer siblings come to equality in their dependency upon one another, the greater their commitment to the sibling system and to one another (Tallman & Gray, 1984). Together, these ideas can be formulated into the following proposition:

> P_2 *When children in a family must rely on one another for a variety of desired rewards, both dependency and interdependency within the sibling system will increase and sibling bonding will be strong.*

Turner (1970) suggests that family members' self/other conceptualizations develop in a family atmosphere characterized by a freedom to express what one thinks and feels. While the freedom of expression varies between families, it nevertheless exists in families to a greater extent than is true of other groups in society. This lack of reserve within the family means that children not only develop their own identities, personalities, traits, values, and so forth in a less inhibited environment, but they acquire knowledge and understanding of their brothers' and sisters' traits, personalities, values, and idiosyncrasies as well.

Within this relatively free environment there are a variety of conditions that foster or inhibit the development of certain personality traits. For example, one condition is the extent of competition that prevails among siblings. The family as a group has finite resources, and in some families there may be competition among children for these resources (Ross & Milgram, 1982). Children may compete with one another for parental approval or attention; they may compete for friendship among their peers; or they may compete for the last serving of cereal in the box. Turner (1970) claims that the type and timing of parental rewards and sanctions in the allocation of resources (which fosters competition or harmony) is important in developing self/other conceptualizations. The extent to which competition over scarce resources prevails among siblings is conducive to developing expectations, personality traits, and values that are different from those in a setting in which cooperation prevails. These differences ultimately affect sibling relationships (Ihinger, 1975).

Family distribution rules that determine the allocation of scarce resources are based on a variety of factors. In some families, allocation is determined by age. In other families, sex may be the determining feature. And in still others, both age and sex may prevail. Merit is yet another basis for distribution. The recipient of the greater share of resources in any group is an important factor in determining status and power (Smelser, 1968). In families, the children who have the most resources will have greater status and probably greater power within the family. They are, therefore, more likely to possess what other siblings need or want. As mentioned earlier, Turner (1970) suggested that differential status dictates different patterns of interaction, expectations, and response. This means that age, sex, and birth order (status characteristics) will affect how siblings feel toward one another, nurture one another, engage in conflict with one another, cooperate with one another, and so on. Status has been found to be associated with attachment. Data consistently show that sisters feel closer to their siblings than brothers, and younger siblings feel closer to, and admire their older siblings more than is the opposite case (Adams, 1968; Bowerman & Dobash, 1974; Cicirelli, 1980; Latts, 1966). These ideas about self/other conceptualizations, distribution rules and differential status are formulated into the following proposition:

> P_3 *In the developmental process a child's sense of "self" and his/her perceptions of siblings' "selves" are influenced by (1) the family's distribution rules, (2) the extent of cooperation or competition encouraged by parents, and (3) the status of each child within the sibling group.*

To summarize, it is proposed that certain conditions in the family are instrumental in establishing close sibling bonds. In an environment that necessitates siblings meeting each other's needs when parents fail to meet them, siblings will increase their dependency upon one another, and consequently will be more tightly bonded. In an atmosphere of privacy, with freedom to express emotions, siblings will have greater opportunity for self-expression, a condition that can foster increased mutual understanding. This understanding leads to assessments of compatible or incompatible personalities that in turn can foster bonding between siblings. Age, sex, and birth spacing determine the degree of access siblings have to one another, and ultimately influence compatibility and shared experience. The family's distribution rules that determine how a family allocates resources will influence sibling attachment, as will the extent of conflict/cooperation concerning resources that is tolerated or encouraged in the household. Finally, resource possession, age, sex, and birth order convey status within the sib-system and status is complexly linked to the bonding process.

Other Microsystems, Mesosystems, Exosystems, and the Macrosystem

The home has been considered the primary microsystem of the child. However, after a parental divorce, a child can move between two parental households, living, as Ahrons (1979) says, in a "binuclear" family.[2] Two parental households can exert different influences on a child in terms of the environments they provide, especially in terms of socioeconomic differences, family customs, and childrearing practices. If and when one or both parents remarry, a new adult enters the child's life and each stepparent may bring stepsiblings or halfsiblings into the home. These aspects of the microsystem must be taken into account when analyzing children's and siblings' behavior after divorce.

In addition to the household, other microsystems such as schools, churches, and play/friendship networks are important to sibling bonding. Interest in these systems centers on the fact that throughout childhood siblings are companions in such settings. Or, if birth spacing and sex do not foster companionship, children often blaze or follow a path laid down for or by their siblings. Conversely, in some cases siblings serve as anti-role models for each other, for example, a younger sibling carves out an opposite path from that of an older brother or sister. Thus, in extra-familial settings siblings are role models against which a child compares and measures his/her capabilities and performance, and against which he/she is measured by others.

Mesosystems provide the relationships or connections between microsystems. According to Garbarino (1982), the number and quality of connections is a measure of the richness of mesosystems for the child. A child's community connections are a function of the family's integration within the community, and associated with the extent of connectedness is the number of adults and children in the family. A child's mesosystem changes when his/her parents divorce. With divorce, mesosystem connections may either (1) divide and reduce when two parental households are established and a child lessens or even loses contact with the nonresidential parent, or (2) multiply and expand when two households are established and the child has the benefit of both networks. Expansion again occurs if one or both parents remarry. This point will be considered later when stepsibling bonding is discussed. It is conceivable that remarriage could reduce a child's mesosystem if a nonresidential parent becomes more involved with stepchildren than with his/her biological child (Furstenberg, 1981; Furstenberg, Spanier, & Rothschild, 1982).

Exosystems are community settings in which a child does not take a direct part but which nevertheless affect his/her well-being. Such settings are parental workplaces, judicial courts, community-based help programs (such as day-care facilities, youth organizations, and counseling programs), and other community agencies that indirectly affect a child's life, such as police, health care, and social welfare organizations. While exosystems have an impact upon children's well-being, they affect sibling relationships only indirectly. For example, courts have the power to separate siblings even though the general rule is that siblings should remain together. According to Kram and Frank (1982),

> It is now generally held that when the circumstances of the case warrant it, and the best interests of the child require it, courts will not hesitate to award custody of one or more children to one parent, and the custody of a sibling or siblings to the other. (p. 49)

The final system of the four-tiered model that Bronfenbrenner (1979) describes is the macrosystem—the laws, norms, values, and ideologies that prevail in the greater society within which the child grows and develops. There appears to be consensus between researchers who study remarriage and clinicians who counsel stepfamilies that there are few clearcut norms to guide stepfamily behavior (Cherlin, 1978). This can result in a great deal of confusion as to what behaviors are to be expected from a stepparent or stepchild. A first-married family is the ideological "model" with which stepfamily members most frequently compare themselves, and there is a tendency to ignore or deny the differences that exist between the two types of families (Fishman & Hamel, 1981; Jacobson, 1979; Messinger, 1976).

The macrosystem is the "general organization of the world as it is and as it might be" (Garbarino, 1982, p. 24), and it can affect sibling relationships in many ways. Cross-culturally it determines how siblings are normatively bound to one another, if they will grow up in one another's environment after they pass the age of 5 or 6, or whether they must avoid being alone in each other's company (Stephens, 1963). In America, there are cultural norms that prescribe sibling behavior, such as the protective actions brothers take for sisters or older siblings take for younger ones. There also may be differences based on class, ethnicity, and race. The role that societal and cultural elements play in relationship to sibling bonding is summarized in the following premise:

> 1. *A variety of environments must be identified and analyzed in order to understand fully the factors influencing sibling bonding processes. These environments are characterized by four social structures, labeled the micro-, meso-, exo-, and macrosystems. The specific conditions that prevail within each of these structures are hypothesized to influence sibling bonding outcomes.*

In summary, sibling relations are affected at each structural level described by Bronfenbrenner (1979): in primary settings such as home, school, and neighborhood; in secondary settings in which parents work and play and through which they link the child to non-family settings; in community agencies and bureaucracies that affect children indirectly through the opportunities and services they provide for family members; and lastly, by the legal, moral, and normative systems that prescribe and proscribe behavior for those who live within a particular culture. We consider now the specfic conditions within the four systems that influence sibling bonding when parents divorce.

Consequences in the Sibling System When Parents Divorce

Earlier in this essay I reported Bank and Kahn's (1982) hypothesis that inadequate parenting was a precondition for strong sibling bonds to develop. It is reasonable to assume that over the course of the childrearing years there are many ways, and many times, that parents fail to meet their children's needs. Further, it can be assumed that inadequate parenting is not conscious, intentional, malicious, or pathological in nature. Parental inadequacy may be defined most simply as situations in which one or both parents, for whatever reason, do not nurture and guide a child in ways that provide for his/her optimum development. Adequacy is a variable that changes with changing family circumstances, varying within as well as between families.

There are some family situations where intentional parental divisiveness rather than inadvertent inadequacy may interfere with the development of close relations between children. Such a situation exists when one or both parents encourage conflict between siblings, when they make invidious comparisons between children, or when they flagrantly favor one child over another. I propose that if the conditions specified in proposition P_l hold, a strong, positive relationship between siblings will develop regardless of differential treatment by a parent or parents. Thus, the following proposition is offered.

P₄ In a family environment where parenting skills and techniques are inadequate but where sibling access is high, where siblings share common experiences, and where they meet each other's needs, strong sibling bonds will develop.

Divorce is a life event that is often associated with a period of inadequate parenting (Hetherington, Cox, & Cox, 1979; Wallerstein & Kelly, 1980). As parents work to resolve problems and come to some mutual understanding of their situation, children's needs may be given minimal attention. Divorce also may shatter a child's sense of reality, order, and security. Under these conditions, given the conditions of sibling access and shared experiences, siblings will look to one another for need fulfillment. Bank and Kahn (1982) offer a similar proposition concerning the consequences of parental divorce:

> . . . many young siblings whose parents have decided to divorce, rely heavily on one another. Afraid of taking opposite sides in a marital war, younger sibs tend to clump together in a spirit of mutual protection as contention between the parents escalates. (p. 64)

There are situations wherein sibling bonding is not enhanced by divorce. One such situation is when siblings each strongly identify with different parents, thus creating child–parent alliances rather than parent–parent and child–child alliances in the family. Another situation is where a judicial decision is made to separate siblings, thus limiting their access to one another. A decision to award custody to one parent versus another may weaken sibling bonding when siblings strongly identify with or "prefer" different parents. These latter decisions are lodged in the exosystem, but they have an impact on sibling relations.

The family microsystem is not the only system that is affected and changed by divorce. Other microsystem experiences change as well. For example, some children's self-confidence diminishes after their parents divorce, and this can affect peer interaction and/or school performance (Guidubaldi, Cleminshaw, Perry, Nastasi, & Lightel, 1986; Parish, 1981; Parish & Parish, 1983; Rosenberg, 1965; Wallerstein & Kelly, 1980). When one parent leaves the family, mesosystem connections that previously were provided by two adults now are reduced. This is especially true if little contact is kept with the absent parent. Divorce is usually accompanied by lower economic status of the wife/mother (Weitzman, 1985). When mothers have custody, this lowered economic level is often accompanied by residential changes such as a dislocation from home, neighborhood, or school; in other words, microsystem settings become altered (Asher & Bloom, 1983). If custody is contested, the exosystem makes itself felt through judicial decisions about the most salient issue concerning children: where and with whom they will live. Finally, if divorce is a relatively uncommon behavior and/or it is negatively sanctioned in the macrosystem, children will perceive their divorce experiences as embarrassing and shameful. If siblings share this experience and the negative emotions resulting from a violation of macrosystem norms, divorce might serve to strengthen the bonds they feel.

Remarriage follows divorce in about 78% of all cases (Glick, 1984). In 1980, two thirds of all remarriages experienced by children involved a previously married man. Since most remarried men have children from their previous marriage it is expected that a majority of children in stepfamilies have stepsiblings, although the exact number cannot be calculated (Bumpass, 1984). The probability of a child acquiring a halfsibling born in the new marriage is associated with the age of existing children—reflecting in part the age of the parents. Bumpass (1984) estimates that about one half of the children under age 5 at the time of remarriage have a halfsibling from the new marriage while only 16% of children aged 10 to 13 gain a halfsibling. These ideas about the consequences of divorce on sibling relationships are summarized in the following premises:

> 2. *A child's family situation following parental divorce—including economic circumstances, nonresidential parent contact and involvement, and custody disputes—strongly affects sibling bonding processes.*
>
> 3. *As a disruptive family experience, parental divorce creates the circumstances for children to "acquire" a stepsibling or halfsibling.*

The final section of this chapter discusses stepsibling relations and attempts to identify the factors that lead to the development of close ties between stepsiblings.

Stepsibling Bonding

A fundamental assumption underlying the theory presented here is that siblings generally feel positive about one another, despite occasional disputes, rivalries, and so forth. This assumption stems from the prevailing norms making affection virtually obligatory between family members (Adams, 1968).

This assumption is important precisely because of the lack of norms surrounding stepfamily member behavior (Cherlin, 1978). To the extent that people in ambiguous situations or relationships generalize from norms that are appropriate in other similar situations or relationships, we may say that norms are "borrowed." (For example, the clinical literature discusses the "myth of instant love," wherein stepparents believe that because they love their new spouse they will automatically love their spouse's children [Schulman, 1972; Visher & Visher, 1978]. Thus, societal norms are borrowed in the absence of norms evolving from actual stepfamily experience.) The theory assumes, then, an underlying expectation that the various children brought to the new union will be predisposed to like one another, everything else being equal. The earlier discussion specified the initial conditions that facilitate this predisposition. That is, when children are close in age, of the same sex, have mutual dependencies, and share common experiences and/or values, they will be more likely to form attachments and develop positive bonds.

Earlier it was established that bonding is facilitated when an individual perceives some benefit gained from interaction. For example, a child may perceive as beneficial an increase in the amount of time, attention, resources, or affection he/she receives from a new stepparent and/or stepsiblings. The opposite situation holds true also. When a child perceives greater cost than gain involved in interaction, interaction will be viewed less positively, or rejected entirely. Or, perceived loss of attention may be viewed as costly, thus inhibiting interaction. Therefore, we can expect that the initial assessments children make of their potential gains and losses associated with the formation of a new family and the acquisition of new siblings will strongly influence their predisposition to like or dislike the new stepsiblings. The possible costs involved are many, but they include a perceived reduction or loss of time, attention, resources, and affection from their own parent. They may have to share their friends and possessions (rooms, toys, pets) or they may have to give up these things altogether if they change residence. This situation is well illustrated by a quote from a young teenager who, 3 months after moving with her mother into the home of her new stepfather and stepsiblings complained, "We've had to give up everything, and they haven't even changed the kind of hair conditioner they use."

One "natural" cleavage within a new sibling group occurs when stepsiblings have different last names. In some families stepfathers legally adopt their stepchildren, thus eliminating this problem. Another solution occurs when children informally adopt a stepfather's last name but no legal change is effected. Adopting a common last name helps to unify the stepfamily and the sibling group, making it in their eyes closer in appearance to the nuclear intact "ideal" family.

One benefit accruing from a parent's remarriage and the addition of a stepparent and stepsiblings is the expansion of a child's mesosystem. A child's familiarity with and interaction in multiple community settings can enhance his/her competencies and opportunities and expand the affiliative network. The more connections or links across community settings the child has, the more he/she can benefit from what the community and its citizens have to offer. The activities and associations of a stepparent and stepsiblings contribute to an enlarged community network.

I mention only in passing the association between socioeconomic status and mesosystem involvement. When a parent remarries across class lines, new and different influences are provided from the meso-, exo-, and macro-systems upon his/her children. Cross-class movement associated with remarriage can have repercussions upon the new sibling system insofar as the two uniting families have different family "cultures," values, and so on that are related to social class lifestyles. In such an instance, personality variables affect the bonding process, for a child's proclivity or resistance to adapt to new circumstances may influence the rate and degree of attachment that develops between new siblings. The following proposition summarizes these ideas:

> P_5 When stepsiblings perceive a mutual benefit of association and feel that they share equally or equitably the costs associated with their changed circumstances and their new joint living arrangements, then strong emotional bonds will develop between them.

To summarize, stepsiblings are assumed to be predisposed to like one another, all else being equal, because of the normative pressure to hold affectionate feelings for family members. This pressure is assumed to exist for acquaintances (sometimes even strangers) who become "family" via remarriage just as it does for members of first families who add family members through childbirth, adoption, or marriage (in-laws). In addition, stepsibling bonding is hypothesized to occur most rapidly under conditions of similarity (age, sex, experience, values), interdependency, perceived mutual benefit of association, few perceived personal costs, and approximate equality in relinquishing aspects of a former life style. Conversely, stepsiblings are predicted to dislike one another and not develop intimate bonds under conditions of dissimilarity, and when perceived costs of association such as loss or reduction of resources, status, and so forth are perceived as exceeding the benefits of such an association.

CONCLUSION

In this chapter, I have employed concepts and insights from a number of scholars of child and human development to formulate a theory that seeks to explain the factors involved in sibling bonding, how divorce affects sibling bonding, and the conditions under which stepsiblings develop positive bonds. Bronfenbrenner's (1979) conceptualization of ecosystems, Elder's (in press) call for attention to personality as well as behavior and social structure linkages, and Turner's (1970) insightful analysis of the bonding process were the starting points for establishing this theoretical framework. I have attempted to illustrate how structural factors exemplified in Bronfenbrenner's (1979) four-tiered model affects the sibling system, and how the relative privacy and intimacy of the family environment helps to develop and maintain individual-member personalities, provide a background for children to learn interaction and role skills, and foster member-bonding.

Parental divorce jeopardizes established family behavior patterns and meaning systems. After divorce, adjustments must be made to accommodate the loss of one or more members, the changes in interaction patterns between family members, and changed interaction patterns between the family and extended kin. It is likely that even under the best of circumstances, parenting under these conditions will become less adequate. Because of this situation, an opportunity exists for sibling bonds to become more intense and for intimacy to grow. The theoretical formulation presented discusses the factors that facilitate this development. The theory also attempts to explain the conditions under which children develop bonds with stepsiblings when their parents remarry, or conversely, why stepsibling bonding is inhibited after remarriage. Appendix 7-1 summarizes the assumptions, premises, and propositions of the theory.

The large number of adults who end a first marriage and begin a new one are establishing a new family environment that is different in many ways from their "first" one. One of the essential differences between first and second (or subsequent) marriages is the potential power of children to enhance or destroy the new union. Children who are the biological offspring of a couple have a vested interest in its maintenance, even during the rebellious adolescent years. (During this stage of the family life cycle the child may try to establish independence from parents/family, but still wishes the family to be an intact unit.) Children have little power over their biological parents' decision to divorce or to remarry. Children whose parents make such choices may wish heartily that the divorce never happened and that the new union be dissolved. At this point they have some power to accomplish the latter end. Children's individual behavior as well as sibling coalitions can disrupt and/ or destroy an adult remarried relationship. Data show that remarriages with children are more vulnerable to trouble, unhappiness, and dissolution (Becker et al., 1977; DeMaris, 1984; Pasley & Ihinger-Tallman, 1982; White & Booth, 1985). Therefore, it may be that children, and the children's subsystem within the family (i.e., the sibling system), have been raised to new importance as the effects of children's power and influence on the success and stability of their parent's remarriage is recognized. The attachments children build to new stepparents and to the strangers who become their brothers and sisters thus become critical factors in the successful functioning and longevity of the new marriage.

APPENDIX 7-1

A Theory of Sibling Bonding: Theoretical Statements

Assumptions

1. Over the course of the childrearing years there are many times, and many ways, that parents fail to meet their children's needs; in other words, they inadequately perform the parenting role.
2. Inadequate parenting is not conscious, intentional, malicious, or pathological in nature.
3. Siblings generally feel positive about one another despite occasional disputes, rivalries, and so forth.

Premises

1. A variety of environments must be identified and analyzed in order to understand fully the factors influencing sibling and stepsibling bonding processes. These environments are characterized by four social structures labeled the micro-, meso-, exo-, and macrosystems. The specific conditions that prevail within each of these structures are hypothesized to influence sibling bonding outcomes.
2. A child's family situation following parental divorce—including economic circumstances, nonresidential parent contact and involvement, and custody disputes—strongly affects sibling bonding processes.
3. As a disruptive family experience, parental divorce creates the circumstance for children to "acquire" a stepsibling or halfsibling.

Propositions

1. In family environments where (1) sibling access is high, (2) children share common experiences, and (3) siblings meet each other's needs, sibling bonds will be strong.
2. When children in a family rely on one another for a variety of desired rewards, both dependency and interdependency within the sibling system will increase and sibling bonding will be strong.
3. In the developmental process a child's sense of "self" and his/her perceptions of siblings' "selves" are influenced by (1) the family's distribution rules, (2) the extent of cooperation or competition encouraged by parents, and (3) the status of each child within the sibling group.
4. In a family environment where parenting skills and techniques are inadequate but where sibling access is high, where siblings share common experiences, and where they meet each other's needs, strong sibling bonds will develop.
5. When stepsiblings perceive a mutual benefit of association and feel that they share equally or equitably the costs associated with their changed circumstances and their new joint living arrangements, then strong emotional bonds will develop between them.

180 *Ihinger-Tallman*

NOTES

1. *Quasi-kin* is a term coined by Bohannan (1970). It refers to a formerly married person's ex-spouse, the ex-spouse's new husband or wife, and his/her blood kin.

2. Ahrons (1979) invented the concept binuclear family to describe a family style that does not force the child to sever the bond with either parent and which allows both parents to continue to enact their parental roles after divorce (p. 499).

REFERENCES

Adams, B. N. (1968). *Kinship in an urban setting.* Chicago: Markham.
Ahrons, C. (1979). The binuclear family. *Alternative Lifestyles, 2,* 499–517.
Asher, S., & Bloom, B. (1983). Geographic mobility as a factor in adjustment to divorce. *Journal of Divorce, 6,* 69–84.
Bank, S., & Kahn, M. D. (1975). Sisterhood–brotherhood is powerful: Sibling sub-systems and family therapy. *Family Process, 14,* 311–337.
Bank, S., & Kahn, M. D. (1982). *The sibling bond.* New York: Basic Books.
Baptiste, D. (1984). Marital and family therapy with racially/culturally intermarried stepfamilies: Issues and guidelines. *Family Relations, 33,* 373–380.
Becker, G. W., Landes, E. M., & Michael, R. T. (1977). An economic analysis of marital instability. *Journal of Political Economy, 85,* 1141–1187.
Bohannon, P. (1970). Divorce chains, households of remarriage, and multiple divorces. In P. Bohannon (Ed.), *Divorce and After* (pp. 127–139). Garden City, NY: Double Day & Co.
Bowerman, C., & Dobash, R. (1974). Structural variations in inter-sibling affect. *Journal of Marriage and the Family, 36,* 48–54.
Bronfenbrenner, U. (1979). *The ecology of human development.* Cambridge, MA: Harvard University Press.
Bumpass, L. (1984). Some characteristics of children's second families. *American Journal of Sociology, 90,* 608–623.
Cherlin, A. (1978). Remarriage as an incomplete institution. *American Journal of Sociology, 84,* 634–650.
Cicirelli, V. (1980). A comparison of college women's feelings toward their siblings and parents. *Journal of Marriage and the Family, 42,* 111–118.
DeMaris, A. (1984). A comparison of remarriages with first marriages on satisfaction in marriage and its relationship to prior cohabitation. *Family Relations, 33,* 443–449.
Dunn, J. (1983). Sibling relationships in early childhood. *Child Development, 54,* 787–811.
Elder, G. H., Jr. (in press). Families, kin, and the life course: A sociological perspective. In R. Parks (Ed.), The *Family.* Chicago: University of Chicago Press.
Fishman, B., & Hamel, B. (1981). From nuclear to stepfamily ideology: A stressful change. *Alternative Lifestyles, 4,* 181–204.
Furstenberg, F. F., Jr. (1981). *Renegotiating parenthood after divorce and remarriage.* Paper presented at the Biennial Meeting of the Society for Research in Child Development, Symposium on Changing Family Patterns, Boston, Massachusetts.
Furstenberg, F. F., Jr., Spanier, G. B., & Rothschild, N. (1982). Patterns of parenting in the transition from divorce to remarriage. In P. W. Berman & E. R. Ramey (Eds.), *Women: A developmental perspective* (pp. 325–348). Washington, DC: U.S. Department of Health and Human Services.

Garbarino, J. (1982). *Children and families in the social environment.* New York: Aldine.

Glick, P. (1984). How American families are changing. *American Demographics, 6,* 20–24.

Guidubaldi, J., Cleminshaw, H. K., Perry, J. D., Nastasi, B., & Lightel, J. (1986). The role of selected family environment factors in children's post-divorce adjustment. *Family Relations, 35,* 141–151.

Hetherington, E. M., Cox, M., & Cox, R. (1979). Family interaction and the social-emotional and cognitive development of children following divorce. In V. Vaughn & T. Brazelton (Eds.), *The family setting priorities* (pp. 89–128). New York: Science and Medicine Publishing Company.

Hunter College Women's Studies Collective. (1983). *Women's realities, women's choices: An introduction to women's studies.* New York: Oxford University Press.

Ihinger, M. (1975). The referee role and norms of equity: A contribution toward a theory of sibling conflict. *Journal of Marriage and the Family, 37,* 515–524.

Jacobson, D. S. (1979). Stepfamilies: Myths and realities. *Social Work, 24,* 202–207.

Kram, S. W., & Frank, N. A. (1982). *The law of child custody: Development of the substantive law.* Lexington, MA: D.C. Heath.

Latts, M. S. (1966). *The four-child, equi-sexed, intact family: Its organization and interaction patterns.* Doctoral dissertation, University of Minnesota.

Messinger, L. (1976). Remarriage between divorced people with children from previous marriages: A proposal for preparation for remarriage. *Journal of Marriage and Family Counseling, 2,* 193–200.

Parish, T. (1981). Young adults' evaluations of themselves and their parents as a function of family structure and disposition. *Journal of Youth and Adolescence, 10,* 173–178.

Parish, T., & Parish, J. (1983). Relationship between evaluations of one's self and one's family by children from intact, reconstituted, and single-parent families. *Journal of Genetic Psychology, 143,* 293–294.

Pasley, K., & Ihinger-Tallman, M. (1982). Remarried family life: Supports and constraints. In N. Stinnett, J. DeFrain, K. King, H. Lingren, G. Rowe, S. Van Zandt, & R. Williams (Eds.), *Building Family Strengths,* (Vol. 4; pp. 367–383). Lincoln, NE: University of Nebraska Press.

Rosenberg, M. (1965). *Society and the adolescent self-image.* Princeton, NJ: Princeton University Press.

Ross, H. G., & Milgram, J. I. (1982). Important variables in adult sibling relationships: A qualitative study. In M. E. Lamb & B. Sutten-Smith (Eds.), *Sibling relationships: Their nature and significance across the lifespan* (pp. 225–249). Hillsdale, NJ: Erlbaum.

Rubin, L. (1985). *Just friends.* New York: Harper & Row.

Schvaneveldt, J. D., & Ihinger, M. (1979). Sibling relationships in the family. In W. Burr, R. Hill, F. I. Nye, & I. Reiss (Eds.), *Contemporary theories about the family,* (Vol. 1; pp. 453–467). New York: The Free Press.

Shulman, G. L. (1972). Myths that intrude on the adaptation of the stepfamily. *Social Casework, 53,* 133–139.

Smelser, N. J. (1968). *Toward a general theory of social change: Essays in sociological explanation* (pp. 102–108). Englewood Cliffs, NJ: Prentice-Hall.

Smith-Rosenberg, C. (1983). The female world of love and ritual: Relations between women in nineteenth-century America. In M. Gordon (Ed.), *The American family in social-historical perspective* (pp. 411–435). New York: St. Martin's.

Stephens, W. N. (1963). *The family in cross-cultural perspective.* New York: Holt, Rinehart & Winston.

Tallman, I., & Gray, L. (1984). A theory of commitment, group formation, and group functioning. Research Proposal submitted to National Institute of Mental Health, Washington, DC.

Turner, R. (1970). *Family interaction.* New York: Wiley.

Visher, E. B., & Visher, J. S. (1978). Major areas of difficulty for stepparent couples. *International Journal of Family Counseling, 6,* 70–80.

Wallerstein, J., & Kelly, J. (1980). *Surviving the breakup: How children and parents cope with divorce.* New York: Basic Books.

Weitzman, L. (1985). *The divorce revolution: The unexpected social and economic consequences for women and children in America.* New York: The Free Press.

White, L. K., & Booth, A. (1985). The quality and stability of remarriages: The role of stepchildren. *American Sociological Review, 50,* 689–698.

THE EXPERIENCE OF STEPFAMILY LIVING

8

Family Relations Six Years after Divorce

E. MAVIS HETHERINGTON
University of Virginia

This paper presents part of the findings of a 6-year follow-up of a longitudinal study of divorce and focuses on family relations at that time. Children from divorced families who initially resided in mother custody households and their divorced parents were studied at 2 months, 1 year, 2 years and 6 years following divorce. A summary of the results of the first 2 years of the project are reported in Hetherington, Cox, and Cox (1982). In this chapter family functioning and parent–child relations at 6 years following divorce are examined in an expanded sample of 180 families including 124 of the families from the original longitudinal study.

Most studies, including this one, find that the first 2 to 3 years following divorce might be regarded as the crisis period during which most children and many parents experience emotional distress, psychological and behavior problems, disruptions in family functioning and problems in adjusting to new roles, relationships, and life changes associated with the altered family situation. However, by 2 years following divorce, the majority of parents and children seem to adapt reasonably well and certainly show great improvement as compared to the first year after divorce. In the 2-year assessment period in this study, some continuing problems were found in the adjustment of boys and in relations between custodial mothers and their sons. These boys from divorced families in comparison to boys from nondivorced families showed more antisocial, acting out, coercive, noncompliant behaviors in the home and in the school, and they exhibited difficulties in peer relations and school achievement. In contrast, girls from divorced families were functioning well and had positive relations with their custodial mothers.

In considering these results, two things must be kept in mind. First, this study involves mother-custody families, and there is some evidence that children may adjust better in the custody of a parent of the same sex (Santrock & Warshak, 1986; Warshak & Santrock, 1983). Second, the age of the child may be an important factor in sex differences in children's responses to divorce. In this study, children were an average age of 4 years at the beginning of the study, 6 years at the 2-year assessment, and 10 years at the time of the 6-year assessment. Reports of more severe and long-lasting disruption of behavior in boys than in girls following their parents' divorce have tended to come from studies of preadolescent children. However, investigations of adolescent girls from divorced families have found problems in the adjustment of the girls in heterosexual relationships and in parent–child relations (Hetherington, 1972; Wallerstein, 1982).

A difficulty in attempting to assess the long-term effects of divorce on parents and children and the factors that may mediate these outcomes is that family members may encounter widely varying family reorganizations and family experiences following divorce. For most parents and children divorce is only one in a series of family transitions that follow separation. Life in a single-parent household following divorce is usually a temporary condition since 80% of men and 75% of women will remarry. About 20% to 30% of children will spend some time in a stepparent family before they are young adults (Glick, 1979; Glick & Lin, 1986). Moreover, since the divorce rate is higher in remarriages than in first marriages, some parents and children encounter a series of divorces, periods in single-parent households, and remarriages.

In this chapter we examine relations between parents and 10-year-old children in nondivorced families, families in which there is a divorced custodial mother, and remarried families with a divorced mother and a stepfather 6 years after the mother's divorce.

METHOD

Subjects

The original sample was composed of 144 middle-class, white children and their parents. Half of the children were from divorced, mother-custody families, and the other half were from nondivorced families. Within each group, half were boys and half were girls. The children were an average of 10.1 years of age at the time of the follow-up study. As might be expected, by this time many rearrangements in marital relations had occurred.

In the 6-year follow-up, the subjects were residential parents and children in 124 of the original 144 families who were available and willing to continue to participate in the study. Sixty of the original divorced families and 64 of the original nondivorced families agreed to participate, although there had been many shifts in marital status in the time since the study began. In the 60 available originally divorced families, only 18 of the custodial mothers had remained single (10 with a target daughter and 8 with a target son), and 42 had remarried (20 with a target daughter and 22 with a target son). Two of the parents had redivorced, and there had been six changes in custody or residence from the mother to the father (5 sons, 1 daughter). Of the 64 originally nondivorced families, 53 were still married (30 sons, 23 daughters), 11 were divorced (7 daughters, 4 sons). It should be noted that the greater willingness to divorce in families with daughters than in those with sons is in accord with the findings of J. Block (personal communication, 1985), D. Baumrind (personal communication, 1986), and Glick (1979). In the newly divorced families, only one of the children, a son, was in the custody of the father.

The parents, for the most part, were well-educated and middle-class. All had at least a high school education and most had advanced training beyond high school. At 6 years following divorce, the household income of the non-remarried divorced mothers was significantly lower than that of the nondivorced or remarried families. Average household incomes were as follows: divorced, nonremarried mothers, $16,010: remarried mothers, $35,162: nondivorced families, $36,900.

A new cohort of families was added to the group of participating original families for whom we had complete data (except for noncustodial father measures) in order to expand the size of the groups to 30 sons and 30 daughters in each of three groups—a remarried mother/stepfather group; a mother-custody, nonremarried group; and a nondivorced group—a total of 180 families. For some analyses, the remarried group was broken down into those remarried less than 2 years and those remarried longer than 2 years. The additional subjects were matched with the original subjects on family size, age, education, income, length of marriage, and, when appropriate, length of time since divorce and time of remarriage.

The cross-sectional analyses of child and parent adjustment and of the relationships among family interaction, child adjustment, parent adjustment, and marital adjustment here utilize the expanded sample. Inconsistencies in the 6-year follow-up data reported in Hetherington *et al.* (1982) and in this chapter occur because only the original sample is used in the first paper while the expanded sample is used here.

Procedure

Partial data were available in the follow-up study on 124 of the original families. For the additional families in the expanded sample, only families on which all measures were available were included in the study. In all cases (including the original study), interviews, tests, and home observations of the residential parents and child were available. In 18 of the original families, complete school data, which included a peer nomination measure, were not available because of lack of willingness of the schools to participate in the study, although with 10 of these families, measures were available from teachers who were contacted directly and who agreed to participate. In addition, telephone interviews and/or take-home questionnaire and test material could not be obtained for six of the noncustodial fathers. As was true in the three waves of data collection in the original study, multiple measures of family relations, stresses, support systems, and parent and child characteristics and behavior were obtained from the child and residential parent, and when possible from the nonresidential parent. These involved standardized tests, interviews, and observations. In addition, teacher and peer evaluations of behavior, observations in school, and information from school records were obtained when possible. More details on the measures used in the first three waves of data collection at 2 months, 1 year, and 2 years following divorce, are available in Hetherington, Cox, and Cox (1978, 1979a, 1979b, 1982). In addition, more information on the child outcome measures in wave four, 6 years following divorce, are available in Hetherington, Cox, and Cox (1985). Only the measures in the analyses presented in this chapter will be described.

Parent interviews. Parents were interviewed separately on a structured parent interview schedule designed to assess discipline practices, the parent–child relationship, expectations for the child, sibling relations, the relationship of the child with the spouse and ex-spouse, the marital relationship, the relationship with the ex-spouse, spouse characteristics, support systems outside of the household, stresses, family roles and responsibilities, family organization, areas of desired change, satisfaction and happiness, and personality. Each of the categories was rated by two judges and the parent. In some cases the category involved the rating of only a single 5-point scale, however most categories involved multiple ratings. The interjudge reliabilities ranged from .58 to .95 with a mean of .85. The parent–judge reliabilities range from .40 to .95 with a mean of .67.

Child interviews. Children also were interviewed on a structured interview schedule covering many of the same topics as those in the parent interview, including discipline practices, parent–child relationships, relationships with the stepparents and noncustodial parents, the quality of their parents' marital relationships, family roles and responsibility, household organization, sibling, peer, and school relations, stresses and support systems, and areas of desired change. Rating procedures were the same as in the parent interviews. Interjudge reliabilities averaged .80. When parents and children were rating the same scales, mother–child reliabilities were .52 and father–child reliabilities averaged .64. As will be seen later, this varied with sex of child, sex of parent, and family type.

Parent personality inventories. The parent personality measures include the Personal Adjustment Scale of the Adjective Checklist (Gough & Heilbrun, 1965), the Socialization Scale of the California Personality Inventory (Gough, 1969), Rotter's Internal–External Locus of Control (I-E) Scale (Rotter, 1966), the Speilberger State–Trait Anxiety Scale (Speilberger, Gorsuch, & Lushene, 1970), and the Beck Depression Inventory (Beck, 1979).

Child adjustment measures. Measures of child adjustment were obtained from parents, teachers, peers, and the children. In the 6-year follow-up this included parents and teachers rating scales of the children's behavior, parents' and teachers' reports on the Child Behavior Checklist (Achenbach & Edelbrock, 1983), modifications of scales used in the three initial waves of the study, and a peer nomination measure based on a modification and extension of the Pupil Evaluation Inventory (Pekarik, Prinz, Liebert, Weintraub, & Neale, 1976). In addition, the child made self ratings on the Pupil Evaluation Inventory and on the Harter Perceived Competence Scale (Harter, 1982).

Twenty-four-hour behavior checklists. On ten different occasions, residential parents and children were asked to record and report in a telephone interview whether 40 child behaviors, 20 types of parent–child conflict, 10 types of husband–wife conflict, and 10 types of parent–child interaction thought to show involvement or warmth, had occurred in the past 24 hours. Using a split-half reliability of temporal stability for the first 5 days versus the second 5 days, reliabilities average .71 for fathers, .73 for mothers, and .69 for children. Average agreement between mothers and fathers across the three dimensions was .70. Agreement between parents and children was lower: .62 for mother and child and .60 for father and child. Children filled out this checklist only at the 6-year follow-up (time 4).

Home observations. Home observations were made on six occasions for a minimum of 3 hours. On three of these occasions, recording was done with raters present, and on three occasions the family interactions were videotaped and coded later. These tapes were coded using three different coding systems. One was a sequential interactive code. The second was a code, focusing only on the child's behavior, that measured internalizing, externalizing, and socially competent behaviors. This coding system is described in greater detail in Hetherington *et al.* (1985). Finally, the tapes were coded on global rating scales described below under observer impressions. In the sequential coding, a focal subject coding system was used, where each family served as the focal subject for 10-minute periods in rotation. The behavior of the child of interest in this study was oversampled, so that he/she served as the focal subject three times more often than did the other family members. All behaviors of the focal subject and all the reactions of other family members to the focal subject were coded at 6-second intervals. In addition, each content code was coded for positive, negative, or neutral affect.

Reliabilities, which averaged .79 for agreement between categories in each 6-second unit, were obtained from two coders coding 20% of the tapes. Cohen's kappas were always significantly above chance levels of agreement.

Structured family problem solving interactions. Husband/wife dyads, parent/child dyads, husband/wife/target child triads, biological sibling dyads, biological/step sibling dyads (when available), and a group of all of the residential family members were involved in 10-minute structured problem-solving interactions. Each dyad, triad, or family group discussed and attempted to reach solutions about issues they individually had reported earlier as continuing problems between them. The order of these structured family problem-solving interactions was randomized, and the interactions were spread across two sessions spaced over about a 2-month period. The coding system was similar to the sequential code used in the free home observations. However, additional codes focusing on problem-solving processes were included.

Observer impressions. The investigators who interviewed the families and observed and videotaped them in the home in free and structured family problem-solving sessions completed a set of 5-point rating scales describing parents' and childrens' behavior toward each other family member. They viewed the tapes after the last data gathering session and then made their ratings. In addition to rating the characteristic level of interaction for each family member on each scale, observers also rated the highest and lowest extreme level to occur at any time in any of the sessions. Thus, a family member's characteristic level of hostility might be 2, but if they behaved in a particularly vicious way on one occasion, they would obtain a rating of 5 on the most extreme high coding. In addition, each parents' overall parenting style was characterized as authoritarian, authoritative, permissive, or disengaged. Finally, the family as a whole was rated on a set of family dimensions which will not be discussed here.

Dyadic adjustment scale. Both spouses took the Dyadic Adjustment Scale (Spanier, 1976). This scale yields an overall measure of marital adjustment and subscales assessing satisfaction, consensus, cohesiveness and expressiveness.

School observations. In the first 3 time periods, each child had been observed in the classroom for eighteen 10-minute sessions. The child's behavior and the behavior of the person with whom the child was interacting was recorded every 6 seconds. In addition, affect during play had been assessed. The same code used in the original study combined with affect codings was used in the follow-up study. (See Hetherington *et al.* [1979b] for more details on this procedure.)

Life Experiences Survey (LES). An extension of the Sarason, Johnson, and Siegal (1978) Life Experiences Survey with ten items added to more intensively study changes in family relations was administered to parents at time 4. Parents were asked to indicate the occurrence of certain events in the past year and in the past 6 year's time since divorce, followed by separate subjective ratings of the event as positive or negative on 7-point scales. A similar, shorter survey was constructed for children and administered at time 4. This measure was read to the children.

Analysis

First and second order factor analysis with oblique rotation and internal consistency analysis involving interview, 24-hour-behavior checklist, observational measures, observer impressions, and test measures were used to develop subscales of parenting behavior, husband/wife relationships, and the child's relationship to parents and siblings. A factor loading of .4 was set as significant. However, in a few cases where items had a priori been assumed to be related to a construct and loaded at .35 or above on a factor, it was retained in that factor. All factors had Cronbach's alphas above .69 with an average alpha of .79.

Separate factor analyses were performed for fathers and mothers, and the same factors emerged for both. However there was variation in the loadings of the factor subscales for fathers and mothers. The parenting constructs are presented in Table 8-1. These factors are similar but not identical to those found in another ongoing longitudinal study of remarriage and divorce by Hetherington and Clingempeel (1986).

Multivariate analyses, followed by univariate analysis of significant multivariate effects, with sex of the child and family types as the independent measures were performed on the composite indices of parent and child behavior. In addition, analyses were performed for factors derived separately from mothers', fathers', and children's reports. It was thought to be important to look at reports from individual family members as well as the composite measures since variations in the perceptions of different family members are often important indicators of family dynamics, and discrepant perceptions have been found to be related to family conflict (Hagan, 1986) and marital distress. The expanded sample of 30 families of boys and 30 families of girls in each of the three family groups was used in this analysis. However, the remarried families group was further broken down into those remarried less than 2 years (early remarriage [ER]), and those remarried more than 2 years

Table 8-1. Dimensions of Parenting

Warmth/responsiveness	*Conflict/irritability*
Expressive affection	Coercion
Social Involvement	Punitiveness
Instrumental involvement	Mood
Control	Conflict over parental authority
Rule setting, restrictiveness	Conflict over household and personal
Firmness, firm versus lax enforcement	issues
Power	Conflict over character development
Monitoring	and deviance
Monitoring strategies	*Maturity Demands*
Successful monitoring	Maturity expectations
	Maturity demands and enforcement

(late remarriage [LR]); thus, there were four family groups. This was based on the assumption that families who were in the first 2 years of a remarriage would be adapting to another life transition, in contrast to families who had been in their current marital situation for more than 2 years. The analyses of residential fathers involved only three family types (early remarriage, later remarriage, and nondivorced).

RESULTS

Parent Adjustment

There were few differences in the adjustment of mothers in the remarried and nondivorced families with the exception that mothers in the first 2 years of remarriage report greater life satisfaction and marital satisfaction. They appear to be in a honeymoon period of adjustment. There are no differences between those mothers remarried for longer periods of time and nondivorced mothers. In contrast, the nonremarried, divorced mothers report less general life satisfaction, less internal control over the course of their lives, more loneliness, and more depression. Loneliness is correlated with scores for depression on the Beck Depression Inventory. The pervasive loneliness of nonremarried divorced women occurs in spite of the fact that by 6 years after divorce they have built up new social networks and have more contact with their families of origin than do mothers in nondivorced families. Wallerstein (1986), in a 10-year follow-up of her longitudinal study of divorce, also comments on the overwhelming loneliness of nonremarried women. Other studies have found that loneliness is much less marked for women who have never married. For divorced women, involvement in a new intimate relationship is the critical factor that alleviates loneliness. Nonworking mothers, divorced mothers of sons, and mothers in blended families in which children from two families have been merged reported less life satisfaction, more depression, and less internalized control of their fate than did other mothers. Maternal depression and state anxiety were related to more irritable and inconsistent parenting behavior and less warmth and positive responsiveness, especially toward sons.

There are few differences between the personalities and adjustment of fathers in nondivorced and remarried families, except that newly remarried fathers report more marital satisfaction than do the other groups of fathers. In addition, both groups of remarried fathers report that the relationship with their stepchildren adversely affects their marital relationship. All groups of fathers report more marital satisfaction and general life satisfaction than do mothers.

Parent–Child Relations

How do nondivorced, divorced nonremarried, and remarried mothers behave with their children? The findings of our study suggest that mother–son relations are problematic in the divorced nonremarried families, as are those between parent and child in the early remarried families, particularly those with stepdaughters. It is important to note that these divorced families are what we might call "stabilized divorced families." The parents have been divorced for 6 years, and the families are well beyond the 2- or 3-year crisis period following divorce. However, divorced nonremarried mothers are continuing to exhibit many of the behaviors with their sons 6 years after divorce that were seen 2 years after divorce. Although interview and observational measures suggest that there are few differences among the three groups of mothers in the physical and verbal affection they direct toward their children, divorced mothers with sons tend to spend less time with their sons and report feeling less rapport and closeness to them. In addition, mothers in all three family types showed more expressive affection toward girls than toward boys.

Divorced mothers are distinguished from mothers of other family types more by differences in control attempts and punitive, coercive behaviors than by warmth and affection. Divorced mothers are ineffectual in their control attempts and give many instructions with little follow through. They tend to nag, natter, and complain to their sons. Although the divorced mothers are as physically and verbally affectionate with their children as are mothers in the other family groups, they more often get involved with their sons in angry, escalating coercive cycles. Spontaneous, negative "start-ups" (i.e., negative behavior initiated following neutral or positive behavior by the other person) are twice as likely to occur with mothers and sons in divorced families as with those in nondivorced families. Moreover, once these negative interchanges between divorced mothers and sons occur, they are likely to continue significantly longer than in any other dyad in any family type. Patterson (1982) has noted that the vast majority of normal children emit a single coercive behavior and then stop. This is not the case with sons and their divorced custodial mothers. As can be seen in Table 8-2, the probability of continuance of a negative response is higher in the divorced mother–son dyad than in any other parent–child dyad with the exception of daughters behavior toward stepfathers in the early stage of remarriage. It should be noted that the sons of divorced women recognize their own aggressive, noncompliant behaviors and report that their mothers have little control over their behavior; however, they also report and exhibit high levels of warmth toward their mothers. It might be best to view this relation between divorced mothers and sons as intense and ambivalent rather than purely hostile and rejecting.

Both sons and daughters in divorced families are allowed more responsi-

Table 8-2. Probability of Negative Response Continuance in Family Dyads

	Nondivorced		Divorced		Remarried Early		Remarried Late	
	Son	*Daughter*	*Son*	*Daughter*	*Son*	*Daughter*	*Son*	*Daughter*
Mother interacting with child	.11	.09	.26	.08	.20	.15	.15	.13
Child interacting with mother	.12	.07	.33	.09	.21	.19	.13	.19
Sibling interacting with child	.19	.15	.27	.24	.30	.28	.20	.20
Child interacting with sibling	.18	.16	.29	.23	.29	.30	.19	.24
Stepfather interacting with child	.10	.05	—	—	.07	.03	.14	.18
Child interacting with stepfather	.03	.02	—	—	.10	.31	.06	.18

bility, independence, and power in decision making than are children in nondivorced families. They successfully interrupt their divorced mother and their mother yields to their demands more often than in the other family types. In some cases, this greater power and independence results in an egalitarian, mutually supportive relationship. In other cases, where the emotional demands or responsibilities required by the mother are inappropriate, are beyond the capabilities of the child, or interfere with normal activities of the child (such as in peer relations or school activities), resentment, rebellion, or psychological disturbance may follow.

Finally, divorced mothers monitor their childrens' behavior less closely than do mothers in nondivorced families. They know less about where their children are, who they are with, and what they are doing than do mothers in two-parent households. On their 24-hour-behavior checklists, boys in divorced families reported being involved in more antisocial behavior that the mother did not know about than did children in any other group, although this discrepancy was also high in the mother–daughter reports in the stepfamily groups. In addition, children in the single-parent households were less likely than those in the two-parent households to have adult supervision in their parent's absence. Both Robert Weiss (1975) and Wallerstein and Kelly (1980) report that one way children may cope with their parents' divorce is by becoming disengaged from the family. In our study, boys from divorced families were spending significantly less time in the home with their parents or other adults and more time alone or with peers than were any of the other groups of children.

In contrast to divorced mothers and sons, there are few differences in the relationship between divorced mothers and daughters and that of mothers and daughters in nondivorced families. However, girls in divorced single-parent households do have more power and are assigned more responsibilities. They do, in the words of Robert Weiss (1975), "grow up faster." Mothers and daughters in divorced nonremarried families 6 years after divorce express considerable satisfaction with their relationship. There is an exception to this happy picture. Interview measures of pubescent status had been obtained from the parents, and their children and interviewers had made ratings of pubescent status. As might be expected, few children had entered puberty by this time since they were only 10 years old. However, 26 of our 90 girls were early maturers and were beginning to show some signs of puberty. Family conflict was higher in all three family types for these early-maturing girls versus late-maturing girls, and it was most marked between mothers and daughters in the single-parent households. Early maturity in girls was associated with a premature weakening of the mother–child bonds. These early maturing girls, especially in the divorced nonremarried families, were alienated and disengaged from their families, talked less to their mothers but interrupted them more, and became involved in activities with older peers. Past research suggests that divorced mothers and daughters may experience problems as daughters become pubescent and involved in heterosexual activities (Hetherington, 1972). The difficulties in interactions between these early maturing girls and their divorced mothers may be precursors of more intense problems yet to come.

One should distinguish between those families in the early stages of remarriage, when they are still adapting to their new situation, and those in the later stages of remarriage, when family roles and relationships should have been worked through and established. In some ways the early stage of remarriage may be a honeymoon period where the parents at least want to make the family relationship successful.

Further, in discussing stepfamilies, it becomes particularly important to identify which family members' perspective is being discussed, since they vary widely. For instance, family members agree that mothers in remarried families are as warm to their children as mothers in other types of families. However, children and stepfathers rate remarried mothers as having less control over their children's behavior than these mothers rate themselves as having. Both interview and observational data indicate that remarried mothers have greater control over her son than do nonremarried divorced mothers, but less control over her daughter than do mothers in either of the other two family types. Control over both daughters and sons is greater for mothers who have been remarried more than 2 years. In the first 2 years following remarriage, conflict between mothers and daughters is high. In addition, these daughters exhibit more demandingness, hostility, coercion, and less warmth toward both parents than do girls in divorced or nondivorced families. Their behavior improves over the course of remarriage. However, even 2 years after remarriage these girls are still more antagonistic and disruptive with their parents than are girls in the other two family types. This noxious behavior is supported by the reports of both parents and children and the observational findings.

In the first 2 years following remarriage, stepfathers reported themselves to be low on felt or expressed affection for their stepchildren, although they spend time with them attempting to establish a relationship. They express less strong positive affect and show fewer negative, critical responses than do the nondivorced fathers. Biological fathers are freer in expressing affection and in criticizing their children for poor personal grooming, not doing their homework, not cleaning up their rooms, or fighting with their siblings. However, they also are more involved and interested in the activities of their children. Initially, stepfathers are far less supportive to stepsons than to stepdaughters. In the interactions in the first 2 years of the remarriage, the stepfathers' interaction is almost that of a stranger who is attempting to be ingratiating, is seeking information, and is polite but emotionally disengaged. These stepfathers are remaining relatively pleasant in spite of the aversive behavior they encounter with their stepdaughters. By 2 years after remarriage, they are more impatient. Although they try to remain disengaged, they occasionally get into extremely angry interchanges with their stepdaughters. These conflicts tend to focus on issues of parental authority and respect for the mother. Stepdaughters view their stepfathers as hostile, punitive, and unreasonable on matters of discipline. The interchanges between stepfathers and stepdaughters and the conflicts between divorced mothers and sons are rated as the highest on hostility of any dyad. Stepfathers make significantly fewer control attempts and are less successful in gaining control with both sons and daughters than are nondivorced fathers. Their control of stepsons but not stepdaughters is better in longer remarriages.

The situation with stepsons is very different than that with stepdaughters. Although mothers and stepfathers view sons as initially being extremely difficult, their behavior is perceived as improving over time. In the families who have been remarried for over 2 years, these boys show no more aggressive noncompliant behavior in the home or problem behaviors, as measured on tests such as the Children's Behavior Checklist, than do boys in nondivorced families (see Hetherington *et al.* [1985] for more details on the adjustment of children). However, mothers, sons, and teachers report these boys as having more positive behavior than do stepfathers. Although stepfathers continue to view stepchildren, especially stepdaughters, as having more problems than do nondivorced fathers, they report improvement in the stepsons' behavior and exhibit greater warmth and involvement with them than with the stepdaughter. In those families remarried for a longer period of time, the stepsons frequently report being close to the stepfather, enjoying his company and seeking his advice and support. As was found in divorced families, monitoring of children's behavior is often not effective in stepfamilies.

Parent Typologies

One of the things that was noteable in these data was the greater variability on measures of both parents' and children's behavior in the divorced and remarried families than in the nondivorced families. It may be that stressful life transitions accentuate the diverse adaptive abilities and varied coping patterns of family members. We thought we might capture the patterning in these variations by looking at family typologies. A cluster analysis was performed on the parenting behaviors of mothers in the three family types and of fathers in the divorced families and in stepfamilies. Four parenting clusters emerged for mothers and fathers. The first was a *permissive parenting style* that was moderately high on warmth, high on involvement, and low on coercion, control, conflict, monitoring, and maturity demands. The second was a *disengaged parenting style* that was high on hostility and low on involvement, warmth, monitoring, control, and maturity demands. This second group involved adult-oriented parents who want to minimize the amount of time, effort, and interference with their own needs that childrearing entails. (It should be noted that when the child becomes demanding or inconveniences disengaged parents, things often become extremely hostile. The ratings of the most extremely hostile behavior that occurred during interactions were highest in disengaged and authoritarian parents.) The third group was an *authoritarian parenting style* that was high on involvement, control, conflict, monitoring attempts, punitiveness and coercion and low on warmth. The fourth was an *authoritative parenting* group that exhibited high warmth, involvement, monitoring, and maturity demands, moderately high but responsive control, and relatively low conflict. It is apparent that with the exception of the disengaged cluster, these are the same parenting typologies identified by Baumrind (1971). Table 8-3 presents the distribution across these four parenting typologies of mothers and fathers of boys and girls in stepfamilies and nondivorced families, and of divorced, nonremarried mothers.

The differences among parenting types are less marked for mothers than for fathers. The most frequent parenting style for all groups of mothers, with the exception of divorced mothers of boys, is authoritative parenting. In contrast, fathers in stepfamilies tend to be much less authoritative and more disengaged than are fathers in nondivorced families. Moreover, although the number of authoritative stepfathers increases over time for boys, authoritative behavior by stepfathers with daughters decreases and disengagement doubles as the remarriage goes on. In addition, even for boys after 2 years of

Table 8-3. Number of Responses in Various Types of Parenting Styles

	Permissive		Disengaged		Authoritarian		Authoritative	
	Mother	*Father*	*Mother*	*Father*	*Mother*	*Father*	*Mother*	*Father*
Nondivorced								
Boys	6	3	4	3	4	8	16	16
Girls	4	1	5	7	4	2	17	20
Divorced								
Boys	8	—	5	—	10	—	7	—
Girls	8	—	3	—	4	—	15	—
Remarried early								
Boys	6	5	4	14	8	7	12	4
Girls	6	7	5	10	5	4	14	9
Remarried late								
Boys	7	3	5	15	4	4	14	8
Girls	3	1	4	20	7	5	16	4

remarriage, disengagement remains the predominant parenting style of step-fathers.

Disengaged parenting and permissive parenting tend to be associated with poor impulse control, noncompliance, and antisocial behavior in children. However, early delinquent behavior and low social competence was more common in the sons of disengaged parents. Authoritarian parenting in nondivorced parents and in divorced mothers was associated with moody, irritable, anxious behavior and low self-esteem in girls. In boys, it is related to these same attributes but also to impulsive aggressive behavior in the school setting.

In general, authoritative parenting is associated with high social competence and low rates of behavior problems, especially with low externalizing problems, and especially in boys. The exception to this is in stepfathers' parenting. Both authoritative and authoritarian parenting in stepfathers is related to high rates of behavior problems in both stepdaughters and in stepsons in the first 2 years of remarriage. After 2 years, authoritative parenting by stepfathers is related to fewer behavior problems and greater acceptance of the stepfather by stepsons but is not at this time significantly related to stepdaughters' behavior. The best strategy of the stepfather in gaining acceptance of the stepchildren seems to be one where there is no initial active attempt to take over and try to actively shape and control the child's behavior either through authoritarian or the more desirable authoritative techniques. Instead, the new father should first work at establishing a relationship with the children and support the mother in her parenting. This period can then be effectively followed by more active, authoritative parenting, which leads to constructive outcomes, at least for boys.

The Impact of Spousal Support on Parents' and Children's Adjustment and on Parenting Behavior

Belsky (1984) has suggested that the marital relationship and support from a spouse may affect the parents' well-being, their relationship with their children, and consequently their children's adjustment. It might be thought that support from the spouse would be particularly important in new stepfamilies since divorced women often are reported to suffer from economic duress, social isolation, task overload, and childrearing problems. The shift to a new marital relationship might offer supports and resources from the stepfather that would help in coping with these problems. In addition, it has been proposed that there is considerable stress and role ambiguity in becoming a stepfather. Support by the mother may assist the stepfather in identifying, establishing, and enjoying his new role and responsibilities.

Six types of support were examined: (1) financial support, (2) emotional support, (3) support in household maintenance, (4) direct childrearing participation in shared activities and in emotional support of children, (5) active participation in character development and discipline, (6) support and encouragement for the spouse in his/her childrearing role. Separate canonical regressions for mothers and fathers were used to examine the relations between these six types of spousal support and parents' adjustment, parent–child relationships, and children's adjustment. Financial support was based on the spouse's income. Emotional support was based on a composite score that included the spouse's score on the Dyadic Adjustment Scale (Spanier, 1976), percentage of positive to positive plus negative scores on the observational measures, global ratings of warmth, and interview reports of closeness and involvement. Support in household maintenance was assessed by a composite measure involving amount of participation in household tasks and satisfaction with the amount of participation in household responsibilities. It should be noted that although these measures are moderately correlated ($p < .10$) as a single predictor of our outcome variables of interest, satisfaction with participation explains twice as much of the variance as does amount of participation. Satisfaction appears to involve an interaction between expectations and performance. Direct childrearing participation (shared activities and emotional support) was comprised of amount of time spent with the child and quality of the relationship with the child based on the 24-hour-behavior checklists, interview measures, and molecular and global observational measures of warmth/involvement. Discipline involved giving and enforcing directions as assessed by interviews and observations. Finally, support for the spouse in his/her childrearing activities was based on interview measures and molecular and global observational measures involving approval, sympathy, or disciplinary support for the spouse in dealing with the child.

The measures of personal adjustment used in this analysis were the Beck Depression Inventory (Beck, 1979), Speilberger's State–Trait Anxiety Inventory (Speilberger *et al.*, 1970), the Helmreich and Stapp Texas Social Behavior Inventory (Helmreich & Stapp, 1974), the Personal Control Scale of the Rotter I–E scale (Rotter, 1966), interview measures of life satisfaction, and the Socialization Scale of the California Personality Inventory (Gough, 1969). The assessment of the parent–child relationship involved the composite measures of warmth, control, and conflict obtained from interviews and 24-hour-behavior checklist and global and molecular observational measures. Finally, the child outcome measures involved measures of externalizing, internalizing and socially competent behavior based on observations, interviews, 24-hour-behavior checklists and standardized tests.

The relationship among the support variables and outcome variables differed in the remarried and nondivorced families, although those for couples remarried more than 2 years were becoming more similar to the nondivorced couples. There are more relationships between spousal support, on the one hand, and adjustment and personal well-being, on the other, for women than for men. For both women in nondivorced families and for spouses in the remarried families, the quality of the marital relationship was related positively to life satisfaction and negatively to depression scores. For women in all three family groups (early remarried, late remarried, and nondivorced), it also was related to state anxiety, and, for mothers in the early stages of remarriage, the quality of the marital relationship was associated with greater feelings of internalized control over the things that happened to them. Only for the mothers in the first 2 years of remarriage was economic support a significant predictor of maternal well-being. Economic support was related not only to internalized control but also to low depression, and low state anxiety, and to high life satisfaction, but only in this group of women. For most of the remarried women, household income had more than doubled following remarriage, and this may have relieved many of the stresses encountered while they were in one-parent households. Many remarried women spoke of the increased options in their lives offered by their newly obtained economic security. About 10% of these women stopped working for a short time following the remarriage but most returned to work. Twenty-three of the women in the early stages of remarriage were employed at least part time, 25 of those remarried more than 2 years were employed full-time, 25 nondivorced mothers were employed, and 27 of our nonremarried women were employed.

For nondivorced men, the quality of the marital relationship was related only to general life satisfaction, and this was a very modest relationship. Apparently, men's views of themselves and their life situation is largely determined by factors external to the marital relationship. Men also view their marriages and life situations more positively than do women. It may take an extremely disrupted marriage to affect masculine adjustment. However, research suggests that men are as distressed as women in response to separation and divorce and that they more often report not being aware of serious marital problems leading up to the divorce. When the marital dissolution does occur, they, as well as their wives, are likely to experience pervasive changes in self concept, emotional distress, and problems in relationships outside of the family (Hetherington *et al.*, 1982).

The effects of spousal support on three aspects of the parent–child relationship—control, warmth, and conflict—were examined. None of the paternal support variables were related to maternal control in the stepfamilies remarried for less than 2 years. However, support by the father for the mother's childrearing practices was related to more effective maternal control. especially over boys in both the longer remarried and nondivorced families, and direct participation in the rearing of boys by the father also was related to maternal control in nondivorced families. In addition, active participation in childrearing by the father and support of the mother in her childrearing were both related to maternal warmth in the longer remarried and nondivorced families. Again, in the couples remarried less than two years, support of the mothers' childrearing but not active intervention led to greater maternal warmth. The quality of the marital relationship was related to maternal warmth toward children only in nondivorced families.

Only in nondivorced families was active participation in childrearing by the father associated with lower conflict between mothers and sons. In the stepfamilies, there occurs what might appear to be an anomalous finding. A close marital relationship is associated with high levels of conflict by children in stepfamilies, especially daughters with their mothers and stepfathers. For sons, this relationship is significant in the early but not later stages of remarriage. How can we explain these unexpected results? It seems likely that in the early stages of remarriage the new stepfather is viewed as an intruder or a competitor for the mother's affection. Since boys in divorced families often have been involved in coercive or ambivalent relations with their mothers, they may, in the long run, have little to lose and something to gain from the remarriage. In contrast, daughters in single-parent households have played more responsible, powerful roles than girls in nondivorced families and have had more positive relations with their divorced mothers than have sons. They may see their independence and their relationship with the mother threatened by the introduction of the stepfather and therefore resent the mother for remarrying. This is seen in resistant, ignoring, critical behavior by the daughter toward her remarried mother. In addition, it is reflected in the sulky, negativistic, hostile behavior observed in stepdaughters with their stepfathers and in the girls own reports of their negative, rejecting attitudes toward the stepfathers. It is notable that the positive behavior of the stepfather toward stepdaughters does not correlate with her acceptance of the stepfather in the early stages of remarriage. No matter how hard the stepfather tries the daughter rejects him.

For nondivorced fathers, a close marital relationship, support by the mother for his childrearing participation, and direct participation by the mother in childrearing are related to paternal warmth and low father–child conflict. Again, the pattern differs in the remarried families, with fathers' reports of a close marital relationship being associated with higher levels of fathers' conflict with daughters in the longer-remarried families. In the early stages of remarriage, stepfathers are behaving in a relatively restrained fashion while they are actively attempting to make the new family situation work. Later in remarriages, there is more reciprocity of negative behavior between stepfathers and stepdaughters.

Finally, let us turn to the relation between the marital relationship, spousal support, and children's adjustment. In nondivorced families marital satisfaction, active involvement of the father in childrearing, and the father's support of the mother in her childrearing role were related to less externalizing behavior in boys and greater social competence in both boys and girls. In the longer-remarried families, support of the mother in her childrearing role and participation in child rearing not mainly as a disciplinarian but in the role of a friend and confidant also led to less externalizing behavior in boys. Boys from the small group of authoritative stepfathers in the late remarriage group had fewer total behavior problems than did boys with stepfathers in the other three parenting typologies. In contrast, active participation in childrearing by the stepfather and a close marital relationship actually led to an increase in acting out behavior and in depression in stepdaughters. Only paternal financial support was associated with fewer total behavior problems in girls in newly remarried families.

In nondivorced families, active involvement of the mother in childrearing and her support of the father in childrearing were related to lower externalizing behavior in boys. No other relationships between maternal support of the father and child outcomes were found.

In summary, financial support appears to be more important in the adjustment of newly remarried mothers and their daughters than in other families perhaps as a contrast with the previous state of financial deprivation experienced in a single-parent household. Parental participation in household tasks had no effects on our outcome measures. The main factors affecting the adjustment of parents and children and parent–child relations appeared to be those related to marital satisfaction, direct involvement in childrearing, and support for the spouse as a parent. Although marital satisfaction tends to be related to the psychological adjustment of the spouses, especially the women in all three family groups, the pattern of other relations differed in stepfamilies and nondivorced families. In stepfamilies, in contrast to nondivorced families, marital satisfaction was related to an increase in problems in parent-child relations and in children's adjustment, particularly with daughters. In addition, in stepfamilies support by the stepfather for the mother's parenting seems to be an efficacious strategy for successful parenting, whereas in nondivorced families active involvement of the father in childrearing also appears to have a particularly salutary effect on mothers' parenting behavior and on the adjustment of sons.

CONCLUSION AND SUMMARY

Family relations change in the 6 years following divorce, and these changes to some extent are related to ensuing marital arrangements. Custodial mothers who do not remarry in the 6 years following divorce have more emotional problems and are less satisfied with their lives than are remarried or nondivorced mothers. Even 6 years after divorce mothers continue to be involved in intense, ambivalent relationships and in coercive cycles with their sons, whereas their relationships with their daughters is a positive one. This is reflected in the adjustment of their 10-year-old children. Daughters in mother-custody homes, with the exception of early-maturing girls, are well adjusted. However, sons in these families show many behavior problems, especially in noncompliant, impulsive, aggressive externalizing behavior.

When divorced mothers remarry, their psychological well-being and life satisfaction increases. The marital relationship and various types of support from spouses affects parenting behavior and the adjustment of both parent and children. The relation of these support factors varies for parents in nondivorced, divorced, and remarried families. One notable finding is that, whereas marital satisfaction is related to positive parenting in nondivorced families, in the remarried families it is related to increased family conflict and behavior problems, especially in stepdaughters. Whereas boys in divorced nonremarried families have more problems both inside and outside of the home, boys in remarried families gradually adapt to and may benefit from contact with a supportive stepfather. Although stepdaughters also gradually adapt to the remarriage, they continue to have more problems in family relations and adjustment than do girls in nondivorced families or in families with custodial mothers who have been divorced for 6 years and who have not remarried.

The types of parenting patterns and their impact on children vary for children in divorced, nondivorced, and remarried families. Authoritative parenting in mothers is the most common parenting style, with the exception of divorced mothers with sons. Moreover, authoritative parenting is related to fewer behavior problems in children in homes with divorced, nonremarried custodial mothers and in nondivorced families. In stepfamilies, a different pattern of relations occurs. Attempts by the stepfather to directly exert control, even authoritative control, over the child's behavior or disengagement early in the remarriage are associated with rejection of the stepfather by the children and with children's problem behavior. A stepfather who first establishes a warm relationship with the stepson and supports the mother's parenting and later moves into an authoritative role has the greatest probability of gaining acceptance and facilitating the adjustment of stepsons. In contrast, even when the stepfather is supportive and gives appropriate responses to a stepdaughter, her acceptance is difficult to gain. A troubling finding in this study is that disengaged parenting is the most common parenting style of stepfathers and disengagement with stepdaughters increases over time.

Past research (Hetherington *et al.*, 1978) has reported that coping strategies that lead to positive outcomes for one family member may adversely affect the adjustment of another member of the family during divorce. This also seems to be the case in remarriage. In order to understand the complex network of factors involved in this adjustment process, it is necessary to view the family not solely in terms of intrafamilial factors as has been done in this paper but also in terms of the families larger ecological framework. This will be done in future papers ensuing from this project.

REFERENCES

Achenbach, T. M., & Edelbrock, C. S. (1983). *The Child Behavior Checklist*. Burlington, VT: University of Vermont.

Baumrind, D. (1971). Current patterns of parental authority. *Developmental Psychology Monographs, 4* (1; Pt. 2).

Beck, A. T. (1979). *Depression: Causes and treatment*. Philadelphia, PA: University of Pennsylvania Press.

Belsky, J. (1984). The determinants of parenting: A process model. *Child Development, 55*, 83–96.

Glick, P. (1979). *Who are the children in one-parent households*. Paper presented at Wayne State University, Detroit, MI.

Glick, P. C., & Lin, S. (1986). Recent changes in divorce and remarriage. *Journal of Marriage and the Family, 48*, 737–747.

Gough, H. G. (1969). *Manual for California Personality Inventory*. Palo Alto, CA: Consulting Psychologists Press.

Gough, H. G., & Heilbrun, A. B., Jr. (1965). *The Adjective Checklist*. Palo Alto, CA: Consulting Psychologists Press.

Hagan, M. S. (1986, April). *The effect of discrepant perceptions and conflict on marital satisfaction and child adjustment in remarried versus nondivorced families*. Paper presented at the Southeastern Regional Meeting of the Society for Research in Child Development, Nashville, TN.

Harter, S. (1982). The Perceived Competence Scale for children. *Child Development, 53*, 87–97.

Hetherington, E. M. (1972). Effects of father absence on personality development in adolescent daughters. *Developmental Psychology, 7*, 313–326.

Hetherington, E. M., & Clingempeel, G. (1986). The adjustment of parents and children to divorce and remarriage. Symposium presented at the Southeastern Regional Meeting of the Society for Research in Child Development, Nashville, TN.

Hetherington, E. M., Cox, M., & Cox, R. (1978). The aftermath of divorce. In J. H. Stevens, Jr. & M. Matthews (Eds.), *Mother–child, father–child relations* (pp. 110–155). Washington, DC: National Association for the Education of Young Children.

Hetherington, E. M., Cox, M., & Cox, R. (1979a). Family interaction and the social, emotional and cognitive development of children following divorce. In V. Vaughn & T. Brazelton (Eds.), *The family: Setting priorities* (pp. 89–128). New York: Science and Medicine Publishing Co.

Hetherington, E. M., Cox, M., & Cox, R. (1979b). Play and social interaction in children following divorce. *Journal of Social Issues, 35,* 26–49.

Hetherington, E. M., Cox, M., & Cox, R. (1982). Effects of divorce on parents and children. In M. E. Lamb (Ed.), *Nontraditional families: Parenting and child development.* (pp. 233–288). Hillsdale, NJ: Erlbaum.

Hetherington, E. M., Cox, M., & Cox, R. (1985). Long-term effects of divorce and remarriage on the adjustment of children. *Journal of the American Academy of Psychology, 24*(5), 518–530.

Patterson, G. (1982). *Coercive family patterns.* Eugene, OR: Castalia.

Pekarik, E. G., Prinz, R. J., Liebert, D. E., Weintraub, S., & Neale, J. M. (1976). The Pupil Evaluation Inventory. *Journal of Abnormal Child Psychology, 4,* 83–97.

Rotter, J. B. (1966). Generalized expectancies for internal versus external control of reinforcement. *Psychological Monographs, 80,* (1; Whole No. 609).

Santrock, J. W., & Warshak, R. A. (1986). Developmental relationships and legal/clinical considerations in father-custody families. In M. E. Lamb (Ed.), *The father's role: Applied perspectives* (pp. 135–163). New York: Wiley.

Sarason, I. G., Johnson, J., & Siegal, J. (1978). Assessing the impact of life change: Development of the Life Experience Survey. *Journal of Consulting and Clinical Psychology, 46,* 932–946.

Spanier, G. B. (1976). Measuring dyadic adjustment: New scales for assessing the quality of marriage and similar dyads. *Journal of Marriage and the Family, 1,* 13–26.

Speilberger, C. D., Gorsuch, R. L., & Lushene, R. (1970). *State–Trait Anxiety Inventory.* Palo Alto, CA: Consulting Psychologists Press.

Wallerstein, J. S. (1982, July). *Children of divorce: Preliminary report of a 10-year follow-up.* Paper presented at the 10th International Congress of the International Association for Child and Adolescent Psychiatry and Applied Professional, Dublin, Ireland.

Wallerstein, J. S. (1986). Women after divorce: Preliminary report from a ten-year follow-up. *American Journal of Orthopsychiatry, 56*(1), 65–77.

Wallerstein, J. S., & Kelly, J. B. (1980). *Surviving the breakup: How children and parents cope with divorce.* New York: Basic Books.

Warshak, R., & Santrock, J. W. (1983). Impact of divorce, father-custody, and mother-custody homes: The child's perspective. In L. A. Kurdek (Ed.), *Children and divorce* (pp. 29–46). San Francisco, CA: Jossey-Bass.

Weiss, R. (1975). *Marital separation.* New York: Basic Books.

9

Family Boundary Ambiguity: Perceptions of Adult Stepfamily Members

KAY PASLEY
Colorado State University

INTRODUCTION

The literature identifying and discussing the problems facing persons in remarriage often includes mention of "boundary ambiguity" (Boss, 1977) and "boundary maintenance" (Messinger, 1976; Robinson, 1980; Visher & Visher, 1979). To date, only one research study on family boundaries has focused on remarriage and examined boundary maintenance as part of a series of factors influencing marital stability (Ihinger-Tallman & Pasley, 1981). The research reported here stems from this earlier work and attempts to examine these concepts—as well as boundary permeability—in greater detail. Specifically, the purpose of this study was to describe the degree and assess the prevalence of boundary ambiguity found in a sample of remarried couples.

The concept of family boundary derives from family systems theory and refers to system and subsystem rules regarding participating members, in other words, who, when, and how members participate in family life (Minuchin, 1974; Minuchin, Montalvo, Guerney, Rossman, & Schumer, 1967). Boundary ambiguity has to do with the uncertainty among family members regarding "their perceptions about who is in or out of the family and who is performing what roles and tasks within the family system" (Boss & Greenberg, 1984, p. 536). Boss has suggested that boundaries include both physical and psychological phenomena which serve to foster a sense of identity that differentiates the members of a group (family) from one another and from other groups (families) (Boss, 1977, 1980b; Boss & Greenberg, 1984).

Boundary ambiguity, defined as a lack of clarity or misalignment of boundaries within the family, has been related to increased family stress and overall family dysfunction (Boss & Greenberg, 1984; Minuchin, 1974). Specifically, Boss (1980a) proposed that individual and family perceptions of who is inside or outside the family are related to the nature of interaction

206

within that system and between that system and the outside world. She suggests that some consensus about family membership (i.e., clarification of the ambiguous state) must occur before the family can function optimally. If the family is unable to clearly determine its membership, it has difficulty determining the roles and rules by which to live. For example, if all members in the new family do not perceive non-residential children who "visit" as part of the family, these children will likely not be assigned the same roles and tasks, nor will they have to act according to the same rules as those children who reside within the family on a daily basis. Residential children may come to resent this differential treatment, and hostile, angry interaction among children or between children and parents may result. Using systems ideas, this means that productive change is blocked and the system (family) remains static. Change becomes impossible because of the confusion that exists regarding membership, roles, and tasks, and movement toward resolution of the confusion cannot occur.

Research suggests that a high degree of boundary ambiguity in any family may cause dysfunction. Boss (1975, 1977) found family functioning was diminished in families of soldiers who were Missing in Action (MIA). Wives in such families perceived the father as still a member of the family (psychological presence) while he was, in fact, physically absent. Further, Boss (1980a) reported that the best predictor of high family functioning in "MIA families" was congruence in the wife's perception of the father's absence, that is, he was perceived as both psychologically *and* physically absent. These findings emphasize the importance of both the psychological and physical dimensions of boundary ambiguity. In the case of remarriage following the death of a spouse, the former spouse (now deceased and therefore physically absent) may continue to influence the newly formed family, particularly if remarriage occurs quickly and the mourning process remains incomplete. Children in such a family, where the mother refers to the biological father as if he were still an active participant in childrearing, may become confused about family membership or the amount of parental authority the new stepfather has over the child's behavior. This type of ambiguity can be referred to as psychological presence coupled with physical absence.

Unclear family boundaries also occur in situations where the physical presence of a family member is coupled with psychological absence, as in the case of a new stepparent who is treated as an outsider by the stepchildren in the new family. In a family discussion, the stepfather may be ignored or talked about as if he was not present or part of the family. Or, it may be that a stepfather is psychologically preoccupied with the needs of his own biological children who reside elsewhere, a preoccupation which diminishes his interest in and ability to be involved with his stepchildren. In both cases, he is physically present in the new family but psychologically absent.

Some literature on remarriage suggests that unclear family boundaries are more common in remarriages than in first marriages (Messinger, 1976; Robinson, 1980; Walker & Messinger, 1979) due to potentially greater permeability and the need to redefine membership. Permeability has to do with the openness of boundaries, or the flow of people in and out for various purposes. At least one study of remarried individuals suggests that permeability influences the adjustment and integration process for family members (Ihinger-Tallman & Pasley, 1981). This study examined boundary permeability as one of several factors contributing to marital instability in remarriages. Data from 788 remarried persons were analyzed. Boundary permeability was measured with four separate scales: degree of access by other people into the family home, frequency with which other people visited the home, frequency of contact with formal agencies or organizations, and frequency with which problems and troubles were shared with others. The findings suggested there were no significant differences between persons in stable and unstable remarriages when reporting the number of people allowed to enter the house without knocking (degree of access). Significant differences *were* found between those in stable and unstable marriages in reports of frequency of contact with formal agencies and organizations and with acquaintances, friends, neighbors, and relatives. For persons in stable marriages, there was greater contact with acquaintances, friends, neighbors, and relatives and less contact with formal organizations and agencies. This is reminiscent of Bernard Farber's finding that families undergoing a crisis have more contact with professionals and less with relatives and former friends (Farber, 1964).

Gender differences were also identified on another measure of boundary permeability: reports of the frequency with which problems were shared with persons outside the family. On this item, females in stable remarriages shared less frequently with others but perceived their husbands as sharing more. No significant differences were found in the men's reports. It was concluded that family boundaries in stable remarriages were more permeable to close associates and less permeable to formal, institutional contacts. While these findings provide limited information about the existence of different types of boundary permeability, they offer no information about the incidence of unclear family boundaries in remarriage nor whether unclear family boundaries are more characteristic of certain types of remarried families. The study reported in this chapter examines these issues.

This study compares the frequency with which remarried couples are categorized as having ambiguous boundaries, as well as the frequency with which four degrees of boundary ambiguity appear. This analysis utilizes Boss's (1980a) conceptualization: (1) low boundary ambiguity indicated by congruence between psychological and physical presence (both high or both low); and (2) boundary ambiguity as indicated by incongruence between psychological and physical presence (one high, the other low). Degree of boundary ambiguity is identified for different types of remarried families, and several structural variables are controlled in the analyses: length of marriage, way in which the former marriage ended (death versus divorce), presence of adolescent children, and social class. Literature relevant to this investigation follows.

SOURCE OF BOUNDARY AMBIGUITY

Boundary ambiguity, or the lack of congruence in perceptions regarding family membership, is influenced by boundary permeability and boundary clarity. Boundary permeability is defined as (1) the amount of interaction between the family and its environment (Messinger, 1976) and/or specific others in the environment who have access to the family (Ihinger-Tallman & Pasley, 1981); and/or (2) the volition for such interaction (Boss, personal communication, 1986). Boundary clarity refers to the consistency of patterns of contact between family members and others (Minuchin, 1974). These two aspects of boundaries are different for first families and those established by remarriage.

In first-marriage families, membership is defined biologically, legally, and spatially, and is characterized by explicit boundaries. A child may not only physically resemble his/her parents, but birth certificates are "proof" of consanguine relationships. Shared surnames are another means of explicitly demonstrating family membership. Extended kin such as grandparents are usually experienced positively and considered "family"—their input is usually welcomed, being seen as stemming from care and concern. Spouses have clearly defined legal ties to their children, and siblings have recognized legal ties to each other because they share the same parents (Wald, 1981). This first family is regarded as a physically defined system with fairly impermeable boundaries.

Remarried families are most likely to be characterized by more subjectively determined boundaries, considering both the frequency of contact and volitional nature of boundaries (Boss, personal communication, 1986; Walker & Messinger, 1979). The common household and surname maintained by both biological parents and their children in a first-marriage family are physical boundary markers unavailable in remarried families. Children brought to remarriages usually hold membership in two households simultaneously, that of their residential parent and that of their non-residential parent. Depending on custody and visitation arrangements, children, as well as other family members (e.g., stepgrandparents, stepsiblings), may or may not consider their "new" siblings to be members of the remarried family. While the new siblings may be considered as family members by their biological parent, their stepparent may have some confusion about their membership in the new family. Also, the stepparent and non-residential parent (usually the stepfather and father) may share economic responsibility for the children as well as some degree of parental authority in terms of daily child care, but the legal rights of stepparents are ill-defined or non-existent.

Thus, in the remarried family, the family boundary is not clearly defined, particularly where non-residential children from a prior marriage are concerned. There may not be consensus about whether these children are "in" the family. Some children, for example, may visit only 2 weeks out of a year. For children who regularly reside within the remarried family, there may be some confusion regarding whether these visiting children are actually "members" of their family. The biological parent of the residential children may share this confusion about the membership of these visiting children. Alternatively, there may be no face-to-face contact at all between the current family members and those from the prior marriage, also creating confusion about family boundaries via perceptions of membership.

Boundaries also become more ambiguous when contact is expanded to include extended kin and quasi-kin[1] as per legal arrangements (as in the case of grandparent visitation rights), less formal agreements, and prior patterns of interaction. Such contact forces the boundaries separating the remarried family and those outside the family to be more open. Thus, for the newly formed stepfamily, boundaries may be biologically, legally, and spatially unclear. Such lack of clarity means members may be confused about family membership—confusion is less likely when members interact on a regular basis (physical presence) and come to see one another as belonging to the existing family unit (psychological presence). Overall, remarried family members interact with an increased number of kin, and the nature of this interaction is not guided by social conventions that apply to a first-marriage family. Norms for appropriate behavior in the multitude of relationships are ill-defined or non-existent (Cherlin, 1978).

Boundary clarity, or consistency of the pattern of contact, is a concept used to measure family functioning. While researchers typically use boundary clarity and boundary permeability interchangeably, arguments have been made against this usage (Boss, personal communication, 1986; Clingempeel, 1981). If a spousal subsystem is to be defined as "healthy," it must have clearly defined boundaries that protect it from the demands of the parent–child subsystem. In families where a strong parent coalition does not exist, enmeshment results, and the roles and functions of family members, parents and children, become blurred (Olson, Russell, & Sprenkle, 1983). Such is sometimes the case in a new remarriage, when during the single-parent phase the mother and child have each served as the emotional support for the other in handling the divorce (Hetherington, Cox, & Cox, 1979). As such, the roles of parent and child become blurred. If the single-parent household contained an older child, that child likely also assumed some adult responsibilities during that time. Upon remarriage, these adult responsibilities are reassigned to the new spouse/stepparent, resulting in a greater distinction between adult and child roles and responsibilities. Such change requires the child and biological parent to redefine their earlier roles and identities.

In other families the pattern of contact between members is nonexistent or is so inconsistent that members of the new stepfamily (particularly children) become confused. For example, the parental subsystem of a "disengaged" family might be minimally involved in the parenting process, and characterized by a stepparent who is unwilling or unable to assume any parental responsibility and authority for the stepchild.

The boundary ambiguity in remarried families may result from several things. Ambiguous boundaries are expected in the transition from one life style to another (i.e., from divorce to remarriage). Yet, this ambiguous state becomes problematic when it continues and is not resolved by the redefinition of roles and rules. Because of the absence of social norms (Cherlin, 1978) and/or the existence of negative stereotypes regarding "step" members (see Coleman & Ganong, Chapter 2), it is often the case that boundary ambiguity is not lessened in stepfamilies. Visitation of children residing outside the remarried family often causes confusion which results in ambiguous boundaries. The lack of social norms for visitation and maintenance of nonresidential relationships does not clarify the boundaries for these families. Consider the stepchild who has been told that his/her new stepfather also has children, but the stepfather rarely sees the children and dislikes talking about them because of his own guilt and emotional pain. Family membership in this case would be less clear for the stepchildren since they are unable to get the "facts" about whether the other children are in or out of the family. On the other hand, we also see boundary ambiguity resulting from the conscious or unconscious ignoring or denial of the existence of family members. The single-parent tells the child that their other parent is "dead" or that a new stepparent is an unloving and "wicked stepmother," when such is not the case at all.

It has been suggested also that other aspects of our society impede the development of clear boundaries in remarried families. The mass media may impede the development of positive social attitudes toward stepfamilies (Perkins & Kahan, 1979; Visher & Visher, 1979). However, as Clingempeel, Brand, and Segal have noted in Chapter 4, no empirical research has tested this hypothesis. Further, the lack of legal sanctions (an example of the lack of social norms) for stepparents is another indication of the extra-legal status of this family type, leading to confusion regarding parental responsibilities and rights. Stepparents have no legal rights where stepchildren are concerned, as exemplified in the situation where a stepchild needs medical treatment and the stepparent is not permitted to authorize such treatment. Stepparents also have no legal rights to custody and/or visitation of their stepchildren who resided with them prior to the end of the remarriage via death or divorce (Kargman, 1983). In fact, joint custody legislation (where the non-residential parent must be consulted on childrearing matters) does not apply to the stepparent when the remarriage ends. Thus, for members of stepfamilies in particular, the legal sanctions and normative expectations for parental responsibility in biological families are nonexistent, which implicitly suggests their ambiguous status.

FACTORS INFLUENCING BOUNDARY AMBIGUITY

Several factors have been identified that influence family boundaries (Boss & Greenberg, 1984; Wood & Talmon, 1983). These factors include: family context, time or stage in the family lifecycle, and length of transition between marriages. These are discussed below.

Family Context

According to Wood and Talmon (1983), "context" involves one's cultural background, family style, and/or the extent of community support available to a particular member or family group. Some families encourage more interaction between generations than do others. Boundary ambiguity is different in a family whose cultural background encourages few generational ties than in one where clarity and definition regarding the interaction between generations is emphasized. Different types of families have different degrees of boundary ambiguity. One family may have blurred boundaries where, for example, generational boundaries are not clearly defined; another family may have extremely open boundaries, where family members and other people come and go freely. In addition, the utilization of community support systems by a particular family may result in more ambiguous boundaries because of the greater outside contact (greater permeability) than a family which has limited interaction with persons and agencies within the community.

Moreover, in the case of remarriage, the concept of "context" must be expanded to include certain structural characteristics which likely influence the boundaries differentiating subsystems within the family, as well as the family as a group from other families in the external environment. Remarriages of greater structural complexity would be expected to have more ambiguous boundaries than structurally simple families and would be characterized also by more permeable boundaries. For example, a remarriage that includes only one spouse with prior marital experience and only his/her children from that prior marriage (the other spouse is not a parent) would likely come to define its boundaries with greater ease than a remarriage where both adults have children from prior marriages and one set resides with the newly married couple and the other set of children "visits."

In addition to the structural complexity of remarried families, the manner in which the prior marriage ended (death versus divorce) likely influences family boundaries. The clinical literature suggests that stepfamilies formed after the death of a spouse confront different issues (e.g., idolizing the deceased parent) than those formed following divorce (Robinson, 1980; Theis, 1977; Visher & Visher, 1979). A remarriage immediately following the death of a spouse may find the survivors referring to the perceived wishes of the deceased spouse/parent in matters dealing with the children, as if the parent were still an active partner (psychologically present) in the parent–child subsystem. However, empirical studies have not examined this potentially important variable (Ganong & Coleman, 1984).

Time or Stage

Time refers to a particular point in the family life cycle when an event such as divorce and remarriage is more likely to influence family boundaries. It is developmentally appropriate early in the family life cycle for the childless couple in a first marriage to be more cohesive and have less permeable boundaries as they attempt to develop a clear sense of identity (Olson, McCubbin, Barnes *et al.*, 1983). This is seen as functional family behavior. Similarly, as children are added to a marriage through pregnancy and birth, boundaries may continue to remain less permeable than later when family members begin to clarify membership and roles. This, too, would be viewed as functional family behavior. As children move to middle childhood and adolescence, family boundaries become more permeable. Peers are brought into the home, and children become more involved in activities outside the home. As children become young adults, marry, and have children of their own, family boundaries become more blurred with the addition of new members to the original family (e.g., in-laws, grandchildren).

Should divorce and remarriage occur, family boundaries are less clearly defined and can become more permeable, as members adjust to new family routines. During adolescence, for example, the adults in a new stepfamily may exert pressure for *all* members to spend time together to solidify the family identity and sense of belonging, a desire which may be unwanted and unheeded by the adolescent. Here the needs and tasks of two different stages in the family life cycle compete: The tasks of the establishment phase and those of parenting adolescent children come into conflict. Pasley and Ihinger-Tallman (1984) reported that 100% of their sample of 784 remarried individuals highly valued "a close family and many shared times," but few reported that this value was translated into reality within their own marriages. This finding suggests that complications may be caused by overlapping stages in the family life cycle. For adolescents who become members of a stepfamily, a decision must be made regarding how much energy he/she wants to invest in the new family, given that limited time is available before the child moves out of the family and becomes independent (Pasley & Ihinger-Tallman, 1982).

Length of Transition between Marriages

Boss and Greenberg (1984) suggest that knowledge of the duration of transition is essential for understanding the influence of boundary ambiguity on the family. When separation and divorce occur, family boundaries lose clarity and family membership becomes confused as the father or mother moves in and out of the home. However, boundaries become less ambiguous over time, as consensus among family members regarding membership develops and a consistent pattern results. Psychological perception regarding who is in and not in the family also becomes clearer with the passage of time and consistent routines.

When remarriage follows divorce, boundaries once again become ambiguous, as members try to define roles, rules, and routines and develop a consistent pattern of interaction. Again, over time boundaries would be expected to become less ambiguous. For families unable to define roles and rules, and whose routines continue to be inconsistent, dysfunctional family behavior can result (Boss & Greenberg, 1984). This is illustrated in the following example: A wife (who has children from a prior marriage residing with her new family) resents her spouse's attachment to his biological child who visits monthly. Over time, resentment continues as she attempts to deny the reality of his prior marriage by rejection of his child. This denial impedes productive family behavior, as the husband becomes increasingly confused by his wife's behavior and is later angered by it. Over time a consistent pattern of visitation develops, making denial of the child's reality and the spouse's prior marriage impossible. If the issues are not resolved and the couple fails to develop a shared perception regarding family membership which includes both sets of children, productive family interaction will be diminished.

The psychological dimension of boundary ambiguity cannot be overstated. Both spouses and children bring to the newly formed family a prior family history—memories and experiences which shape their concept of family membership and feelings of belonging. Incorporating new members, as in the case of remarriage, requires that a different perspective about one's meaning of "family" be formed. A young child, for example, whose concept of the family likely includes only one father, experiences confusion, as he/she attempts to assimilate the new stepfather into his/her concept of family. Because the stepfather does not "fit" cognitively, he can more readily be ignored psychologically, at least for a time. However, over time it becomes harder to ignore the psychological reality of a stepparent. Such psychological distancing is easier when the child does not reside with the stepparent on a daily basis. Lack of frequent contact means that the child's perception and his/her reality do not come into conflict as often. Such would also be the case in stepfamilies where one set of children from the prior marriage visit infrequently.

In summary, both boundary permeability and boundary clarity serve as sources for the development of boundary ambiguity. There are few, if any, societal guidelines available to assist families in eliminating such ambiguity within remarriage. Because the contextual environment is more complex and the family is likely faced with overlapping stages in the family life cycle, boundary ambiguity is more likely. To date, however, no investigation has examined the prevalence of boundary ambiguity in remarriage or the conditions under which boundary ambiguity appears. The present study explores boundary ambiguity in remarriage by (1) determining the prevalence of boundary ambiguity in a sample of remarried couples; and (2) describing the types of boundary ambiguity in remarriages of differing structures. Future research needs are also discussed.

THE STUDY

Sample

The sample for this study ($N = 272$ couples) was taken from a larger project (Pasley & Ihinger-Tallman, 1980). Respondents for the larger study were drawn from the records of marriage license applications issued in Spokane County, Washington, between January 1975 and December 1979. A list of 6935 couples in which at least one of the pair reported prior marital experience was obtained from these records. From this group, 3,160 couples' names appeared in the then current (1980) telephone directory. A random sample of potential participants was drawn from the list of couples whose names appeared in the directory, and about 250 couples were selected from each year ($N = 1281$). Participants were potentially included in the study if (1) they could be contacted by telephone, and (2) they were currently married. The randomly selected couples were mailed a letter introducing the study and inviting participation. An attempt was made to contact each household by telephone to determine willingness to participate in the study by completing a questionnaire. These calls revealed that 170 couples did not meet the criteria for inclusion (e.g., spouse had died, the couple had separated, divorced, or had actually not married once making application); another 257 couples could not be reached by telephone after repeated attempts (i.e., wrong number, disconnected, moved with no new listing). Of those contacted, 267 couples refused to participate. Overall, 587 couples

216   *Pasley*

agreed to participate and two copies of a 14-page questionnaire were mailed
to these couples. Fifteen of the 587 couples separated between the initial
contact and the end of the 7-week follow-up procedure. Completed questionnaires were returned by 359 couples and 66 individuals (only one spouse
responded). The final response rate was 46.8% (the number returning the
completed questionnaires [784 individuals] divided by the number who met
the criteria for inclusion [1678 individuals]). No follow-up was attempted for
those who could not be contacted, refused to participate, or failed to complete the questionnaire.

For this study couples who had adult children (no children under 19
years residing in the home or with the other parent) and childless couples
were excluded from the analysis. Thus, the findings reported here are based
on data obtained from 272 couples.

Table 9-1 presents information regarding the principal demographic
characteristics of the couples in this sample. As can be seen in this table, most

Table 9-1. Number and Percent of Couples in Terms of Demographic Characteristics

Demographic Characteristic	Number	Percent
Number of persons living in the household		
Two (only non-residential children)	34	12.6
Three (one child)	84	31.0
Four (two children)	91	33.6
Five (three children)	41	15.1
Six (four children)	14	5.2
Seven or more (five or more children)	7	2.5
Presence of adolescents		
Yes	86	31.7
No	185	68.3
Prior marital experience		
Only one spouse	132	48.5
Both spouses	140	51.5
Way prior marriage ended, if any		
Death only	6	2.4
Divorce only	247	96.5
Combination of death and divorce	13	5.1
Type of remarried family		
Non-custodial children only	35	13.2
Common children only	47	18.4
Custodial children only	74	27.9
Variations of the above	102	40.4
Social class		
White collar	129	54.7
Blue collar	107	45.3

remarried couples had one or two children residing with them, and few remarried couples (2.6%) had what is considered a large family (five or more children). Among those with children present, about one third of the couples had an adolescent child present in the home while the remaining two thirds had no children over 12 years of age residing in the home. The sample was divided about equally by the number of couples in which only one spouse reported prior marital experience versus couples in which both reported prior marital experience.

Several designations of remarried family type were reported. The majority of couples (40.4%) reported some type of complex family structure, couples with custody of a child/ren from a prior marriage plus a common child/ren, or couples with custody of a child/ren from a prior marriage plus a non-custodial child/ren from a prior marriage, or couples with a common child/ren and non-custodial child/ren from a prior marriage, or couples with custody of a child/ren from a prior marriage plus a non-custodial child/ren and a common child/ren. Fewer couples reported a simple family structure with only children from a prior marriage (13.2%).

Couples were classified as either white or blue collar families on the basis of husband's occupation. On the basis of this socioeconomic characteristic, 54.7% were designated as white collar couples and 45.3% were designated as blue collar couples.

As might be expected, the majority of couples entered this marriage following divorce (96.5%). Only 2.35% were remarried following death of a spouse. Another 5% were remarriages where one spouse had ended their prior marriage by divorce while the other had remarried following the death of a spouse.

Instruments

Boundary ambiguity was assessed using items that measured both psychological and physical dimensions. The responses from both spouses on separate questionnaires were used to classify *couples* in one of several different types of boundary ambiguity discussed below. Important to the analysis, boundary ambiguity is measured as a couple construct.

Psychological ambiguity was derived from individual responses to a question which asked: "Please tell us who are the people you consider to be your family members. List them, their age and sex, beginning with yourself." Prompts of "Who? (husband, wife, son, stepson, etc.)" were offered to increase the chances respondents would label relations as accurately as possible. If spouses reported the same children, whether the children were biological, "step," or "common," they were coded as having low psychological ambiguity. When spouses did not perceive the same family membership (i.e., exclusion of a child or children), the couple was seen as having high psychological ambiguity.

Physical ambiguity was derived from individual responses to two questions. The first question asked "The following questions ask about you and the other members of your present family. Please tell us who lives in your home with you at this time. List them, their age, and sex." Again a prompt was offered, "Who? (son, stepdaughter, wife, etc.)" to enhance the chances that relationships were labeled accurately. A second question asked about the children or stepchildren who did not live with the couple. Spouses identifying the same children on these two questions were classified as having low physical ambiguity. Spouses who did not report the same children were designated as having high physical ambiguity.

These two questions were used together because, after examining responses on only the first question, it was discovered that some stepmother families with children residing outside the home would have been inaccurately classified as having physical ambiguity when in actuality both adults acknowledged the nonresidential stepchild in the second question. The same situation was true for nonresidential mother–stepfather families. Using responses to both questions permitted the inclusion of all types of stepfamilies.

Data Analysis

The purpose of this study was to assess the prevalence and describe the degree of boundary ambiguity in this sample of remarried couples. Therefore, frequency counts were made of (1) the number of couples characterized as having high (some) or low (none) boundary ambiguity; (2) the number of couples categorized as having different types of boundary ambiguity (the different types being low psychological and low physical, low psychological and high physical, high psychological and low physical, or high psychological and high physical); and (3) the types of remarried families classified as having ambiguous boundaries.

Chi-square analysis was performed to determine if significant differences exist between couples by various subgroups or demographic characteristics such as (1) income level, (2) social class, (3) length of marriage (less than 2 years, 2 to 4 years, and 4 or more years), (4) prior marital experience (one only vs. both), (5) manner in which the prior marriage terminated (death, divorce, or combinations of these two)[2], (6) number of children in the household (less than 2, 3 to 4, more than 4), (7) presence or absence of adolescent children (at least 12 years), and (8) type of remarried family (nonresidential children only, children born to the current marriage only, residential children from a prior marriage, or a combination of these). For the *chi*-square analysis boundary ambiguity groups were designated as low or high only.

FINDINGS

Prevalence of Boundary Ambiguity

Of the 272 couples, 164 (60.7%) were classified as having low psychological and low physical boundary ambiguity. Spouses in these couples shared the same perception regarding family membership (psychological presence) and also reported the existence of the same children as residing inside and/or outside the home (physical presence).

The remaining 108 couples (39.3% of the sample) were classified as having ambiguous boundaries (see Table 9-2). Twenty-two couples (7.7%) were classified as sharing the same perception regarding family membership (psychological dimension), but disagreed on the children who resided inside and/or outside the home (physical presence). These couples were labeled as having low psychological and high physical ambiguity. Another 36 couples (13.2%) were classified as failing to share the same perception regarding family membership while agreeing on the children residing inside and/or outside the home (high psychological and low physical ambiguity).

The largest segment of the group having ambiguous boundaries consisted of couples who neither shared the same perception regarding psychological family membership nor reported the same children physically residing inside and/or outside the home (50 couples or 18.4% of the sample). These couples were classified as having both high psychological and high physical boundary ambiguity. Clearly these data suggest many of the couples in this sample have some degree of confusion over family boundaries as defined here.

Table 9-2. Number and Percent of Couples by Type of Boundary Ambiguity

Degree of Boundary Ambiguity	Number	Percent
Low psychological + low physical[a]	164	60.7
Low psychological + high physical[b]	22	7.7
High psychological + low physical[b]	36	13.2
High psychological + high physical[b]	50	18.4

[a]Couples with this type of boundary ambiguity are referred to as having a "low" degree of ambiguity.

[b]Couples with this type of boundary ambiguity are referred to as having a "high" degree of ambiguity.

Types of Remarried Families

The data pertaining to the comparison of boundary ambiguity by type of remarried family are presented in Table 9-3. The least frequent type of remarried family is the one in which there are children from each previous marriage, as well as from their current marriage to each other. The most frequent types are those with children from *his* previous marriage and the marriages with children from both previous marriages. The greater frequency of the Husband (H), Wife (W), H's children type than the H, W, W's children type is very likely a reflection of the fact that men with children find it easier to remarry than women with children—one reason for this being that the wives are more likely to have custody.

These data are more important in the present analysis for what they say about boundary ambiguity. At one extreme are those remarriages with common children only. For these married individuals, family boundaries are (by our definitions) almost uniformly unambiguous, as might be expected. At the other extreme are the H, W, H's children units, more than three quarters of which are high in ambiguity. This, of course, is most likely the result of the fact that in most cases his children do not live with them, so that the wife excludes them from her family definition, while the husband more often than not includes them.[3] All the other family types are in between these extremes in ambiguity, ranging from 24% to 50% high in ambiguity. Although there are too few cases to generalize, it should not surprise us if, given more cases, the

Table 9-3. Type of Remarried Family and Percent with Low or High Boundary Ambiguity

Type of Remarried Family (not based on shared household)	Number	Boundary Ambiguity	
		% Low	% High
H, W, [a]their child(ren)[b]	44	95	5[c]
H, W, W's children	40	70	30
H, W, H's children	64	23	77
H, W, his or her children, their children	42	76	24
H, W, H's children, W's children	76	58	42
H, W, H's children, W's children, their children	6	50	50

[a]H = Husband; W = Wife.

[b]Their children "means children that have been produced by the couple since the remarriage.

[c]The two instances of high ambiguity with only children in common are cases where an infant born to the current marriage was omitted by one of the spouses.

situation of "his, hers, and our" children would produce a considerable amount of ambiguity, given its complexity.

Ambiguity by Demographic Characteristics

Findings relevant to the differences between remarried types in boundary ambiguity by demographic characteristics are not presented in table form. In an initial analysis, these data were cross-tabulated to determine whether couples classified as having ambiguous boundaries differed by income level, socioeconomic status, length of marriage, prior marital experience, manner in which the prior marriage terminated, number of children in the household, and presence or absence of adolescents in the household. Results of these chi-square analyses were all non-significant. Thus, the data suggest that for these remarrieds, such demographic characteristics do not distinguish couples in terms of the likelihood of boundary ambiguity.

DISCUSSION

These data support the finding that high boundary ambiguity seldom occurs in remarriages where only common children exist. When children exist from a previous marriage, however, ambiguity is more likely. As Cherlin (1978) suggested, steprelations have few social conventions to guide them. Biological and legal complications often lead to boundary ambiguity. In addition, these findings indicate that ambiguous boundaries are most frequent when children exist from the *husband's* former marriage. "Forgotten" children, or children most often unreported, are those of the husband. These children were usually not residing with the remarrieds and, interestingly enough, they were as likely to be forgotten or omitted by their own parent as by the stepmother. It is likely that lack of contact, or an inconsistent pattern of contact between a father and his nonresidential children influences perception of the child as not being a member of "the family." It may also be the case that a stepmother resents her husband's children and the financial and emotional drain they make on the remarriage. There are no statistical data to test these assumptions, but informal comments by the respondents do support their plausibility. Findings from other studies indicate that this lack of contact may literally reflect an "out of sight, out of mind" attitude in these fathers and their new wives. This, then, contributes to our understanding of Boss's concept of psychological presence or absence, as well as boundary ambiguity.

In those cases of ambiguity involving other combinations of previous and common children, it was again the non-resident child or children who is the source of the ambiguity. There is some evidence to suggest that the birth of a child within a remarriage fosters adjustment and integration among members of the new family (Duberman, 1975). The "common" child provides a unifying element for the new family; however, this does not necessarily mean that ambiguity is avoided concerning children of the former marriage or marriages. In fact, were we to generalize from the findings of Table 9-3, we would argue that *residential location* is the most important factor determining ambiguity, while *complexity*, or the sheer number of relationships existing, is the second most important explanatory factor.

Recall that the major demographic variables did not appear to affect ambiguity in any patterned way. This may be because such variables are structural rather than perceptual, and boundary ambiguity is basically a perceptual construct. Perhaps other variables with a value component, including religious beliefs and affiliation and marital expectations, may better measure the perceptual context. Future research warrants consideration of such variables.

It also seems that length of time between marriages should have some effect on ambiguity. While length of *current* marriage did not have explanatory value, Boss and Greenberg (1984) suggest that uncertainty regarding duration of the ambiguous state, that is, how long it will last, causes higher boundary ambiguity. In other words, remarrieds whose time between marriages is longer may experience greater ambiguity than those who move quickly from one marriage to the next. However, the divorce literature suggests that patterns of contact stabilize at 2 to 3 years after divorce (Hetherington, Cox, & Cox, 1979; Troph, 1984; Wallerstein & Kelly, 1980). This would suggest that the longer the period between marriages, the less the ambiguity, as uncertainty subsides and boundaries "firm up." Thus, the effect of time between marriages deserves attention as an independent variable.

CONCLUSIONS

Overall, this study suggests that both physical and psychological indicators of boundary ambiguity are part of stepfamily or remarried life. Remarrieds with only "their" children have little basis for ambiguous boundaries, while those with children by the husband's former marriage are likely to have perceptual problems with whether those children are in or out of the family.

The need for additional investigation is obvious, particularly regarding adjustments and integration experiences of "stepmother" families. Most research on remarriages has focused on residential units, and thus the H, W, H's nonresidential children family type has been omitted. This study has indicated the importance of considering all the various biological combinations, but has only begun the task. The complexities referred to by Duberman, Cherlin, and others for residential units are compounded when nonresidential relationships are included as well. Further, longitudinal research would help to examine changes in boundary ambiguity over time in relation to various remarried configurations. It would also assist in determining the influence of boundary redefinition on members of both new and prior families experiencing the shared transitions of separation, divorce, and remarriage.

NOTES

1. Quasi-kin is a term used by Bohannan (1970) to refer to a former spouse, his/her new spouse, and former in-laws.
2. Comparison of degree of boundary ambiguity by manner in which prior marriage ended was impossible since few couples (19 or 7.48%) experienced termination by death of a spouse.
3. Analysis with the household as the unit of analysis will be the focus of a subsequent paper that I plan to write. At this point, my major concern is all biological relationships, though household cannot be completely ignored in the explanation.

REFERENCES

Bohannan, P. (1970). *Divorce and after: An analysis of the emotional and social problems of divorce.* New York: Doubleday.

Boss, P. (1975). *Psychological father presence in missing in action (MIA) family: Its effects on family functioning.* Proceeding from the Third Annual Joint Medican Meeting Concerning POW/MIA Matters. San Diego, CA: Center for Prisoner Studies, Naval Health Research Center.

Boss, P. (1977). A clarification of the concept of psychological father presence in families experiencing ambiguity of boundary. *Journal of Marriage and the Family, 39,* 141–151.

Boss, P. (1980a). Normative family stress: Family boundary changes across the lifespan. *Family Relations, 29,* 445–450.

Boss, P. (1980b). The relationship of wife's sex role perceptions, psychological father presence, and functioning in the ambiguous father-absent MIA family. *Journal of Marriage and the Family, 42,* 541–549.

Boss, P., & Greenberg, J. (1984). Family boundary ambiguity: A new variable in family stress theory. *Family Process, 23,* 535–546.

Cherlin, A. (1978). Remarriage as an incomplete institution. *American Journal of Sociology, 84,* 634–650.

Cherlin, A., & McCarthy, J. (1985). Remarried couple households: Data from the June 1980 current population survey. *Journal of Marriage and the Family, 47,* 23–30.

Clingempeel, W. G. (1981). Quasi-kin relationships and marital quality in stepfather families. *Journal of Personality and Social Psychology, 41,* 890–901.

Clingempeel, W. G., Ievoli, R., & Brand, E. (1983). Structural complexity and the quality of stepfather–stepchild relationships. *Family Process, 23,* 547–560.

Clingempeel, W. G., & Segel, S. (1986). Stepparent-stepchild relationships and the psychological adjustment of children in stepfather and stepmother families. *Child Development, 57,* 474–484.

Duberman, L. (1975). *The reconstituted family: A study of remarried couples and their children*. Chicago, IL: Nelson-Hall.

Farber, B. (1964). *Family organization and interaction*. San Francisco: Chandler.

Ferri, E. (1984). *Stepchildren: A national study*. Berkshire, England: Nfer-Nelson Publishing Co.

Ganong, L., & Coleman, M. (1984). The effects of remarriage on children: A review of the empirical literature. *Family Relations, 33*, 389–406.

Hetherington, E. M., Cox, M., & Cox, R. (1979). Stress and coping in divorce: A focus on women. In J. Gullahorn (Ed.), *Psychology of women in transition* (pp. 95–128). Washington, DC: B. H. Winston & Sons.

Ihinger-Tallman, M., & Pasley, K. (1981). *Factors influencing stability in remarriage*. Proceeding from the 29th International Sociological Association, Committee on Family Research Seminar on Divorce and Remarriage. Leuven, Belgium: Catholic University.

Kargman, M. W. (1983). Stepchild support obligations of stepparents. *Family Relations, 32*, 231–238.

Messinger, L. (1976). Remarriage between divorced people with children from previous marriages: A proposal for preparation for remarriage. *Journal of Marriage and Family Counseling, 2*, 193–200.

Minuchin, S. (1974). *Families and family therapy*. Cambridge, MA: Harvard University Press.

Minuchin, S., Montalvo, B., Guerney, B. G., Rossman, B. L., & Schumer, F. (1967). *Families of the slums: An exploration of their structure and treatment*. New York: Basic Books.

Olson, D., McCubbin, H. I., Barnes, H., Larsen, A., Muxen, M., & Wilson, M. (1983). *Families: What makes them work*. Beverly Hills, CA: Sage.

Olson, D., Russell, L. S., & Sprenkle, D. H. (1983). Circumplex model VI: Theoretical update. *Family Process, 22*, 69–83.

Pasley, K., & Ihinger-Tallman, M. (1980). *Problems and problem-solving strategies in remarried families*. Grant funded by the Grant-in-Aid program, Washington State University, Pullman, WA.

Pasley, K., & Ihinger-Tallman, M. (1982). Stress in remarried families. *Family Perspectives, 16*, 181–190.

Pasley, K., & Ihinger-Tallman, M. (1984, October). *Consensus on family values in happy and unhappy remarried couples*. Paper presented at the annual meeting of the National Council on Family Relations, San Francisco, CA.

Perkins, T. F., & Kahan, J. P. (1979). An empirical comparison of natural-father and step-father family systems. *Family Process, 18*, 175–183.

Robinson, M. (1980). Step-families: A reconstituted family system. *Journal of Family Therapy, 2*, 45–69.

Theis, J. M. (1977). Beyond divorce: The impact of remarriage on children. *Journal of Clinical Psychology, 6*, 59–61.

Tropf, W. (1984). An exploratory examination of the effect of remarriage on child support and personal contacts. *Journal of Divorce, 7*, 57–73.

Visher, E. B., & Visher, J. S. (1979). *Stepfamilies: A guide to working with stepparents and stepchildren*. New York: Brunner/Mazel.

Wald, E. (1981). *The remarried family: Challenge and promise*. New York: Family Service Association of America.

Walker, K. N., & Messinger, L. (1979). Remarriage after divorce: Dissolution and reconstruction on family boundaries. *Family Process, 18*, 185–192.

Wallerstein, J. S., & Kelly, J. B. (1980). *Surviving the breakup*. New York: Basic Books.

Wood, B., & Talmon, M. (1983). Family boundaries in transition: A search for alternatives. *Family Process, 22*, 347–357.

10

Parenting in the Binuclear Family: Relationships between Biological and Stepparents

CONSTANCE R. AHRONS
University of Southern California
LYNN WALLISCH
University of Wisconsin

INTRODUCTION

The process of change in any given family that is set in motion by marital disruption boggles the mind: It frequently requires a complex computation to chart and understand the kinship relationships that are affected. Given current remarriage rates (see Chapter 1 of this volume), most divorced families will move through a series of stressful transitions and structural changes that will have profound impacts on the lives of the adults and children involved. These structural changes give rise to a host of disruptions in roles and relationships, and each transition may be weathered with varying amounts of stress and turmoil.

Projections from current trends indicate that between 40% and 50% of American children born in the 1970s will spend some portion of their minor years in a one-parent household. If current remarriage rates continue, it is also projected that approximately 25% to 30% of the children will live for some period of time in a remarried household (Glick, 1984). Although we do not have accurate cohabitation statistics, we can assume that many of these children will also live for some period of time in a cohabiting household, which may or may not develop into a remarriage household. This means that at least 25% to 30% of the children will have more than two adults who function simultaneously as parents. Even more complex kinship structures result from the increasing rate of redivorce.

It is abundantly clear from these statistics that large numbers of American families will experience major transitions such as divorce and remarriage. The resulting pattern of serial marriage has ushered in rapid changes in family life as it has been known in the past.

Consider the following case example (see Figure 10-1):

BINUCLEAR FAMILY DIAGRAM

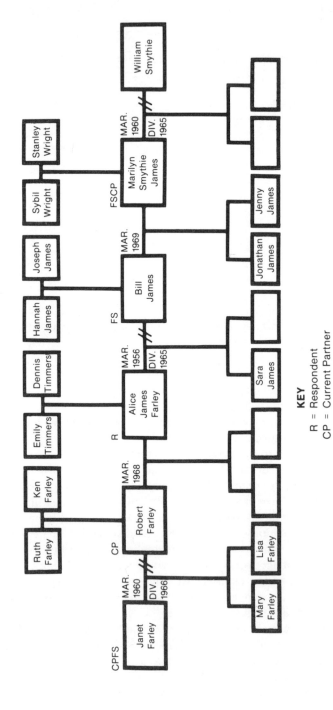

KEY

R = Respondent
CP = Current Partner
FS = Former Spouse
CPFS = Current Partner's Former Spouse
FSCP = Former Spouse's Current Partner

Figure 10-1. Binuclear family diagram.

When Sara James was 8, her parents separated and she lived with her mother, Alice, spending weekends and vacations with her father, Bill. She lived in a one-parent household with her mother until she was 11, at which time her mother remarried. Her new stepfather, Robert, also had been divorced, and he was the noncustodial parent of two daughters, Mary and Lisa, ages 5 and 7 respectively. His daughters spent about 10 days each month living in his household. A year later, when Sara was 12, her father remarried. Within the next 3 years, he and Sara's stepmother, Marilyn, had a son and a daughter (Jonathan and Jenny). At age 15, a picture of Sara's family looked like this: she had two biological parents, two stepparents, two stepsisters, a half-brother, and a half-sister. Her extended family had expanded as well: she had two sets of stepgrandparents, two sets of biological grandparents, and a large network of aunts, uncles, and cousins.

In addition to Sara's complex network of kin, she had two households of "family." By the time she was 15, she had lived in a nuclear family, a one-parent household, and a remarried household.

The Binuclear Family

As exemplified in the case example of Sara's family, the reorganization of a family through divorce frequently results in the establishment of two households: maternal and paternal. These two interrelated households, whether each is a one-parent or a remarried household, form one family system—a "binuclear" family system. The centrality of each of these households will vary among postdivorce families. Some families (such as those with sole custody) make very distinct divisions between the child's primary and secondary homes, whereas in other families (such as those with joint physical custody) these distinctions are blurred with both homes having equal importance. Hence, the term "binuclear family" represents the structural concept of a family system with two households, irrespective of the importance of each in the child's life experience. The coining of the term is a first step in developing language to identify a postdivorce family structure (see Ahrons, 1979, 1980a, 1980b).

Although Sara's family transition is highly discrepant with our notion of the traditional American family, a sizeable minority of American children will experience similar developmental transitions and will spend major portions of their lives as part of a binuclear family system. Our knowledge about these transitional processes is extremely limited. We have focused attention in the last decade on the process of marital disruption and have only very recently begun to explore and identify the changes in all family relationships that the divorce initiates. Of central concern now are questions such as: How do parents who live in separate households continue to parent? How do any new partners, who may or may not reside with their own children, relate to their stepchildren? How, when there are two recoupled households responsible for the rearing of the same child, do parental responsibilities get shared or divided? What are the interrelationships among all the adults who are involved in parenting the same child but who do not share the same household?

Lack of formal "rules of relationship" are thought to be one source of stress in the divorce experience as well as in remarriage (Mead, 1970; Messinger, 1985; Pasley & Ihinger-Tallman, 1982). The type of continuing interaction former spouses work out may have to be renegotiated when one or both join with a new partner. For example, where it may have been acceptable for a divorced mother to call upon her former husband to do certain household tasks like fix a broken garage door, it may no longer be acceptable once he has remarried. A recoupling of one of the divorced parents requires their dyadic relationship to somehow integrate the new partner, as well as other family members acquired from the new union. As there are no societal norms for such relationships, these norms have to be worked out ad hoc. In fact, society has tended to discourage continued interaction between former spouses, and thus, postdivorce relationships are often fraught with tensions.

The family, as a system of interacting interdependent parts, undergoes radical change in the divorce process. A major task in the process of reorganizing into a binuclear family is the redefining of parental roles and relationships. Divorced parents need to establish new rules for determining how they will continue their parenting roles and obligations while living in separate households. This coparenting relationship, defined by Bohannan (1970) as that aspect of the relationship between former spouses that is concerned with childrearing, is the most difficult and complex task of the divorce process.

The rules and patterns of coparenting that divorced spouses establish during the divorce process are likely to undergo changes again when a remarriage takes place and a new partner, the stepparent, enters the binuclear family system. For example, if the father recouples, the mother might feel she has to deal with two people instead of one on any issue related to the child. The father might also feel conflicts in trying to meet the needs of his new family as well as those of his first family and may have to change the nature of his coparenting relationship with his former spouse. Thus, the recoupling of one parent usually requires another transition and reorganization of the coparental subsystem. New rules need to be constructed not only for the coparental relationship but for the relationship between first and second spouse—mother and stepmother, father and stepfather—as well. Many of the old angers and conflicts may arise again at this time. If the child was used as a pawn in the struggle for power between the couple in their divorce, he or she will probably be put in that role again as the family juggles positions and roles to establish a new equilibrium. Then, if the other parent recouples, another reorganization and redefinition of family roles may occur.

Because our thinking about divorce has been so steeped in a pathological, "social ill" framework, we have almost no theory-based knowledge of what a healthy divorced family looks like as it develops. The family-theory literature, including work from both the developmental and systems perspectives, does not adequately address the postdivorce family. As social scientists, we may have moved beyond thinking that a family must be contained in one household, but we have not yet worked out how a family continues to function as a family across two, or even three, households.

In the following sections of this chapter, we will draw on data from a study-in-progress of divorced families to begin to identify some of the major relationship and role changes in the transitions of parenting that commonly result from divorce and remarriage.

THE STUDY

Sampling

The Binuclear Family Research Project is a longitudinal investigation that takes the family as the unit of analysis and focuses on the consequences of divorce and remarriage for the family system. Gathering data from 98 pairs of former spouses and their current partners at approximately 1, 3, and 5 years after divorce, this study has a number of unique characteristics. First, unlike most studies of divorce, the sample was drawn from divorce court records with the intent of identifying a sample that would be more representative of a typical population of divorcing couples. Drawn from the divorce court records of Dane County, Wisconsin, the major restrictions on the sample were related to residency within the county on the part of both spouses, the presence of minor children, and contact between the nonresidential parent and child at least once in the 2 months prior to the first interview. Second, data were collected from both former spouses as well as from new partners acquired postdivorce. Due to the small number of joint- and father-custody cases in 1977, divorces finalized in 1978 and the first 6 months of 1979 were reviewed for identification of additional non-mother-custody cases. Therefore, the sample consisted of a random sample of mother-custody cases drawn from the 1977 court records, and the total population of non-mother-custody cases in 1977, 1978, and the first 6 months of 1979.

This sampling procedure yielded a final pool of 379 potentially eligible couples. Letters explaining the study and requesting participation were sent to all eligible individuals ($N = 758$). The letters were then followed by phone calls in which those who did not meet the criteria for participation were identified. Of the eligible and locatable sample, 51% agreed to participate. This yielded a final sample of 98 couples: 54 had mother custody, 28 had joint custody, and 16 had father or split custody. At Time 2, 3 years postdivorce, 176 of the original 196 divorced parents (90%) were reinterviewed. This resulted in at least one respondent from 96 and both respondents from 80 of the original 98 families. These original 176 study participants identified 122 new partners, either married or cohabiting, and of these, 91 (75%) were interviewed. A partner was defined as cohabiting if he or she lived with the respondent 12 or more nights per month. At Time 3, 5 years postdivorce, the total number interviewed was 178 which included several respondents who had been lost at Time 2. There were 115 new partners of whom 85 (74%) were interviewed.

Data Collection

In-depth, semi-structured interviews were conducted in the respondents' homes. The interview contained both open-ended and structured questions, two modified Q-sort procedures, and a paper-and-pencil Hopkins Symptom Checklist. Multiple indicators were used for most of the major variables under investigation, and the interviews were conducted by graduate students in social work with clinical interviewing experience. The interviewers were matched by sex with the subjects because it was felt that respondents might talk more candidly to a member of their own sex and because this would also ensure that information from one spouse would not be passed on to the other. The interviews focused on a wide range of topics designed to assess the extent and quality of the relationship between former spouses, their relationship with their children, their new partners, if any, their new partner's former spouse and their own former spouse's new partner. The interviews averaged 1½ hours at Time 1 and ranged from 1 to 4 hours at Times 2 and 3, depending on the binuclear family structure, that is, whether they were remarried, whether their new partner had children from a prior marriage, and so forth. (For further details on the methodology of the study, see Ahrons, 1981, 1983; Bowman & Ahrons, 1985.)

As we devised the interview schedules for the 3- and 5-year postdivorce follow-up interviews, we encountered serious dilemmas with terminology. One clear indication of the lack of societal norms for binuclear families is the absence of terminology for the complex network of interrelationships. This language deficit became problematic to our research team in the development of the interview schedule.

For example, one of our major goals was to obtain a picture of the relationship between the biological mother or father and their former spouse's current spouse or cohabiting partner. The dilemma was: how could we keep asking the respondent questions that began, "Do you and your former spouse's current partner _____?" without both distancing and confusing them? No kinship term exists for that relationship—the one between mother and stepmother, or father and stepfather, and even less so, between stepmother and stepfather (the current partners of the former spouses).

Over time, as a research staff, we developed our own shorthand for these relationships: the relationship between mother and stepmother, for instance, became the relationship between "R" and "FSCP" (respondent and former spouse's current partner). If the mother's new husband was also previously married, she then had a potential relationship with his former wife, that is, her "CPFS" (current partner's former spouse). (If her new husband had children of his own, the biological mother then also became a stepmother herself, although in this study we continued to refer to the original former spouses as biological parents and to their partners as stepparents.) However, we realized that we could not ask the respondents questions in this cumbersome way or use our own notations or symbols without defeating our goals by depersonalizing a family system in which we were trying to identify continuing kin relationships.

Out of confusion came creativity: We ended up by diagramming the binuclear system (see, for example, Figure 10-1). In so doing, we realized we needed to use two legal-sized sheets of paper taped together in order to include the entire system in the diagram. Hypothetically, at 3 years post-divorce, the binuclear family system could include two parents, two stepparents, four sets of grandparents, and five sets of children (the children of the formerly married pair, each new partner's children from a first marriage [stepsiblings of the biological children], and two sets of new children of the remarried pairs [half-siblings of the biological children]). We then moved to what seemed like a simple conclusion, once decided upon: to start the interviews with a binuclear diagram and have the interviewer and respondent fill in the diagram together. For the remainder of the several-hour-long interview, the interviewer referred to each member in this extended system by first name rather than by relationship. These diagrams turned out to be an invaluable research and clinical tool. At the same time, they helped establish rapport between interviewer and respondent and permitted both to have a visual picture of the family. Although the term "binuclear" has not yet gained societal acceptance, it is now a household word for 98 families in Dane County, Wisconsin—an unintended result of the research.

The findings presented here are concerned with the complex family systems created by the remarriage of one or both former spouses, who are parents, to new partners who may themselves be parents. The information is based primarily on data from the second interview, at 3 years postdivorce. At this time, 58% of the divorced women and 76% of the divorced men had recoupled (were remarried or cohabiting). Because little research has been done on the postdivorce family relationships of reconstituted families, the data presented here will be primarily descriptive in nature.

Characteristics of the Sample

The biological parents were, on the average, in their mid-30s and had been married for about 11 years prior to their divorce. Two thirds of the couples had been separated before filing for divorce; these separations were about 1 to 2 years in length. About half of the respondents had completed college, and almost all (both men and women) were engaged in paid employment at the time of both interviews, slightly over half of them in professional, managerial, or administrative positions. The average household income prior to divorce was approximately $21,000 for both men and women. After divorce, it had dropped to about $15,000 for women while remaining the same for men.

At the time of the original data collection, the number of children per family ranged from one to six, with an age range of 2 to 18 years. Seventy percent of the sample had more than one minor child, with an average number per family of two children. At the first interview, 90% of the women and 49% of the men reported at least one child under 18 living in their household. This overlap probably represents not only the cases of split custody in which each parent had custody of one child, but the fact that in many cases of joint custody, both parents considered the same child as part of their household.

By 1 year after divorce, approximately 14% of the women and 22% of the men had remarried, and another 13% of each were planning remarriage in the near future. By the second interview, 3 years postdivorce, 35% of the women and 55% of the men had remarried. Another 23% of the women and 21% of the men had cohabitors. The new partners were similar in education and employment to the biological parents. Two thirds of the respondents' new partners had themselves been married before, and somewhat over half had children from their previous relationships. Seventy percent of the new wives and 30% of the new husbands with children had the children residing with them in the new remarried household. About 10% of the married or cohabiting couples had a new child born to this relationship.

Although the sample is similar to that of other recent longitudinal studies of divorce (e.g., Hetherington, Cox, & Cox, 1976; Wallerstein & Kelly, 1980), the findings should be generalized with caution. That is, the findings are probably typical of a "normal" (non-clinical) population of divorced people who are white, middle-class, and living in a somewhat "liberal" community.

Measurement of the Principal Variables

Remarriage

The divorced couples were classified by their marital status at 3 years post-divorce: For 11%, neither former spouse had remarried. For another 11%, only the wife had remarried, while only the husband had remarried for 29% of the former couples, and both former spouses had remarried in 48% of the cases. Table 10-1 shows the variety of family structures of the respondents at 3 years postdivorce and, for comparison, the changes at 5 years postdivorce. The terms "remarriage" and "new spouse" were extended to cover couples who were cohabiting at least 12 nights per month, and in the following discussions, no distinction will be made between having "recoupled" and being legally married.

Coparental Interaction

The interaction between the former spouses focusing on parenting biological children was measured by a "coparental sharing" scale. Respondents were asked to indicate how often they shared with their former spouse childrearing

Table 10-1. Family Structure at 3 and 5 Years Postdivorce (Numbers Are N's Except Where Percentages Are Indicated)

	3 years $(N = 96)^a$	5 years $(N = 95)^a$
NEITHER PARENT RECOUPLED	11 (11%)	17 (18%)
MOTHER RECOUPLED, FATHER SINGLE	11 (11%)	11 (12%)
Neither partner nor recoupled pair has children	2	2
Only partner (CP–CPFS) has children	7	2
Only recoupled pair (R–CP) has children	2	2
Both partner (CP–CPFS) and recoupled pair (R–CP) have children	0	1
FATHER RECOUPLED, MOTHER SINGLE	28 (29%)	30 (32%)
Neither partner nor recoupled pair has children	6	8
Only partner (CP–CPFS) has children	17	15
Only recoupled pair (R–CP) has children	4	5
Both partner (CP–CPFS) and recoupled pair (R–CP) have children	1	2
BOTH PARENTS RECOUPLED	46 (48%)	37 (39%)
No new kids	6	3
Only mom's partner has children	15	10
Only dad's partner has children	5	3
Both partners only have children	6	5
Only one recoupled pair has children	4	5
Both recoupled pairs only have children	0	0
One partner + one recoupled pair have children	6	8
One recoupled pair + both partners have children	3	1
Both recoupled pairs + one partner have children	0	1
Both partners + both recoupled pairs have children	1	1

[a]Missing cases were filled in from information from spouse who was interviewed, if available. Percentages may not total to 100 due to rounding.

activities in ten different areas, such as making major decisions concerning the children, discussing the children's problems, planning special events in the children's lives, and so on. A 5-point Likert-type scale, ranging from "never" (1) to "always" (5) was used to measure the extent of sharing. (See Appendix 10-1 for the ten questions comprising this scale as well as for the questions comprising each of the following scales.) Each respondent was given a score representing the average of their responses to these ten questions, with a high score indicating a greater amount of interaction or sharing.

The amount of *conflict* and amount of *support* in coparental interaction was also measured by 5-point scales. Conflict was assessed by four questions asking how often respondents argued or disagreed about childrearing; support was measured by six questions asking how much the former spouses helped or supported each other in childrearing matters.

Satisfaction

Respondent's satisfaction was assessed in five areas: the custody arrangement, the amount of time they or their former spouse spent with their noncustodial children, the amount they shared with their former spouse in regard to the children (as measured by the coparental sharing scale), the coparenting relationship in general, and their life overall.

Involvement with Children

The former spouses were asked how involved they were with their children in 14 different areas, such as discipline, dress and grooming, celebrating holidays, recreation, schoolwork, and so on. Respondents were asked to indicate their involvement on a 5-point scale ranging from "not at all" (1) to "very much" (5), and as with the coparental sharing scale, they were given a score representing their average response on these questions. They were also asked to rate how involved their former spouse was in the same areas. (Custodial mothers were assumed to be very highly involved with their children and were not asked to rate themselves, nor were their former spouses asked to rate them for involvement. Joint- and split-custody parents were asked about their involvement with their noncustodial or nonresidential children, if there were any. If the amount of involvement differed for different children, involvement with the youngest child was used.)

Nonparental Interaction

The amount of interaction former spouses had with each other in areas not related to parenting was measured on a 6-point scale, ranging from "never" (1) to "once a week or more" (6). Fourteen items, such as talking about old friends in common, talking about personal problems, having physical contact, and so forth, were included.

"Psychological" Variables

Five-point scales were also developed to measure the former spouses' continuing psychological closeness and attachment to one another, their anger, their positive feelings and their attitude toward each other as parents.

OVERVIEW OF THE FINDINGS

Coparenting between Former Spouses: Is It Affected by Remarriage?

Since the divorced couples all had at least one child still under 18 at 3 years postdivorce, they all had a "coparental relationship" of sorts that could range from minimal interaction to high involvement with each other in areas relating to the children. Overall, former spouses still shared a moderate amount of coparenting at 1 year after divorce. At that time, about 21% of the former spouses "always" or "usually" shared in seven or more of the ten areas asked about, and another 21% "rarely" or "never" shared in seven of ten areas. The remaining 59% "sometimes" shared in these areas. There was a significant decrease in the amount of coparental sharing by 3 years postdivorce, at which time only 9% still had a high degree of sharing. There was also a significant decrease over that period in the amount of time they spent together with each other and their children. At both 1 and 3 years, satisfaction with the amount of sharing was positively related to the actual amount of sharing. However, while the amount of sharing decreased over time, the respondents' satisfaction with this amount did not significantly change. Satisfaction with the coparenting relationship overall did decline over the 3-year period for the fathers, although not for the mothers. The amount of conflict and of support in the coparenting relationship did not change between 1 and 3 years postdivorce. There were no significant differences between former husbands and wives in the amount of coparental sharing, conflict, support, or satisfaction reported at either time period.

The remarriage of one or both of the former spouses might reasonably be expected to decrease the amount of coparenting between them since a person involved in a new family might have less interest in or time to spend with a former spouse, or may even feel pressured by the new spouse to limit involvement with the first spouse. While we do not have enough information to determine the reasons, a deterioration in coparental relations after remarriage was evident among our respondents. This was especially true if only the husband had remarried. For instance, the number and frequency of childrearing activities shared between the former spouses (the "coparental sharing scale") was highest when neither partner had remarried and lowest when only the husband had remarried. The amount of support in coparental interaction was highest and conflict lowest when neither partner had remarried, while conflict was highest and support lowest when only the husband had remarried. If neither former spouse had remarried, they were also most likely to spend time together with each other and their children; they were least likely to do so if only the husband had remarried. Table 10-2 presents these rather complicated relationships more graphically.

Remarriage was not associated either positively or negatively with the husband's satisfaction with the amount of coparental sharing. Husband's satisfaction with the coparental relationship overall was highest, however, when neither former spouse had remarried or when only the mother had remarried; his overall satisfaction was lowest when both partners or only the father had remarried. For the wives, satisfaction with the amount of coparental sharing and overall satisfaction with the coparental relationship was highest when both partners had remarried or only the wife had remarried. It was lowest when only the husband had remarried (see Table 10-2).

Table 10-2. Differences on Parenting Variables by Recoupled Status at 3 Years Postdivorce

	Recoupled Status			
Variable	Neither	Mother Only	Father Only	Both
Coparental Sharing				
Mothers	$+^a$		−	
Fathers	+		−	
Support				
Mothers	+		−	
Fathers	+		−	
Conflict				
Mothers	−		+	
Fathers	−		+	
Spend Time With Former Spouse and Children				
Mothers	+		−	
Fathers	+		−	
Satisfaction with Amount of Coparental Sharing				
Mothers		+	−	+
Fathers				
Overall Satisfaction with Coparental Relationship				
Mothers		+	−	+
Fathers	+	+	−	−

^{a}+ indicates higher values on the variable, − indicates lower values, blank indicates no significant difference for that recoupled group.

STEPPARENTS: ROLES AND RELATIONSHIPS

Because all of the former spouses in our sample had children, any new partners became *de facto* stepparents, although they may not have functioned actively in that role. Their actual involvement in parenting their partner's children depended on the custody and living arrangements of those children as well as on the degree of involvement of the children's biological parent. Although the new partners may have had children of their own from a previous relationship, our interest here was on their role as stepparents, both in relation to their new spouses and in relation to their stepchildren.

The Coparenting Relationship of Stepparents and Biological Parents

Remarried parents have potentially two coparenting relationships, one with their former spouse and one with their new partner. It might be expected that these two relationships are related in some way. For instance, perhaps the more the former spouses share with each other, the less need there is to share with the new partner. Alternatively, there might be a "sharing" type of person who shares a great deal with both former and new spouse. However, we found no association, either positive or negative, between the amount of coparental sharing that occurred between former spouses and that was reported between new spouses (as measured by a similar coparental sharing scale).

Overall, the amount of coparental sharing between biological parents and their new partners was high, with 62% of stepmothers and 73% of stepfathers "always" or "usually" sharing in seven or more of the ten areas asked about, and less than 10% "rarely" or "never" sharing seven or more activities. The apparent greater participation of stepfathers in coparenting is due in part to the fact that, because women are more likely to get custody of their children, stepfathers more often have stepchildren in residence. However, even when legal custody was held constant, stepfathers had higher levels of sharing than stepmothers: 70% of stepmothers and 81% of stepfathers whose partners had custody "always" or "usually" shared seven or more coparenting activities. A variety of factors may account for this gender difference: more interest or involvement on the part of stepfathers (at least as perceived by them), a more positive reaction of children to stepfathers, or the fact that biological mothers may allow their new partner to share more than biological fathers do. Unfortunately, we do not have enough information from these data to determine the cause.

Stepparents' satisfaction with their amount of coparental sharing was not related to the actual amount they shared. However, stepfathers, who reported sharing more than stepmothers, were also more satisfied in general: 89% of stepfathers and only 63% of stepmothers were "very" or "somewhat" satisfied, and only 8% of stepfathers and 24% of stepmothers were "very" or "somewhat" dissatisfied (the rest had "mixed" feelings).

Stepmothers reported slightly fewer differences between themselves and their partners in their ideas for dealing with the partners' children concerning bedtime, mealtime schedules, household tasks, discipline, behavior expectations, and problem-solving style: About 81% of stepmothers and 86% of stepfathers reported differences in these areas. Of those stepparents who did report differences, however, stepmothers were more likely (52%) than stepfathers (43%) to think that these caused problems. However, none of the problems in these areas were considered "serious" by any respondent.

About 15% of both stepmothers and stepfathers reported that, when they had problems with their partner's children, they "let the partner handle them." Seventy-eight percent of the stepfathers and 62% of the stepmothers said they "handled the problems themselves." The rest noted that either both dealt with the children together or that the parent who was on the scene handled the problem, irrespective of the exact nature of it.

Stepmothers more than stepfathers (65% vs. 54%) thought that their partners' children had affected the relationship between them and their partners in some way. Of those who thought so, 21% of the stepmothers felt that the effect had been negative, but no stepfathers shared this feeling.

The research on stepparent roles is still a new area of study with many unanswered questions. As noted by Mills (1984), definitive knowledge is lacking both about the roles stepfamily members develop over time and how these roles then relate to overall family satisfaction. The issue of stepparental bonding requires negotiation and limit-setting (Visher & Visher, 1979). The remarriages in our study are in the early stages of their development and issues of coparenting are still in flux. From these limited data, however, it appears that these stepparents are experimenting with adopting a shared parental role. Stepfathers seem to have a more clearly defined coparental role than do stepmothers: They share more coparenting activities, are more satisfied, consider differences in childrearing styles to be less problematic, and less often feel that their current marital relationship has been negatively affected by their stepchildren. However, as suggested by Mills (1984), more longitudinal data over a time period of at least 5 years is needed before valid conclusions can be drawn.

Stepparents' Interaction with Their Stepchildren

Stepparents were asked how involved they were with their stepchildren (using the "involvement with children" scale discussed above), and biological parents were also asked to rate the involvement of their partners with the biological children on the same scale. The involvement of the stepparents as assessed by the biological parents and as assessed by the stepparents themselves correlated fairly highly (.64 for stepfathers and .77 for stepmothers), and the following discussion is valid whichever scale is used.

About one quarter of the stepparents might be considered to be very involved with the children, since they were "much" or "very much" involved in 10 or more of the 13 areas asked about. Just under one fifth of the stepparents had a very low degree of involvement, interacting only "a little" or "not at all" in 10 out of 13 areas. There was no significant difference in the level of involvement between stepmothers and stepfathers. Of the 13 activities, stepparents were most involved in celebrating holidays and significant events with their partners' children, and least involved in attending school- or church-related functions, planning for the children's future, religious or moral training, helping the children with schoolwork, and dress and grooming.

The degree of involvement of the stepparents was, as might be expected, related to the degree of involvement of the biological parents themselves (as measured by the same scale), although this was more so for stepfathers (.49 correlation with their partner's, the biological mother's, involvement) than for stepmothers (.29 correlation with biological fathers). Stepfathers whose partners had sole or joint custody were more involved with the children than those whose partners did not have custody. For stepmothers, however, there was no difference in involvement by whether or not the biological father had custody.

A high degree of stepparent involvement with the children was apparently considered desirable. About 60% of the biological parents (both mothers and fathers) felt that the amount of their partner's involvement with their children was "about right;" the rest would have liked them to be more involved. Biological parents whose partners were more highly involved were also more satisfied with the amount of involvement. About 65% of the stepfathers were satisfied with their own current level of involvement, while only 46% of the stepmothers were; virtually all of the other stepparents wished for more involvement.

Stepfathers were generally more satisfied (81%) than stepmothers (64%) with the relationship they currently had with their partner's children; 14% of the stepfathers and 25% of the stepmothers were dissatisfied, and the rest had mixed feelings. Stepfathers reported slightly more often (89%) than did stepmothers (80%) that they felt "comfortable" with their partners' children. When stepparents were asked what kind of relationship they had with their stepchildren, stepmothers tended to see themselves more as friends or companions (42% vs. 35% of stepfathers), while stepfathers saw themselves more as parents (49% vs. 28% of stepmothers). However, when asked if they considered themselves or not to be "stepparents" to their partner's children, more stepmothers (54%) than stepfathers (40%) said they did.

Stepparents were also asked a battery of Q-sort questions about their feelings and experiences as a stepparent (see Appendix 10-2 for the questions). Overall, stepfathers seemed to have more positive feelings about their competency and status as a stepparent, to feel that they got more support from their partners, and to think that their stepchildren liked them more than did stepmothers. An equal percentage of stepfathers and stepmothers, however, acknowledged that "it's more difficult to be a stepparent than a natural parent."

Again, just as stepfathers seemed to have a more successful coparenting experience, they also appeared to have more positive interaction with their stepchildren. While the actual amount of their involvement was no higher than that of the stepmothers, they were more satisfied with the amount and nature of this involvement and with their overall experiences as a stepparent.

Are Stepparents "Substitute" Parents or "Additional" Parents?

Given the lack of norms for parenting in binuclear families in which one or both partners have recoupled, stepparents may experience confusion about appropriate role behavior. The label "stepparent" in our society carries negative connotations and ambiguous role prescriptions that may result in confusion for both the adults and children (see Chapter 2, this volume).

The relationship a child has with a stepparent might be expected to affect the child's relationship with his/her biological parent and vice versa. The child may perceive a conflict in having two fathers or mothers, and closeness to one may be balanced by distance from the other.

One measure of how close the child feels to his/her stepparent might be whether or not the child calls them "mom" or "dad" at home or when talking about them to others. Since the children themselves were not interviewed, we have to rely on information from the parents and stepparents about the children's relationship with them. One third of the stepfathers interviewed said their partner's children called or referred to them as "dad" but only 12% of the stepmothers were called "mom." In families where the stepfather was called "dad," the biological father was less involved with his own children than in families where the stepfather was not called "dad." However, the stepfather's being called "dad" did not make the biological father any more likely to say that he felt like a visitor in his children's lives, nor to be dissatisfied with the amount of time he spent with his children.

Whether or not the stepmother was called "mom" did not seem to affect the biological mother's involvement with her children at all. This may be because so few stepmothers were, in fact, called "mom" or because most biological mothers had custody of their children, and so the stepmothers were not as salient in the children's lives.

The stepparent's being called "mom" or "dad" did not have any effect on the amount of coparental sharing between the former spouses, nor did it affect their nonparental relationship. These findings on stepparent involvement again suggest that the development of the stepparent role and the stepparent–stepchild relationship are difficult and complex transitions. Because our sample is small, we are not able to examine the variables of complexity of family structure, sex, and age of child in relationship to stepfamily involvement. The existing research (e.g., Clingempeel, Brand, & Ievoli, 1984; Crosbie-Burnett, 1984) suggests that these variables are critical in determining the role of the stepparent. But again, as in the preceding area, the issue of stepparent gender differences seems to be another important variable in assessing the amount and satisfaction of stepparent–stepchild involvement.

OTHER NEW FAMILY RELATIONSHIPS

Mothers and Stepmothers, Fathers and Stepfathers

About half of the divorced respondents whose former spouses had recoupled now had contact with their former spouse's new partner (the stepparent), and another quarter had contact at one time but discontinued it. As might be expected, this contact centered mainly on the children and had to do with visiting arrangements, childrearing issues, and the like. Respondents distinguished between "having contact" and "having a relationship" with the stepparent. Only about one third of those who had contact said they had made some efforts to actually develop a relationship with these stepparents. The reasons given for discontinuing contact by those who had contact in the past clustered in three groups: (1) the spouses (biological parent) did not want the new and old partners to relate; (2) there was anger between the first and second partner based on a previous relationship, for example, "she used to be my former husband's secretary," "we were friends before he married my former wife"; and (3) there was no occasion to relate because the biological parent had little involvement with the children.

To explore further the relationship between mothers and stepmothers and fathers and stepfathers, we asked the biological parents several questions about the nature and quality of their relationship. Most of the biological parents (75%) considered the stepparents to be "acquaintances" rather than friends or relatives. Their interactions appeared to be distant but polite. Few reported arguments, anger, or hostility in their contacts, and about half said they would "usually" or "always" accommodate the stepparent if he/she needed to make changes in the visiting arrangements for the children. Again, half felt the stepparent to be supportive of the biological parent's special needs as a parent. About half of the biological fathers and two thirds of the biological mothers had ever said "thank you" to the stepparents for their help with the children. However, only about 20% considered the stepparent to be a resource to them in raising their children, and fewer still had ever sought help from them regarding the children. About half the biological mothers and only 20% of the biological fathers felt that they and the stepparent sometimes or more often had basic differences of opinion about issues related to child-rearing, although only a quarter of the mothers and 8% of the fathers reported they "usually" or "always" had these differences.

The biological parents completed a pencil-and-paper series of 16 questions about their feelings toward the stepparent. The answers suggested that they felt primarily detached from them rather than either openly hostile or friendly. About one quarter of biological mothers and fathers expressed feelings of competition with the stepparent, or resentment of them, or wishing the stepparent would "just disappear." Ten to fifteen percent admitted they had feelings toward the stepparent of jealousy, dislike, anger, or desire to punish him/her. About a quarter of the mothers and 10% of the fathers said they cared about the stepparent's welfare or had warm feelings toward him/her, and one quarter of both men and women "really liked" the stepparent. It is important to note, however, that about 30% to 40% of the biological parents said they most frequently felt indifferent toward the stepparent. Except where noted, there was little difference between fathers and mothers in these feelings.

In an attempt to see if we could distinguish "typologies" of parent–stepparent relationships, the questions tapping positive, negative, and indifferent feelings were combined into three scales. On these measures, about 26% of mothers and 13% of fathers most frequently had positive feelings toward the stepparent, 8% of both mothers and fathers most frequently had negative feelings, and about 40% of both mothers and fathers most frequently felt indifferent toward them. The others reported only rarely having feelings of either liking, disliking, or indifference toward the stepparent; we can perhaps interpret this as extreme indifference as well.

The biological parents seemed to be able to disassociate their personal feelings about their former spouse's new partner from their feelings about him/her as a stepparent. This ability was evident in the finding that about half the mothers and 65% of the fathers acknowledged that the stepparent was "usually" or "always" a caring person with the biological children, and 40% of both mothers and fathers felt that the stepparent was a good influence on the children. Only about 20% thought that the stepparent was sometimes or more often irresponsible with the children.

Overall, the fathers were somewhat more satisfied with their interactions with the stepfathers than the mothers were with their interactions with the stepmothers: 78% of fathers and 61% of mothers were mostly satisfied, while 6% of fathers and 15% of mothers were mostly dissatisfied. The rest had mixed feelings.

These findings suggest wide variations in the relationships between mothers and stepmothers and fathers and stepfathers in the initial stages of the stepparents' entry into the binuclear family system. About three quarters of divorced parents whose former spouse had remarried had at some time had contact with their former spouse's new partner, but the nature of this contact could range from hatred to close friendship. The patterns of relationships formed a continuum similar to the relationship patterns of former spouses (Ahrons & Wallisch, 1986). Most reported feeling cordial but detached from the new stepparent. But at either end of the continuum, there were some— more women than men—who had positive feelings and some who had negative feelings. However, most of the biological parents were able to transcend their personal feelings toward the stepparent to recognize that they could, indeed, be a good parent to their children.

The Stepmother–Stepfather Relationship

When both former spouses with children remarry, do their partners (the stepmother and stepfather) have contact with each other? About one fifth of the stepparents did have, at the time of interview, direct contact with the other stepparent, and another 14% had contact at sometime in the past. Of those who never had contact, fewer than one fifth said they would have liked to have some contact. Some of the reported contact was through friends or social acquaintances in common, but few of the stepparents had made any special efforts to develop a relationship with the other stepparent, mostly because they were just "not interested." Only 17% saw any benefits to having a relationship with the other stepparent, while 62% did not, the others were undecided. Fourteen percent considered that there were actually disadvantages to such a relationship, and another 12% were undecided. However, 22% thought there were some similarities and common interests between themselves and the other stepparent, and about as many said they would hypothetically choose the other stepparent as a friend. It is likely that many of the new partners of former spouses have had no occasion to become acquainted, since about half of them said that they did not know if they would like to become friendly with the other stepparent or not.

Most of the contact that did occur between the stepparents was centered around the children of their spouses, and took the form of family activities in common. However, the stepparents did not, on the whole, feel that they were a resource to each other in their relations with these children. The stepparents, for the most part, considered the other stepparent to be an "acquaintance" rather than a "family member." Almost all expressed satisfaction with the kind of interaction they had with each other and felt that their partners (the biological parents) were equally satisfied.

Extended Family Relationships

About 36% of the biological parents said that their children's relationship with their paternal or maternal grandparents changed since the divorce, and for three quarters of them, the change had been for the worse with at least one set of grandparents. The children's relationship with their grandparents was least likely to have changed if neither partner had recoupled, and most likely if only the father had recoupled. However, there was no systematic association between which parent had recoupled and which grandparents it was with whom the children's relationships had deteriorated. Instead, the deterioration appeared to be more related to the perception of the parent: Mothers felt that relations had become worse with the paternal grandparents, while fathers thought they had become worse with the maternal grandparents. This may, in fact, be a reflection of the decline in relations between the respondent and his/her in-laws, with the respondent projecting the same change to the relationship between the grandparents and the children.

A similar "reporting bias" can be seen when recoupled parents or their former spouses were asked about their children's relationship with their "step" grandparents. In many instances, it may be that the respondent simply did not know what kind of relationship the children had with his or her former spouse's new in-laws. When both former spouses had recoupled, 46% of the mothers and 31% of the fathers reported that their children had a relationship with both sets of grandparents; 26% of the mothers and 12% of the fathers said that they had a relationship with the stepfather's parents only; and 17% of the mothers and 34% of the fathers said that they had a relationship with the stepmother's parents only. The others reported no relationship at all with stepgrandparents.

The Effect of Having Stepchildren or Children From the New Marriage on Roles and Relationships of the Divorced Parent

Acquiring a new family through remarriage—either because the new partner had children of his/her own or because the new couple decides to have children together—can increase the stresses and strains already created by the divorce (Pasley & Ihinger-Tallman, 1982). It can lead to role conflict, as the person strives to accommodate both the new and old families and determine where primary loyalties lie. It can affect the relationship with the former spouse, the new spouse, and the children from the first marriage.

In this section, we examine stepparenting from the other point of view—

that of the original former spouses of our sample. About one third of the former spouses acquired stepchildren from their new marriages, and 10% had new children born to the remarriage. In the following discussion, respondents who had stepchildren only and those with new children only or new children and stepchildren will be considered together, since there was little difference in the analyses done on the groups separately.

Fathers and mothers who had stepchildren and/or new children perceived themselves to be less involved with their biological children from the former marriage than those who had no step- or new children. This was true regardless of whether or not they had custody of the biological children. However, having step- or new children did not affect the amount of coparental sharing between the former spouses.

There was little evidence that role conflict was higher among respondents who had new families. Respondents were asked how often, if at all, they felt torn between responsibilities to job and family, friends and family, their former spouse and their new spouse, or their new spouse and their children from the previous marriage. There was no association between having step- or new children and the extent to which respondents felt conflicts in these areas. The few respondents who had a new child born to the marriage did not feel that it had affected their relationship with their former spouse; however, many of them felt that having a new child had created problems in their relationship with their other children.

Parents with or without step- or new children were equally satisfied with the amount of time they spent with their noncustodial children, their coparenting relationship with their former spouse, their new marriage, and their life overall.

Being a stepparent, however, does not necessarily imply extensive involvement with one's stepchildren. The stepchildren may be nonresident, and even their own parent (the new spouse) may not have much continued interaction with them. In addition, then, to examining the impact of having stepchildren at all on a person's other family relationships, we attempted to determine whether the actual amount of involvement with those stepchildren had an effect on the person's relationship to their former spouse, their new spouse, or their biological children.

In general, it did. The more a person was involved with his/her stepchildren, the better were the relations with the new partner (the stepchildren's parent) as well as with his/her own biological children from the former marriage, and the worse the relations with the former spouse. However, these associations were much stronger for women than for men (see Table 10-3). Women with more involvement with their stepchildren had, when compared to women with less involvement, less nonparental interaction with their former husband, and less psychological closeness, attachment, or good feelings toward him. They also had somewhat less coparental interaction with

Table 10-3. Correlation of Involvement with Stepchildren with Variables Measuring Relationship with the Former Spouse, the Current Partner, and the Biological Children

	Women	Men
Relationship with Former Spouse		
Conflict Scale	−.04[a]	.08
Support Scale	−.16	.02
Nonparental Interaction Scale	−.36*	−.19
Coparental Sharing Scale	−.19	−.07
Psychological Closeness Scale	−.42*	−.01
Anger Scale	−.19	.01
Attachment Scale	−.51**	−.28*
Attitude to Former Spouse as Parent Scale	−.16	.23
Positive Feeling Scale	−.46**	−.44**
Respondent Likes Amount Of Time Shared With Former Spouse Related to Children	.50**	.17
Respondent Likes Parenting With Former Spouse	.57**	.24
Relationship with Current Partner		
Dyadic Adjustment Scale	.68**	.34*
Overall Life Satisfaction	.34*	.09
Relationship with Own Biological Children		
Involvement with Biological Children Scale	.48	−.11
Respondent Feels Like Visitor in Noncustodial Children's Lives	−.59*	−.24
Respondent Satisfied With Amount of Time Spent With Children	.77**	.02
Respondent Satisfied With Custody Arrangement	.35*	−.20

Note. For description of scales used, see Appendix 10-1.

[a]Correlations are pairwise, and thus may be based on different *N*s for each question. Double asterisks indicate a significance level of .01, single asterisks of .05.

their former spouse, but were more likely to be satisfied with this interaction. They were more involved with their own biological children, more satisfied with the custody arrangement, and more satisfied with the amount of time they spent with their noncustodial children, if any. They were also less likely to say they felt like a visitor in the lives of their noncustodial children. Women more involved with their stepchildren were also more satisfied with their relationship to their new partner, and with their life overall at this time. For men, the only strong findings were that men more involved with their stepchildren showed less attachment to and good feelings for their former spouse and had a better relationship with their new partner.

These findings suggest that relationships within the stepfamily are related to continuing relationships in the binuclear family. Involvement with a new stepchild and satisfaction with the stepparent role is likely to result in attenuation of the relationship between former spouses. Especially for mothers, the more involved they are with their new stepchildren, the less they are involved in any type of relationship with their former spouse. And the more involved they are with their new stepchild, the more satisfied they are with their new marital partner. Crosbie-Burnett (1984) found in her study of stepfather families that the stepfather–stepchild relationship was more central to family happiness than was the marital relationship. She notes that an unsatisfactory stepparent–stepchild relationship places stresses on the new remarriage relationship. Our preliminary findings support the importance of a satisfying stepparent–stepchild involvement to remarital satisfaction.

SUMMARY AND CONCLUSIONS

Any conclusions drawn from these preliminary findings of the relationships between biological and stepparents in the binuclear family are best offered as hypotheses to be tested in future research rather than as definitive results. These families are structurally complex systems with wide variations that form a continuum from the simplest (neither partner recoupled) to the most complex (both partners recoupled to other divorced parents and have children of both prior marriages and the new unions). Further, when we divided the sample by gender, custody type, and categories of response, small subsamples were the result. It also must be noted that these families are in the early stages of stepfamily development, being recoupled, on the average, only about 2 years.

Taking into account the above limitations, some patterns related to gender appear to emerge. For example, the finding that interaction between former spouses decreases significantly when the father remarries but not when the mother does so is important to note. Taken in conjunction with the findings that stepmothers are less satisfied with their relationship to their stepchildren, feel their relationship with their husband (the biological father) is more negatively affected by the presence of his children, are more dissatisfied with their role and are less involved with their stepchildren, we can conclude that the father's remarriage is the more stressful transition for both the former spouses and the new partners. Although we have no data directly from the children, it seems reasonable to infer that this transition may be more stressful for them as well. The findings of Clingempeel, Brand, and Ievoli (1984) suggest that the father's remarriage is more problematic for girls than for boys. They speculate that the presence of a stepmother may pose a major threat to the father–daughter relationship.

The relationship between mothers and stepmothers also appears to be a more difficult one than that between fathers and stepfathers. The women reported more differences of opinion and less satisfaction with their interactions. At the same time, mothers had, on the whole, more positive or caring attitudes toward stepmothers than did fathers toward stepfathers. Rather than being contradictory, these findings might suggest that female parents are more involved, both negatively and positively, with each other than are male parents. Carol Gilligan's (1982) suggestion that women are more relationship-oriented than men may indeed provide a basis for interpreting these findings. As the sociological literature has informed us, "women are the kinkeepers of the family." Because of the centrality of family in women's lives, their feelings about relationships in the family, whether nuclear or binuclear, may be more intense than men's. If true, this might also help explain the more stressful transition of the father's recoupling. Adding another woman parent to the family may pose a more serious threat and result in more stress and dysfunction to both mothers and stepmothers and, as Clingempeel, Brand, and Ievoli (1984) note, to stepdaughters as well.

Summarizing the findings about the nature and quality of relationships in the binuclear system is more difficult. In general, we found that most of the adults perceived their counterparts in the other "nucleus" of the family more as acquaintances than as family members. Most reported feeling somewhat detached or indifferent toward each other. The stepfamilies (whether remarried or cohabiting) are in the early stages of their development: The assimilation process results in confusion that reverberates throughout the family system (Crosbie-Burnett & Ahrons, 1985; Papernow, 1984). One could speculate that this pattern may resemble the early stages of relationships with in-laws in a first marriage. One major difference, however, is that the norms in our society support and sanction good relationships with in-laws whereas the norms for binuclear families tend to prescribe either negative or dissolved relationships.

These normative expectations raise an interesting but unanswerable question: If the norms for divorced families included the expectation that obligations to children require a continuation of relationships, would actual perceptions of relationships be different? In other words, if mothers, fathers, and stepparents had norms for relationships similar to those of new first spouses toward in-laws, would they indeed begin to perceive themselves as family? And if so, would it change the nature of the relationship between stepparents and same-sex biological parents and between stepmothers and stepfathers in the binuclear system?

The one present similarity in both types of extended kin systems is the negative stereotype often depicted in the public media of both mothers-in-law and stepmothers as nasty, meddling family members with whom it is difficult to establish good relationships. The fact that the women in these kin relation-

ships are singled out again suggests that the role of women and the relationships between women family members are more salient in families than those
of male members.

One major conclusion we can draw from these data, perhaps, is that the
maternal and paternal subsystems of the divorced family are indeed interdependent. In these early postdivorce stages, we have found a variety of patterns, with most families having continuing relationships based on a common
offspring. They range from friendly to hostile with the majority being somewhat distant but cordial. Given the early stage of development, we are left
with more questions about how these relationships may change over time.
Will time cause the two family subsystems to drift apart? Or will family events
(graduations, marriages) or the inevitable family crises (illness, death, redivorce) create the need for continued interaction and provide a shared family
history that may keep feelings of kinship in the binuclear family alive? And
how will the birth of a grandchild—a further link between the subsystems—
affect the binuclear family? These questions can only be answered by more
extensive, longitudinal research on the postdivorce family. Such variables as
former-spouse relationships, custody arrangements, and individual psycho-
dynamics need to be studied to shed more light on the patterns of postdivorce
relationships. As we focus our attention upon the transitions of family change
that result from divorce, we will need to examine the impact on the extended
kinship system as well. Whether extended kin are added, retained, or relin-
quished in binuclear families may depend on a complex interaction of factors
that will, in turn, affect the functioning of the family (Ahrons & Bowman,
1982; Cherlin, 1978; Furstenberg & Spanier, 1984).

To shift from a perspective of pathology to a perspective of normalization requires that we reconceive much of our earlier thinking about divorce
and family change. It requires us to extend our theorizing about families to
include families after divorce as continuing, rather than dissolved, family
units. It means we will need to develop new models of divorced families that
include the new families of the original biological couple. Only with a new
paradigm of divorced families can we provide role models for divorcing
families that give them some direction for the changes they will experience
through divorce. Such a paradigm may not alter the distress experienced by
families as they move through the reconstruction process, but it can provide
them with guidelines for family functioning that do not disrupt the bonds of
family. A normalization model means that we must begin to think of remarriage in terms of adding family members instead of replacing family
members. The stepfamily unit is part of a larger system of kin and may be
thought of as one nucleus of a "binuclear" family system. As such, it requires
a different systemic model than the traditional nuclear family (Ahrons &
Rodgers, 1986).

APPENDIX 10-1

Questions comprising scales and variables discussed in text

Coparental Interaction Scale

At the present time, which of the following do you share with your former spouse?
(1 = never, 2 = rarely, 3 = sometimes, 4 = usually, 5 = always)

       a. Making major decisions regarding your children's lives
       b. Making day-to-day decisions regarding your children's lives
       c. Discussing personal problems your children may be experiencing
       d. Discussing school and/or medical problems
       e. Planning special events in your children's lives
       f. Talking about your children's accomplishments and progress
       g. Talking about problems you are having in raising the children
       h. Discussing how the children are adjusting to the divorce
       i. Discussing problems you are having with the coparenting relationship
       j. Discussing finances in regard to your children

Reliability: .94, women; .93, men*

Conflict Scale

(1 = never, 2 = rarely, 3 = sometimes, 4 = usually, 5 = always)

       a. When you and your former spouse discuss parenting issues, how often does an argument result?
       b. How often is the underlying atmosphere one of hostility or anger?
       c. How often is the conversation stressful or tense?
       d. Do you and your former spouse have basic differences of opinion about issues related to childrearing?

Reliability: .84, women; .88, men

Support Scale

(1 = never, 2 = rarely, 3 = sometimes, 4 = usually, 5 = always)

       a. If your former spouse has needed to make a change in visiting arrangements, do you go out of your way to accommodate?
       b. Does your former spouse go out of the way to accommodate any changes you need to make?
       c. Do you feel that your former spouse understands and is supportive of your special needs as a custodial (or noncustodial) parent?

  *Determined by using Cronbach's alpha.

    d. When you need help regarding the children, do you seek it from your former spouse?

    e. Would you say that your former spouse is a resource to you in raising the children?

    f. Would you say that you are a resource to your former spouse in raising the children?

Reliability: .84, women; .74, men

Satisfaction

(1 = very dissatisfied, 2 = somewhat dissatisfied, 3 = mixed, neither satisfied nor dissatisfied, 4 = somewhat satisfied, 5 = very satisfied)

    a. How satisfied are you with the custody arrangement?

    b. How satisfied are you with the amount of time you (your former spouse) spend(s) with the [noncustodial] children?

    c. How satisfied are you with the amount that you share with each other in relation to the children [as measured by coparental sharing scale]?

    d. How satisfied are you with the present parenting relationship between you and your former spouse?

    e. In general, how satisfied are you now with your life as a whole?

Reliability not available.

Involvement with Children Scale

(1 = not at all, 2 = a little, 3 = somewhat, 4 = much, 5 = very much)
How involved are you (is your former spouse) with the children in the following areas?

    a. Disciplining the children
    b. Dress and grooming
    c. Religious or moral training, if any
    d. Running errands for/with the children
    e. Celebrating holidays with the children
    f. Celebrating significant events (e.g., birthdays) with the children
    g. Taking the children for recreational activities (e.g., sports)
    h. Attending school or church-related functions
    i. Discussing problems with the children that they might be having
    j. Taking the children for vacations
    k. Social activities with friends or extended family, grandparents
    l. Helping children with schoolwork
    m. Discusssing children's social activities (e.g., friendships, dating, parties, over-nights)
    n. Planning for the children's future (e.g., education, career, marriage)

Reliability: .88, women; .93, men   (rating of self)

Reliability: .95, women; .93, men   (rating of former spouse)

Nonparental Interaction Scale

There are a number of different ways that some former spouses continue to relate to one another after divorce. Think back over the past year and tell me how often you and your former spouse have related in these ways.
(1 = never, 2 = once or twice a year, 3 = every few months, 4 = once a month, 5 = twice a month, 6 = once a week or more often)

> a. Talking about old friends in common
> b. Discussing finances not related to the children
> c. Talking about your past marriage to each other
> d. Talking about your families (mother, father, etc., but not the children)
> e. Talking about new experiences you are having in your present lives
> f. Talking about personal problems
> g. Talking about reconciling (marrying each other again)
> h. Talking about why you got divorced
> i. Having sexual intercourse
> j. Helping each other with household tasks not related to the children
> k. "Dating" each other
> l. Having physical contact (e.g., hugging, kissing) without sexual intercourse
> m. Going out to dinner without the children
> n. Talking about new partners

Reliability: .93, women; .90, men

Psychological Closeness Scale

(1 = always, 2 = often, 3 = sometimes, 4 = rarely, 5 = never)

> a. I feel neutral about my former spouse
> b. I feel detached from my former spouse
> c. I feel indifferent toward my former spouse

(1 = never, 2 = rarely, 3 = sometimes, 4 = often, 5 = always)

> d. I feel emotional extremes of hating and then loving my former spouse

Reliability: .51, women; .59, men

Attachment Scale

(1 = never, 2 = rarely, 3 = sometimes, 4 = often, 5 = always)

> a. I find myself wondering what my former spouse is doing
> b. I find myself spending a lot of time thinking about my former spouse
> c. I feel I will never get over the divorce
> d. Sometimes I can't believe we got divorced

Reliability: .77, women; .65, men

Anger Scale

(1 = never, 2 = rarely, 3 = sometimes, 4 = often, 5 = always)

      a. I feel angry for the hurt I have gone through
      b. I blame my former spouse for the divorce
      c. I don't feel my former spouse deserves to be happy
      d. I want revenge for wrongs done to me
      e. I hope my former spouse has problems in new relationships
      f. I think my former spouse should be punished
      g. I want to get back at my former spouse for what's been done to me
      h. I hate my former spouse

Reliability: .82, women; .78, men

Positive Feelings Scale

(1 = never, 2 = rarely, 3 = sometimes, 4 = often, 5 = always)

      a. I love my former spouse
      b. I care about my former spouse's welfare
      c. I have warm feelings for my former spouse
      d. I feel compassion for my former spouse

Reliability: .85, women; .86, men

Attitude toward Former Spouse as a Parent Scale

(1 = never, 2 = rarely, 3 = sometimes, 4 = often, 5 = always)

      a. My former spouse is a caring parent
      b. My former spouse is a good parent to the children

(1 = always, 2 = often, 3 = sometimes, 4 = rarely, 5 = never)

      c. My former spouse is an incompetent parent
      d. My former spouse is an irresponsible parent

Reliability: .93, women; .90, men

Dyadic Adjustment Scale

This is a 32-item scale measuring the current relationship of the newly recoupled pair (i.e., divorced parents and their new spouses or cohabiting partners). It consists of questions asking about the frequency of disagreements in various areas, such as family finances, household tasks, making major decisions, sexual relations, philosophy of life, and so on; questions asking about the amount the partners engage in mutual activities; and questions tapping the respondent's general assessment of the relationship (How often do you think things are going well between you and your partner? Do you ever regret having remarried?). A high score on this scale indicates a higher level of "dyadic adjustment".

APPENDIX 10-2

Q-Sort Questions

(1 = never, 2 = rarely, 3 = sometimes, 4 = often, 5 = always)

1. I feel I am a good stepparent.
2. I feel I am a caring stepparent.
3. I feel I am a competent stepparent.
4. I feel I am a responsible stepparent.
5. I feel I have a positive influence on my partner's children.
6. I feel I do not live up to others' expectations of me as a stepparent.
7. My partner appreciates what I do for his/her children.
8. I feel insecure as a stepparent.
9. I feel inadequate as a stepparent.
10. I feel it is more difficult to be a stepparent than a natural parent.
11. Being a stepparent creates problems for me.
12. I like being a stepparent.
13. I resent being a stepparent.
14. I worry about being good enough as a stepparent.
15. I feel my partner's children need me.
16. I feel my partner's children do not need me.
17. I feel I am trying too hard to be a good stepparent.
18. I feel people judge me strictly as a stepparent.
19. I feel I receive support from others as a stepparent.
20. I feel my partner's children do not respect me as a parent.
21. I feel my partner's children do not respect me.
22. I feel my partner's children like me.
23. I feel it is difficult to know what a stepparent is allowed to do.
24. I feel it is difficult to know what a stepparent is supposed to do.
25. I feel my partner understands my role as a stepparent.
26. It is difficult for me and my partner to discuss stepparent problems.
27. I worry that my performance as a stepparent will hurt my marriage/relationship.
28. I feel like an outsider in my partner's family.
29. I feel my partner thinks I am trying too hard to be a good stepparent.
30. I feel my partner thinks I am not trying hard enough to be a good stepparent.
31. I feel my partner's family acknowledges my effort at being a good stepparent.

32. I feel my own family acknowledges my efforts at being a good stepparent.
33. I feel others compare me with my partner's former spouse.
34. I feel insecure about my place in my partner's family.
35. I feel I compete with my partner's children for his/her time.

REFERENCES

Ahrons, C. R. (1979). The binuclear family: Two households, one family. *Alternative Lifestyles, 2*, 499–515.

Ahrons, C. R. (1980a). Divorce: A crisis of family transition and change. *Family Relations, 29*, 533–540.

Ahrons, C. R. (1980b). Joint custody arrangements in the postdivorce family. *Journal of Divorce, 3*, 189–205.

Ahrons, C. R. (1981). The continuing coparental relationship between divorced spouses. *American Journal of Orthopsychiatry, 51*, 315–328.

Ahrons, C. R. (1983). Predictors of paternal involvement postdivorce: Mothers' and fathers' perceptions. *Journal of Divorce, 6*, 55–59.

Ahrons, C. R., & Bowman, M. (1982). Changes in family relationships following divorce of an adult child: Grandmothers' perceptions. *Journal of Divorce, 5*, 49–68.

Ahrons, C. R., & Rodgers, R. H. (1987). *Divorced families: A multidisciplinary developmental view*. New York: Norton.

Ahrons, C. R., & Wallisch, L. (1986). The relationship between former spouses. In S. Duck & D. Perlman (Eds.), *Intimate relationships: Development, dynamics and deterioration* (pp. 269–296). Beverly Hills, CA: Sage.

Bohannan, P. (1970). The six stations of divorce. In P. Bohannan (Ed.), *Divorce and after* (pp. 33–62). New York: Doubleday.

Bowman, M. E., & Ahrons, C. R. (1985). Impact of legal custody status on fathers' parenting postdivorce. *Journal of Marriage and the Family, 47*, 481–488.

Cherlin, A. J. (1978). Remarriage as an incomplete institution. *American Journal of Sociology, 84*, 634–650.

Clingempeel, W., Brand, E., & Ievoli, R. (1984). Stepparent–stepchild relationships in stepmother and stepfather families: A multimethod study. *Family Relations, 33*, 465–474.

Crosbie-Burnett, M. (1984). The centrality of the step relationship: A challenge to family theory and practice. *Family Relations, 33*, 459–464.

Crosbie-Burnett, M., & Ahrons, C. R. (1985). From divorce to remarriage: Implications for families in transition. *Psychotherapy and the Family, 1*, 121–137.

Furstenberg, F. F., Jr., & Spanier, G. B. (1984). *Recycling the family: Remarriage after divorce*. Beverly Hills, CA: Sage.

Gilligan, C. (1982). *In a different voice*. Cambridge, MA: Harvard University Press.

Glick, P. C. (1984). Marriage, divorce, and living arrangements: Prospective changes. *Journal of Family Issues, 5*, 7–26.

Hetherington, E., Cox, M., & Cox, R. (1976). Divorced fathers. *Family Coordinator, 25*, 417–428.

Mead, M. (1970). Anomalies in American postdivorce relationships. In P. Bohannan (Ed.), *Divorce and after* (pp. 107–125). New York: Doubleday.

Messinger, L. (1985). *Remarriage*. New York: Plenum.

Mills, D. (1984). A model for stepfamily development. *Family Relations, 33*, 365–372.

Papernow, P. L. (1984). The stepfamily cycle: An experiential model of stepfamily development. *Family Relations, 33*, 355–364.

Pasley, K., & Ihinger-Tallman, M. (1982). Stress in remarried families. *Family Perspective, 16*, 181–190.

Visher, E., & Visher, J. (1979). *Stepfamilies: A guide to working with stepparents and stepchildren.* New York: Brunner/Mazel.

Wallerstein, J., & Kelly, J. (1980). *Surviving the breakup.* New York: Basic Books.

11

Family Type, Visiting Patterns, and Children's
Behavior in the Stepfamily: A Linked Family System

DORIS S. JACOBSON
University of California, Los Angeles

INTRODUCTION

There has been much discussion in professional journals about whether we
are experiencing the decline of the American family. The remarriage rate
belies this and suggests that, while there is an inability on the part of an
increasing number of people to achieve satisfaction the first time around, a
second attempt seems worth the effort. Many of those who remarry have
children from a prior marriage and are custodial and/or non-custodial parents. Thus, the stepfamily has emerged in large enough numbers to be
considered one of several types of families that are part of contemporary
American social structure—a variant rather than a deviant form of family
life. The substantial number of adults and children now living in stepfamilies
will likely continue if the divorce and remarriage rates remain high. This
family form includes new configurations of interaction, including an increased number of dyadic and triadic relationships. Children and adults
potentially must relate to two households, that of the custodial and the
noncustodial parent. For adults, many of whom have grown up in intact
families, and for adults and children who must now relate to adults in two
households, adjustment can involve a kind of "culture shock." As individuals
find themselves faced with a new reality, complicated yet basic questions are
raised, such as "What is a family?" A survey of literature indicates that the
number of empirical studies of the stepfamily is limited. Research has not
kept pace with the changing American family, and there is need for new
conceptualization for this increasingly important family form and for further
empirical study.

This chapter is divided into three parts. First, a brief examination of
demographic characteristics of the changing American family is presented.
Second, a new conceptualization of the stepfamily as a "linked family
system" is offered. A typology of linked family systems, in which the types of
family to which a child of divorce and remarriage can belong, is presented.

257

Finally, selected findings from a recently completed study on stepfamily interaction are reported with special attention to children's behavior as related to types of family structure identified in the typology.

THE CHANGING AMERICAN FAMILY

A few statistics concerning the changing demographic characteristics of the American family with particular attention to divorce and remarriage makes the prevalence of the stepfamily clear. A profile of the changing structures can be seen in Table 11-1. The "typical" American family (referring to a first remarried couple living with their biological children) seems to be on the way to losing its majority status. While 73% of all children under 18 lived in traditional families in 1960, the figure was 63% in 1978, and only 56% are projected to do so in 1990. In 1978, 10.2% of all children lived in a stepfamily; an additional 18.6% were living with a single parent. A large majority, 74% of those living with single parents were in situations where parents were separated or divorced. Children living with single parents are the fastest growing group and are projected to include 26.5% of all children in 1990 (Glick, 1979, 1984). It should be kept in mind that living with a single parent is often a temporary status as children (and parents) move from intact family to single-parent household to a remarriage or stepfamily arrangement. For those who redivorce, the chain of events is repeated, and the number of those who have ever experienced a single parent and/or a remarried situation is greater than the figures for any specific moment in time indicate. According to unpublished research involving projections by A. Norton of the United States Census Bureau, about 59% of all children born in the 1980s may be expected to live with only one parent for at least one year before the age of 18. More than two thirds of these children (close to 35% of all children) may expect to live with a remarried parent in a stepparent family for a part of their childhood (Glick, 1984). It is important to note that children, even while living in a single-parent household,[1] are part of a stepfamily, if a noncustodial (visited) parent has remarried. In that event, the child has a stepparent and is part of a stepfamily in the visited household.

The above figures reflect the rapid changes that have occurred, particularly between 1960 and 1980, during which period the divorce rate increased 2.5 times (United States National Center for Health Statistics, 1981). While the divorce rate declined slightly in 1982 and 1983, the number in the population estimated to experience divorce at some time continues to go up. Based on projections by age groups, about one half of the first marriages of young adults today are estimated to end in divorce. Furthermore, a large

---

[1]This according to the definition developed for the study that will be reported and presented in the discussion of the "linked family system" in the next section of this chapter.

Table 11-1. Living Arrangements of Children Under 18 Years of Age in the United States 1960–1990 (Percentages)

	1960 (64,310,000)[b]	1970 (69,523,000)	1978 (63,206,000)	1990[a] (64,776,000)	Trend: 1960–1990
Living with two biological parents: married once	73.2%	68.7%	63.1%	56%	−17.3%
Living with two biological parents: one or both previously married	5.7%	5.0%	4.1%	4%	−1.7%
Living with one biological parent and one stepparent	8.6%	9.4%	10.2%	10%	+1.4%
Living with one parent	9.1%	13.4%	18.6%	26.5%	+17.4%
Living with neither parent	3.4%	3.5%	4.0%	5%	+ 1.6%

Note. Data derived from Glick, P. C. (1979). Children of divorced parents in demographic perspective. *Journal of Social Issues, 35*, 171–172; also, Glick, P. C. (1984). Marriage, divorce and living arrangements. *Journal of Family Issues, 5*, 7–26.
[a]Projection.
[b]Total number of children under 18.

proportion of divorced persons remarry (five out of six divorced men, and three out of four divorced women), creating an unprecedented number of new marriages in which one or both spouses have been previously married (Glick, 1984). About one half of all remarriages take place within 3 years after divorce (Cherlin, 1981). Recent estimates of the National Center for Health Statistics project a somewhat greater risk of disruption for the remarried after divorce; 49% of first marriages are likely to end in divorce as compared to about 60% of remarriages (Glick, 1984). The higher probability of divorce for remarrieds may be related to the complexity of adjusting to a family structure that includes children (custodial and/or noncustodial) and adults who relate to two households (Crosbie-Burnett, 1984; Pasley & Ihinger-Tallman, 1982).

THE CONCEPT OF STEPFAMILY AS A LINKED FAMILY SYSTEM

With the changing characteristics of families, we need to rethink the manner in which stepfamilies are conceptualized; we need an approach not tied to conventional terms such as "nuclear," "intact," or "broken." Concepts are needed that reflect the web of interrelationships and the dynamic complexity of the new phenomena. This is important for the development of theory, practice, program planning, policy, and research. To meet this need, the definition of "stepfamily" is different in this chapter and the study to be reported from that found in most professional and popular literature. Ordinarily, the term refers to the custodial household. This is the household in which a child lives with a custodial remarried parent and his/her spouse, most commonly characterized by a biological mother and a stepfather. This limited definition is the one upon which most statistics are available and on which most research is based. The new definition presented here is different in a way that gives attention, in each instance, to the two households to which a child of divorce and remarriage relates: the custodial (live-in) and the noncustodial (visited). This new concept of stepfamily is called the "linked family system."[1] In it, the child is seen as related to both households, each of which is viewed as a subsystem of a dual-household family system. People in both households are seen as part of the child's environment. The child is viewed as the "link," influencing and being influenced by those in both households. To illustrate: A child is part of a stepfamily as a linked family system if he/she lives with a single mother and visits a remarried father and his wife (the visited stepmother). The child, as link between the two households, is a major channel of communication, overt and covert. Much of the communication between the two households is about or through the child. However, communication may also be about other matters such as an ongoing attachment and/or hostility between the parents (being former spouses). The child may be integrated into the family life of those in the live-in household, those in the visited household, those in both, or neither of the households. Figure 11-1 illustrates the child as part of a linked family system. The circles represent the two households, and the passageway reflects the child as link, who, by foot, bicycle, car, or plane moves back and forth between them. This conceptualization reflects the reality of the environment of the child and the stepfamily in a way addressed in no other research. The figure is simplified for purposes of research in that it focuses on only one child in each linked family system.

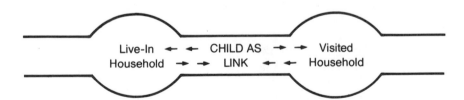

Figure 11-1. The child in a linked family system.

VISITED FAMILY

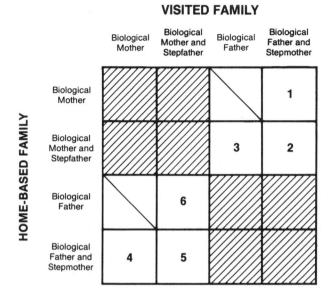

Figure 11-2. Typology of linked family systems (stepfamilies).

Once defined as a linked family system, stepfamily structures need to be described. A typology of major linked family system types to which a child of divorce and remarriage can potentially belong has been articulated and is shown in Figure 11-2.

In Figure 11-2, column headings reflect structures of the custodial family, and row headings reflect those of the non-custodial family. The cells with numbers represent the six possible family types to which a child of divorce and remarriage can belong, three in which a child lives with a mother, and three in which a child lives with a father. The numbers in these cells refer to family types in the study that will be reported in the next section of this chapter. The cells with the lines through them reflect linked family systems that are not part of this stepfamily typology because both parents have remained single. While these are dual-family systems for the child, there is no stepparent and therefore no stepfamily.

In regard to stepfamilies as linked family systems, there are six possible family types, three in which a child lives with a mother and three in which a child lives with a father. The six family types are as follows:

Type 1. Child lives with a single mother and visits a remarried father.
Type 2. Child lives with a remarried mother and visits a remarried father.

In this instance, the child has two stepparents—one in the live-in household and one in the visited household.

Type 3. Child lives with a remarried mother and visits a single father.

There are three parallel types of families in which a child lives with the father and visits the mother as seen in Family Types 4, 5, and 6.

TESTING THE MODEL

The research that is presented here is exploratory: It should not be viewed as hypothesis testing, but rather on the order of model development. The linked family system typology on which the study is based provides guidelines for research on stepfamily interaction by proposing a more inclusive conceptualization of stepfamily life. In general, it incorporates the idea of multiple role incumbents with whom the child interacts as well as expanded possibilities for attention to intra- and inter-family interaction. Therefore, it takes into account a greater variety and complexity of interactions in stepfamilies than the traditional definition of stepfamilies can include. One thesis that underlies this perspective is that variation in contemporary family life is not adequately represented by the simple dichotomies (intact vs. other, two-parent vs. one-parent) found in much of the literature. In fact, there may be as much variation within the so-called non-traditional families as there is between them and the more traditional family type. If so, social research requires a model or models that more appropriately reflect this social reality. Of particular importance is the view questioning whether children's behavior can be understood in relation to the dichotomies mentioned above. It seems reasonable to suppose that children's behavior is influenced by a host of factors, and especially by the nature and quality of interactions among the expanded number of significant persons, including parent figures, with whom they interact. The typology proposed suggests the many dimensions along which stepfamilies may vary (i.e., number of adults in parenting roles, visiting arrangements, conflicts between those in the two households). Thus, a second major assumption of the research presented is that children's behavior in stepfamilies can best be explained by paying attention to dynamic variables rather than only static, demographic classification.

The Study: Stepfamily Interaction and Children's Behavior

The purpose of this study was to make a contribution to understanding interactions in stepfamilies defined as linked family systems, with particular attention to the well-being of children. This report presents information not readily available in the literature about life in linked family systems. Research results focus on the examination of the relationship between: (1) family type and adjustment-related children's behaviors, and (2) contact time of the child with the non-custodial parent and adjustment-related children's behaviors. Additionally, descriptive information is presented concerning visiting patterns of children with noncustodial parents in diverse family types.

There has been limited research concerning the relationship between being part of a stepfamily and children's behavior. A recent review of the empirical studies of children who have experienced parental divorce and remarriage suggests that few clear and unambiguous conclusions can be drawn from existing research. Major areas in which studies are needed were identified (Ganong & Coleman, 1984). For example, studies are needed that examine the factors that contribute to the well being of children who live in different types of stepfamily structures. Almost all existing research compares children in mother/stepfather families with those in intact families. Often there is an underlying assumption that stepchildren are in a disadvantaged position. This assumption is not necessarily warranted, and investigations using alternative frames of reference are needed. Studies are needed that focus attention on children who live with fathers and stepmothers. Finally, no researchers to date have reported data on non-custodial stepchildren. The study reported here addresses these areas, and attempts to fill some of the identified gaps in knowledge.

Sample Selection and Measures

The sample consisted of 176 children and the adults in both households of their linked family system: 50 in Family Type 1, 51 in Family Type 2, 42 in Family Type 3, and 33 in Family Type 4. This includes children in all three mother-custody linked family systems types, and children in one father-custody type. Only one father-custody was chosen because of anticipated difficulty of recruitment. (It is estimated that only 10% of children of divorce live with fathers [Glick, 1984].) Within each family type, children were stratified by sex and age (8–12, 13–17). Individual interviews were held in the homes with each focal child and with the parents and stepparents in the two households to which each child was linked. In all, interviews were held with the 176 children, their 352 parents, and their 227 stepparents in 352 households.

The sample was recruited primarily from the marriage records of the Los Angeles Superior Court in Los Angeles, California. Records were scanned for a one-year period. Of the 5,828 identified as potential informants, 32% (1,879) were actually located; of those, 34% (645) qualified for inclusion in the study. Fifty-seven percent (370) of those in the first family of the linked family system agreed to participate, 44.7% (288) of those in both families agreed to participate, meaning that 12.7% of those originally recruited were lost because the "second family" refused to be part of the study. Of those who qualified and agreed to participate, some were used to pretest interviews and for training interviewers, and some did not qualify by the time the research interview took place (for example, a parent had moved out of the area). A small number refused after initial acceptance. Criteria for inclusion were as follows: (1) at least one marital partner had a previous marriage that ended in divorce; (2) the existence of at least one child age 8–17 from that former marriage; (3) both marital partners had at least a high school education; (4) both parents lived within a 150-mile radius of Los Angeles; (5) the child had been in place, that is, living in the same living situation, for a least one year prior to interview; (6) the child had seen his/her non-custodial parent at least once in the year prior to interview; (7) the child, parents, and stepparents in both households agreed to participate in the study. The study, therefore, focused on middle-class families from the general population in which there was some interface between those in the two households of the linked family system in the year prior to interview. It focused on those who lived relatively close to each other and in which the child's living situation was somewhat stable. It included only those families in which the child, parents, and stepparents in both households agreed to participate.

Data collection was carried out by ten mental health professionals, all of whom had masters degrees in social work or psychology and several years of clinical experiences. Those in each household of the linked family system were assigned to different interviewers to maximize sensitivity and to reassure the informant of confidentiality. If there were two adults in a household, they were seen back to back by the same interviewer or simultaneously by two interviewers. Those in the two households were, for the most part, seen within a month of each other.

Child behavior was measured by the use of the Achenbach Child Behavior Checklist (CBCL) (Achenbach, 1978). This is a self-report measure designed to obtain parents' reports of children's problems and competencies in a standardized format. The instrument includes 118 items describing behaviors about which a respondent is asked to indicate "very true," "somewhat true," or "not at all true" of the child at the time of interview or over the previous 6 months. All parents and stepparents in each linked family system completed the forms. Standardized scores are available separately from Achenbach for a normal and a clinical population, and within each of these groups separately for boys and girls for two age groups. The instrument generates two broadband subscales referred to as "Internalizing" and "Externalizing." The internalizing subscale designates fearful, inhibited, over-controlled behavior while the externalizing subscale involves aggressive, anti-social, under-controlled behavior. In this research, analysis was carried out using Achenbach's standardized scores for normal populations. There is little question that there are assets and liabilities to the use of self-report measures in general and as related to children's behavior. On the one hand, there is the potential bias of the reporter, and on the other, the importance of parent observations. This instrument was chosen because there are adequate reports of reliability and validity; normalized scores are available for comparison by age and sex for both a general and a clinical population (Achenbach & Edelbrock, 1983).

Because reports from multiple-parent and stepparent role incumbents were involved in each family situation, an important decision for the research was whose report should be accepted as the measure of the child's behavior. The CBCL was originally developed in studies on intact families in which it was administered primarily to mothers. The most comparable source in this study is the live-in biological parent (mothers in Family Types 1, 2, 3, and fathers in Family Type 4), and these sources were chosen for the study. The decision to use the report of the live-in parent was based on three considerations:

1. In this sample, the noncustodial or visited parent (mother or father) sometimes had infrequent contact with the child.

2. Achenbach and Edelbrock (1981) found that fathers' and mothers' reports of children's behavior in intact families were highly correlated. In the present study, the correlation between mother's and father's reports was significant ($r = .37$), but not highly correlated enough to consider averaging.

3. There exists no research evidence of stepparents' reports of children's problems as it compares with those of the live-in biological parents.

The measures of children's problems are therefore based on reports of live-in biological parents standardized against the Achenbach and Edelbrock scores within each of the age and sex groups. This measure was considered the most appropriate empirically, and the one which resembled most closely that used in the development of the instrument. A recognized weakness of this choice is that there may be systematic differences in perceptions of children's behavior among custodial mothers (Family Types 1, 2, and 3) and custodial fathers (Family Type 4).

The obtained CBCL scores were compared with Achenbach's normal and clinical populations separately. Older boys and girls in this sample had significantly higher behavior problem scores (higher scores indicated more behavior problems) than those in the Achenbach normal sample for both total problem scores and for the two broad-band subscales. Scores obtained for younger children indicated similar patterns, however, the differences were not significant. While CBCL scores were higher than those for the Achenbach normal sample, they were significantly lower than those for the Achenbach clinical sample for all age and sex group comparisons. This suggests that children in linked family systems, for the most part, are more stressed than others, but as a group are not identified as seeking or needing help.

Findings

Family Type and Children's Behavior

To address the relationship between selected aspects of children's behavior and family type, a three-way analysis of variance was used to test for the effects of family type, sex, and age and their interaction on reports of children's behavior problems, as measured by the standardized total score on the CBCL. As presented in Table 11-2, there was a main effect by family type ($F = 3.4$, $MS = 48.5$, $p < .03$). No interactions were found to be significant.

As Table 11-2 indicates, the highest scores for the total behavior problem score and both broad-band scales were for children in Family Type 4, the only father-custody family included in the study. Conversely, the lowest scores (fewest behavior problems) were for children in Family Type 2, the only family type in which both parents of the child have remarried. The Duncan Multiple Range Test was used to test for the pattern of significant differences between family types. Mean scores for children in Family Type 4 were significantly higher than those for children in two of the three mother-custody family types: Type 1, in which the child lives with a single mother and visits a remarried father, and Type 2, in which the child lives with a remarried mother and visits a remarried father. There was no significant difference between children in Family Type 4 and those in Family Type 3 in which the child lives with a remarried mother and visits a single father. Overall, children living with a remarried father are reported to have more behavior problems than those living with a mother.

Table 11-2. Duncan Multiple Range Test[a] of Mean Scores[b] on CBCL Scales by Family Type

Variable	4[c] (N = 33)	3 (N = 42)	1 (N = 50)	2 (N = 51)
Mean of Total Adjustment Score	57.4	55.3	51.3	50.7
Mean of Externalizing Scale Score	57.5	56.8	52.6	51.4
Mean of Internalizing Scale Score	57.5	57.3	53.1	52.9

[a]Means contained by a "∟_____⌐" are not significantly different ($p \leq .05$).
[b]All means are standardized within age and sex groups.
[c]See Figure 11-1 for description of family types.

The findings must be considered with caution. While parents in father-custody families report more problems in their children, there are fewer of this type of family in the study. Since this is a correlational study, an association does not imply a causal relationship between father-custody and children's problems. Nevertheless, it is possible to speculate on the meaning of these findings. It is still relatively rare for children of divorce to live with their fathers. From a psychological point of view, it is possible that such an arrangement emerges more readily when children had behavior problems prior to or immediately after divorce. A single mother may see herself, or be seen by others (former spouse, court systems), as less able to deal with a problem child. This can be complicated if she sees herself or is seen by others as having problems herself that interfere with child care, with or without a problem child. From a sociological view, children and parents may receive less support from significant others and/or the broader community in the father-custody arrangement. One consequence of less support may be more behavior problems. Finally, there may be intervening interpersonal variables. For example, is a father-custody arrangement more likely to occur when there is high interparent conflict regarding child custody? Is there more likely to be parent–stepparent conflict in father-custody situations? Subsequent analysis of data will include attention to some of these dimensions. Nevertheless, research by Colvin (1981), Santrock, Warshak, and Elliot (1982), and Zill (1978) lends some support to these findings. Colvin found that adolescents from father-custody families reported a significantly higher amount of family stress than those in intact mother-custody families. And Zill found that a significantly higher proportion of children in father-custody families were reported as having had or needing psychological care. The study presented here, however, includes only one of the three possible father-custody arrangements that can exist. There is much to learn about the reasons for such an arrangement being chosen or imposed on parents and children.

Visiting Patterns with the Noncustodial Parent and Children's Behavior

Time spent visiting with the noncustodial parent was measured by asking each parent the precise number of hours the child spent with that parent during the 2 weeks prior to interview. Careful attention and considerable interview time was given charting "time spent." Parents were asked whether or not hours reported were "typical" for a 2-week period and, if not, what was. Biological mothers' and fathers' reports of "typical" time spent were highly correlated ($r = .79$, $p < .01$), and therefore could be combined.

The mean typical time spent with the non-custodial parent in a 2-week period, as an average of mothers' and fathers' reports, is presented by family type in Table 11-3.

As is evident in Table 11-3, children in Family Type 2 averaged the most

Table 11-3. Mean "Typical" Time Spent with Visited Non-Custodial Parent by Family Type

	4[a] (N = 33)	3 (N = 42)	1 (N = 50)	2 (N = 51)
Hours per 2-week period	x = 27.23 SD = 24.61	x = 31.69 SD = 23.86	x = 35.99 SD = 27.17	x = 41.01 SD = 24.42

[a]See Figure 11-1 for description of family types.

"time spent" with the visiting non-custodial parent, and those in Family Type 4 averaged the least. Type 2 is the only family type in which parents in both households are remarried. There was a significant difference between "time spent" by children in Family Type 2 and Family Type 4 ($p < .05$); children in Family Type 2 spent significantly more time with the non-custodial parent than those in Family Type 4. As reported previously, children in Family Type 4 have the highest behavior problem score, and those in Family Type 2 the lowest. One can speculate that there may be more comfort about time spent when *both* parents have invested in remarriage. For these children, there may be less concern about divided loyalties which can include a need to "protect" a parent who is single and "alone."

An ANOVA was performed relating time spent and family type, age and sex. This revealed a significant difference only for time spent by age of the child, $F = 16.94$ (1, 175), $p < .01$. Younger children spent more time visiting than older children in all family types except Family Type 2 in which both parents are remarried. In that family type, there was no significant differences; considerable time was spent with the non-custodial parent by children in both age groups. However, even when not significant by family type, the direction for all children was the same: younger children of both sexes saw non-custodial parents more time on the average than did older children.

Whatever the family type, the amount of "typical time spent" is impressive for those in this sample. While the range was wide, 27 hours in a 2-week period was the lowest mean for any family type. This is more than a half day each week or one full day every other week, depending on arrangements. This finding emphasizes the importance of linked family systems and indicates that there are a substantial number of children who have not, over time, "lost" a parent by divorce, and who are *not* part of a "one-parent" family but rather a two-parent, "two-household" family. There are a considerable number of families for whom visiting time and arrangements are important in decision making and in arranging lifestyles—families for whom a greater understanding of interpersonal relationships within this new family form is important.

In the analysis of "time spent" as related to children's behavior, no significant correlations were found between time spent and the total problem score or the broad-band scale scores for the total sample, or by family type. This finding differs from findings in my previous research (Jacobson, 1978) in which a significant positive relationship was found between time spent and child adjustment within the first year after parental divorce with similar measures of time spent and adjustment. In the study reported in this chapter, parents had been separated an average of 6½ years before the research interview. Further, the current work excludes the extremes, that is, children whose noncustodial parent had not seen the child at least once in the year prior to interview and those who had joint physical custody. Inclusion of children in these situations would have provided a wider range of variance that might have influenced the findings (Furstenberg, Nord, Peterson, & Zill, 1982). Finally, all custodial parents and their spouses (when they existed) had to agree to participate in an extensive interview, even when there was limited contact; so, selection bias may, in part, have influenced the results.

SUMMARY AND DISCUSSION

In summary, these findings suggest that the children of divorce and remarriage defined in this study are somewhat more stressed than those in the general population but should not be regarded, as a group, as needing treatment. Within this context, some variables associated with higher behavior problem scores were identified. Findings indicate that children in the father-custody family type in this study have significantly higher behavior problem scores than children in two of the three mother-custody families studied. This finding must be interpreted with caution, since association does not imply a causal relationship. Several interpretations of this finding have been suggested, including the potential impact of intervening interpersonal variables. No association was found between time spent visiting by the child with the noncustodial parent and the report of the child's behavior on the CBCL. This finding may be influenced by the fact that the study design excluded children who had spent no time with the noncustodial parent in the year prior to interview and those who were experiencing joint custody. Overall, the amount of time spent with the noncustodial parent was impressive. These findings indicate the importance for a greater understanding of the increasing number of families that extend across two households, those in which children maintain regular contact with both parents in the linked family system.

Additional observations from the informal reports of informants are of importance in thinking about further research and in sensitizing helping professionals to issues that may arise in the linked family system. These observations indicate that in many instances the two families must take each other into account in daily decision making much more than many had anticipated. Some linked family systems appear to live "in tandem," friendly or not, and must make arrangements that include attention to the "other family" in planning schedules, weekend arrangements, vacations, and so forth. Reactions to happy or distressing life events in one household (death, marriage, taxes) can spill over to the "other" household through the child who is wittingly or unwittingly the communicator between the two. Former husbands and wives reported an unexpected sensitivity of feelings in relating to each other, even after an average of 6½ years postdivorce, stating that contacts through children involved a constant reminder of the previous relationship. The children reported the delicacy of working out relationships with two families who often had different values, lifestyles, and ideas about discipline. Children had the potential for having a comfortable relationship in one household, two households, or neither. They could be the focus of loving concern in one, both, or neither. Or, children could be overlooked in both, as adults dealt with the complex responsibilities and relationships in their lives and interacted with the quantitatively increased number of "actors" in the family "drama." In the latter situation, questions concerning who has the major responsibility for the child's well-being arise.

For both clinicians and researchers, it is important that any inclination to draw a line around the custodial household be reconsidered in understanding children and adults of divorce and remarriage. This does not mean that all members of both households need participate in treatment, or that all be part of an empirical study, but rather that their impact on a current situation be seriously considered (Jacobson, 1979, 1980). The legal system, too, can benefit from a grasp of the potential importance of the linked family system. Some custody adjudications concern themselves primarily with the relationship between the biological parents who are involved. The concept of the linked family system can apply to other than stepfamily situations, such as those in foster homes and those in which adults cohabit. These can also be arrangements in which children relate to two households. Overall, the interactions between those in the linked family system are a challenge to remarried families, many of whom are negotiating the new territory well—but rarely, as observation in this study indicates, without investing considerable time, preoccupation, and experiencing considerable stress. It is a challenge to clinicians to help families develop plans that take into account the increased number of persons involved in the two families in a way in which everyone's "space" is considered, in which no one is the object of debasement even when a parent or stepparent is unable to do what might be considered in the best interests of the child. It is a challenge to researchers to identify and measure the complex interactions involved. The research reported in this paper suggests that the linked family system is an important concept for understanding the changing American family for which further attention in practice and research is indicated.

NOTE

1. Constance Ahrons is one of the few researchers who has given attention to the importance of a dual household conceptualization for adults and children of divorce and remarriage (see Ahrons, 1981, and Chapter 10, this volume).

ACKNOWLEDGMENT

This report is based on the project titled "Stepfamily Interaction and Child Adjustment" supported by a basic research grant from the National Institute of Mental Health, Division of Social and Behavioral Sciences, #MH33908.

REFERENCES

Achenbach, T. M. (1978). The child behavior profile: I. Boys aged 6–11. *Journal of Consulting Clinical Psychology, 46*, 478–488.

Achenbach, T. M., & Edelbrock, C. S. (1981). Behavior problems and competencies reported by parents of normal and disturbed children aged 4–16. *Monographs of the Society for Research in Child Development, 46* (Serial No. 188).

Achenbach, T. M., & Edelbrock, C. S. (1983). *The Child Behavior Checklist*. Burlington, VT: University of Vermont.

Ahrons, C. (1981). Continuing coparental relationships between divorced spouses. *American Journal of Orthopsychiatry, 51*, 315–328.

Cherlin, A. (1981). *Marriage, divorce and remarriage*. Cambridge, MA: Harvard University Press.

Colvin, B. (1981). *Adolescent perceptions of intra-marital stress in stepfamilies*. Unpublished doctoral dissertation, Florida State University.

Crosbie-Burnett, M. (1984). The centrality of the steprelationship: A challenge to family theory and practice. *Family Relations, 33*, 408–418.

Furstenberg, F. F., Jr., Nord, C. N., Peterson, J. L., & Zill, N. (1982, April). *The life course of children of divorce: Marital disruption and parental conflict*. Paper presented at the Meeting of the Population Association of America, San Diego, CA.

Ganong, L. H., & Coleman, M. (1984). The effects of remarriage on children: A review of empirical literature. *Family Relations, 33*, 389–407.

Glick, P. C. (1979). Children of divorced parents in demographic perspective. *Journal of Social Issues, 35*, 171–172.

Glick, P. C. (1984). Divorce and living arrangements. *Journal of Family Issues, 5*, 7–26.

Jacobson, D. S. (1978). The impact of divorce on children: I. Parent–child separation and child adjustment. *Journal of Divorce, 1*, 341–360.

Jacobson, D. S. (1979). The stepfamily: Myths and reality. *Social Work, 224*, 202–207.

Jacobson, D. S. (1980). Crisis intervention with stepfamilies. In G. Jacobson (Ed.), *New directions for mental health services: Crisis intervention in the 80's* (Vol. 6, pp. 35–43). San Francisco: Jossey-Bass.

Pasley, K., & Ihinger-Tallman, M. (1982). Stress in second families. *Family Perspectives, 16*, 181–190.

Santrock, J., Warshak, R., & Elliot, G. (1982). Social development and parent–child interaction in father custody and stepmother families. In M. E. Lamb (Ed.), *Non-traditional families: Parenting and child development* (pp. 284–314). Hillsdale: Erlbaum.

United States National Center for Health Statistics (1981). *Monthly Vital Statistics Report* (Vol. 29, No. 13). Washington, DC: Author.

Zill, N. (1978, February). *Divorce, marital happiness and mental health of children.* Findings from the FCD National Survey of Children, prepared for the National Institute of Mental Health Workshop on Divorce and Children, Bethesda, MD.

12

Parent–Child Relationships in Stepmother Families

JOHN W. SANTROCK
University of Texas at Dallas

KAREN A. SITTERLE
Timberlawn Psychiatric Hospital

FAMILIES IN TRANSITION

Remarried families, those in which one or both of the spouses has been married and bring children from the first marriage to live in the newly formed stepfamily, are among the fastest growing social phenomena in the United States. Divorces in this country are being granted at a rate of 1.2 million a year, and most involve minor children. Four out of five of these divorced adults remarry within 3 years (Glick, 1980). Thus, many of the children of divorce become children of remarriage. By one estimate, if present rates of childbearing, divorce, and remarriage continue, as many as 25% to 33% of *all* children will be a member of a stepfamily by 1990 (Glick, 1984). These statistics indicate that marital disruptions and rearrangements of family ties are increasingly common experiences in the lives of many children (Hetherington, 1981).

Remarried families are families in *transition*. Remarriage represents just one transition in a long sequence of events that follows in the wake of family disruption. Remarriage is best conceptualized as one life event in a sequence of experiences involving transitions in the lives of parents and children, rather than as a single event. The first transition period following separation and divorce is characterized by disequilibrium and disorganization in which family members are experimenting with a variety of coping mechanisms, some more effective than others (Hetherington, 1981). Ideally, this period is then followed by reorganization and the eventual attainment of a new pattern of equilibrium in the single-parent household. However, when a single parent remarries a new family is formed and a second disequilibrium occurs. Family members may be confronted with a number of major changes including an increase or decrease in financial status, relocation of residence and school,

273

assumption of new roles and responsibilities, reorganization of household routines, and new attachments—all leading to the eventual formation of a new family system. An important research question focuses on how this sequence of life events affects the subsequent development and adjustment of children who have experienced the divorce and remarriage of their custodial parent.

While research efforts in recent years have begun to document the effects of divorce on children (Hetherington, Cox, & Cox, 1979, 1982; Santrock & Sitterle, 1985; Wallerstein & Kelly, 1980), little is known about what happens to children when their custodial parent remarries. Unfortunately, most of what we know about stepfamilies is colored by fairytales (such as the myth of Cinderella and her wicked stepmother) while studies are plagued by methodological problems. Stepfamily research is at present in a very formative stage of development. Investigators must contend not only with the complexities of research measurement and design involved in doing family research in general, but also with the problems specific to working with stepfamily populations (Esses & Campbell, 1984). Some of the major problems include the reliance upon data collected from surveys and questionnaires that are given to only one family member, either the stepparent or stepchild (Bowerman & Irish, 1962; Wilson, Zurcher, McAdams, & Curtis, 1975). Other studies use clinical reports of unknown reliability (Bohannan, 1975; Fast & Cain, 1966; Visher & Visher, 1979). Most of the stepfamily studies also fail to include a control group of intact families, do not include behavioral observations of the family members, or combine stepmother and stepfather families into a single group when conducting statistical analyses. Not surprisingly, the stepfamily research provides a confusing and mixed picture of children's development and adjustment in stepfamily homes. Some studies indicate that children from stepfamilies are less well-adjusted (Bowerman & Irish, 1962; Fast & Cain, 1966; Langer & Michael, 1963), while others claim that children in stepparent homes are functioning just as well as their counterparts living with both biological parents in non-divorced families (Bernard, 1956; Burchinal, 1964; Duberman, 1973; Wilson *et al.*, 1975).

As the number of stepfamilies continues to increase, it becomes imperative that rigorous empirical studies be carried out. In one review (Esses & Campbell, 1984) some valuable guidelines for stepfamily research were offered. First, researchers need to clearly define the types of stepfamilies they intend to study (e.g., remarried mothers with children, remarried fathers with children, or blended families where both spouses bring children into the family). Second, researchers need to collect information from multiple family members to increase the reliability and validity of their findings as well as to provide greater insight into the family's functioning. Third, researchers need to move beyond the use of self-report measures and use direct measurement techniques for assessing couple and family interactions. In particular, the use of behavior observations is encouraged. And, perhaps most importantly, the positive coping mechanisms used by stepfamily members and the factors associated with stepfamily success need to be charted.

Since custody dispositions are awarded solely to the mother in 90% of divorce cases (Sanders & Spanier, 1979), stepmother families are relatively rare. However, there is evidence that more men are now seeking custody of their children (Bodenheimer, 1977), and consequently, the percentage of stepmother families may be increasing. In our research, we refer to stepmother families as families in which the father obtains custody of his children following divorce and later remarries, adding a stepmother to the family. In the next section, we will briefly review the prior research on family relations in stepmother families. We will then present the findings from our own research investigation.

SUMMARY OF STEPMOTHER FAMILY RESEARCH

Methodologically adequate studies of parent–child and stepparent–stepchild relationships in stepmother families are virtually nonexistent. The little research that has been done on stepmother families is filled with many of the same problems found in the stepfather family research. In general, investigations of stepmother families confirm what clinical reports suggest: that stepmothers experience a great deal more stress, anxiety, depression, and anger regarding their family life compared to mothers in other family structures (Barry, 1979; Draughton, 1975; Nadler, 1976). However, these studies do not shed much light on how this stress affects the children growing up in stepmother families.

One investigation of stepmother families (Nadler, 1976) did include several different measures in a comparison of stepmother and intact-family mothers. The Multiple Affect Adjective Checklist was used to measure anger, anxiety, and depression. The Marriage Adjustment form was included to assess marital relations, several TAT cards were selected to provide a projective indication of anger, anxiety, and depression, and a conflict questionnaire was developed to assess conflict in family life, with relatives, and in the community. Nadler (1976) found that stepmothers experienced more intrapersonal conflict and had more feelings of anxiety, depression, and anger regarding family relations than did mothers from intact families. In a review of marital conflict, Barry (1979) also concluded that stepmothers experience a good deal of discord when compared with mothers in other family structures.

Two studies also examined the children's perceptions in addition to those of the stepmother. Bhatt and Mehta (1975) studied children, ages 12 to 15, from intact-family and stepmother homes. They asked these youngsters about their perceptions of their relationship with their mothers and step-mothers. Children in stepmother homes reported more negative relationships with their stepmothers than children living with their natural mothers.

A recent behavioral study by Santrock, Warshak, and Elliott (1982) compared boys and girls from stepmother, father-custody divorced, and intact families. Families were matched for socioeconomic status, family size, and the child's age at the time of his/her parent's separation. This study used behavioral observations of the child interacting with his/her parent and stepparent. Variables rated from observations included warmth, self-esteem, anxiety, demandingness, maturing, sociability, and independence. They found that boys from stepmother families were less affectionate with their fathers than boys in single parent father-custody families or girls from intact families. Girls from intact families showed more self-esteem and social maturity with their fathers than the remainder of girls or boys. In contrast, boys in stepmother families were less sociable with their fathers than boys in single parent father-custody families and girls from intact families.

Different results were found when the children were observed interacting with their mothers or stepmothers. Overall, boys tended to be less socially competent than the girls. In the group of intact families, boys showed the lowest self-esteem and girls were less demanding. According to the authors, this pattern of results suggested that children from stepmother families exhibited more socially mature behavior with their stepmother than with their natural father. They also concluded that remarriage and the entry of a stepmother is associated with more positive effects for girls and less competent social behavior for boys.

In the multimethod investigation by Clingempeel, Brand, and Ievoli (1984) the stepmother–stepchild relationship was examined using both behavioral observations and self-report measures. These researchers found that the stepmother's relationship with her stepdaughter was more negative and detached than the stepmother's relationship with her stepson. These girls used more negative problem-solving behavior and less positive verbal behavior in their observed interactions with their stepmothers than boys with their stepmothers. Stepmothers, however, did not differ in their responses with their stepsons or stepdaughters on any of the behavioral measures. Unfortunately, no comparisons were made between stepchildren and children growing up in intact families.

It is difficult to draw conclusions about stepmother families from such a limited number of studies. There has been a noticeable absence of studies that include multiple measures and observations from several sources and across multiple settings. Furthermore, there have been no investigations that have systematically compared boys and girls living in stepfather and stepmother families using the multimethod and multisource approach advocated in the review of Esses and Campbell (1984). As seen next, in the present investigation we have adopted a multimethod and multisource approach to the study of interpersonal relationships within stepmother and stepfather families. This study includes the use of observations in different contexts: home, school, and with peers.

METHODS

Subjects

Sixty-nine children and their parents and stepparents from three types of family structures participated in the study: (1) families where the father retained custody following a divorce and has remarried; (2) families where the mother retained custody following a divorce and has remarried; and (3) two-parent or "intact" families where both biological parents live in the home and there has been no history of divorce. Of the 69 families, 18 children lived in stepmother families (10 girls, 8 boys), 26 children lived in stepfather families (13 girls, 13 boys), and 25 children lived in intact families (12 girls, 13 boys). The children were all from white, middle-class families and only one child in the family between the ages of 7 to 11 served as the target child. In all the stepparent families, the reason for dissolution of the child's biological parents' marriage was divorce and the biological parent in the stepfamily was always the parent who had received custody of the child following the divorce. The stepparent families must also have lived together for at least one year, and children with identified emotional problems were excluded. In addition, an attempt was made to match parents/stepparents on age, education, and socioeconomic status.[1]

Participating children and their families were recruited from the Dallas–Ft. Worth metropolitan area using a variety of procedures. These included referrals from university students, churches, the Dallas Stepfamily Association, and responses to newspaper articles, and radio and television advertisements. As might be expected, the stepmother families were the most difficult to obtain. An elaborate and prolonged search for these families was pursued over an 18-month period, and was finally terminated after obtaining 18 of the families meeting the criteria.

Description of the Subjects

Table 12-1 lists the means and standard deviations for a series of demographic characteristics of the 69 intact stepmother and stepfather families. The mean age of the children was 9 years 6 months, and the average grade level was the fourth grade. The overall income of the families was $47,000, indicating that the participating families were clearly from the middle to

Table 12-1. Means and Standard Deviations of Demographic Variables for Boys and Girls in Stepmother, Stepfather, and Intact Families

| Demographic Variables | Stepmother Families | | | | Stepfather Families | | | | Intact Families | | | |
| | Boys | | Girls | | Boys | | Girls | | Boys | | Girls | |
	M	SD	M	SD	M	SD	M	SD	M	SD	M	SD
Child's age	9.7	1.5	9.5	1.7	9.6	1.3	10.0	1.6	9.5	1.5	9.3	2.0
Child's grade	3.7	1.4	3.8	1.9	4.1	1.4	4.5	1.6	3.8	1.8	3.9	1.6
Number of children	1.8	1.0	2.3	.7	2.8	1.0	3.2	2.0	2.1	.6	2.0	1.2
Length of current marriage (in years)	3.08	2.25	3.33	2.0	3.83	2.41	3.66	2.25	14.16	2.0	14.75	4.66
Combined income of both parents (thousands of dollars)	49.0	24.0	51.0	20.0	47.0	28.0	60.0	36.0	45.0	16.0	48.0	21.0
Male parent's education	16.4	3.5	15.3	3.2	15.1	2.7	15.8	4.3	16.1	2.0	15.9	2.6
Female parent's education	16.0	2.9	13.9	2.5	12.7	2.0	14.5	1.7	14.3	1.4	14.8	1.6
Hours worked by male parent	45.0	7.0	41.0	5.0	49.0	17.0	47.0	11	49	13	42	15
Hours worked female parent	19.0	17.0	26.0	20.0	19.0	19.0	28.0	18.0	10.0	15.0	11.0	16.0
Male parent's age (years)	36.0	6.0	40.0	6.0	35.0	8.0	39.0	7.0	38.0	4.0	37.0	7.0
Female parent's age (years)	31.0	5.0	32.0	6.0	33.0	5.0	35.5	5.0	35.0	2.0	36.0	6.0

upper-middle class. The male parents (remarried fathers, stepfathers, and intact fathers) in the sample tended to be in their mid- to late-30s, were high school graduates, and the majority had completed some college or advanced training beyond high school. The female parents (remarried mothers, step-mothers, and intact mothers) were somewhat younger and less well-educated than their spouses. Nevertheless, most of the women were in their early- to mid-30s and had completed high school. One difference between the male and female parents is worth noting. The male parents were all working 40 hours or more a week, while most of the female parents worked on a part-time basis, with the women in the stepparent groups more likely both to be holding down full-time or part-time jobs, and to have been working for a longer period of time than their counterparts in intact families. As antici-pated, the parents in intact families had been married significantly longer than the couples in the stepparent groups, nearly 15 years as compared to 3 years. However, the two stepparent groups were closely matched on length of marriage.

Demographic Characteristics of Stepmother and Stepfather Families

Information regarding a number of demographic characteristics pertaining only to the stepmother and stepfather families was obtained. The means and standard deviations of these variables are shown in Table 12-2. Analyses revealed that the stepmother and stepfather family groups were fairly well matched. In general, the children in stepparent families were about 3½-years old when their parents separated and about 6-years old when their custodial parent remarried. The average length of the remarried parents' first marriages was about 7½ years, and they tended to wait about 2 years before marrying again. It was also found that the noncustodial parent, much like the other parents in this sample, had completed some college or advanced training beyond high school. Not surprisingly, the income of remarried fathers was nearly twice as much as remarried mothers during the time they were single parents. Also, as expected, noncustodial fathers were making greater annual child support payments compared to the almost negligible payments made by noncustodial mothers.

Procedure

In our investigation of children's development in stepfamilies, we adopted an approach to the study of family interaction that derives information from a variety of data sources. For example, parents and stepparents were inter-viewed and given a battery of questionnaires to complete; children were included as informants via paper-and-pencil tests, interviewed, and observed interacting with peers in a laboratory playgroup (Sitterle, 1984); parent–child

Table 12-2. Means and Standard Deviations for Demographic Characteristics for Stepmother and Stepfather Families

| Demographic Variable | Stepmother Families | | | | Stepfather Families | | | |
| | Boys | | Girls | | Boys | | Girls | |
	M	SD	M	SD	M	SD	M	SD
Age of child at separation	4.4	2.4	3.6	1.6	2.8	2.4	3.5	2.4
Remarried parent's income as single parent (thousands of dollars)	16.9	4.0	32.1	13.0	10.8	7.6	20.9	18.4
Non-custodial parent's education	13.5	2.3	13.7	1.9	13.3	2.9	15.5	2.9
Length of remarried parent's first marriage	7.2	3.1	8.4	3.9	7.9	5.5	8.2	3.6
Age of child at time of remarriage	6.7	1.5	6.2	1.1	5.6	2.2	6.3	2.3
Child support payments by non-custodial parent (annually)	82.5	233.3	57.9	173.3	1,432.5	1,583.3	2,329.4	2,384.6
Interval between separation and remarriage years	1.7	1.5	2.1	1.6	1.8	2.0	2.3	1.6
Number of children of stepparent who are biological children living in residence	.38	.52	.38	.52	.16	.58	.67	1.72
Number of children of stepparent who are biological children living elsewhere	.13	.35	.38	1.06	.42	.90	.83	1.03
Number of children of stepparent who biological children total (Residential plus non-residential)	.50	.53	.75	1.39	.58	1.00	1.50	1.83
Number of stepchildren in residence (Total family size in residence [New children produced by stepparent marriage + biological children of stepparent])	1.38	.74	1.50	.53	1.66	.78	1.83	.72
Number of half-siblings produced by newly formed stepfamily	.12	.35	.37	.52	.92	1.08	.33	.65

and stepparent–stepchild dyads were observed interacting with each other in the laboratory; and teachers were asked to rate the children's adjustment and behavior in the school setting.

Using multiple data sources rather than a single data source tends to minimize problems with distortion and incorrect inferences that might be drawn when relying upon only a single family member or data source (Maccoby & Martin, 1983). The point is to make the best use of what each method has to offer in trying to measure each variable. Although a variety of measures are being used in this investigation, only those relevant to the findings reported in this chapter are described in detail.

Parent–Child Laboratory Interaction

Each parent and stepparent were observed separately interacting with the child in the laboratory. The parent–child and stepparent–child dyads were asked to engage in two 10-minute structured tasks in which the parent and child were asked to: (1) plan an activity together, and (2) to discuss the main problems in their family. These tasks were adopted from a procedure used by Lewis, Beavers, Gossett, and Phillips (1976) in their research on family functioning, and were placed in this order because the second task has been found to be more anxiety-producing. The interaction sessions with each parent and stepparent were scheduled on different days, separated by at least a 2-week interval. All sessions were videotaped behind a one-way mirror to permit the use of multiple coding of behavior. The children's, parents', and stepparents' behaviors were coded independently on a series of 9-point rating scales.[2] The behavior categories for children and parents/stepparents are listed in Table 12-3.

Most of the parent categories are derived and modified from those developed by Baumrind (1971). Her categories of "authoritarian," "authorit-

Table 12-3. Parent and Child Observation Coding Categories

Parent/Stepparent's Behavior	Child's Behavior
Control	Warmth
Encourages emotional independence	Self-esteem
Engages in verbal interactions	Anxiety
Attentive to child	Anger
Directive versus facilitative	Demandingness
Authoritarian parenting	Maturity
Authoritative parenting	Sociability
Permissive parenting	

ative," and "permissive" refer to styles of parenting. For example, *authoritarian parenting* emphasizes firm limits and controls on the child, with little give-and-take. The orientation is punitive with a high value placed on obedience. This type of parenting behavior is linked with the following social behaviors of the child: anxiety about social comparison, failure to initiate activity, and ineffective social interaction. *Authoritative parenting* encourages the child to be independent but still places limits, demands, and controls on their actions. There is extensive verbal give-and-take, and parents demonstrate a high degree of warmth and nurturance toward the child. This type of parenting behavior is associated with social competency, particularly self-reliance and social responsibility. *Permissive parenting* places relatively low demands, limits, and controls on the child's behavior. The child is given considerable freedom to regulate his/her own behavior, with parents taking a nonpunitive stance. Parents are not very involved with their child. This type of parenting is associated with immature, regressive behavior on the part of the child, poor self-restraint, and inability to direct and assume leadership. The child categories were chosen to represent personality characteristics and outcomes associated with healthy or poor adjustment. These categories have been used in previous research on the effects of divorce on children by the first author (Santrock *et al.*, 1982).

The videotapes of remarried parent–child and stepparent–stepchild interactions were coded by highly trained coders who were blind to the hypotheses under investigation. The child's and parent/stepparent's behaviors were coded independently. Twenty percent of the videotapes were observed and coded by a second rater as a reliability check. Interrater reliability was calculated using the formula of (agreements + 1/agreements + disagreements) × 100. Reliability for the behavior categories ranged from 61% to 93% with a mean of 87.5%.

Parent Involvement Scales

A series of 5-point scales were designed to assess the degree of parental involvement ranging from discipling the child to celebrating special holidays and occasions with the child (see Table 12-4). This measure was adapted from Ahrons (in press). The parental involvement scale was designed to provide a global rating of the degree to which the parent or stepparent is emotionally and physically available to the child both in their day-to-day activities as well as the low frequency, but salient events in the child's life (e.g., Christmas holidays and birthdays). The scale is meant to measure the emotional responsiveness and sensitivity of the parent to the child's needs as well as the degree to which the parent or stepparent is a stable and dependable object in the child's life.

Both parents and stepparents were asked to complete this questionnaire regarding their own involvement with the target child. In addition, the

Table 12-4. Areas of Parental Involvement

Areas of Parental Involvement
Disciplining
Moral or religious training
Running errands for/with child
Celebrating significant events (e.g., birthdays) with child
Taking child to and from recreational activities (e.g., sports, special classes)
Participating in or observing reactional activities
Attending school or church related functions
Discussing problems with child that he/she might be having
Taking child on vacations
Providing comfort, sympathy when child is upset

remarried parents were also asked to complete this questionnaire regarding the noncustodial parent's current involvement with the target child.

Child Involvement Scales

A child involvement scale measuring parental involvement was similarly constructed and adapted for use with the children in the study. This scale included the same 11 dimensions of parental involvement as assessed by the form completed by parents and stepparents. The child's version, however, was converted into a nonverbal task rather than a pencil-and-paper task in order to minimize the differences in cognitive and reading ability and to increase their interest. A felt covered board was constructed with five different colored pockets, ranging in size with the largest pocket corresponding to the most involvement to the smallest pocket corresponding to the least amount of involvement. Each involvement dimension was phrased as a question and printed on a card with a picture depicting the activity being inquired about. The child was then asked to place the card in the pocket that best described the amount of involvement by the parent. The child was asked to complete the involvement tasks regarding the remarried parent, the stepparent, and the noncustodial parent's current involvement with him/her at separate times during the interview process.

Data Analysis

The basic analysis was a multivariate analysis of variance involving sex of child and family composition (stepmother, stepfather, and intact families). In some of the analyses, the intact families were used as the comparison group for the stepmother families, while in others the comparison group was the set of stepfather families. Pearson *r* correlations were also computed in order to look at linkages between certain demographic variables and the nature of the child's social competence and parent–child relationships. The results will not be presented separately for each measure. Rather, information presented here represents the combined findings from videotaped observations of parent–child interaction and self-report measures of involvement and the nature of parent–child relationships completed by the remarried father, the step-mother, and the child. In our discussion, we will compare the relationship patterns in stepmother families with the interaction patterns in intact families and stepfather families.

RELATIONSHIP PATTERNS IN STEPMOTHER FAMILIES

Stepmother Families and Intact Never-Divorced Families

Remarried and Intact Family Fathers

When we examined the videotaped interactions, we found no differences between remarried father–child and intact-family father-child interactions. In our study it seemed that remarried fathers behaved much like never-divorced fathers when interacting with their children. We observed that both groups of men encouraged their children to be independent and at the same time provided firm limits and controls on their children's behavior. They were attentive to their children and engaged in spontaneous discussion with them. The pattern of parent–child interaction showed considerable congruence between observations and self-report measures. Remarried fathers were as actively or more actively involved in their children's lives as never-divorced fathers. In fact, remarried fathers reported that they were more likely to take their children with them on vacations than were never-divorced fathers.

Spouses (stepmothers and mothers from intact families) concurred with these reports, feeling that their husbands were equally involved in a variety of childrearing activities. However, stepmothers reported one area in which these two groups of men differed in their relationships with their children. According to their wives, remarried custodial fathers appeared to take a more active role in the discipline and moral training of their daughters than was true for fathers in intact families. Children living in stepmother families also reported several ways in which they believed their fathers were more involved with them than never-divorced fathers were with their children. These chil-dren claimed that their fathers were more sensitive and responsive to their emotional needs. Custodial fathers in stepmother families were also more likely to talk with their children about their feelings and problems and these children were more likely to view their fathers as someone who was available to comfort them when they needed it.

Stepmothers and Intact Family Mothers

We found strong agreement between stepmothers, their husbands, and children that never-divorced mothers were more involved with their children than stepmothers with their stepchildren. This pattern held across both the behavioral measures and the self-report data. For example, in their behavioral interactions with their stepchildren, stepmothers encouraged less emotional independence, particularly with their stepsons, compared to never-divorced mothers. Never-divorced mothers demanded more autonomous and mature behavior of their children, particularly their sons, whereas stepmothers more often gave into the demands of their stepchildren. We also found differences between the perceptions of stepmothers and intact-family mothers, in addition to the differences we observed in their interactions with their children. At the same time, our group of stepmothers made it very clear that they felt less involved with their stepchildren in a number of important areas of parenting and childrearing. For example, compared to never-divorced mothers, stepmothers were less likely to take their children to and from recreational activities, attend events in which their children were participants, or run errands with their children. Thus, they did not seem to have available a number of excellent opportunities for face-to-face interaction with their stepchildren in which to share the day-to-day events in their children's lives, as did the mothers from intact families.

Spouses confirmed these feelings. Fathers from intact families felt their wives were more apt to take the children with them when they were running errands and were more responsive to the emotional needs of their children. According to their husbands, the women from nonstepfamily homes were more sympathetic and more likely to comfort their children when they were distressed than were the stepmothers. However, when it came to disciplining the children, the parent that was more active seemed to depend on the sex of the child. Never-divorced mothers took a more active role in the discipline of their daughters whereas stepmothers were more involved in the discipline of their stepsons. From the child's perspective, stepmothers were detached and uninvolved in nearly every facet of the child's upbringing including their moral training, sensitivity to their problems, and taking them on vacations or to the neighborhood store. This was not true when children of mothers from never-divorced homes were asked their perceptions of their mothers' involvement with them.

Remarried Fathers and Stepmothers

We also wanted to know how the child's relationship with the biological parent (remarried father) compared with the child's relationship with his/her stepmother. We were interested in seeing how parental and childrearing responsibilities were shared in these families. We found a number of important differences in the relationships children had with their biological parent (remarried fathers) versus their stepparent (stepmothers). As might be expected, the child's relationship with his/her biological father was closer, more nurturant, and more involved than the child's relationship with his/her stepmother. There were distinct differences between remarried fathers and stepmothers in their observed interactions with their children—a pattern of differences that again seemed to depend upon the sex of the child. Remarried fathers were more permissive and indulgent with their daughters and more restrictive with their sons. Interestingly, these same fathers expressed less confidence in the rearing of their daughters than of their sons. In contrast to their husbands, stepmothers felt more confident in the parenting of their stepdaughters. Along similar lines, stepmothers were likely to be more involved in the moral training of their stepdaughters with custodial fathers assuming the more active role in the moral training of their sons. Apart from these differences, remarried fathers and stepmothers reported equal involvement and responsibility in childrearing and parental activities.

When the children's perceptions of their relationship with their fathers and their stepmothers were compared, a slightly different picture emerged. The children in stepmother families consistently perceived their fathers as more involved than their stepmothers on every dimension of the involvement scale.

Stepmother Families and Stepfather Families

A comparison of various aspects of relationships in stepmother families to similar relationships in stepfather families revealed that the role of the biological parent and the stepparent in these two kinds of stepparent families often were very different. For example, we found that remarried mothers in stepfather families were much more involved in a variety of matters pertaining to the child's everyday living than were remarried fathers in stepmother families. The remarried mothers were more involved in discipline, more often took their child on shopping errands, participated and observed the child's recreational activities more, discussed problems with the child more, and provided the child with more comfort and sympathy than remarried fathers. These differences were consistently reported by both the remarried parents and the stepparents. However, children were less likely to report such differences, although in one instance they did indicate that remarried mothers took them on vacation more than was true for remarried fathers. Overall, then, it appeared that remarried mothers were more actively involved in the child's life than were remarried fathers. However, it is important to remember that for the most part, the picture of the remarried father was one of much more active involvement and parenting than is true for fathers in general.

Analyses of the comparison of stepmother–stepchild relationships with stepfather–stepchild relationships were among the clearest findings obtained in our research. Stepmothers were much more likely to be highly active participants in the lives of children than were their stepfather counterparts based on both their own and their children's perceptions. Children from stepmother families perceived their relationship with their stepparent as more positive than children from stepfather families.

The Noncustodial Parent

Out of all the parenting demands that custodial parents must contend with, perhaps the most difficult is the relationship they and their children have with the noncustodial parent. If the children have a satisfactory amount of contact with their noncustodial mother or father, their adjustment to living with their custodial mothers and fathers will be smoother. In turn, the residential parent will have an easier time raising the children and dealing with the other areas of parenting if their relationship with their ex-spouse is relatively conflict free. When divorced parents continue to argue about the terms of their relationship, life is unpleasant for everyone with the children usually losing most of all.

Virtually everything we know about the relationship between the custodial parent and noncustodial parent is based on the situation in which the mother has custody of the children and the father is the visiting, noncustodial parent. Frequent contact and availability with the noncustodial father even after remarriage is associated with positive adjustment in children, particularly boys (Camara, Weiss, & Hess, 1981; Hetherington *et al.*, 1982). Unfortunately, evidence to date suggests that involvement and visitation by noncustodial fathers diminishes markedly after remarriage (Furstenberg, Spanier, & Rothschild, 1980; Hetherington, *et al.* 1982). Frequently, noncustodial fathers reduce their participation in their first family as they become involved in a new relationship, particularly when the former spouse remains single. Moreover, following their own remarriage, noncustodial fathers are less likely to maintain contact with their daughters. They not only visit their sons more often and for longer periods of time following divorce, but this visiting pattern continues following remarriage (Camara *et al.*, 1981; Furstenberg *et al.*, 1980).

Grief (1985) found that noncustodial mothers were slightly more likely to visit when the father was raising only girls than when he was raising only boys. In addition, as the children got older, visitation and the number of overnights spent together became less frequent over time. It remains unknown how the nature of the child's relationship with their noncustodial mothers changes following their father's marriage. However, it is interesting to note from the above discussion, that there is greater involvement on the part of noncustodial parents with their same-sexed children, similar to the prior research on stepfathers and custodial parents.

In our study, we examined the nature of children's relationships with their noncustodial parent—and how that relationship might have changed since the custodial parent's remarriage. We asked both custodial parents, stepparents, and the children to describe how involved they felt the noncustodial parent was with the child. In general, children in stepmother families felt their noncustodial parent was more involved with them than did children in stepfather families. Specifically, the children in stepmother families reported that they felt their natural mothers were more sensitive to their emotional needs and would comfort them and support them when they needed it compared to noncustodial, biological fathers. They also mentioned that their natural mothers spent more time with them in face-to-face interaction, during daily activities, and celebrating special occasions. In addition, on an independent measure of the quality of the noncustodial parent–child relationship obtained during the child interview, these children endorsed the view that they had a more positive relationship with noncustodial mothers than did children with noncustodial fathers. The children in stepmother families reported that their natural mother communicated with them more, talked with them about the things that happened during the day and about their thoughts and feelings. The measure confirmed that children in stepmother families felt their natural mothers were more sensitive and emotionally involved with them than children perceived their noncustodial fathers to be.

Interestingly, custodial parents and stepparents were not different in their perceptions about the quality of the child's relationship with their noncustodial parents. That is, they reported that visiting fathers were as involved with their children as were visiting mothers. It is unclear why such a discrepancy exists between the reports of the adults and the children, but visitation patterns, the relationship between the custodial and noncustodial parents, and the child's wishes about their noncustodial parents may all be important factors. For example, remarried fathers may report that their ex-wives are less involved in their children's lives than they really are because of resentment and bitter feelings during or after their marriage. The child, on the other hand, may portray his/her noncustodial mother in a more positive light for other reasons. This child's perceptions may be colored by fantasies of how he/she wishes their relationship to be, rather than accept the fact that he/she has a limited mother–child relationship. The absent mother may be idealized so the child can avoid the psychological pain of abandonment and maintain ties with the absent parent. Similar findings have emerged with children of divorce who experienced repeated rejection of their efforts to maintain a relationship with their noncustodial fathers (Wallerstein & Kelly, 1980). However, although we can at present only speculate about the reasons, children in stepmother families obviously feel quite strongly that their natural mothers are actively involved in their lives and are emotionally responsive to their needs, irrespective of the viewpoint held by their fathers and stepmothers.

Demographic Variables: The Parent–Child Relationship and the Child's Social Competence

A number of demographic variables have been identified as contributing to individual differences in the child's ability to cope with the changes in the stepparent situation (Esses and Campbell, 1984). In the present investigation, recall that we systematically controlled for many of these factors, such as economic status, the reason for parental absence, and the child's age. That is, each of our family groups did not differ from each other with regard to a number of demographic variables. Pearson r correlations between 13 demographic variables and summary indices of the child's social competence and the quality of the parent–child relationship within stepmother families were performed in order to further investigate the relationship between these two sets of variables. Significant results were obtained for five of the demographic variables. Three involved the complexity and size of the stepfamily and the other two variables focused on income and the employment of the stepparent.

One set of significant correlations focused on the degree of complexity in the stepmother family. Hetherington *et al.*, (1982; see also Chapter 8 in this volume) defined a complex stepfamily as one in which both the stepparent and the remarried parent bring children to live in the newly formed stepfamily. By contrast, a simple stepfamily was defined as one in which only the remarried parent has brought children into the newly formed stepfamily. They found that children were better adjusted in simple than complex stepfather families. In the present study, we found highly significant correlations between the child's self-worth (as rated by the child and his/her parents— $p < .003$ and $p < .007$ respectively) and the complexity of the stepmother family. That is, children in simple stepmother families were more likely to report a more positive sense of self-worth. In addition, children in complex stepmother families were more likely to feel separation anxiety than their counterparts in simple stepmother families.

The second demographic variable that was associated with children's social competence in stepmother families was a "step-procreation" variable. The step-procreation variable refers to a child who is born to the stepmother and the remarried father following the remarriage. From one perspective, step-procreation families are functionally intact families with children from a previous marriage. For the most part, we found that when stepmother families produced a new child, it seemed to have a negative effect on the stepparent and custodial parent's ability to work together as a team regarding parenting of the other children.

A third demographic variable we found to be significantly associated with the child's social competence in the stepmother family was the number of total children living in the household. In our sample, the total number of children living in the stepmother family ranged from one to four children. Interestingly, we found that as the number of children in these families increased, the more likely the remarried father was to report an increase in conflict following the remarriage and entry of the stepmother into the household. A fourth demographic variable found to be significantly associated with social competence was the combined annual income of both the remarried father and stepmother. In our sample of stepmother families, the annual income ranged from \$20,000 to \$100,000. We found that greater income was associated with positive self-worth in the children and more competent social interactions between the stepmother and the children. (The latter correlation was significant at the $p < .005$.)

DISCUSSION

In general, remarried fathers appear to be actively involved with their children—and in some areas are even more involved than fathers from intact families. Most remarried fathers felt very satisfied with their relationship with their children and with how their children were progressing. From their own point of view, these fathers were "good" parents. They felt comfortable disciplining their children and doing activities with them. Remarried fathers also seemed to be particularly sensitive and responsive to the emotional needs of their children. They were the adults their children turned to for comfort and when they needed to talk about their feelings and problems. Traditionally, these nurturing activities have been associated with the maternal role. Perhaps in the absence of the child's natural mother, this group of fathers assumed these maternal caretaking activities as single parents. They continued to be nurturing and affectionate with their children even with the presence of a new "maternal" figure in the household. This group of custodial fathers seemed to have a more androgenous view of the paternal role—one that combined both traditional masculine and feminine characteristics. These men may have been this way for many years, and doing many of these kinds of activities before their divorce. Overall, our group of remarried fathers appeared to be highly competent parents. They had good father–child relationships and carried a fair share of the weight in responding to their children's emotional, social, and physical needs. These fathers felt very positive about their relationship with their children and these feelings were reciprocated by their children.

In contrast, our group of stepmothers felt they were less involved with their stepchildren compared to mothers from intact families. Nevertheless, we sense that these women were struggling to establish a good relationship with their stepchildren. In fact, these women were sharing many of the parental and childrearing activities with their husbands. Despite the stepmothers' persistent efforts to become involved, their stepchildren tenaciously held onto the view of them as somewhat detached, unsupportive, and uninvolved in their lives. Not surprisingly, stepmothers seemed to have reached a similar conclusion about their role within the family system.

There are several possible explanations for the child's negative view of their stepmothers and their stepmothers' own negative view of their relationship with their stepchildren. First, given the biological and attachment history between the child and their custodial fathers, it is logical that the child's relationship with their custodial fathers would be closer and more positive than their relationship with their stepmothers. However, this does not explain the children's strong negative feelings toward their stepmothers. It may be that the stepmother's presence threatens the child's attachment to his/her natural noncustodial mother, which is already strained by physical separation. The remarriage may also have a particular significance for the children involved, as it may signify the finality of the parents' divorce, ending not only the child's fantasies of reconciliation but also their hopes of their mother's return. The stepmother's presence may act as a constant reminder to the child that the loss or absence of his/her mother is final. It may be that these children displace their anger, hurt, and disappointment toward their noncustodial mothers, and even their fathers, onto their stepmothers.

Also, the adjustment of children within the stepmother family system may be influenced by the lack of social support and recognition for this type of family within our culture. With rising divorce and remarriage rates, stepfamilies have become a more predominant way of life for many children. The continued tendency of the courts to award custody to mothers (Lindemann, 1977) has placed the stepfather family alongside intact families as a well-accepted family alternative. In contrast, the stepmother family continues to be more of a "nontraditional" family system. The few studies of stepmothers (Draughton, 1975; Nadler, 1976) consistently point out that there is little definition or social affirmation for the role of stepmother within the family. Further, investigators also point to the stepmother's difficulty in escaping the psychological effects of the "wicked stepmother" myth. Children are typically sensitive to social norms and want to "fit in" during the elementary school years. It may be that children in stepmother families feel stigmatized, and this concern is reflected in the quality of their relationship with their stepmother.

It is not clear why stepmothers felt more confident in their parental role with their stepdaughters or were less involved in the moral training of their stepsons. Logically, one "does best" what one "knows best" and there may be a greater familiarity with the same-sex child. Sexual issues that are always prominent in moral training highlight the differences parents may feel with their opposite-sex children. Most fathers, for example, leave discussions of birth control and feminine hygiene up to their wives. Similarly stepmothers may feel somewhat "out of bounds" talking to their stepsons about their emerging sexuality.

Regardless of whether we were observing or interviewing stepmother or stepfather families, we sensed the significance of an enduring, secure attachment to the custodial parent (Santrock, Sitterle, & Warshak, 1987). Children in stepparent families have undergone considerable disruption in their lives—in the families we studied, the divorce of parents and then the remarriage of parents. One of the major problems faced by children living in stepparent families is the multiple number of close relationships they must deal with. The one longstanding, enduring attachment they have is with their custodial parent, whether it be a remarried mother in a stepfather family or a remarried father in a stepmother family. We sensed that the positive nature of the relationship between the remarried parent and the child was a key ingredient in helping the child through the disruption and disequilibrium they are confronted with as the family moves from the status of intact to divorced to stepfamily.

It is also important to consider the demographic variables that were associated with more competent social adjustment and healthier parent–child relationships in stepmother families. The fact that such variables as complexity of the stepfamily, a child who is born to the remarried father and the stepmother, total number of children in the household, and annual income were related to the child's self-worth and the quality of parent–child relationships suggests that certain kinds of stepmother families may be associated with more adjustment problems than others. For example, we found that children seemed to adjust better in a stepmother family when only the remarried father had children from his previous marriage, when a new child was not produced by the remarried father and the stepmother, when there were fewer children, and the annual income was reasonably high.

With regard to the simple/complex distinction, the complex stepfamily introduces another set of close relationships for the child to contend with—that of stepsiblings. Sibling rivalry occurs in virtually every family with two or more children. But in the case of stepsiblings, conflict may be greater as siblings from different biological origins compete for attention and affection from both their natural parents and stepparents and compare themselves with each other. Complex stepfamilies are often larger than simple stepfamilies. We found that in larger stepmother families, remarried fathers reported more conflict than remarried fathers in smaller stepmother families. As stepmother families increase in size, there is less time to devote to each child. This may be particularly important in stepparent families because these children have undergone considerable disequilibrium in their lives and may require more affection and involvement on the part of parents for optimum development. Larger stepfamilies also cost more to maintain. In this regard, we found that annual income was related to the child's self-worth and competent social interaction between the child and the stepmother. Thus, while it has been found that economic matters are salient concerns of divorced families, especially mother-custody households, we also found that money was an important factor in stepmother families. And economic matters are likely to become even more critical in the case of larger stepfamilies.

Finally, we also found that the birth of a new child to the stepmother and the remarried father, what we called step-procreation, had a negative impact on parenting of the stepchild. In understanding the step-procreation variable, it is important to review the theme that the child has undergone considerable disequilibrium, and that attachment to the remarried parent is critical in the child's adjustment. In this regard, the presence of a new stepsibling may produce feelings of insecurity on the part of the child. The child now has to observe parents giving attention to a child that is biologically related to both of them, whereas he/she has only one biological parent in the household. Of course, even in intact families with never-divorced parents, it is not unusual for parents to give the newborn infant more attention than his/her siblings (e.g., Lamb & Sutton-Smith, 1982). However, such increased attention to the new child in a stepmother family may have a greater negative impact on older siblings than in the intact family because of past stress and dissequilibrium, the presence of only one biological parent, and the painful reminder of their own mother's absence. In a stepmother family, the child has already had to cope with the change and loss of important relationships during the divorce. Having lost one attachment figure, the threatened loss of the other is always frightening.

Limitations of the Present Research and Suggestions for Future Research

Our research focused on elementary school children from middle-class, white families, and was conducted with a small sample. Future research should be extended to other age groups, working-class families, and larger samples of stepmother families. Stepmother families were particularly difficult to obtain in comparison to stepfather families, undoubtedly because of their lower incidence. However, one other reason for our difficulty in locating these families may have been related to the fact that we had a number of criteria on which were were matching stepparent families and intact families. We also matched stepmother families as closely as possible on factors such as the age of onset of the separation/divorce, age of the child, and socioeconomic status to a sample of father-custody and mother-custody single-parent families on which we had previously collected data. As we searched the Dallas–Ft. Worth metropolitan area for stepmother families, we actually turned away a large number of stepmother families who did not meet the criteria set for our sampling. Researchers should note that we found a particularly large number of stepfamilies with adolescents whom we did not study.

While our study focused on children, future research should be extended to other age groups. We know little about the development of infants and adolescents in stepmother families, but for many reasons, we could speculate that family processes may differ in stepmother families with either younger children than we studied or adolescents.

Unlike adolescents in intact families, teenagers in stepfamilies have a handy tool when things are not going their way or when their world becomes stressful: the threat that they will leave and move to the residence of the noncustodial parent. Even under the best of circumstances it takes a considerable amount of cooperation and communication to avoid manipulation by the adolescent in a stepfamily.

The cognitive development of the adolescent also makes his/her experience of the relationships in stepfamilies different from that of a younger child. He/she probably has a better understanding of the implications the remarriage has for both his/her present and future life. The concomitant consolidation of identity in adolescence may also take a different form in stepfamilies. Also, the emerging sexuality of the adolescent only adds to the already complex attachments in stepfather families. The need to deal with sexuality within a stepfamily can create more tension than in a nuclear family. For example, there may be more open displays of affection between the newlyweds which may be stimulating to teenagers, in contrast to children in nuclear families, who are not so aware of their parents' sexuality (Visher & Visher, 1979). Thus, we believe a ripe area of research inquiry focuses on possible developmental differences in the way children and adolescents experience life in various stepfamily arrangements.

Those studying the results of our investigation may want to consider the possibility that families in our sample may be better adjusted than stepfamilies in the general population. Because of the limited number of current studies on stepfamilies it will probably be some time before adequate comparative analyses can be made with other findings from similar explorations. Nonetheless, we encourage other investigators to examine the motivation their families might have to participate in such a project. It may be that the better adjusted families can tolerate more scrutiny because they are more willing to learn about themselves and improve their situation. Indeed, we eliminated stepparent families who had any history of emotional problems. Less well-adjusted families are more apt to be seen in clinical populations and may show different characteristics. On the other hand, some of the families that volunteer to participate in studies of stepparent families may be seeking solutions to family difficulties and see such participation as one way to obtain this information. Clearly, though, it is important for researchers to recognize the motivation of the participants who agree to be in a research study and the extent to which they represent a clinical or a nonclinical sample. It is obvious that the children and parents (particularly remarried parents) we observed and interviewed were better adjusted than a comparable clinical sample.

We also recommend that future studies be conducted in a multi-method, multi-source, multi-context format (see also Chapter 3 in this volume). We had hoped that our behavioral observations would reveal important information about parent–child interactions in stepmother families. However, in our analysis of parent–child relationships, the interviews and involvement scales given to the child, the remarried parent, and the stepparents, when pieced together, revealed more insights about stepmother family processes. In particular, the involvement scales, completed by both the parents and the child, provided valuable information about the daily events in stepparent family life. It may be that the brief time allowed for the videotaped interactions simply did not permit the full nature of parent–child interaction to unfold. Therefore, future research in this area may need to include microanalytic coding systems, longer observation sessions, and possibly conduct such observations on a number of occasions to obtain a more accurate portrayal of stepparent family life. Nonetheless, we encourage the use of behavioral observations in future research on stepparent families. It may well be that as we continue our analyses of the data that the videotaped observations of parent–child relationships will link up in important ways with demographic variables and family-process variables, such as the child's and the remarried parent's reconstruction of the divorced family, the child's relationship with the noncustodial parent, and so forth. Indeed, as reported in this paper, we found that step-procreation was associated with videotaped observations of less socially competent parenting on the part of the stepmother.

In the introduction of this chapter we pointed to the importance of considering the stepparent family in terms of a sequelae of equilibrium and disequilibrium across a number of years rather than as a single event. Quite clearly, longitudinal studies would be beneficial in discovering valuable information about the unfolding of lives through intact, divorced, and stepfamily configurations. Even when longitudinal studies are not possible, it is wise for researchers to discover the manner in which the members of the stepfamily reconstruct the past and carry forward previous relationships (Sroufe & Fleeson, 1985). Such reconstruction of past family relationships could be expected to influence the nature of present parent–child interactions in the family. It is also important to learn about how the nature of relationships in one context, such as the family, influence relationships in other interpersonal contexts, such as interaction with peers. While Hetherington *et al.* (1979) revealed how mother-custody divorce influences children's play and peer interaction, we have virtually no information about how entrance into a stepfamily and continued life there might influence the way children interact with peers. We have collected extensive information about children's peer relationships in stepfather and stepmother families, including videotaped observations (Sitterle, 1984), and these will be reported at a later time.

Finally, the nature of the attachment process in stepfamilies may be an important variable in the quality of functioning of the various family members. While extensive information has been collected on the attachment of infants in intact families, we know little about the nature of attachment itself in divorced or stepparent families. We believe the concept of secure attachment, as developed by Ainsworth (1979), Bowlby (1969), and Sroufe and Fleeson (1985), needs to be carefully looked at in stepfather and step-mother families. Secure attachment is an important concept not just in infancy but throughout the lifespan (Bretherton & Waters, 1985), and little is directly known about this process in stepparent families from an empirical standpoint.

Along similar lines, investigators should approach a broader range of relationships in stepfamilies including intergenerational attachments. Entrance into a stepfamily increases not only the number and type of "parents" children must relate to, but also the number and type of grandparents and other kin as well, particularly in a complex stepparent family. There have been very few investigations of interpersonal or intergenerational relationships in stepparent families, although studies of children in intact families are beginning to appear that reveal how the attachment process and the nature of parent–child relationships are carried through generations to influence the nature of the child's development (e.g., Main, Kaplan, & Cassidy, 1985; Uhlenberg, 1974). In one investigation (Furstenberg & Spanier, 1984), it was found that grandparents were included in the kinship network of stepparent families and not excluded from participation. However, this investigation did not touch on the developmental outcomes of such experiences for children and how intergenerational experiences are carried forward in time.

Research into the nature of life in stepparent families is complex and time-consuming. As yet, we have a limited empirical base on which to build generalizations about stepmother families. Nonetheless, we hope the present study will be one of many that challenge the fairytales and stereotypes of stepmother families that are rampant in our culture.

NOTES

1. One of the intents of this investigation was to obtain children who could be closely matched to a group of children from single-parent father custody and single-parent mother custody families who had been previously studied (Santrock & Warshak, 1979; Santrock, Warshak, & Elliott, 1982).

2. A rating scale method versus a behavior frequency count was used for several reasons. Raters tend to report the central tendency of an individual's behavior,

averaging out the moment-to-moment changes in situations or eliciting conditions. Ratings, therefore, minimize situational components and maximize the person component (Cairns & Green, 1979).

ACKNOWLEDGMENTS

A number of people contributed in substantial ways to this research. Cathy Dozier performed the duties of project coordinator with organization and cheer. Marjorie Stephens provided valuable help with data coordination and statistical analysis. Pam Blumenthal also provided helpful comments on an earlier version of this paper. This research was made possible through a grant from the National Institute of Mental Health #5-R01-MH-34954. Also a grant from the Hogg Foundation of Mental Health provided continued support of this research.

REFERENCES

Ahrons, C. R. (in press). Predictors of paternal involvement post divorce: Mothers' and fathers' perceptions. *Journal of Divorce.*

Ainsworth, M. D. S. (1979). Infant–mother attachment. *American Psychologist, 34,* 932–937.

Barry, W. A. (1979). Marriage research and conflict: An integrative review. *Psychological Bulletin, 73,* 41–45.

Baumrind, D. (1971). Current patterns of parental authority. *Developmental Psychology Monographs,* 4 (Pt. 2).

Bernard, J. (1956). *Remarriage: A study of marriage.* New York: Holt, Rinehart & Winston.

Bhatt, K. K., & Mehta, M. S. (1975). The perceived parental perception as a function of the mother–child relationship. *Indian Journal of Clinical Psychology, 2*(2), 113–117.

Bodenheimer, B. M. (1977). Progress under The Uniform Child Custody Jurisdiction Act and remaining problems: Punitive decrees, joint custody, and excessive modification. *California Law Review, 65,* 978–1014.

Bohannan, P. (1975). *Stepfathers and the mental health of their children.* LaJolla, CA: Western Behavioral Sciences Institute.

Bowerman, C., & Irish, D. (1962). Some relationships of stepchildren to their parents. *Marriage and Family Living, 24,* 113–121.

Bowlby, J. (1969). *Attachment* (Vol. 1). London: Hogarth Press.

Bretherton, I., & Waters, E. (Eds.). (1985). Growing points of attachment theory and research. *Monographs of the Society for Research in Child Development,* Vol. 50, Nos. 1–2, (Serial No. 209).

Burchinal, L. G. (1964). Characteristics of adolescents from unbroken, broken, and reconstituted families. *Journal of Marriage and the Family, 26,* 44–50.

Camara, K. A., Weiss, C. P., & Hess, R. D. (1981, April). *Remarried fathers and their children.* Paper presented at the biennial meeting of the Society for Research in Child Development, Boston.

Clingempeel, W. G., Brand, E., & Ievoli, R. (1984). Stepparent–stepchild relationships in stepmother and stepfather families: A multi-method study. *Family Relations, 33*(3), 465–473.

Draughton, M. (1975). Stepmother's model of identification in relation to mourning in the child. *Psychological Reports, 36*(1), 183–189.

Duberman, L. (1973). Step-kin relationships. *Journal of Marriage and the Family, 35*, 283–292.

Esses, L., & Campbell, R. (1984). Challenges in researching the remarried. *Family Relations, 33*(3), 415–424.

Fast, I., & Cain, A. (1966). The stepparent role: Potential for disturbance in family functioning. *American Journal of Orthopsychiatry, 36*, 485–491.

Furstenberg, F. F., Jr., Spanier, G. B., & Rothschild, N. (1980). *Patterns of parenting in the transition from divorce to remarriage.* Paper presented at the NICHD, NIMH and NIA Conference: "Women, A Developmental Perspective."

Furstenberg, F. F., Jr., & Spanier, G. B. (1984). *Recycling the family: Remarriage after divorce.* Beverly Hills, CA: Sage.

Glick, P. C. (1980). Remarriage: Some recent changes and variations. *Journal of Family Issues, 1*, 455–478.

Glick, P. C. (1984). Prospective changes in marriage, divorce, and living arrangements. *Journal of Family Issues, 5*, 7–26.

Grief, G. (1985). *Single Fathers.* Lexington, MA: Lexington Books.

Hetherington, E. M. (1981). Children and divorce. In R. Henderson (Ed.), *Parent–child interaction: Theory, research and prospects.* New York: Academic.

Hetherington, E. M., Cox, M., & Cox, R. (1979). Play and social interaction in children following divorce. *Journal of Social Issues, 35*, 26–49.

Hetherington, E. M., Cox, M., & Cox, R. (1982). Effects of divorce on parents and children. In M. E. Lamb (Ed.), *Nontraditional families: Parenting and child development* (pp. 284–314). Hillsdale, NJ: Erlbaum.

Lamb, M. E., & Sutton-Smith, B. (Eds.). (1982). *Sibling Relationships.* Hillsdale, NJ: Erlbaum.

Langer, L., & Michael, S. (1963). *Life stress and mental health.* New York: Macmillan.

Lewis, J. M., Beavers, W. R., Gossett, J. T., & Phillips, V. A (1976). *No single thread: Psychological health in family systems.* New York: Brunner/Mazel.

Lindeman, J. (1977). *Contested custody and the judicial decision-making process.* Ph.D. dissertation, Florida State University, College of Social Sciences.

Maccoby, E., & Martin, J. (1983). Socialization in the context of the family: Parent–child interaction. In E. M. Hetherington (Ed.), *Handbook of child psychology: Social development.* New York: Wiley.

Main, M., Kaplan, N., & Cassidy, J. (1985). Security in infancy, childhood and adulthood: A move to the level of representation. In I. Bretherton & E. Waters (Eds.), Growing points of attachment theory and research. *Monographs of the Society for Research in Child Development*, Vol. 50, Nos. 1–2 (Serial No. 209).

Nadler, J. H. (1976). The psychological stress of the stepmother. Doctoral dissertation, California School of Professional Psychology, Los Angeles. *Dissertation Abstracts International*, 1976, 37, 5367-B. (University Microfilms No. 77-6308, 261).

Sanders, R., & Spanier, G. B. (1979). Divorce, child custody and child support. *Current Population Reports.* Washington, DC: U. S. Bureau of the Census.

Santrock, J. W., & Sitterle, K. A. (1985). The developmental world of children in divorced families: Research findings and clinical implications. In D. C. Goldberg (Ed.), *Contemporary marriage: Special issues in couples therapy.* Homewood, IL: Dorsey Press.

Santrock, J. W., Sitterle, K. A., & Warshak, R. A. (1987). Parent–child relationships in stepfather families. In P. Bronstein & C. P. Cowan (Eds.), *Fatherhood today: Men's changing role in the family.* New York: Wiley.

Santrock, J. W., & Warshak, R. A. (1979). Father custody and social development in boys and girls. *Journal of Social Issues, 35*, 112–135.

Santrock, J. W., Warshak, R. A., & Elliott, G. W. (1982). Social development and parent-child interaction in father custody and stepmother families. In M. E. Lamb (Ed.), *Nontraditional families: Parenting and child development* (pp. 289–314). Hillsdale, NJ: Erlbaum.

Sitterle, K. A. (1984). Peer relations of children in stepmother, stepfather, and intact families. Unpublished doctoral dissertation, University of Texas Health Science Center, Dallas, Texas.

Sroufe, L. A., & Fleeson, J. (1985). Attachment and the construction of relationships. In W. W. Hartup & Z. Rubin (Eds.), *Relationships and Development* (pp. 51–72). Hillsdale, NJ: Erlbaum.

Uhlenberg, D. (1974). Cohort variations in family life cycle experiences of U.S. females. *Journal of Marriage and the Family, 36,* 284–292.

Visher, E. B., & Visher, J. S. (1979). *Stepfamilies: A guide to working with stepparents and stepchildren.* New York: Brunner/Mazel.

Wallerstein, J. S., & Kelly, J. B. (1980). *Surviving the breakup: How children and parents cope with divorce.* New York: Basic Books.

Wilson, K., Zurcher, L., McAdams, D., & Curtis, R. (1975). Stepfathers and stepchildren: An exploratory analysis from two national surveys. *Journal of Marriage and Family, 37,* 526–536.

PROSPECTS FOR FUTURE DEVELOPMENT

13

The Evolution of a Field of Investigation: Issues and Concerns

KAY PASLEY
Colorado State University

MARILYN IHINGER-TALLMAN
Washington State University

After reviewing the chapters of this volume and pondering the addition they make to the existing literature, we continue to believe that the closing remarks made by Ihinger-Tallman (1984) in the special issue of *Family Relations* on this topic reflect the state of research and theory on remarriage and stepparenting: "There is much to do—but we have a beginning" (p. 487).

The growth of information on remarriage and stepparenting has been phenomenal when the number of publications are considered. The Focus Group on Remarriage and Stepparenting, sponsored by the National Council on Family Relations, began preparing a comprehensive bibliography on the topic in 1981. This bibliography included citations appearing in both the professional and lay literatures. The first edition of this bibliography (Pasley & Ihinger-Tallman, 1982) included 287 citations, some dating back to the 1930s. We identified 43 lay publications (books only). The following year, the addendum (Pasley & Ihinger-Tallman, 1983) included an additional 65 citations from the professional literature, and three additional popular books. The 1984 edition of the bibliography (Coleman, Ganong, & Rogers, 1984) included 472 citations from the professional literature and 93 popular books. The 1985 addendum included 41 additional professional citations and 47 popular books (Coleman & Ganong, 1985), bringing the total to 513 citations from the professional literature and 140 popular books. Most recently, the 1986 Addendum (Crosbie-Burnett, Giles-Sims, & Rogers, 1986) included 42 new citations in the professional literature and 10 citations in the popular literature. Thus, to date, 555 professional citations have been located and 150 popular citations are noted.[1]

Further, in a review of the articles published in popular magazines (e.g., *Ladies' Home Journal* and *Redbook*) between 1940 and 1980, some 119 articles focused on the topic of remarriage and stepparenting (Pasley & Ihinger-Tallman, 1985). While examining the most recent publications in popular magazines (1980–1985), we found an additional 64 articles had been published—a number almost equal to that found for the entire decade of the 1970s.

Not only have both the professional and popular literatures expanded, but increased interest has clearly been demonstrated within professional organizations. For example, the Focus Group of the National Council on Family Relations, a special interest group, meets during the organization's annual conference. At the annual meeting of the American Orthopsychiatric Association, an Institute on Stepfamilies has been offered since 1976. The primary purpose of this institute is to educate clinicians about the nature and complexities of stepfamily life. The Society for Research in Child Development sponsored the study group whose work resulted in this volume.

At the national and international levels interest has been evident also. The National Institute on Child Health and Human Development sponsored a conference entitled "The Influence of Divorce, Single-parenting and Remarriage on Children" in May of 1985. Twenty-five scholars from across the U.S. were invited to discuss findings from their various research projects. Four scholars presented summaries of their work on remarriage and stepparenting. In 1981, the International Sociological Association Committee on Family Research sponsored a seminar on divorce, single-parenting and remarriage. One hundred and twenty-five scholars from around the world met in Lueven, Belgium to present and discuss papers on these topics. While most of the papers focused on divorce and single-parenting, two papers were devoted to remarriage.

Here in the final chapter of this book, we attempt to identify the strengths and weaknesses of the research on remarriage and stepparenting and the ways the research reported here eliminates some of these weaknesses. Lastly, we summarize how the chapters in this volume contribute to a better understanding of remarriage and stepparenting.

COMPLICATIONS IN THE SEARCH FOR KNOWLEDGE

Research on remarriage and stepparenting is fraught with a number of problems, most of which are common to family research in general. These problems have made it difficult to compare findings across studies and have inhibited the ability to make definitive statements about stepfamily life. Several authors have identified and discussed the common methodological problems facing researchers who investigate remarriage (see Chillman, 1983; Esses & Campbell, 1984; Ihinger-Tallman & Pasley, 1987; Price-Bonham & Balswick, 1980). We briefly review these problems below.

Theoretical Problems

For the most part, studies of remarriage and stepparenting are atheoretical. Because theory helps to explain behavior and leads to a better understanding of family life, it ideally serves as the foundation for research design and data interpretation. Instead of grounding studies in theory, however, researchers have typically incorporated the "deficit comparison" model (Ganong & Coleman, 1984) mentioned earlier in this volume (see Chapter 5).

However, not all research on the topic has been atheoretical, nor have all investigators employed the deficit model. In several cases, various family theories have been applied to the study of remarriage and stepparenting. For example, Crosbie-Burnett (1984) used general systems theory to guide her research. Exchange theory has also been used by Giles-Sims (1984a), and she has applied concepts from role theory to the study of stepparent roles (Giles-Sims, 1984b). Recently, Hill (1986) used family development theory to examine the marital transitions experienced by many of today's families. He discussed transitional stages of divorce, single-parenthood, and remarriage and commented on how these experiences meet the developmental needs of the family.

This volume also provides evidence of a continued commitment by scholars to place their work within a theoretical framework. For example, Clingempeel, Brand, and Segal integrated family development theory with the concepts from Bronfenbrenner's (1979) ecological model to identify areas of needed research. Giles-Sims borrowed from social exchange principles to explain three basic aspects of remarriage: mate selection, power-dependency, and the development of stepfamily norms. Ihinger-Tallman also applied the ecological model to explain stepsibling bonding—an unexplored area of stepfamily life.

Scholars interested in remarriage and stepparenting have reviewed the extant literature on divorce, single-parenting, and remarriage to identify and codify key hypotheses that may be useful for directing future research (see as examples Rodgers [1983] and Ihinger-Tallman [1984, 1986]). In this volume, Ganong and Coleman's work takes a somewhat similar approach: They codify questions in order to identify future research problems. They discriminate between two main literatures, comparing and contrasting their similarities and differences, and emphasizing recent progress made in integrating them. In terms of theory, these authors found that clinical scholars work from a theoretical base more often than do empirical scholars.

Methodological Problems

As in family research in general, the study of remarriage and stepparenting has been limited by a myriad of sampling, measurement, and analysis problems. Information on this topic is limited by the fact that, while there are accurate data available on the characteristics of the remarried population, there are no reliable data describing the stepfamily population. This presents a problem since approximately 65% of all remarriages involve children (Glick, 1980, 1984) and much of the concern about the effects of living in a stepfamily has focused on the effects that it has on children. While there is some estimate of the number of stepfamilies in which children are in residence and some information about their general characteristics (Bumpass, 1984; Cherlin & McCarthy, 1985; Hofferth, 1985), we have no estimates of the characteristics of stepfamilies with nonresidential stepchildren. Furthermore, the information on residential stepfamilies is admittedly underestimated because it only accounts for remarriage and stepfamilies formed after divorce.

Lack of information about the remarried and stepfamily populations increases the difficulty of generalizing from research findings to the broader population. Another difficulty inhibiting generalization stems from the fact that researchers have tended to draw "convenience samples" (as opposed to random samples). This has resulted in findings based upon small numbers of white, middle-class couples or individuals. Small sample size also limits the ability to investigate the influence of multiple variables in any one study.

The empirical studies reported within this volume have attempted to eliminate these problems. For example, Furstenberg, Pasley, Ahrons and Wallisch, and Jacobson report the findings from studies using large, random samples limited only by the criteria for inclusion in the study, e.g., contact with children from the prior marriage within the previous year, ability to contact subjects by telephone. More specifically, Furstenberg's findings come from a large, randomly selected, national sample as well as those from a smaller sample randomly drawn from the divorce records in Pennsylvania. The findings reported by Pasley are also from a large, random sample drawn from the marriage license applications in an eastern Washington State county. Although their final sample size was smaller than those in the Furstenberg and Pasley studies, both Jacobson and Ahrons and Wallisch identified their potential respondents from public records also.

Measurement issues are problematic in many studies of the family. Across studies, variables may often be conceptualized in the same way but are operationalized differently. For example, achievement (a common dependent measure of child outcome) has been assessed (operationalized) by school grades, achievement scores, and/or teacher ratings. In addition, many early studies used instruments that were designed especially for that study. In creating new measures, researchers failed to assess or measure reliability and validity. There is evidence of a commitment to the use of valid and reliable instruments and more common operationalization of constructs in the research reported in this volume. For example, both Hetherington and Jacobson used the Achenbach Behavior Checklist (Achenbach & Edelbrock, 1983) as the measure of child outcome. In the four studies reported by Coleman and Ganong, the same measure was used as a means of determining negative stereotyping of stepfamily members.

Further, family researchers studying remarriage commonly limit their investigations by (1) using a single research method, (2) gathering data from only one respondent per household, and (3) measuring variables with a single item. That is, data typically are collected via paper–pencil questionnaire from one spouse or parent in the family and use one question to measure the key dependent or independent variable, marital happiness for instance. Additionally, one individual in a household is often asked to report on the behavior or attitudes of other family members. Most studies in this volume have obtained data from multiple sources. That is, Hetherington and Santrock and Sitterle obtained data from both adult members of the family as well as a target child. Pasley analyzes findings from a study where data were obtained from both spouses. Jacobson and Ahrons and Wallisch report findings from both spouses plus their new partners/spouses, and Jacobson includes data from a target child as well.

Finally, there is need for researchers to study family life with longitudinal designs. This is especially salient when studying remarriage and stepfamilies since the literature suggests that the process of adjustment and integration takes considerably longer than first believed (Clingempeel, 1981; Mills, 1984; Papernow, 1984; Stern, 1978). Four studies reported in this volume have used longitudinal designs. Furstenberg reports findings from the National Survey of Children (Furstenberg, Nord, Peterson, & Zill, 1983) in which the sample of children was followed over a period of 5 years, and data were collected at two time periods. Ahrons and Wallisch discuss their findings from a sample of 98 couples studied three times over a period of 5 years. Jacobson's study reports findings from a 3-year longitudinal investigation. Hetherington summarizes findings on the effects of divorce and remarriage on families at four time periods.

Other scholars not represented here also are committed to eliminating the methodological problems we have mentioned. For example, a longitudinal design is being employed in the on-going study by Clingempeel and Hetherington which examines stepfamily life and adult and child outcomes with a sample of 250 families (200 stepfamilies and 50 first-married families) identified primarily via marriage license records. Koren and his colleagues (1983) also conducted a longitudinal study of 63 stepfamilies in Oregon. Efforts to use similar instruments to measure the same variables also are apparent in the work of others. This practice will allow for the comparison of findings across studies in the future.

Data Analysis Concerns

Family research has been criticized for its use of single-source data collection (Esses & Campbell, 1984). It has been argued that to obtain a true picture of family life, more than one member's perception is essential. However, working with multisource data is more complicated than single-source data, and difficulties arise in deciding which statistical methods to use to analyze data from multiple respondents. Several alternatives have been suggested, such as discrepancy scores, additive scores, averaging scores, and correlational scores (Pasley, Ihinger-Tallman, & Coleman, 1984; Olson, McCubbin, Barnes, Larsen, Muxen, & Wilson, 1983). The development of typologies to classify multisource data has also been recommended (Olson *et al.*, 1983; Snyder & Smith, 1986). The findings reported in this volume demonstrate the use of typologies and other forms of analysis for examining multisource data (see as examples the chapters by Pasley and Jacobson).

While multisource data are complicated to analyze for first-married families, this problem becomes amplified in remarried families. Investigations of first-married families have fewer persons that are part of the "family" to study, while remarriage incorporates additional family members. For example, Ahrons and Wallisch report data obtained from both parents *and* their new spouses. Jacobson collected data from two parents, one or two stepparents, *and* a target child. Furstenberg discusses the findings from his Pennsylvania study where reports about grandparents, stepgrandparents, parents, and children were included.

Discipline Bias Issues

Scholars who study the family usually do so from a particular and specific academic discipline. A consequence of this is that those who study remarriage are influenced by an epistemological bias which dictates the focus of investigation. Sociologists commonly study families by observing group-orientation, focusing on a small group, or conducting a societal level analysis. Psychologists, on the other hand, usually approach the study of the family from the perspective of the individual.

Epistemological biases are clearly evident in the fact that psychologists are less likely to publish the findings from their studies in sociological journals and vice versa. A consequence of this is that cross-fertilization of ideas, similarity of research methods, and operationalization of variables is hard to achieve. Additionally, wide exposure to what scholars in other disciplines are thinking and discovering is lessened.

Ganong and Coleman reveal the differences between two primary sources of information on remarriage: the empirical and the clinical. The lack of cross-disciplinary interaction is evident here. Comparing the writings of empirical researchers and clinicians who study remarriage, there appears to be little similarity between the questions asked, the methods used, and the conclusions drawn. As Ganong and Coleman suggest, the two groups have much to learn from one another, and they fortunately report that more cross-fertilization is evident in the most recent literature.

Historically, there has been little cross-fertilization between disciplines.

Research has shown that rarely do memberships in discipline-specific professional organizations overlap (Brody & Endsley, 1981; Endsley & Brody, 1981). While professional meetings provide only one of several avenues for dialogue among scholars, they are ideal settings for such interaction. Because the study of the family is multidisciplinary, it requires interdisciplinary dialogue and cross-disciplinary commitment to research. The chapters in this book demonstrate this commitment, stemming from the study process involving most of the scholars represented here that provided an arena for multidisciplinary dialogue. Further, the collaboration of the authors of these chapters shows clear evidence of discipline cross-over.

NEW CONTRIBUTIONS

Readers of this volume who are familiar with the literature on remarriage and stepparenting will find that its content makes a new contribution in several ways. Not only do the studies presented here represent research that has eliminated some of the common problems of research, but new conceptual frameworks are included, as well as reports of findings which have common themes. This volume is rich with guidelines for future research. Clingempeel, Brand, and Segal use theoretical constructs and familiarity with a particular area of investigation in the identification of gaps in the existing knowledge about remarriage and stepparenting. Ihinger-Tallman and Giles-Sims both provide a series of propositions grounded in theory to further stimulate the study of remarriage. While identifying both the similarities and differences in the clinical and empirical literature on the effects of remarriage on children, Ganong and Coleman not only provide research questions, but they also offer encouragement in that the most recent work they reviewed shows greater commitment to improved methodology, an incorporation of theory, and an increase in cross-discipline orientation.

The remaining chapters make contributions to the existing literature primarily via their findings. Synthesizing the findings reported here, we can draw several conclusions:

1. Stepfamilies and members of stepfamilies are held in lower esteem compared to members of first-married families.

2. The daily life in a stepfamily is more similar than dissimilar to that of a first-married family, with members holding similar conjugal expectations and performing the same tasks where children and household maintenance are concerned.

3. About 50% of the nonresidential fathers have little or no contact with their children from the prior marriage, suggesting that shared parenting—or the binuclear or linked family systems—are not representative of the majority of remarried families.

4. For families where continued contact occurs, the relationship be-

tween biological parents and stepparents is characterized by detachment and distance. (This should not suggest that there is conflict, as evidence presented here suggests that these adults treat one another politely.)

5. Stepparents play a unique role—a role which is distinct from that of parent, and one which is more difficult.

6. Adult members of stepfamilies appear confused about family membership—confusion which may not become clarified over time. Such is not the case in remarriages where children are the biological offspring of the remarried couple.

7. Stepparenting is characterized by a disengaged parenting style, with stepfathers using more authoritative and authoritarian parenting behaviors than stepmothers. While authoritative parenting behaviors by stepfathers are related to less problematic behavior in children, such is not the case for stepmothers, especially where stepdaughters are concerned.

8. The quality of the stepparent–stepchild relationship influences marital satisfaction such that marital satisfaction is negatively related to conflict between stepparent and stepchild, particularly where stepdaughters are concerned.

9. Family structure alone is not a good predictor of child outcome. Instead it appears to be the interaction of a variety of variables which influences child behavior and adjustment to stepfamily living.

These last two conclusions warrant greater discussion since much of the evidence presented in the reports from the research projects discussed here, as well as other research available, suggests that stepmother families experience greater stress than stepfather families, and female children in these families show evidence of more negative child outcomes. The findings reported here indicate that stepmothers are less satisfied with their relationship to their stepchildren, feel that their marital relationship is negatively affected by their husband's children, are more dissatisfied with their role, and feel that the relationship between them and the biological mother is more difficult. Stepmothers also report themselves to be less involved with their stepchildren and have more conflictual relationships with them. Interestingly, structural complexity, step-procreativity, total number of children in the household, and annual income were related to the child's sense of self-worth and the quality of the parent–child relationship. This additional information suggests that certain types of stepmother families may be associated with child adjustment difficulties. Boundary ambiguity commonly appears in stepmother families, particularly where family membership is unclear regarding nonresidential children. Again the stepmother family and those stepfamilies with greater structural complexity (albeit not those with children in common) tend to have more ambiguous boundaries.

Not only do stepmother families appear to be more problematic, but children in stepmother families also appear to be at "greater risk." Jacobson reported that children in father-custody families (stepmother families) had the highest behavior problem scores and that these children were the least likely to spend a good deal of time with their mothers. Hetherington found that girls in stepmother families were characterized by more noxious behavior, which, unlike boys, did not diminish over time. Furstenberg also reported that the relationship between stepmothers and stepdaughters is commonly conflictual—conflict that does not lessen with increased experience in the stepfamily. Taken together, the studies included in this volume provide an expanded picture of stepmother families and the potential outcomes for children and adults. Many of these findings are consistent with those from earlier studies:

10. Stepfathers appear to be more involved than do stepmothers in the parenting process.

11. The stepmother family is characterized by the most problematic relationships.

The content of this volume hopefully offers the new scholar valuable guidelines for research while providing the seasoned scholar with more "food for thought." It has attempted to demonstrate the importance of interdisciplinary dialogue and research, as well as to advance our knowledge about remarriage and stepparenting. It is hoped that we have continued to progress in our search for greater understanding of this family form and its impact on the various family members.

NOTE

1. The increases are not limited to only those articles published in a particular year, but rather include all publications to that date including any publications from previous years not already referenced in an earlier bibliography.

REFERENCES

Achenbach, T. M., & Edelbrock, C. S. (1983). *The Child Behavior Checklist*. Burlington, VT: University of Vermont.

Brody, G. H., & Endsley, R. C. (1981). Researching child and families: Differences in approaches of child and family specialists. *Family Relations, 30,* 275-280.

Bronfenbrenner, U. (1979). *The ecology of human development*. Cambridge, MA: Harvard University Press.

Bumpass, L. (1984). Some characteristics of children's second families. *American Journal of Sociology, 90,* 608-623.

Cherlin, A., & McCarthy, J. (1985). Remarried couple households: Data from the June 1980 Current Population Survey. *Journal of Marriage and the Family, 47,* 23-30.

Chillman, C. S. (1983). Remarriage and stepfamilies: Research results and implications. In

E. D. Macklin & R. H. Rubin (Eds.), *Contemporary families and alternative lifestyles* (pp. 147–163). Beverly Hills, CA: Sage.

Clingempeel, W. G. (1981). Quasi-kin relationships and marital quality. *Journal of Personality and Social Psychology, 41,* 890–901.

Coleman, M., & Ganong, L. H. (1985, November). *Comprehensive bibliography on remarriage and stepparenting: 1985 addendum* (Available from M. Crosbie-Burnett, University of Wisconsin, Madison, WI.)

Coleman, M., Ganong, L. H., Rogers, R. (1984, October). *Comprehensive bibliography on remarriage and stepparenting: 1984 addendum* (Available from M. Crosbie-Burnett, University of Wisconsin, Madison, WI.)

Crosbie-Burnett, M. (1984). The centrality of the step relationship: A challenge of family theory and practice. *Family Relations, 33,* 459–463.

Crosbie-Burnett, M., Giles-Sims, J., & Rogers, R. (1986, November). *Comprehensive bibliography on remarriage and stepparenting: 1986 addendum* (Available from M. Crosbie-Burnett, University of Wisconsin, Madison, WI.)

Endsley, R. C., & Brody, G. H. (1981). Professional isolation of child and family specialists as revealed in a time series analysis of parent–child relationship research methods. *Family Relations, 30,* 5–15.

Esses, L., & Campbell, R. (1984). Challenges in researching the remarried. *Family Relations, 33,* 415–424.

Furstenberg, F. F., Jr., Nord, C. W., Peterson, J. L., & Zill, N. (1983). The life course of children of divorce: Marital disruption and parental conflict. *American Sociological Review, 48,* 656–668.

Ganong, L. H., & Coleman, M. (1984). Effects of remarriage on children: A review of the empirical literature. *Family Relations, 33,* 389–406.

Giles-Sims, J. (1984a, October). *Stepfamily cohesion, expressiveness and conflict by stepfather–outside parent relationship.* Paper presented at the annual meeting of the National Council on Family Relations, San Francisco, CA.

Giles-Sims, J. (1984b). The stepparent role: Expectations, behaviors, sanctions. *Journal of Family Issues, 5,* 116–130.

Glick, P. C. (1980). Remarriage: Some recent changes and variations. *Journal of Family Issues, 1,* 455–478.

Glick, P. C. (1984). Marriage, divorce and living arrangements: Prospective changes. *Journal of Family Issues, 5,* 7–26.

Hill, R. (1986). Life cycle stages for types of single parent families: Of family development theory. *Family Relations, 35,* 19–29.

Hofferth, S. L. (1985). Updating children's life course. *Journal of Marriage and the Family, 47,* 93–115.

Ihinger-Tallman, M. (1984). Epilogue. *Family Relations, 33,* 483–487.

Ihinger-Tallman, M. (1986). Member adjustment in single parent families: Theory building. *Family Relations, 35,* 215–221.

Ihinger-Tallman, M., & Pasley, K. (1987). *Remarriage.* Beverly Hills, CA: Sage.

Koren, P. E., Lahti, J. I., Sadler, C. A., & Kimboko, P. J. (1983). *The adjustment of new stepfamilies: Characteristics and trends.* Portland, OR: Regional Research Institute for Human Services, Portland State University.

Mills, D. (1984). A model for stepfamily development. *Family Relations, 33,* 365–372.

Olson, D. H., McCubbin, H. I., Barnes, H., Larsen, A., Muxen, M., & Wilson, M. (1983). *Families: What makes them work.* Beverly Hills, CA: Sage.

Papernow, P. (1984). The stepfamily cycle: An experiential model of stepfamily development. *Family Relations, 33,* 355–363.

Pasley, K., & Ihinger-Tallman, M. (1982, October). *Comprehensive bibliography on remarriage and stepparenting.*

Pasley, K., & Ihinger-Tallman, M. (1983, October). *Comprehensive bibliography on remarriage and stepparenting: 1983 addendum.*

Pasley, K., & Ihinger-Tallman, M. (1985). Portraits of stepfamily life in popular literature: 1940–1980. *Family Relations, 34,* 527–534.

Pasley, K., Ihinger-Tallman, M., & Coleman, C. (1984). Consensus styles among happy and unhappy remarried couples. *Family Relations, 33,* 451–457.

Price-Bonham, S., & Balswick, J. O. (1980). The noninstitutions: Divorce, desertion, and remarriage. *Journal of Marriage and the Family, 42,* 959–972.

Rodgers, R. H. (1983, October). *Developing a propositional theory of the consequences of separation/divorce/remarriage.* Paper presented at the annual meeting of the National Council on Family Relations, Minneapolis, Minnesota.

Snyder, D. K., & Smith, G. T. (1986). Classification of marital relationships: An empirical approach. *Journal of Marriage and the Family, 48,* 137–151.

Stern, P. N. (1978). Stepfather families: Integration around child discipline. *Issues in Mental Health Nursing, 1,* 49–56.

Index

315